PASSING FOR WHITE

PASSING FOR WHITE

Race, Religion, and the Healy Family, 1820–1920

James M. O'Toole

UNIVERSITY OF MASSACHUSETTS PRESS   Amherst and Boston

Copyright © 2002 by University of Massachusetts Press

All rights reserved

Printed in the United States of America

LC 2002000351   ISBN 1-55849-341-7

Designed by Mary Mendell   Set in Minion

Printed and bound by Maple-Vail Book Manufacturing Group

Library of Congress Cataloging-in-Publication Data

O'Toole, James M., 1950–

Passing for white : race, religion, and the Healy family, 1820–1920 / James M. O'Toole.

p. cm.

Includes bibliographical references and index.

ISBN 1-55849-341-7

1. African Americans—Biography. 2. African American families. 3. Healy family.
4. Interracial marriage—United States. 5. African Americans—Race identity. 6. Racially mixed
people—United States—Biography. 7. United States—Race relations—Case studies. 8. Passing
(Identity)—United States—Case studies. 9. Religious tolerance—United States—Case studies.
10. Jones County (Ga.)—Biography. I. Title.

E185.96 .095 2002

973'.0496073'00922—dc21

2002000351

British Library Cataloguing in Publication data are available.

For
George A. O'Toole (1910–1996), *pater familias*
Mildred B. O'Toole (1910–), *mater alma*
and
Winifred L. O'Grady (1906–), *parens tertia*

CONTENTS

ILLUSTRATIONS

ACKNOWLEDGMENTS

Some authors like to cite the Book of Ecclesiastes (12:12)—"Of the making of books there is no end"—to explain (or perhaps to justify) how long it takes to produce a finished volume. The making of this one has taken a while, but it has not really seemed endless. Apart from the joys of research, often reducible to the simple thrill of reading other people's mail, the process has been sped by the help of many collaborators, and as always, it is a pleasure to acknowledge them. These are the old friends, new friends, and strangers who contributed to the effort, sometimes without knowing it.

At the head of the list are the archivists, librarians, and curators who made available the source materials in their care. The records pertaining to the Healy family are scattered all across the country, and my visits to those repositories were both pleasant and efficient, thanks to these often unsung heroes of the scholarly world. My particular thanks go to Ronald Patkus, Phyllis Danchy, and Robert Johnson-Lally of the Archives of the Archdiocese of Boston; Sister Therese Pelletier, S.C.I.M., of the Archives of the Diocese of Portland; Mark Savolis and the Reverend Paul Nelligan, S.J., of the Archives of the College of the Holy Cross; Jon Reynolds (R.I.P.) of the Georgetown University Archives; the Reverend Peter Hogan, S.S.J., of the Archives of the Josephite Fathers; Sister Florence Bertrand, C.N.D., of the Congregation de Notre Dame; Sister Nicole Bussières, R.H.S.J., of the Religieuses Hospitalières de Saint Joseph; Brenda Banks and Edward Weldon of the Georgia Department of Archives and History; Peter Blodgett of the Huntington Library; the Reverend William O. Harris of the Speer Library of the Princeton Theological Seminary; Amy Roberts of the Presbyterian Historical Society; Cindee Herrick of the U.S. Coast Guard Museum; and several members of the staff of the National Archives and Records Administration.

Friends and colleagues have read some or all of the manuscript; more charitably, they have tolerated my talking about it at the slightest provocation. They have earned my heartfelt thanks, and where I have been foolish enough to ignore their advice, they have also earned the right to say "I told you so." They constitute a roundup of the usual suspects in my case, but familiarity has only deepened my appreciation to Cyprian Davis, O.S.B., Paul Faler, James Fisher, James Hennesey, S.J., Dan Hurley, Elisabeth Kaplan, John Kendall (R.I.P.), Mary Oates, Thomas O'Connor, Steve Puleo, David Quigley, Alan Rogers, and Helen Samuels. I am grateful too for the general encouragement offered over the years by Adele Logan Alexander, Maria Brooks, Suellen Hoy, John J. McDonald, M.D., Dennis Noble, and especially Paul Wright of the University of Massachusetts Press.

The most particular thanks I owe are to the current generation of the Healy family. I doubt that I would be very welcoming to someone who appeared, out of the blue, investigating my family and proposing to publish a book about them. Family is one's own, isn't it, with outsiders keeping a respectful distance? But the present-day descendants of the Healys have encouraged this work, and I would not have been able to continue without their support. Tom Riley, Bob Riley, Miriam Flecca, Clay Young, and others all know, I think, how important the story of their family is, and I thank them for their magnanimity in allowing me to tell it.

PASSING FOR WHITE

The letter had shaken her badly. Bessie Cunningham was seventy-three, and she hadn't been well. Now, in the winter of 1951, this unexpected letter from a man she had never met only worsened her condition. "Thank God" she had been the one to open it, she wrote back, "as I am not anxious for my children to see the contents." Her correspondent, a historian, thought the matter harmless, but she knew better, for his investigation had come to center on the lives of her grandparents, Michael and Eliza Healy. They had been dead for more than a century, but to Mrs. Cunningham they were still dangerous. "I can see no reason for delving back over a hundred years," she wrote from her home outside Boston; the inevitable result would be "to make my children and their children very unhappy. . . . What good will it do to anyone now?" she wanted to know. "We cannot go back a hundred years to right things, and it surely is not our fault that such things should have happened to our family." Couldn't the historian at least "leave some of the sordid things out"? Better yet, why not just forget the whole business? "Surely God will answer my many and heartfelt prayers to have the Healy family forgotten."[1]

The historian, who happened to be a Jesuit priest named Albert Foley, persisted, but he met resistance again that summer from another branch of the Healy clan, which he had found across the country in Santa Barbara, California. There he met with another widow and her son, who were just as reluctant as their cousin in Massachusetts (whom they did not know) to have the family's story told. They were "afraid of even one word leaking out," Foley told some friends. The son was in a panic, fearful that his wife would leave him if the full historical truth were told. His mother, too, was uneasy, but she was also more clever. After first refusing to see Father Foley, she suddenly called him to her room, saying that she had committed "a great sin" and asking him to hear her confession. The priest shrewdly refused, inventing some excuse. He realized that she was trying "to tie my hands by going to confession to me and getting the whole story under the seal of confession," the solemn vow priests take never to reveal what penitents tell them. Just then, the woman's daughter-in-law returned home, Foley reported, and "I had to leave."[2]

Nor was Foley the first scholar advised to let the family languish, forgotten. A few years earlier, a graduate student had begun to study the Healys, certain that they were historically significant. Before he got very far, however, he was warned off by a senior professor, who had known "for a long time" that there was a family secret. Even so, the older man said bluntly, "it should be investigated no further. The results will do no good." However carefully wrapped in the mantle of scholarship, the story entailed unavoidable peril. "You must know as well as I the effect of any disclosure of this nature," the mentor wrote. Pulling rank, he ordered his pupil to find another topic for research. "In a case like this," he concluded, "silence is golden."[3]

What was it about the Healy family that demanded this secrecy? Why was silence about them golden? What were the "sordid things" about which Mrs. Cunningham worried? Every family's history has its ups and downs, episodes resolutely screened from the gaze of outsiders, and even from younger members of the family. But time smooths these over and eventually the truth comes out, as it did here. In 1954, three years after he had ignored the pleas of Healy family members to drop the matter, Albert Foley published his biography of Michael and Eliza Healy's oldest son.[4] The book divulged the family's supposedly terrible secret: Michael had been an Irish immigrant, and Eliza had been an African American slave.

In the America of the 1950s, an America in which strict racial segregation was the law in many places and the custom in most, a revelation of this kind might indeed be shattering, especially to those who thought of themselves as situated unambiguously on the white side of the color line. To acknowledge that a forebear had been black was to risk reclassification of the subsequent generations. The taint—it was seen as a taint, a bad and "sordid" thing—of "black blood" was permanent and irreparable, and its effects were still potent long afterward. If Eliza Healy had been black, the thinking went, then so were her children, and their children, and all the rest of the family. That was why the wife in California might divorce her husband. If his ancestor had been black, then so was he, no matter what he looked like or how he thought of himself. That in turn meant that she, a white woman, had married a black man; even worse, their children were magically rendered black too. How could she be expected to stay in such a marriage, which so many of her contemporaries would have agreed was sordid and shameful?

But the times were beginning to change in the 1950s, and Americans, many of them reluctantly, were rethinking their attitudes about race, which one foreign observer had aptly defined as the "American dilemma."[5] Albert Foley was among those trying to break down racial barriers, especially in the South, where he lived and taught for most of his career. History might be enlisted in the service of that noble goal, he thought. Examples of past interracial cooperation could promote current and future progress. If an earlier generation of the Healy family had accomplished much in spite of racial obstacles, might they not serve as models in the struggles of the present? Might they not be reimagined as African American heroes, the first black achievers in each of their chosen fields? It was for these purposes that Foley sought to recover them for history—not as a "great sin" to be exposed, but as an encouraging tale of triumph over adversity.

Another half-century has gone by since then, and it is time to examine the Healy family again. The retelling must be informed by our more complex understanding of the idea of race. The Healys and other nineteenth-century Americans assumed that "race" was something real; it was a fixed, biological condition, like brown eyes or left-handedness, which existed objectively and could not be changed. Albert Foley and his contemporaries in the twentieth century made the same assumptions, even as they challenged the political and social consequences of that system of classification. For them, no less than for earlier Americans, racial categories were clear: everybody was something, in racial terms. Today, by contrast, we are coming to recognize that race is not a biological fact, but rather an elaborate fiction that society writes over time. What we make of different individual traits, like skin color, matters more than the traits themselves. Many scholars are demonstrating just how complicated racial categories are and have always been; the apparently clear distinctions are anything but that.[6] This newer view undermines the notion that a person is "really" white, or black, or anything else.

Applying these insights to the Healy family is difficult, in part because the very words we use may obscure as much as they enlighten. The self-sustaining vocabulary of race makes it hard to avoid the assumptions we try to reject. The word "race" itself, for instance, tempts us back into thinking that there really are biological categories and that one stays forever in the category assigned at birth. "Mixed race" is similarly problematic, since it implies that there is such a thing as an unmixed racial group, an impossibility except perhaps for the most isolated of human populations. To speak of a person's racial "heritage" is likewise misleading, for we know that heritage is always assembled out of many available possibilities. "Roots" and "ancestry" have a certain poetry to them, but they mask the ways in which we each select and interpret our family's history. Worst of all is "blood," the strongest metaphor for biological unalterability. Blood, in the end, is just blood, red once oxygenated; there is no such thing as black blood or white blood.

In spite of myself, I will use all these words in discussing the Healys, but I do so reluctantly. Of course, the Healys themselves and their contemporaries did use these words and used them to denote what they took to be real things. But today, we must try to read through those usages even when they become our own, remembering how little reality is behind them. One is tempted to put these words in quotation marks every time they appear, but neither editors nor readers would stand for that clumsiness. Instead, readers might mentally insert them as reminders that we must use them warily and, indeed, that the Healys' example only further subverts them.

The story of the Healy family is a picturesque one, spanning a century in time and the entire continent in geography. It can now be told more fully, thanks to the availability of documents and sources not previously known. We can learn more about the less prominent members of this remarkable family, about the previously invisible sisters, for example. Just as important, for a nation in which racial matters are very different from what they were in the 1850s or the 1950s—not easier to resolve, just different—the Healys may still be able to teach us some valuable lessons. So many details of their story are unlikely ones, given the written and unwritten rules of their day. It even begins in an unlikely place . . .

CHAPTER ONE

Parents: Michael and Eliza

By the time the sun comes up on summer mornings in Jones County, it is already hot. The heat of the day before has not dissipated overnight, and its intensity seems to start today just where it left off yesterday. A cooling breeze occasionally gusts off the river, and the dense pine woods offer the relief of shade, but the moist air still hangs thick. The land rises up sharply from the broad, shallow stream with the tongue-twisting name—Ocmulgee—but then it eases off into rounded hills. Where the bare ground is exposed, the earth has a remarkable appearance. This is not loose, dull-gray soil that sifts easily through the fingers, but a wet, hard-packed clay of startling red, indelibly staining anything it touches. A place like any other, Jones County is just different enough to seem at once familiar and exotic.

For unrecorded ages the land had belonged to the Cherokees and Creeks, tribal names now associated with regions farther west. The first Europeans arrived at the beginning of the eighteenth century, calling the place Georgia in honor of their king. By the end of the revolution that those colonists eventually mounted against their homeland, the territory was increasingly contested, and the movement of white settlers into the backcountry proved irresistible. Repeatedly, the natives were dispossessed of new stretches of territory—"freed from Indian occupancy" was how one early chronicler described it—with the government assuring them that each time would be the last. By the 1820s, the Creeks had to leave the state altogether, and redistribution of the land to the self-proclaimed forces of civilization began in earnest. Seven times in five years, parcels of two hundred acres each were set aside, and ownership was determined by lottery. The names of free white males, widows with children, and minor orphans were placed in one lottery drum, with the numbers of the land lots in another. Local commissioners drew a name and a corresponding piece of land from each drum, and the winners went away happy. Men and women with the nerve to strike out into this territory and the luck to have their names drawn had the chance to secure their future.[1]

It was to this place, so different from the cool and rainy land of his birth, that an immigrant had come in the spring of 1818, ready to swear allegiance to his adopted country. Using the form prescribed by law, this unimpressive newcomer addressed no less a personage than James Monroe, president of the United States, and pretended to tell that worthy his life story. He had been born, the man said, in "the Parish of Kilian, in the County of Gaulway" in Ireland twenty-four years before, but he had left there in 1815 and come to America through the port of New York. On landing, he set out for Georgia, settling first at Augusta and then removing to his present home near the town of Clinton in Jones County, "which last place he intends to make his place of residence." Then he came to the point. It was "his intention at the time of his arrival in the United States + still is to become a Citizen thereof." He wanted to "renounce forever all allegiance + fidelity to any foreign Prince, Potentate, State or Sovereignty, + particularly," he added, no doubt with a pleasure only an Irishman could fully appreciate, "the Kingdom of Great Britain." He assured President Monroe that he had always "behaved himself as a person of good moral Character," that he was "attached to the principles of the Constitution," and that he was "well disposed towards . . . peace + good order." He repeated the formula orally, and his citizenship became official when he signed his abbreviated name to the text of the oath copied into the record book of the county court: "Michl. Healy."[2]

The story he told was accurate enough, if somewhat truncated. Years later, one of his sons, fascinated in old age by genealogy, sketched in more detail. Michael Morris Healy had indeed been born in Ireland on the twentieth of September in 1796, though the precise location was in doubt. The son traced the family to the town of Athlone in County Roscommon, thirty miles from the place his father had claimed, and more distant still from Donoughmore in County Cork, which was home to most of the other Irish Healys. An older brother had died at age twenty-four, and four younger sisters married men from the surrounding countryside: some of these came briefly to the United States, but they all returned to Ireland, leaving Michael alone in North America. There were stories that an unnamed cousin had already found his way to Georgia and an even more picturesque tale that Michael had deserted from the British army in Canada during the War of 1812, but these were probably just family legends that got better with each retelling. The certainty of the Healy story began with Michael's appearance in Georgia to take the citizenship oath. Shortly thereafter, he moved a few miles down the road from tiny Clinton to occupy land he had won in the county, close to the geographic center of the state on the banks of the Ocmulgee.[3]

From the beginning, the purpose of the land lottery had been to encourage people like Michael Healy to settle the frontier, clear their acreage, and put it into production. The task was daunting and, to some, singularly devoid of promise. "There is hardly a poor woman's cow" on Cape Cod, said a skeptical visitor from New England, "that is not better housed and more comfortably provided for than a majority of the white people of Georgia." Most of the settlers had incorrigibly "vagrant and hopeless habits," and they were "coarse and irrestrainable in appetite and temper, . . . almost imbecile for personal elevation." A local commentator was more sympathetic. The pioneers of middle Georgia were "generally polite and affable in their manners," he said, "and hospitable to a fault." An easygoing democracy reigned, with "a man in homespun as good as one in silk or broad-cloth." It was true that some bad habits, especially "drinking, cursing, and Sabbath-breaking," had been evident at first, but these fell off as settlement advanced; "dancing and chicken-fighting" were almost unknown, he reported proudly. Everything seemed new: there hadn't even been time to clear the tree stumps from the just-laid-out streets. All the houses "looked as if they had been put up the day before," a Scottish traveler remarked in 1829, and always in the air was the smell of the sawmill.[4]

Prosperity depended on finding a crop that could be turned into a reliable flow of cash, and an agricultural "king" emerged quickly: cotton. This was, a novelist would write much later, "a savagely red land, blood-colored after rains, brick dust in droughts, the best cotton land in the world." Georgia farmers who set themselves the task of supplying cotton to the mills of Old and New England found an insatiable demand. They were aided by the ingenuity of a wandering Yankee schoolmaster named Eli Whitney, who in 1793 patented a device—a "gin"—that efficiently removed the stubborn seeds from the fiber of the crop. National production soared from a scant 3,000 bales in 1790 to 73,000 in 1800, and it continued steadily upward from there. By the 1820s, just as Michael Healy was starting to make his way, cotton offered the surest path to wealth. In the 1829 season, more than 50,000 bales were produced in Jones and adjacent Bibb Counties; less than a decade later, local production was already over 100,000 bales a year. Prices always fluctuated, bad years might follow good ones, and those who failed to manage their land wisely risked exhausting the soil. Even so, cotton farmers earned a security unfamiliar to most of those who worked the land and depended on the vagaries of the weather.[5]

A planter who hoped really to succeed needed laborers more than anything else because cotton required so much attention. Seedlings were set in straight furrows by hand in March, and after about three weeks they took root. Next, they had to be thinned out and kept free of weeds, tasks that could be done only by hand and, even worse, by constantly bending over. One cotton worker remembered in later life that it was necessary to spend long, successive days going over a field of thirty to fifty acres without straightening up for more than a minute at a time. By July, the hottest month of the year, the cotton began to bloom, and picking started at once. Bolls left on the plant too long popped open and were lost to the wind, so when they were ready to be harvested nothing could stand in the way of that essential task. Picking required as many field hands as possible, and the planter with more of them was better off than the one with fewer. An experienced hand could pick about one hundred pounds in a day, but the more ruthless planters and overseers pressed their workers to bring in amounts approaching twice that quota. Cotton also took a good deal out of the soil, and after two successive crop years a field had to rest for a season, with corn or grass planted and then plowed under to help restore it. This too tilted competitive advantage toward bigger holdings, since the provident farmer always left some productive capacity unused at any given time.[6]

These advantages of scale linked the benefits of cotton to its tragic consequences, for here as everywhere in the American South the farming economy was built on the labor of black slaves. Ever since that fateful day in 1619 when a passing Dutch man-of-war sold twenty Africans to the settlers of Jamestown in Virginia, a captive work force, defined by skin color, had been part of the American experiment. In the 1730s, however, the first white Georgians had deliberately excluded slavery from their territory. Georgia was supposed to be a land of opportunity for the disadvantaged poor of England, a place where the unfortunate might improve themselves through the exertion of their own labors. Slaves would only encourage indolence among their owners, the early trustees of the colony thought, permitting profit without work, thereby undermining the high moral purpose of the settlement. There were also more practical reasons to resist the introduction of slaves. Georgia was a buffer between Spanish Florida and the English colonies to the north; bringing in black slaves would only introduce a "foreign" population that might be tempted to unite with the Floridians against English interests.[7]

Despite these considerations, settlers in the territory demanded the importation of slaves, fearing economic disadvantage without them. Some Georgians simply smuggled slaves in and kept them in defiance of the law. Others went through the fiction of hiring them from South Carolina, "renting" slaves for a fee that looked suspiciously like a purchase price and for a term that was as good as life. Even the clergy relented. George Whitefield, the great itinerant preacher, came to look on slavery as a good thing, and by 1749 the trustees gave legal sanction to slave ownership. White Georgians soothed their consciences with laws limiting masters' power over slaves and providing for the Christian instruction of those in bondage, but, like similar statutes elsewhere, these were honored mainly in the breach. Slaves could be worked regardless of the weather, and white owners even convinced themselves that this was the natural order of things. A so-called climatic theory, the notion that blacks were biologically suited to work in hot climates in a way that whites were not, proved dismayingly durable: not only could slaves be forced to work in the summer's heat but, whites reassured themselves, they actually liked it. The black man was "emphatically the child of the Sun," one Georgian wrote, "happily framed to live and labor, strengthen and exult under his fiercest glare, in the most fiery climes." Once introduced, slavery was there to stay, and the number of slaves in the state increased steadily. Georgia's slave population ranked it fifth among all the slaveholding states in 1790, but by 1860 it was second only to the geographically larger Virginia.[8]

Slaves were essential to cotton cultivation in central Georgia, and those in bondage eventually outnumbered their owners. In 1810, just as the area was settled, whites represented 65 percent of the residents of Jones County, then about 9,000 people altogether; fifty years later, with the total population roughly the same, the black-white ratio in the county had almost precisely reversed, with two black inhabitants for every white one. Moreover, the economy continued to favor the concentration of ownership in fewer and fewer hands. When the federal census of 1850 was taken in Jones, it found more than 6,000 slaves held by 453 masters, an average of about 14 each, but many planters exceeded that number by a wide margin. A man named John Towles owned 109, and Elizabeth Lowther, a widow, held 91. (Women, whether single or widowed, accounted for almost 16 percent of the slaveowners in the county, according to the census.) The average slaveholder across the river in Bibb County had only 8 slaves, though a few of them had acquired many more. The slaves of middle Georgia, who grew and picked cotton, may have lived a little better than those on the harsher rice and sugar plantations along the coast, but that was little consolation in the face of the overwhelming fact of enslavement itself. Some house servants were "as well fed and as well clad as the free domestic servants of many countries of Europe," an English visitor observed optimistically in 1839, but he had to acknowledge that they remained "wholly uneducated, and entirely without the hope of benefiting their condition by any exertions" of their own.[9]

Given the relative sizes of the free and enslaved populations, whites' fears over controlling their slaves could never be entirely allayed. In the 1830s, the citizens of Jones County mobilized twice in response to unfounded rumors of slave uprisings, reports fed by the news of Nat Turner's bloody insurrection in Virginia in August 1831.[10] These fears also found legal expression. At first, the local slave codes had not been so harsh as those of other colonies. Eighteenth-century Georgia had permitted the manumission of slaves by masters, for instance, though the burden of proof was always on blacks to demonstrate that they were free, the law presuming slavery to be their normal state. In 1765, the colony even took the exceptional step of encouraging the immigration of free blacks from elsewhere, providing for their naturalization and even for the possibility that they might enjoy all the benefits of citizenship except voting. This law may have run too far ahead of public opinion, however, and few ever actually tried to take advantage of it.

After the American Revolution, a harsher and more restrictive regime settled into the life of the region. Delegates from Georgia led the fight to protect the slave trade in the Constitution of 1787, accounting it a victory when the new government was blocked from legislating on the subject for twenty years. In 1802, the private manumission of slaves was expressly outlawed in Georgia, and the power to bestow freedom was reserved to the state legislature, to be used only in exceptional cases. In 1818, a loophole in this law was closed, eliminating the possibility that masters could free their slaves in their last will and testament. Blacks were forbidden to own or carry firearms; they could not be taught to read or write; and all free blacks entering the state had to register with local authorities on arrival. Those failing to do so could be jailed pending payment of a fine and, if unable to pay, they could be sold into slavery. Not even those dispensing the consolations of religion were exempt. Any black preacher who wanted to address a congregation of more than seven persons needed a permit, issued only on the recommendation of three white preachers of his denomination. Slavery may have come late to Georgia, but once there, it took hold with no less force than elsewhere in the South.[11]

These "black codes" hoped to ensure that nothing disrupted the shaky social and racial foundations on which the profits from cotton depended. Once grown and picked, however, the cotton had to be collected and shipped to market, and it was at this stage in the process that the region around Jones County assumed a critical importance. The area was just at the geographic fall line, the place where the long coastal plain met the hills of the Piedmont, making it the ideal location for a central shipping point. The rivers were navigable from there to the sea, so the cotton could be loaded onto flatboats, floated down the Ocmulgee to where it flowed into the Altamaha and then into the town of Darien on the coast; from there it was off to the North and to Europe. At the point on the Ocmulgee that was the farthest upstream boats could navigate freely, a town was forming just as Michael Healy arrived to take his oath of allegiance to the United States. The first cabin was put up on the western shore of the river opposite Jones County in 1822; by the end of the decade, more than 2,600 people were living in a town, called Macon after an early senator from North Carolina. The seat for Bibb County, Macon came to dominate the economy of the surrounding countryside. Great effort went into improving the emerging network of roads: every male inhabitant, including every male slave and the rare free black man, was expected to contribute twelve days each year to the construction and maintenance of roads, and he could be fined for failing to appear with his tools at the appointed times. For farmers throughout the region, Macon was the source of supplies and the place where they brought their produce to begin its long way to markets at home and abroad.[12]

The town flourished. "No place has risen up with greater rapidity," one early booster said; "in the character of the people there is much variety," another added. Those who lived in the town were "devoted to business," and their country neighbors were equally "industrious, frugal, and kind." A temporary town hall and market building was put up in 1828, and it was permanently replaced in 1834. The market was open every day from just before dawn until eleven o'clock in the morning. Farmers could sell their crops, buy what they needed, exchange the latest news, and still get home in time for a productive afternoon and evening. Ferries were running across the Ocmulgee as early as 1820, but sturdy bridges that were put up in the 1830s provided an easier way to get goods, livestock, and people in and out of town from the hinterland. The river was dredged several times to improve navigation, and a steamer connected Macon with Darien in 1829, reducing the travel time between the two places to an almost unbelievably fast eight days. By 1836, there was a daily mail stage to Milledgeville, then the state capital; by 1843 a railroad ran to Savannah; and five years later, a telegraph line linked Macon with Augusta and the world. The town had prosperous doctors, lawyers, dentists, and bankers; two weekly newspapers; and four hotels. Nor were the finer things lacking: there were three jewelry stores, two bookstores, and, as of 1842, the shop of a daguerreotypist run by "a pupil of S. F. B. Morse." Churches of several denominations organized themselves, and the town could even point with pride to a handsome "garden-type" cemetery. "The business of the place was rapidly increasing," Macon's earliest historian wrote; "the back country was being settled up with thrifty farmers who, for more than sixty miles around, in various counties, came to Macon as the center of trade."[13]

One such thrifty farmer was Michael Morris Healy. Luck had been kind to him in the early land lotteries: after winning a substantial plot of Jones County acreage in 1823, he took two more parcels in the drawing of 1832. Because it was random, however, the lottery system often produced a complex checkerboard of ownership, with one settler's fields scattered and broken up by those of others. Owners thus tried to consolidate their holdings in the interests of efficiency. Throughout his life, Michael Healy bargained shrewdly with his neighbors—now selling an orchard, now buying a field, now prosecuting an adjacent farmer who encroached—to concentrate his farm on the hills above the river. Eventually he held 1,500 acres, 800 of them "improved" and in use, 700 more "unimproved" and waiting for development or sale. This land was assessed in 1850 at the impressive sum of $7,500, and that placed him near the top of the heap. The census that year listed 412 landowners in the county: in improved acreage, Healy ranked thirty-third; in total land value, he was thirty-sixth.[14] He was well enough off to lend money to the less prosperous and to give them mortgages when they bought portions of his property. As early as August 1822, barely four years after arriving in the state, he had loaned $200 to two men, and when he went to court three years later to recover the defaulted loan, he won the money with interest. Ten times in his life he had recourse to the courts for this purpose, each time successfully getting his money back in amounts that ranged as high as $500.[15] Having to rely on the judicial system was bothersome, of course, but more to the point, he had the money to lend in the first place.

Wealth in the antebellum South was measured not only in land and liquid assets but also in slaves. Here, too, Michael Healy stood out. In 1830, the federal census reported that he owned thirteen—seven men and six women—a respectable number for the time. Over the next twenty years, however, his slave ownership grew just as impressively as the rest of his property. By 1850 he owned forty-nine slaves, well above the local average of fourteen; of nearly five hundred slaveowners in Jones County, he ranked eighteenth. These slaves constituted a small community of their own, consisting of five men, twelve women, and thirty-two children of all ages: the oldest male was forty-five, the oldest woman was fifty, and the children ranged from one month to sixteen years. To supervise their work he hired an overseer, a widower named William Hornaday who had a young son boarding with a nearby schoolteacher. Healy's slaves were estimated to be worth $22,000, but when they were finally sold they brought in almost $34,000, a staggering sum for the time.[16]

Success meant that Michael Healy could live a life of relative comfort, the fond if often unrealized dream of immigrants. His three-room farmhouse and the adjacent barns, slave quarters, and outbuildings do not survive into the present, and there are no reliable contemporary descriptions. Still, a picture of what has been too grandly called "the Healy plantation" emerges from the dry inventories compiled by the census takers and the later executors. This was an active, working farm, full of animals: fourteen horses, about forty milk cows and cattle, more than a hundred hogs, and a few random chickens. There was produce from garden plots to feed humans and livestock alike, together with all the tools one needed: ploughs, hoes, hammers, saws, wheelbarrows, and wagons. Conditions on the frontier were rough by more cosmopolitan standards, but Healy did not lack for refinements. Besides the usual kitchen, parlor, and bedroom furniture, there were carpets on the floors, and he was even able to indulge some genteel tastes. He had wine glasses, framed lithographs on the walls, a gold watch, a handsome birdcage, and a fiddle, which he or someone else in the household could apparently play.[17]

A clearer measure of his quest for a better life was his library of just over one hundred volumes. Those struggling to get by had little time for reading, but Michael Healy seems to have had both leisure and inclination for the life of the mind. His tastes were wide-ranging. Some of his books were practical, including cookbooks and medical texts, the latter essential with the closest doctor ten miles away in Macon. He liked adventure stories, and the more exotic the setting the better: best-selling accounts by explorers in Africa and South America joined narratives of the Lewis and Clark expedition and a timely book for the 1840s, a volume entitled *What I Saw in California*. He enjoyed history and biography: there were lives of Davy Crockett and Napoleon, an early edition of Jefferson's writings, David Hume's history of England, and Edward Gibbon's *Decline and Fall of the Roman Empire*. Literature also figured prominently on his shelves, with all the classics represented, from Shakespeare and Milton to Byron and Walter Scott.

He had an unusual interest in philosophy and religion, though there is no evidence that he himself was ever a member of any church. He read the essays of Locke and Bacon, the sermons of Bossuet, and the histories of Josephus, and he kept a theological dictionary compiled by an English "independent" (that is, Calvinist) minister. Interestingly, he had a translation of the Koran but seems not to have owned a Bible. Though unchurched, he may have been baptized a Catholic in Ireland before his emigration, and perhaps deferring to that ancestral religion, he had three volumes pertaining to the Roman church: a "true Catholic story" that answered the aspersions of nativists; an apologetic work offering "fifty reasons why the Roman Catholic apostolic religion ought to be preferred to all the sects"; and a collection of poems and pious stories called *The Catholic Keepsake*. Moral reform may have been on his mind, but only up to a point. He had a volume exposing "the arts and miseries of gambling," but just in case, he also kept a copy of Hoyle's popular compilation of the rules of card games.[18] Farm life could be isolating, but Michael Healy used some of his wealth to maintain his connection to the literature of the wider world. His bookshelves corroborate the other evidence of his success achieved during the thirty-five years between his arrival in America and his death.

Success was never for oneself alone; it was for family. Pioneers of the American interior ventured into the unknown not just for themselves, but also so that they would have something to pass on to a subsequent generation. When Michael Healy arrived in Georgia he was a bachelor of twenty-two, with marriage and children still ahead of him. Once there, his steady material advancement certainly made him a marriageable prospect, capable of providing for a wife and their children. The decision he made about marriage, however, was startling for his era, running contrary to some of his community's most deeply held beliefs and prejudices. In fact, he never legally married at all. Instead, he spent his life in a common-law marriage with a woman who was at once his wife and his slave.

❧

The origins of Eliza Clark Healy, like those of any other slave, were not considered important enough to write down anywhere. Perhaps her parents were refugees from the revolution in Haiti in the 1790s. Perhaps she was a child of the slave cabins on the nearby plantation of Samuel Griswold, a Connecticut Yankee who settled in Jones County and ran the state's first iron foundry. Perhaps she was the daughter of Major James Smith, a surveyor in Macon, and one of his slaves. Each speculation, equally plausible and equally unprovable, has been advanced. That she had a surname ("Clark") was unusual but not entirely unknown among slaves, and it may simply have been adopted from a former owner. Her birthdate has generally been given as March 3, 1813, making her seventeen years younger than Michael Healy, but this too is uncertain. What is sure is that, beginning in 1829 at the latest, the two lived together faithfully as husband and wife until their deaths within a few months of each other in 1850.[19]

In so doing, they violated perhaps the most powerful taboo of nineteenth-century America: marriage between persons of different races. Horror at this prospect arose from the understanding of what race itself was. For people of their time, the word had a clear, even scientific, definition: race depended, literally, on blood. The content of one's veins determined who one was forever. What came to be called the one-drop rule specified that a single drop of ancestral Negro blood was sufficient to define a Negro. In contrast to South America and the Caribbean, the United States had resisted enumerating identifiable interracial classes, and most Americans believed that it had to be that way. The rigidity of racial distinctions had to be maintained as much as possible. The idea that a person might be able to cross over from one race to another was out of the question. Blood might be diluted over time, but its essence could not be altered; the biological "fact," determined by the presence of even one drop, could not be changed. It was as if blackness were a kind of virus that could never be cured.[20]

Until the early years of the nineteenth century, the one-drop rule sometimes admitted exceptions, but as time went on fewer challenges to the orderliness of domestic racial arrangements were tolerated. The distinction between "white blood" and "black blood" came to seem so fundamental that any attempt to mix the two had to be censured. The twisted logic of slavery depended on the maintenance of clear dividing lines: slaves were black, blacks were slaves, and it had to be that way. If nuances were permissible, little about the peculiar institution could be sure—or at least so the theory went, for interracial sexual contact in fact persisted. The exploitation of black female slaves by their white male masters was consistently condemned in theory, but it was just as consistently countenanced in practice. The better sorts often assumed that interracial passions were particularly unrestrained among the lower ranks of society, but the reality was that white men of all classes took advantage of enslaved black women. Antebellum Southerners and other Americans decried racial "amalgamation" and concealed the evidence of it as much as they could, but it remained a dirty little secret that everyone knew.[21]

The law necessarily addressed this problem, and public authorities were eager to control the mixing of whites and blacks, and, to a lesser extent, whites and Indians. As early as 1630 a white man in Virginia was whipped for "lying with a negro." One colonial legislature after another outlawed what would much later be called "miscegenation," a mocking word coined in the heat of the political campaign of 1864. Statutes imposed stiff fines on ministers who dared preside at weddings involving parties of different colors; fines and possible banishment were also prescribed for the white, free person involved in an interracial sexual act. As slavery settled into the fabric of life in once-reluctant Georgia, that colony in 1750 became the first to declare specifically that black-white marriages were null and void by their very nature. Such unions, while hardly unknown, were not widespread, and thus it was the possibility rather than the actuality that drove the fear. In any case, the law sought to put the community's abhorrence clearly on record.[22]

Where interracial sexuality did occur, the law imposed the most powerful disincentive of all. Recognizing that the white party was most often a man and the black party a female slave—his slave—Southern states established the principle that children would always take on the condition of their mother. A mother's slavery made all her children slaves too. A father's freedom could not devolve onto the sons and daughters he had by a slave woman. There was to be no legitimate intermediary group between free and slave, between white and black; freedom and whiteness were to be jealously guarded. Masters could thus be as promiscuous as they liked, and the consequences, in the persons of their mixed-race offspring, would never threaten the status of their "real" children or the neatness of racial control.[23]

Of course, the dynamics of power between female slaves and their masters had always been fundamentally unequal, and a more perfect expression of that disparity would be hard to imagine. Not only was a slave woman's labor controlled by another, not only might she be sold at any time, but more than that, her very body and its most intimate experiences belonged ultimately not to herself but to someone else. Southern jurists had long agreed that the authority of masters was virtually absolute: "wanton murder" might be punishable, but lesser abuses and all kinds of sexual exploitation certainly were not. Slave women proved remarkably resilient, however, and historians now recognize that they were far from helpless. In spite of everything, they placed a high value on forming stable marital unions of their own, and they believed as strongly as whites in the importance of maintaining the family unit. Slaves' ideas about sexual morality mirrored those of their owners, and they enforced this code among themselves to the extent that they were able: the presumption that premarital pregnancy ought to lead more or less directly to marriage, for example, was no less common in the slave quarters than it was in the big houses of the owners. Relying on their own inner resources and on connections among themselves, slave women tolerated what they had to and waited as necessary for better opportunities. Though many of their experiences conspired to turn them into victims, they resisted victimhood as much as they could.[24]

Female slaves learned their roles and the strategies for dealing with bondage early in life. A slave mother could expect a month or two of rest immediately after giving birth, but then she had to return to her usual duties with only slight accommodation for such necessities as the nursing of infants. Slave daughters spent their earliest years largely at play, but about the age of five or six they were set to easily learned and executed tasks. By the time they were twelve, they could expect to be doing the work that would occupy them for the rest of their lives. Slave girls had more of a chance than their brothers to find work in the house rather than in the field, and the more capable of them—and often those with the lightest complexions—were taught to cook, sew, care for their master's family, and produce household goods. Most owners chose domestic servants from within their own slave ranks, rather than risk acquiring someone unreliable through purchase, and this offered opportunities for advancement among some female slaves, albeit within a limited sphere. If they were always subject to the possibility of sexual advances by their master or his sons, they likewise could exercise some control over the choice of a husband and the raising of their own children.[25]

In other circumstances, Eliza Clark Healy could have looked forward only to such a rigidly bounded life as this. Her history, however, was very different. For reasons that we cannot now recover, Michael Healy chose not simply to use this slave sexually while he married a respectable white woman. That was by far the more normal course for slaveholders, but he rejected the idea of maintaining, in effect, two families, one black and one white. He could never, he knew, formally make Eliza his wife under the laws of Georgia. There is no evidence that he ever approached any religious authority to marry them, something a clergyman would in any case have been forbidden to do. Instead, he married her by what one writer delicately called "frontier process," acting from the first as her only husband and treating her as his only wife. Why he did so must be left to speculation. It may have been a particular sense of honor or perhaps even a phenomenon that historians often overlook: love. Whatever the reason, we are confronted with the fact of their lives together and the only words he ever put on paper about her. She was, he said in 1845, "my trusty woman Eliza, mother of my . . . children."[26] He could not call her his wife, for that was a legal impossibility. Still, in everything but law, that is what she was.

The reasons Eliza Clark entered into this de facto marriage are easier to imagine. In it, she won a freedom that was unachievable otherwise. If she had indeed been the product of a union between a white master and one of his slaves, as one explanation had it, her connection to Michael Healy ensured that her own children could evade the rule that had applied to her: that children inherited only the slavery of their mother, never the freedom of their father. Moreover, her marriage to a white man gave her the opportunity to live a life fundamentally subversive of the culture that had enslaved her because of her color. We do not now know what she looked like, how light or dark her complexion, though it seems probable (given the appearance of her children) that she was light-skinned. In any case, her marriage was an attempt to break out of the American dichotomy that saw only two races, whites and blacks. These prospects of a better life for herself and her children were too tangible to reject once they had been, unexpectedly, offered. To be sure, it was a risky course. She and her husband always faced the possibility of exposure, ostracism, and punishment, and in the future, there might be even more serious consequences. While Michael Healy lived, he could protect her, but the prospects she and her children faced if her husband should die were genuinely terrible, including sale into slavery, a condition all the more bitter for those who had known freedom.

If we cannot fully understand the reasons why Michael and Eliza entered into so unconventional a union, neither can we know all the tensions, social and psychological, they felt as a result of it. For Michael, there was the enduring incongruity of owning other slaves while he himself was married to a slave. His choice of a wife certainly disposed him no more than any of his neighbors to challenge the institution of slavery itself; indeed, he continued to depend on it. He left no evidence of his political or racial opinions, though one of his sons later expressed contempt for those pressing for the abolition of slavery, and there is no reason to doubt that, like most southerners, Michael shared that outlook. Neither did his marital situation prevent him from acquiring more slaves. He owned just thirteen when he married Eliza; by the time he died, that number had more than tripled, through purchase and natural increase. Nor did he shrink from putting those slaves to the hard labor of cotton production. The job of his overseer, Hornaday, was to work them efficiently. Even if that man were not as cruel as the fictional driver Simon Legree, he had the duty to ensure his employer's profits from slaves.

For Eliza, too, the ironies were sharply drawn. Still legally a slave herself, she was now mistress of a household built on the labor of slaves. True, she was not forced, like the slave concubines of otherwise-married masters, to see her own children labor in bondage while their white half brothers and sisters enjoyed the privileges of the big house. Even so, she herself had escaped into freedom, all the while surrounded by those who had not and could not. Scholars have identified many instances of the ownership of slaves by free blacks and former slaves, and, like them, Eliza Healy accepted this rare opportunity to participate in the dominant, white culture. Though she might violate the expected equation of blackness with slavery, she did not present a more generalized challenge to the racial structure of the South.[27]

Even if the Healys themselves were prepared to construct this unusual family, few, if any, of the white inhabitants of Jones County might be expected to sanction so serious a violation of the accepted racial code. Law and popular custom seemed to draw such clear lines between the races that any attempt to blur them would seem an invitation to swift and certain denunciation. Theory often lagged behind practice, however, and there was room in the antebellum South for otherwise unacceptable interracial arrangements. Censorious neighbors might overlook such transgressions, particularly if the principals did not flaunt them. Just two counties northeast of Jones, for example, a nearly exact contemporary of Michael Healy's won tacit acceptance in his community. Nathan Sayre of Sparta, Georgia, was to all appearances a lifelong bachelor, but about 1828 he began what the family's historian called a "permanent monogamous relationship" with Susan Hunt, a free woman of color. They bowed to social convention in many ways, even building their house, ostentatiously called "Pomegranate Hall," so that the living quarters were hidden from the street. There were few other concessions to racial etiquette, however, and Sayre suffered little for his unorthodox domestic situation: he was elected several times to state and county office, for instance. Even in what were thought the most dangerous of interracial relationships—those in which the woman was white and the man was black—whites sometimes tolerated more than they thought they could. In one Virginia case from the 1820s, neighbors openly took the side of a slave who had had a long-term liaison with a local white woman, placing the responsibility for it on her and exacting no punishment on him.[28]

Two factors worked in Michael and Eliza Healy's favor in achieving local acceptance. First, the remoteness of their lands (across the river and several miles from Macon) shielded them from the disapproving eyes of those who lived nearby. Without trying very hard, they could keep largely to themselves, though on at least one occasion Eliza traveled into town with Michael to sit for a daguerreotype, an image that is now, sadly, long lost. Moreover, Michael was wealthy, and he was thus entitled to a measure of deference from the less successful. He never held public office in the county, something a man in his position might have been expected to do, but his economic and social standing was high enough to insulate him from overt disapproval. The couple's situation, however, was always precarious. About 1845, a destructive summer storm blew through the county, and the locals immediately designated it "the Healy storm," almost as if it represented the judgment of heaven against the two of them—and against the county for tolerating this racial apostasy. Another time, neighborliness turned sour when the Healys' domestic life came up. Workers on the Ocmulgee flatboats stopped at the farm one day for refreshment, and one (aided perhaps by homemade whiskey) had the temerity to suggest that the Healy children would command a good price if consigned to the Macon slave auction. Michael reacted angrily, turning his dogs loose to chase the offending revelers away.[29]

In spite of these kinds of uncertainties, Eliza Healy bore ten children with clockwork regularity and, surprisingly enough, all but one of them survived the diseases of infancy and childhood. The oldest came at two-year intervals: James Augustine, born April 6, 1830; Hugh Clark, born April 16, 1832; Patrick Francis, born February 27, 1834; Alexander Sherwood, born January 24, 1836; Martha Ann, born March 9, 1838; Michael Augustine, born September 22, 1839. A baby named Eugene, born June 30, 1842, lived only a few weeks, but he was then followed by a second cluster of siblings: Amanda Josephine, born January 9, 1845; Eliza Dunamore, born December 23, 1846; and a second Eugene, born January 23, 1849.

As in many families, the names chosen for these babies are revealing. A few were common enough: James, Patrick, Martha. Children of each gender got the name of one of the parents, though in neither case was this the oldest child of that sex; a modest concession had already been made by giving Hugh his mother's surname as a middle name. Augustine is slightly more unusual, but it may have been added later by two of the boys. The most striking name is Alexander Sherwood, and this was probably derived from two prominent local men: Elam Alexander, a successful Macon builder who arrived in the region at about the same time as Michael Healy, and the Reverend Adiel Sherwood, a local Baptist minister.[30] Naming a son after two local dignitaries indicates that Michael Healy was not entirely aloof from the surrounding community, in spite of his strange family. The most noticeable name among the girls is probably Eliza Dunamore (also sometimes rendered as "Dunmore" and "Denismore"), the first name that of her mother, the second from the region in Ireland that had traditionally been associated with the Healy clan. Michael had not come from there, but the choice of that name suggests some desire on his part to reestablish an emotional connection with the land of his birth.

More serious than the children's names was the question of their racial identity. Their technical legal status as slaves was always clear, but given contemporary understandings, what were these children in racial terms? Were they black or white or something else? What possible place was there for them in American society? Always the objects of morbid fascination among whites, the offspring of interracial sexuality were denoted by a bewildering variety of terms—quadroon, octoroon, mustifee, griff, marabon, and (the most common) mulatto—all of which tried to specify more precisely than was possible the exact degree of racial mixture. At first, most white Americans were disposed to think mixed-race people su-

perior to supposedly "pure" blacks. After all, they had some "white blood" in
them, and that was presumed to have an upward, civilizing effect. As the nineteenth century advanced, however, the opposite view came to seem more convincing: blackness corrupted more powerfully than whiteness improved, and the
result was a steadily downward spiral for those of mixed heritage. Popular science
concluded that they were biologically weak, morally corrupt, psychologically
troubled, and even incapable of reproduction, just like the animals (mules) from
which the word "mulatto" derived.[31]

On the face of things—literally—white Americans generally supposed it possible to determine race just by looking, but fears also persisted that this was not a
precise enough test. As complexions multiplied, the ability of whites to identify
the allegedly real racial essence, carried in the blood, became more problematic.
This only reinforced another fear: that some blacks could find a way to violate the
American racial code, successfully pretending to be white instead of black. Dread
of "passing" was everywhere. It was not only a contravention of the natural order,
but it was also a sin made all the more grave by the deception that lay at its core
and by the nagging suspicion that inferiors were putting something over on their
betters. The apprehension that someone one knew would turn out to be black instead of white was haunting; the prospect that one's daughter might actually
marry a man practicing this deception was so chilling that it gave rise to the very
cliché itself.[32] Thus, the lightness or darkness of the Healy children's complexions
was critical, but unfortunately the evidence on this score is very thin. Photographs, taken in adulthood, survive for only four of them (James, Patrick, Sherwood, and Michael), and they reveal a wide range. Where their parents were
known, the Healy siblings would have been known to be partially black and thus,
as far as many were concerned, entirely black. Where their family circumstances
were unknown, the possibility that at least some of them might escape facile racial
classification became real.

Like most children, the Healys were born into a life of advantages and disadvantages, but their predicament was more complicated because of their parents'
unconventional marriage. On the one hand, these were the sons and daughters of
a comfortably well-off father. They lived a life of considerable prosperity, especially for the family of a man who had come to Georgia with little but hope only
a few years before. On the other hand, they faced the most potent and apparently
immutable of disabilities. In the eyes of the law, their mother was and must remain a slave; accordingly, they too were and would forever be slaves. No matter
how much wealth Michael Healy might amass, their chances of inheriting it and

using it for their own purposes would always be, strictly speaking, out of the question. Their father could not emancipate them any more than he could free his wife, and they would always remain officially illegitimate. If he tried to bequeath his property to them at his death, the courts would more than likely invalidate his will altogether, and everything he had worked for would be forfeited.[33] Technically, it was even illegal to teach them to read and write, and the prospect that they might one day have careers, successes, and free families of their own was dim.

As Michael Healy considered his family's situation, the only real solution was to get his children out of Georgia. This would not solve all their problems, for disabling racial attitudes were as strong north of the Mason-Dixon line as south of it. Still, the North offered a better chance for them to live the kind of life he had worked to give them. In another state, they could inherit and use his property for their own purposes. They might even be able to disguise their origins and cross the seemingly impenetrable racial barrier that separated black from white. Somewhere else they might pass over the boundaries society had erected around them. Beginning in the early 1840s, therefore, Michael Healy began to search for a means of escape for his children—and perhaps for himself and his wife as well.

CHAPTER TWO

Brothers: James, Hugh, Patrick, and Sherwood

Very few avenues of escape, literal or figurative, were available in the 1840s to those defined by law and custom as slaves. Regardless of their complexion, those designated as blacks had been successfully shut out of the larger community by white Americans. Judged permanently, biologically inferior, slaves and former slaves could find few places, north or south, where they might try to build a life on their abilities alone. Even those parts of the country with reputations for liberality in such matters restricted black people no less enthusiastically than their southern neighbors. In Massachusetts, for instance, home to the abolition movement, blacks had to ride in railroad carriages separate from whites until 1843. The Bay State's colonial-era law against interracial marriage remained in force until that same year; its public schools were segregated until 1849 and public accommodations until well after that. The color of one's skin, even if it contained only the faintest hints of blackness, could be a disabling mark anywhere in the United States. Thus, when Michael Healy sought refuge outside Georgia for his children, he had no delusions about the difficulty they faced. Instead, his calculation had to be a comparative one: where might their relative advantage be better than it was at home?

He looked first to New York City, and it seemed a plausible choice. Anonymity was always an ally to those light-skinned blacks who sought passage into the white world, and a city the size of New York offered that sort of cover. Moreover, Michael had business connections there. In the course of building his prosperous plantation, he had often visited the place that was emerging as America's commercial center, just as he had gone through it on his journey from Ireland to Georgia. He befriended a hardware and dry goods merchant named John Manning, who ran a store on lower Broadway in Manhattan. Manning would eventually serve as guardian of Healy's children, becoming what another friend identified as "really a parent" to them.[1] If they were in New York, the younger Healys might rely on Manning's protection and care.

The metropolitan area also had schools, run by Quakers, that would accept the Healy children without inquiring too closely into their background. The Society of Friends, though never very numerous in America, had taken an early lead in opposing slavery. Since the 1740s, Quakers had denounced slaveholding as contrary to scripture and to the equality implicit in the Christian message. Thus, Michael Healy could readily suppose that his sons—there was as yet little thought of education for his daughters—might fare better with them than elsewhere. He showed no more personal attraction to Quakerism than he did to any other church, but if this group were able to tighten his children's hold on freedom, he was willing to let it. Accordingly, about 1837, he took his oldest son, James, then just seven years old, to New York and placed him in an elementary school of the Quakers at Flushing on Long Island. A year later, Hugh, the next oldest, followed him there, and shortly afterward Patrick, too, joined his brothers; James may also have studied for a time at another Quaker school in New Jersey.[2] Prosperity had given their father the means to get them out of harm's way at home, and there is little reason to suppose that either he or they ever thought of their returning to Georgia.

For children so young, this leave-taking from home was decisive in several ways. It opened up worlds of opportunity otherwise unavailable, but it also underlined the family's enduring predicament. In Georgia they were a legal and social impossibility—at once black and white, at once slave and free—so they had to abandon the security of home and start over somewhere else, largely on their own. That necessity both pulled them apart physically and drew them more closely together emotionally. Denied life together as a family, the siblings knew the risk of breaking apart into so many atomized individuals. For the rest of their lives, they followed each other around the country, and wherever one or two of them settled through the circumstances of career, others soon came too. Their adult correspondence and diaries are filled with deep concern for one another.

The early separation from their parents was also critical. At first, this probably expressed itself as simple homesickness, but as time went on it may also have reinforced a need to distance themselves from the dilemma their father and mother had created for them by marrying in the first place. Removed from their parents, even such parents as society would have judged unacceptable, the siblings had to look elsewhere for the nurture and support that adults are supposed to provide their children. The Healys had to find that sustenance in other individuals and institutions, so much so that, in later years, they almost never spoke of their parents. The less said about their mother the better, of course, but much the same was true of their father. James was the only one ever to recall Michael Morris Healy openly, in middle age recounting a stylized and almost certainly apocryphal story about being calmed by him during a frightening thunderstorm.[3] Michael Healy's material success made new lives possible, and for that his children had to be grateful. At the same time, Eliza Clark Healy's status meant that these children could never enjoy the normalcy of traditional family life.

No records survive of the Healy brothers' early education or of how their fellow students reacted to these racially curious youngsters. Even presuming academic success, there were limits to how far they could advance in the small schools of the Quakers. Just then, however, chance intervened and settled the family's future. In March 1844, Michael Healy undertook one of his periodic trips to the north, attending to business and checking on the progress of his three oldest boys at school in Flushing. He took a train from Macon to Savannah and then proceeded up the coast from city to city by packet boat. On the steamer running between Washington and New York, he fell into conversation with a fellow passenger, a tall Bostonian whose sharp, heroic features frequently invited comparison with Daniel Webster. He was John Bernard Fitzpatrick, a Roman Catholic priest who was returning home from Georgetown College in the nation's capital, where he had just been consecrated an auxiliary bishop of Boston. Fitzpatrick was zealous for the advancement of his church and enthusiastic for its most important recent project, the opening of a college for young men. As Healy and Fitzpatrick talked during the long, slow hours aboard ship, a new option for the planter's children emerged.[4]

Michael Healy would probably never have turned to the Catholic church for a solution to his children's problem had he not unexpectedly encountered the young bishop. He may or may not have been baptized as an infant, but since coming to America he had had no association with the Roman (or any other) church. Irishmen of his generation were generally less likely to practice their faith than those of later eras, after the onset of a so-called devotional revolution that came to Ireland with the terrors of famine. More practically, even if he had been religiously inclined, he would have found it difficult to do anything about it. For most of his life, the Catholic presence in the American South was virtually nonexistent: in 1820, there were only two parish churches in the whole territory between Baltimore and New Orleans. John England, the energetic bishop of Charleston, South Carolina, had passed through Macon as early as 1829, but a resident pastor for the place was not found until 1841. Three years later, that overextended priest withdrew to Savannah, visiting central Georgia only once a month. A small congregation of about fifty Irish railroad laborers gathered in Macon on Sundays for priestless prayer, but they were an unimpressive lot: "extremely lukewarm" and "half Protestant," one missionary said of them. Though they managed to pool their resources to buy a former Presbyterian church building, they fared little better than other Catholics in Georgia, who lingered in what an early chronicler called "spiritual destitution." Michael Healy remained apart from this nascent parish, staying "unchurched" for his entire life.[5] Even so, he found in the encounter with Fitzpatrick a fortuitous shelter for his children.

To an outsider, Catholicism in New England in the 1840s looked more substantial than it actually was. Still very much in the minority then, Catholics had increased to measurable numbers only at the time of the American Revolution. A parish had been organized in Boston in 1789, and a resident bishop had been appointed in 1808. Encompassing all six New England states, the Boston diocese was almost as much of a missionary operation as the church of the South, with few priests and small, scattered congregations. Beginning in the 1820s, the arrival of increasing numbers of immigrants, especially from Ireland, proved both a blessing and a curse. New parishes opened, spreading the institutional presence of the church, but hostility toward the newcomers was never very far beneath the surface of life in New England, sometimes bursting into violence. The "Pope's Day" celebration of the colonial era, a raucous affair in which an effigy of the Roman pontiff was dragged through the streets and then set ablaze, had been suppressed during the Revolution in deference to the alliance with France, but periodic anti-Catholic rioting persisted. Most serious had been the attack on a convent of Ursuline Sisters in Charlestown, Massachusetts (just across the harbor from Boston proper), in the summer of 1834. Incited by lurid rumors of young nuns confined against their will and subjected to the shocking advances of lecherous priests, a mob stormed the convent, chased the inhabitants out, and burned the place to the ground.[6]

Unsuccessful at recovering damages from the state for the convent's destruction, the leaders of Catholic Boston retreated from public visibility, and the new college of which Fitzpatrick had spoken was a part of that retrenchment. Benedict Fenwick, Boston's bishop (whom Fitzpatrick would succeed two years after his meeting with Michael Healy), had bought a small, unsuccessful "academy" and proposed to make it the focus of an educational program for the sons of immigrants. Located in the central Massachusetts town of Worcester, the school was renamed the College of the Holy Cross, and it was entrusted to priests of the Jesuit order. Separated by forty miles from the suspicious eyes and nativist passions of Boston, the school would, the two bishops hoped, offer a safe haven in which Catholic boys could pursue their studies undisturbed.

Combining secondary education with that of a modern-day college, Holy Cross offered a well-defined program that might take up to six years, following the Jesuits' *ratio studiorum* (system of studies). It also had a grammar school of "rudiments" in which the youngest boys, affectionately called "the brats," were prepared to move on to the higher grades. An early prospectus described the school's goals. Students who were "intended for any of the learned professions" followed a traditional curriculum: history, geography, astronomy, chemistry, public speaking, and languages, including English, French, Latin, and Greek. Boys looking to the business world could learn bookkeeping and other useful subjects. Those with an eye toward the priesthood pursued an "ecclesiastical course," covering "the several departments of sacred learning, biblical and theological." Religion was not confined to particular classes, however; rather, "the religious and moral instruction of all is attended to with watchful and anxious care," and there were mandatory lectures "on the principles, doctrines, and ceremonies of the Catholic Church." The cost ($150 per student per year, payable half-yearly in advance) was not cheap, but that fee covered all the basics: "tuition, board and lodging, washing and mending linen and socks." Additional charges were assessed for the study of other modern languages—German, Italian, and Spanish were available—and for such niceties as music, drawing, dancing, fencing, and "medical attendance."[7]

Although Holy Cross was a new undertaking, by no means assured of success, Michael Healy found much to like in the idea of sending his sons there. As his own bookshelves attested, he had keen intellectual interests, and he perhaps hoped for no less in his children. Exposing them to regular religious practice might also have had some appeal, if only because it would enhance their respectability. Beyond that, many successful southerners entrusted the education of their offspring to northerners, either sending them north to school or importing tutors, in the hope that their children might escape the provincialism of the backcountry and become at least partially "Yankified."[8] For some white fathers, removing sons from the temptations of interracial sex on the plantation might also have played a role. Michael Healy, however, had even more pressing reasons to secure his children north of the Mason-Dixon line, given their always uncertain status at home, and the isolation of Holy Cross had many attractions. Set on a hill above a remote town in New England, it offered a different kind of anonymity from that of New York City. Once safely there, his sons could withdraw into a little world of their own. They might still be anomalous, especially to the largely southern faculty—mostly Jesuits from old Maryland families—but the school could still be a hiding place for them.

If the precise reasons why the four Healy brothers were sent to Holy Cross remain partly speculative, their enrollment there at the end of the summer of 1844 is certain. James was fourteen at the time and was found to have been sufficiently prepared by the Quakers for placement in the second year of the high school program; Hugh, age twelve, was likewise judged eligible for that class. Patrick, age ten, still had to spend some time in the lower grades, and Sherwood, age eight, was sent directly from Georgia and enrolled with Patrick in the grammar school. With the exception of Hugh, who went back to Georgia once, none of them ever returned home again.

☙

Holy Cross was small, but it proved a welcoming place. James would later recall that the original faculty had numbered about half a dozen and that, besides himself and his brothers, there were between twenty and thirty students that first year. "There was no playground," he remembered, "no fences," and the scaffolding still stood around the one building that housed all the college's personnel and activities. Discipline was strict: "my teacher strikes me over the head every chance that he can get," one student complained to his parents, no doubt exaggerating. The daily routine was purposeful. The boys were roused from their beds at five in the morning, and they went straightaway to the chapel for prayers and mass. After that, they put in two hours of studying before breakfast. Fifteen minutes of recreation were then permitted before the school day began: two classes in the morning, dinner at twelve, two more classes in the afternoon. In the evening, all were expected in a study hall until eight, at which time they returned to the chapel to say the rosary; they could then enjoy a little free time until bed and lights-out at nine. They got used to this schedule quickly enough—"it comes quite natural to me," a student wrote cheerily to his parents—but it could still take its toll. "I was caught asleep in the class of moral philosophy," James confessed to his diary one day in June 1849.[9]

Drowsiness in class was not the usual demeanor of the Healy brothers, and they quickly distinguished themselves in their studies. A wider world of learning was opening up to them, and they rushed enthusiastically toward it. James read Hamlet (his first encounter with Shakespeare) and pronounced himself "completely charmed by it." He likewise studied the historian William Hickling Prescott and judged him "by far more unprejudiced than the common run of writers." The Healys were bright, even aggressive students, eager to do well. "I make it a constant practice to speak upon every question proposed," James said of one public-speaking class, even when, as in this case, "I was rather beaten, . . . as I had the weakest side." He delivered a short Latin oration at the "exhibition" that concluded the school year in the summer of 1845, and he gave similar performances every year thereafter. The others also declaimed on these occasions, Sherwood offering a dramatic account of the battle of Lepanto and Patrick contributing an allocution on the battle of Bunker Hill—in Spanish, no less. Hugh and two classmates "acquitted themselves in a laudable manner in French" and won "unqualified praise." Sherwood "evinced . . . promptness and accuracy in arithmetic," and he and Patrick placed first overall in their respective grades.[10]

As the oldest, James often acted *in loco parentis* for his younger brothers, a role to which he often recurred in later life. He watched their progress closely and scolded them when he thought they needed to work harder: Sherwood had to be warned against succumbing to a temptation to whisper in class and Patrick against occasional "impudence" and "inattention." Once, the precocious Sherwood, barely thirteen at the time, penned a "long and complaining" open letter about conditions at the college and was officially reprimanded for it. The screed "was very well written, however," the proud older brother could not help but observe. James was not above the occasional transgression himself, once almost getting caught smoking and at least twice swearing off cigars "forever," only to backslide each time. He likewise monitored his siblings' physical well-being, noting Hugh's visit with an eye doctor, Patrick's having two teeth pulled, and Sherwood's recovery after being hit with a stone thrown by a classmate while playing "duck on a rock."[11]

This last incident was apparently accidental rather than deliberate, but it raises the question of how these brothers got along with their fellow students. By enrolling at Holy Cross they had escaped slavery but not the prevailing American attitudes about race. To their fellow students no less than to their father's neighbors back home, these children were supposed to be defined by the "black blood" in their veins. In such circumstances, they had every reason to expect that they would win the acceptance of their peers only grudgingly, if at all. Nor could their family secret be hidden, for it was plain for all to see. Though Patrick's skin was very light and Hugh's complexion is unknown, both Sherwood and James showed unmistakable evidence of African ancestry. As Patrick would later remark, anyone who looked at some of the brothers could easily solve the racial riddle of all of them. Moreover, though it was located securely in the North, the college enrolled a substantial number of boys from the South, which exposed Michael Healy's sons to the very racial problems he had sought to avoid in sending them away.

Even so, race seems to have played no role in how the Healy brothers got along with their classmates. The four boys from Georgia were not merely accepted; they were embraced by the college and its inhabitants, faculty and students alike. Their academic performance proved that they were equal to, and usually better than, any other student, but their classmates never held that against them—perhaps because they were such regular fellows. They were active in student clubs and always joined the impromptu expeditions into the surrounding countryside for swimming in the warm weather and skating in winter. With the other students, they went squirrel hunting and regularly descended the steep hill on which the college stood to take advantage of lecturers and musical reviews stopping in Worcester. Sometimes, they were even the ringleaders of mischief: Patrick and Sherwood were more than once "read out for lines," a punishment for misbehavior that consisted of having to memorize up to 150 lines of Virgil.[12] Regardless of any private, unexpressed feelings, the other students at Holy Cross included the Healys fully in the life of the school. Their racial origins were known but, not for the last time in their lives, came not to matter.

The brothers made friends readily and stood at the center of college life. With so small a student body, the character strengths and foibles of all were always on display. James began the diary he kept during his senior year with "an annotated List of Students," a catalog that shows his wide circle of friendships. It also reveals something of a tendency to be censorious and at ease in judging others, favorably and unfavorably. Two students, for example, both from Maryland, were described respectively as a "good fellow" and "very good," but others earned sharper assessments. One native Bostonian was "smart but silly," a New Yorker was a "loafer," and another Marylander was "lazy." One had a "thick head," and others were characterized variously as "rowdy," "too pert," and "girlish," the last presumably a serious failing in an all-male student body.[13] In later life, James often took the same waspish and even haughty view of others, perhaps a kind of overcorrection for the racial ambiguity that left him and his family always open to challenge. For now, his "annotations" demonstrated how intimately he was a part of college life.

The Healys' success at Holy Cross, both academic and social, was possible because they so willingly and completely attached themselves to the school, its people, and its values. Categorized by society into an uncertain racial position, they quickly realized that the college offered them a path through the complicated problem of identity. Until their enrollment, everywhere they turned they were aberrations: the products of condemned interracial sexuality, they were beset by anomalies. Though defined as black, some of them were light-skinned enough to appear to be white. Defined as slaves, they lived a life of freedom. Defined as chattels with no rights to own property or even to learn how to read, they were the recipients of an advanced education and the opportunities it opened. To continue to live in such a bifurcated mental world would mean a life of unremitting tension, but at Holy Cross they found a way to resolve that tension. The real test of belonging there was full participation in the Catholic church, and they proceeded to pass the test. Unsure about whether they were black or white, they could decide for themselves what they wanted to be. They could be Catholics.

Before their arrival in Worcester they had been blank religious slates. With only the occasional priest in Jones County, they had never been baptized as children. Now under the tutelage of Catholic priests, however, they were expected to participate in all the religious exercises of the college, and this they did. In addition to a daily schedule that included mass and other devotions, the academic year was also marked by a retreat, the first one of which was given in November 1844, shortly after the Healy brothers arrived on campus. For three days, classes were suspended while the Jesuits did what they did best. Mass, pious reading, examination of conscience, recitation of the rosary, and exhortation to conversion were all pursued with such earnestness that even the indifferent found it hard to remain unmoved. When it ended, the retreat had had its desired effect, as the superior of the college noted in the school's record book: "Nov. 18th 1844—At the close of the boys' retreat, the following students were baptized by Father Moore, spiritual father of the College, viz. James Healy, Hugh Healy, Patrick Healy, Alexander Sherwood Healy—sons of Michael Healy of Macon, Bibb County, state of Georgia." Baptized with them were two other students, their classmates William and Henry Brownson, sons of Orestes Brownson, the controversial Transcendentalist convert to the Roman church. Seven months later, in June 1845, the Healys received the sacrament of confirmation at the hands of Bishop John Fitzpatrick, whose chance meeting with their father had made their coming north possible in the first place.[14]

Insofar as we are able to judge such matters, their conversions were sincere, and in later years the brothers always remembered their baptism as a significant turning point, almost literally a day of rebirth. James spoke for all of them. In 1849, he looked back on the occasion and recognized it as the decisive event of his life. "Today 5 years ago," he wrote, "I entered this college. What a change. Then I was nothing, now I am a Catholic." His words had a narrow, literal meaning: he had not been a member of any church before this, and now he was. But the change he felt went deeper than that, a transformation from abject "nothing" into something. The others too were profoundly affected. Patrick would speak of his conversion as the opening of "a new and more perfect life," while Sherwood was described as "wonderfully altered." All four brothers immediately enlisted as altar boys, and when James assisted at mass, the experience touched him deeply: "how the thought of it awed the soul," he wrote in wonder.[15]

Their resort to religion is both expected and not. During slavery and afterward, religion offered many African Americans consolation from the harshness of life, together with an important means of self-expression. The black church afforded a rare opportunity for slaves to act independently of white control. It also provided a means of holding on to older African traditions even while adopting the newer ones of white owners, often fusing tribal religion with their masters' Christianity.[16] In the same way, the Healys might well have seen religion as a device for grounding themselves amid the uncertainties of their background. For the majority of their black and mixed-race contemporaries, however, the religions of choice were various branches of American Protestantism. American slaves and free blacks seemed most at home as Baptists, Methodists, or in other denominations in the so-called low church tradition. Largely because of their unexpected placement at Holy Cross, however, the Healy brothers followed the more unusual course of using the Catholic church as their form of religious expression.

From almost any perspective, it was a very unlikely choice. To begin with, the resurgence of anti-Catholic nativism meant that their decision to become Catholics might represent at best a jump from the frying pan into the fire. The Charlestown convent riot of 1834, still fresh in the public's mind, hardly indicated a hospitable religious environment. Since then, one gothic best-seller after another had portrayed the titillating abuses that supposedly went on behind the walls of Catholic institutions. Closer to home, Holy Cross was in the middle of a twenty-year struggle to secure a legal charter to grant academic degrees. The Massachusetts legislature was withholding the charter partly on the grounds that the college was engaged in spreading the dangerous anti-republican ideas of popery.[17] Already deeply at odds with society because of their racial status, the Healy brothers were only compounding their problems by assuming this suspect religious faith as well. Why should they so deliberately seek yet another reason to stand out as different?

More seriously, the record of the American Catholic church on questions of race had always been decidedly unimpressive. Wherever slavery was legal, Catholics joined the practice if they could afford to: the Jesuit order itself had owned slaves, in Maryland and elsewhere, for two hundred years. The peculiar institution had its vigorous defenders among the clergy and laity to the very end. Papal statements had drawn a fine distinction by denouncing the slave trade as early as the seventeenth century, but church leaders found no immorality in slave ownership. In America, Bishop John England of Charleston actively defended the maintenance of slavery where it already existed. Writing in his diocesan newspaper in 1840 and 1841, England presented a series of open letters addressed to a political figure who had, the bishop said, wrongly associated the Catholic religion with abolitionism. The charge was a calumny, England asserted, reviewing the history of slavery as presented in the Bible and the writings of the church fathers to show that Catholics found nothing inherently wrong with it. John Hughes, the archbishop of New York, considered slavery merely a "comparative" rather than an absolute evil. It was, he never doubted, "infinitely better than the condition in which [Africans] would have been, had they not been seized" and brought to America in chains.[18]

These positions were restated again and again. Bishop Francis Kenrick of Philadelphia maintained as late as 1861 that masters discharged their moral responsibilities so long as they treated their slaves mildly and according to "Christian principles." Archbishop Martin Spalding of Baltimore addressed a long "dissertation" to Rome on the subject in 1863, pointedly assigning historical blame for slavery in the United States to "Protestant England." Catholic laymen also joined the defense. "We cannot alter the fact of negro inferiority," Orestes Brownson wrote bluntly in the middle of the Civil War, expressing the fond hope that, should slaves win their freedom, they would simply "drift away" to Central and South America. The prospect that blacks might live as free men and women was one he dreaded, in part because it increased the likelihood of interracial marriages, which were, he said, "never desirable." He also despaired over the ability of African Americans to recognize true religion. "Why is it that you can scarcely get a single Christian thought into the negro's head," he wondered, "and that with him religion is almost sure to lapse into a groveling superstition?" With characteristic self-assurance, Brownson knew the answer. "Why, because he is a degenerate man, and superstition is degenerate religion."[19] Brownson's own sons were friends and classmates of the Healy brothers, baptized with them, but still the famous polemicist never deviated from American racial orthodoxy. Was this a church that could offer these young men from Georgia a comfortable spiritual home?

That the Healys could so enthusiastically embrace a church whose leading thinkers were convinced of the inferiority of blacks suggests that they were using

Catholicism at least in part to separate themselves from their African American heritage. Their choice of this religious identity provided them a means of escape from their culture's definition of who and what they were, a definition that was based on race alone. The reasons not to be black in their society were perhaps so obvious as to need no elaboration: for them, blackness would mean disadvantage at best, enslavement at worst. Thus, they probably needed little encouragement to think of themselves as white. Still, the transition from one race to the other—the passage from black to white—was difficult and risky. Having been defined as black, they could not simply make another selection without the help of some mitigating, intermediate institutions. Circumstance had presented them with the Catholic church as their intermediary, and they took hold of it. They made their identity simpler by making it more complicated.

Their decision was all the more startling because, society had decreed, they were supposed to have no racial choice at all. Biology had determined who they were, and biology's judgment admitted no appeals. The presence of that "one drop" from their mother had defined them forever as blacks. Suddenly, they had found a way to transcend that imperative. They could set aside the predetermining power that American society assigned to race. They could be something else, and in the process they could ease their way across the color line. Nineteenth-century Catholics were presumed to be white, since almost all of them had their origins in Europe: at the time, most American Catholics traced their origins to Ireland or Germany. By becoming Catholics, the Healys could, in effect, become white too—or at least confirm a decision to associate only with the whiteness of their father. However improbable their choice of religion may have seemed, it allowed them to accomplish another, more difficult choice: the choice not to be black at all, but to be white.

Becoming Catholics may also have appealed to them because it situated them in a larger cultural phenomenon, one that overshadowed even America itself. Here was a church that was international in scope, with a tradition far older than that of the upstart American republic. What better way for the Healys to take a measure of revenge on their society and its racial definitions than by countering with something grander and more ancient? Catholicism was nearly two thousand years old, and in their own time it seemed resurgent and newly vital. The papacy, then in the process of losing its political control over central Italy, was emerging as spiritually triumphant. The reign (1846–1878) of Pope Pius IX proved critical in this transition. In 1854, the pope single-handedly proclaimed a new article of faith, the doctrine of the Immaculate Conception, and a decade later he published a detailed "syllabus of errors," which condemned such far-fetched American notions as the separation of church and state. In 1870, Pius and his successors would be declared infallible in matters of faith and morals, a direct and unerring channel to the Holy Spirit. One might find this assertive church appealing or not, but it gave its adherents a refuge from doubts of all kinds. On most matters Catholics were "so sure," one of them would later write proudly, "so certain and set apart."[20]

A church that took such unabashedly clear positions offered the Healys a certainty that had too frequently eluded them otherwise, and the desire for firm ground was not peculiar to them. Later on, many black Americans would look to the older, if not necessarily religious, cultures of Europe and Africa for liberation from the restricting American notions of race. A desire to find a different rootedness for themselves, to reject misplaced loyalty to America, sent many African Americans in search of a new cultural identity. For some, this was found in an emerging pan-Africanism and a heightened sense of worldwide black solidarity. A reshaped allegiance took the place of his American-ness, W. E. B. Du Bois remembered of his own transformation; "henceforth," he said, "I was a Negro."[21] The Healys followed this course through the rejection of America for something else, but in their case, having already rejected their African heritage as well, the "something else" was the international culture of the Roman church. They would use religion to confirm a white identity. Even before their conversion, they had many reasons to reject the blackness of their mother, but their entrance into Catholicism solidified that decision.

❧

Their intentional grasp on whiteness is evident from the earliest surviving documentation we have about them. From the time of their conversion onward, the Healys consistently separated themselves from African Americans and refused to identify with them. While a student, for instance, James dispassionately repeated in his diary the offhand stories told by fellow students—many of them, like himself, the sons of slaveholding parents—about the "niggers" on the farms back home, apparently satisfied that this fighting word did not apply to him or his brothers. One day, a classmate was describing an effective means for catching squirrels, "after having just been talking about niggers," James wrote matter-of-factly. He then joined in the wild laughter when the audience misunderstood the narrator to be describing a method for hunting down runaway slaves. The offensive term came easily to James Healy. It was uncommon usage among upper-class planters before the Civil War, but it was no aberration. He mimicked supposed black dialect with no indication that he thought it peculiar to do so. Retelling a story from a Boston newspaper about "a negro preacher," he rendered the man's words: "Belubbed bredren, de debil is a big hog." Bemused by such carrying-on, James remarked snidely, "There must have been a revival after that."[22] He had managed to make fun of two things at once: the preacher (whose congregation included "an old grey headed snow ball," a condescending term whites used for aged black men) and the revival style of African American religion, an obvious contrast to the more decorous worship of his own new-found Catholicism.

The Healy brothers even witnessed one of the most racially charged phenomena of their era, the minstrel show. On the evening of James's graduation from Holy Cross in July 1849, an occasion that was surely the most important day of his life so far, he walked into Worcester with Hugh, Patrick, Sherwood, and a friend to celebrate. After strolling around for a while, they bought tickets to see the Ethiopian Serenaders, the foremost blackface troupe of their day. Summoning up more critical hauteur than was probably necessary, James found "too much foolery" and "too much noise" in the performance; "the words were not pronounced distinctly," he commented, as if he were reviewing a more serious production. Even so, they had all "laughed a great deal."[23] So successfully had he and his brothers separated themselves from their black ancestry that they found nothing remarkable either in the availability of this sort of entertainment or in their own enjoyment of it. Absent was any sense that they were part of the racial group being mocked on the stage. Just as important, their friends were equally comfortable with their white identity. Unfortunately, none of his classmates was the informative diarist that James Healy was, so their detailed opinions are unknown. But their silent actions say much. The white adolescent who sat through the minstrel show surrounded by the Healy brothers seems not to have thought of them as any less white than he.

Nor did the Healys have much sympathy for the arguments of abolitionists. As he grew older, Sherwood defended the traditional Catholic position that slavery was not "an evil *in se*" and that slave ownership was permissible even if slave trading was not. Slavery might even help "to control & civilize the negro." He wondered openly whether enslavement would have gained its original foothold had the Protestant Reformation not "shorn [the Catholic church] of her power." Moreover, he concluded, "those in modern times who pity the negro hate the church." His brother shared this view, common among Catholics in New England, that the Yankee Protestant leaders of the abolition movement were too closely aligned with anti-Catholic nativism. James observed with satisfaction that a rally in Worcester, conducted by the fiery William Lloyd Garrison ("a fool," he remarked tersely) had managed to collect only $1.37 in support of its cause. Borrowing an abolitionist newspaper from a friend, he quickly threw it aside, dismissing it as "full of threats against slavery as usual."[24] Hostility toward abolitionists was, of course, the normal, respectable political opinion of most Americans during the 1840s. Still, the ironies of the Healy brothers' stance toward slavery are more pointed—strictly speaking, they were slaves themselves—and these ironies were underlined by the ease with which they spoke about "the negro" as if they were talking about someone else.

Instead of sympathy toward black Americans, their allegiance was given wholly to their new religion. They became devout and regular in their observance, serving as officers of the student sodality, an organization that promoted regular prayer, especially to the Virgin Mary. They gathered with other students to recite the rosary, and they internalized orthodox Catholic habits, often with the special fervor and scrupulosity of the convert. James, for instance, went to confession one Saturday in August 1849 and then, in a highly unusual move, went again the next morning, apparently to confirm that he had been forgiven. On another occasion, he spent several days wrestling with his conscience about an unspecified matter; resolving his concern by recourse to the confessional, he happily reported that he "felt ready for communion this morning." He lost no opportunity to prove his commitment to Catholicism, assessing one author whose work he was reading in class as "very fair for a Protestant." For his part, Patrick devoutly praised "the great change which God . . . wrought in me," and James described Sherwood as "much changed for the better." Sherwood himself proclaimed his faith "a badge, an ensign, a standard"—he was borrowing the words from the Spiritual Exercises of Ignatius Loyola, no doubt to the pleasure of his Jesuit teachers—and he later concluded that "the Catholic religion is too sublime and too difficult of observance to have been invented by man."[25]

Catholicism offered them more than other-worldly reassurance, however; it also gave them a close and accepting community in this world. Here was a readymade set of connections, all the more important to them as adolescents, far from home. The small circle of Catholic New England happily took them in, perhaps because it was itself isolated in an otherwise cool social and religious climate. Beset by hostile nativists even as their church grew, the region's Catholics were prepared to welcome anyone, no matter how improbable, who chose voluntarily to join them. Rare indeed were those outsiders who willingly sought entrance into a church that many detested. In that context, questions about who and what these converts were seemed less important, even though Boston's Catholics had no more tolerant racial attitudes than other Americans. Nevertheless, the very radicalness of the religious decision made by these strangers from Georgia counted in their favor.

The boys spent their vacations from Holy Cross not at home but with the relatives of priests in and around Boston, becoming in effect members of those families. They enjoyed the Christmas holidays of 1848, for example, in these adoptive surroundings. The four left Worcester by train and took up temporary residence in Cambridge with Eleanor and Thomas Boland, the sister and brother-in-law of Bishop Fitzpatrick. There they met their own sister Martha, age ten, who was now boarding permanently with the Bolands. She had been sent north by their father shortly after the boys' enrollment in school, and she had been baptized only a month after them. Like her brothers, she too had settled into the little world of Boston Catholicism. On Christmas morning they all got up early and went to mass, returning home afterward for toasts with eggnog. Next, several of them traveled into the cathedral in Boston to hear a second mass, this one a grander liturgy complete with a string orchestra performing the music of Haydn. In the afternoon there was a sleigh ride and finally, after supper, the exchange of gifts. Fitzpatrick himself and several priests, their day's work done, came in the evening and joined the others for parlor games and the "bagsport," a kind of Christmas grab bag. There was enough friendly horseplay all around that, during the grab, one of the students nearly hit the bishop on the head with a cane.[26] The youngsters from Georgia were no longer exotic outsiders: they were intimate members of a close-knit circle.

They may even have found in this extended religious family a welcome substitute for—or, at least, a supplement to—their own biological family. The degree to which the Catholic church replaced the parents and siblings left behind in Georgia is evident in their relationship with one of their teachers, Father George Fenwick. Part of a long-tailed English Catholic clan that traced its American origins to the first settlements in Maryland, Fenwick had entered the Society of Jesus at Georgetown College in 1815 and studied at various Jesuit houses in Europe. When his older brother Benedict, then the bishop of Boston, opened Holy Cross in 1843, George Fenwick arrived from Washington as part of its first faculty. A teacher of Latin and Greek, he was tall, gaunt, and formidable in appearance, but his outgoing personality made him a student favorite. He took a special interest in the Healy brothers, and they in turn looked to him as a special protector and patron. Tellingly, they even fell into the habit of addressing him as "Dad." Fenwick offered them advice on what they should do with their adult lives—he and James "had some long talk . . . about my future destiny," the young man noted on one occasion—and Fenwick exchanged regular correspondence with the brothers until his death in 1857. They confided in him as they did in no one else, sharing among themselves concerns over his health, just as children do with aging parents.[27]

This familial warmth toward Fenwick stood in contrast to the more distant relationship they had with their own father and mother. At school, the boys exhibited no sentimentality about Georgia and certainly no intention ever to return to it. They never inquired about their four youngest siblings—Michael, Josephine, Eliza, and Eugene—three of whom had been born after their departure for the north. They did, apparently, see their father occasionally: though specific evidence is lacking, Michael Healy came north on business periodically during their years at Holy Cross. His infrequent letters to them were formal affairs, transmitting money to pay their tuition bills and Martha's expenses for room and board with the Bolands. Once out of Georgia, they never saw their mother again and evinced no desire to do so. In his diary, James mentioned her only once, reporting in March 1849 that "Father" had sent him a daguerreotype of her. Interestingly, the young man felt compelled to note that he even "recognised" her "after so long an absence from home."[28] Eliza Clark Healy had become a shadowy figure from the past whom one might or might not recognize. None of their correspondence with their father survives, but many letters to George Fenwick, beginning always "Dear Dad," are extant. They had a remote "Father," spoken of in proper and businesslike terms; a Catholic priest was now their only "Dad."

With the church as their extended family and Fenwick as their surrogate parent, the decision three of the brothers made to pursue lives in religion seems, in hindsight, inevitable. When James and his teacher had their talk about his "future destiny" in January of 1849, both already knew that the young man would enter a seminary in the hope of becoming a Catholic priest. Patrick and Sherwood were inclining toward the same decision, while Hugh was opting for a life in business. The founders of Holy Cross had hoped that many of its graduates would consider the priesthood, in part as a way of developing a native-born American Catholic clergy. They did not expect that all their students would seek ordination, however, and the training of well-educated Catholic laymen was also an important goal. While one of the Healy brothers would choose this latter course, three chose the former. Theirs was not a dramatic religious conversion, to be followed quickly by the cooling of emotion or a gradual falling away. Instead, religion was to be their life.

As the oldest, James went first when his college career came to a close. Classes ended as usual at the beginning of July 1849, followed by a few days of examinations and then preparation for what would be the first commencement in the school's history. Student speakers were drilled beforehand in the hope of making a good impression, and on Thursday, July 26, the ceremonies were held. After morning mass, a procession of students and faculty, led by the school band, marched around the college building and into the lecture hall. James began what he himself called the "speechifying," talking for half an hour on "Moral Principles," an assigned topic. Next came several other boys from each class year, including Sherwood (who, James said, "did excellent well and everybody says so") and Patrick (who, his brother noted reproachfully, "mumbled"). James then took the rostrum again for the valedictory address, "during which I was crying myself and about a dozen of the boys also," as he evoked their college years as "the brightest and happiest days of our existence." Finally came a rendition of "Home, Sweet Home" from the band, the awarding of diplomas, and the reading out of class rank. James placed first among the graduates, with one of the Brownson brothers right behind him and Hugh finishing fourth. Patrick was first in his class, and Sherwood second in his. All the boys received personal congratulations from Bishop Fitzpatrick, who was presiding, and from the day's special guest, Father Theobald Mathew, the famed Irish missionary who traveled America preaching the cause of "total abstinence" from drink. For the graduates, melancholy mixed with celebration: teary good-byes alternated with some last high jinks. During the banquet after the ceremonies, James punned that he and his friends "layed in something to keep our *spirits* up." Happily, Father Mathew had already left for a temperance rally in Boston.[29]

James was now ready to take his next step, armed with "a good resolution of not setting my mind on this world nor the things of this world." His brother Hugh, also a graduate that day, was likewise preparing to leave Worcester, but he would move toward the "things of this world." Returning to Georgia was never an option, so instead he relocated to New York City, where he went to work for his father's friend John Manning. The store that Manning ran at 160 Broadway was prosperous enough to give the young man experience that he might some day take into a business of his own. Beyond that, with James's imminent departure for several years of retreat from the world in a seminary, Hugh as the next oldest assumed the responsibility to look after the others. He later brought Sherwood to New York for a time, allowing him to earn some money for college expenses. He checked up on Martha, still boarding with the Bolands but old enough now (she was twelve) so that a decision would soon have to be made about her future schooling. Another brother, named Michael after his father, followed his siblings from Georgia to Holy Cross in the fall of 1849, and Hugh had to superintend his welfare too.

Thus, by 1850, the course of Healy siblings seemed to have been laid out clearly. Unable to remain in Georgia because of their parents' unorthodox marriage and the disabling racial status it had imparted to them, they had found escape and new lives in the North. They had passed into the white community and into a religious community that, however unexpectedly, was willing to accept them. The continued success of their father's plantation gave them the financial resources they needed to take advantage of these opportunities. At midcentury, their prospects were far brighter than they had any hope to expect, but fortune turned on them quickly. With the sudden deaths of their parents a few months apart, all their uncertainties came rushing back.

CHAPTER THREE

Orphans: Hugh, Martha, and the
Younger Children

By the middle 1840s Michael Morris Healy had succeeded, perhaps beyond his hopes, in securing a future of freedom for his older children, but there was uncertainty amid his success. Economically, times were good. Cotton prices had recovered nicely after bottoming out in the panic of 1837, and he prospered from what one historian has called "the last golden decade" of Georgia agriculture before the Civil War. He left no account books to measure his wealth, but other evidence places him consistently in the top 10 percent of land and slave owners in Jones County.[1] Supporting four boys at Holy Cross cost $600 per year, no mean sum at the time, and the expenses of Martha, boarding with the Bolands, were likewise considerable, but he had both the money to spend and the incentive to spend it. At home, life could seem normal, but it was a fragile normalcy. In his eyes, Eliza Clark Healy was his wife, but because the law counted her a slave, her safety depended entirely on him. If he, a man seventeen years her senior, should die before her, slavery would almost certainly replace her freedom. The same fate might also befall the youngest children: Amanda Josephine (known throughout her life by the second of her names), Eliza Dunamore, and the infant Eugene. Until they were old enough to be sent north, their future too was insecure.

As a provident man, therefore, Michael set out to provide legally for his family, sitting down immediately after Josephine's birth in January 1845 to draw up a will. We do not know what kind of legal advice was available to him, but he recognized that disposing of worldly affairs was trickier for him than it was for other men. There were certain things that he must not say in this document. He could not, for example, actually call Eliza his wife, for the law denied her that status. Nor could he declare her a free woman, since the use of wills for manumission had been expressly illegal in Georgia since 1818. Overreaching on either count raised the possibility that his wishes would be invalidated by the courts and his property forfeited. A contemporary farmer in adjacent Putnam County had tried to evade the law by directing his executors to buy land in Indiana and to settle his slaves on it, but a judge saw through this backhanded attempt at emancipation and broke the will. In another case, a shrewd lawyer in nearby Hancock County had been more successful, ordering those managing his affairs to allow his six slave children to leave for another state, scrupulously reaffirming that "they are not to be emancipated in this state, but are slaves here."[2] Michael Healy too had to navigate in these dangerous testamentary waters.

He began by pretending that his case was a perfectly normal one, leaving his entire estate to "my beloved children in New York: James, Hugh, Patrick, Sherwood, + Martha." It was a bold opening gambit. They certainly could not inherit his property, "both real and personal," if they were Georgians, because if they were Georgians they were slaves. Better, then, that he simply run the bluff, placing them under the laws of New York (even though they actually lived in Massachusetts) by designating his "worthy and trusted friend," John Manning "of the City and State of New York," as their guardian. Healy next ordered that all his property in Georgia, "negroes excepted," be sold and the money invested with Manning for the benefit of the children. The slaves were to be hired out every year "in the usual way"; only after the youngest child came of age were the slaves to be sold, with the proceeds added to the capital of the estate. When the children "now in Georgia shall arrive at the North," he said in words that indicated his intention to send them there, they were to share fully in the estate. Finally, on the status of the children's mother, he chose his words very precisely indeed. He directed that "my trusty woman Elisa [sic], Mother of my Said children, . . . shall be removed to a free State when her Interest will be best consulted," and that the executors were to pay her $120 each year for the remainder of her life.[3] The language was veiled and correct but, in its own way, forthright. Eliza might have been merely his "trusty woman," not his legal spouse, but she was nevertheless publicly acknowledged as the mother of his children. She inherited nothing but would be supported with an annuity for as long as she lived.

Unwilling to leave anything to chance, Michael Healy also took the occasion to specify some other last intentions. Against the future appearance of predatory suitors for his daughters, he declared that their shares of the estate would go "to them and their bodily heirs only," a provision that was becoming common among concerned fathers at the time. He designated several immediate neighbors to act as his local executors, but Manning alone was to be legally responsible for the children. Were Manning to "pay the debt of nature," Healy added poetically, he nominated

Father Thomas Mulledy, the president of Holy Cross College, "to act as guardian for my children and to carry out the provisions of my will." If this priest were unable to carry out these duties, then James Healy, as the oldest son, was empowered to serve as guardian jointly with "some discreet and proper person" of his own selection—perhaps in Michael's mind, Bishop Fitzpatrick or Father Fenwick.

Michael had done as much as he could for his wife and their children within the constraints of the law, but the tensions of life in the present never abated. As national political agitation over slavery grew in intensity and the demand for ever clearer racial dividing lines in the South likewise grew more pressing, Georgia became less and less likely a place for the family. No single event prompted him, but by the time of the birth of the last child in January 1849, Michael Healy seems to have determined to sell off his property in Jones County and reunite the entire family in the North. He and Eliza, together with the babies, would follow the well-worn path to New York or, perhaps, Boston. That summer, James recorded the decision in his diary. "Last evening," he wrote on the day before his graduation from college in July 1849, "Hugh + myself both rec[eive]d letters from home." Next he noted the significant news: "Father"—at first he had written "the old man," but then struck a line through it and substituted the more dignified title—"will be on in the fall of the year, and will leave Georgia next spring."[4]

When the spring of 1850 came, however, it brought a sadder development: the death of Eliza Clark Healy on May 19. We know unfortunately little of it. No member of the family committed mention of it to paper, at least to no paper that has survived, and no mementos of her were preserved as keepsakes.[5] Eliza's death, at age thirty-seven, was surely a stunning blow to her husband, who had devoted his life to this unusual woman. It was all the more distressing because of the children left behind: Josephine was only five, young Eliza but three, and Eugene just fifteen months. Loss of his "trusty woman" probably reinforced Michael's intention to leave Georgia, but that could not be done immediately. The crop was already in the ground that spring as usual, and he thus had to remain for at least one more season before leaving the past behind.

A happier future was not to come for him, as he followed his wife in death three months later on August 27. The summer of 1850 had been one of the hottest on record in Jones County, with afternoon temperatures often standing at 104 degrees, but those extremes may not have contributed to Michael Healy's rapid decline. In New York that July, Hugh had encountered a family friend, visiting from Macon, who reported that "Father is enjoying excellent health." Even so, it is perhaps not too much of a reach to suppose that a lonely melancholy had set in: if anyone may be said to have died of a broken heart, the fifty-three-year-old widower seems a fitting candidate. Like that of his wife, his own death went unremarked by any of his children or by those who knew them. Quietly, Michael was buried next to Eliza on a hill above the Ocmulgee River, and a year later a hired workman enclosed the two graves within a stone wall.[6]

James was out of the country, enrolled by then at a seminary in Montreal, so Hugh as the next oldest assumed the responsibility to see that his father's wishes, expressed in the will, were carried out. He had to think twice, however, about returning to Georgia himself to take charge of things; once there, he might not be able to get back out again. Accordingly, he and Manning had to depend on the trustworthy neighbors who had been designated as executors: Robert Hardeman, William Moreland, and Robert Macarthy. These three set in motion the procedures for disposing of the dead man's property. They hired appraisers who, with a precision that was customary in such cases, went through Healy's house and barns, itemizing everything and assigning a value: tools, household goods, produce, livestock. By the end of September this work was done. The liquid assets of the deceased were meager—only $46.93 in cash, together with a dozen promissory notes, one of them ten years old and marked "uncollectible"—but the total assessment was more impressive. The "perishable property" was valued at just over $9,000, the land at $7,500, and the slaves at more than $22,000. By early December, the land was sold, bringing in over $8,000, a comfortable $500 more than the appraisers had said. Healy's 1,500 acres went all in one piece to a man who thereby became the second largest landowner in the county. The profit margin was not nearly so good when the personal property was auctioned off two weeks later, as a hundred neighbors spent the day walking around the place bidding on the items presented to them.[7]

Such affairs were always a buyer's market. The original owner was dead, unable to haggle for better terms, and the executors, no matter how fond they had been of their deceased friend, were eager to get the whole business over with as quickly as possible. Thus, it was all very well for the appraisers to say that Healy's fancy eight-day clock was worth $10, but a buyer picked it up for only $6 under the auctioneer's gavel. The livestock appreciated or depreciated under the shrewd scrutiny of experienced eyes. The cattle were valued at $5 per head; one went for $12 but most for less than $3. One man paid $150 ($25 more than the asking price) for the gray mule named Mouse, but another walked away with the bay mare Skylark, said to be worth $85, for only $77. Healy's overseer, William Hornady, picked up some things he had probably had his eye on for some time. He got a prize stallion named Dunganon, together with its blankets and a racing saddle, for $260 and a double-barreled shotgun for $17. When the day was over, the proceeds came to just under $5,200, barely half the hoped-for amount, a take then reduced even further by the auctioneer's commission.[8]

For now, the most valuable commodities, the slaves, were left out of the calculation, and it is here that the sad irony of Michael and Eliza Healy's children comes crashing home. Still legally slaves themselves, they were now slaveowners. Today we marvel that the ownership of other humans was thinkable for anyone, let alone for those who understood enslavement better than any white master could. The institution was so pervasive, however, as to be unavoidable. "Everybody in the South," Frederick Douglass said sarcastically, "wants the privilege of whipping somebody else." Free black slaveholders were hardly unknown: the pioneer black historian Carter Woodson counted more than sixty of them in Georgia in 1830 alone. Some were even reputed to be especially hard masters, and they may have had their reasons to be strict. Free blacks were always in a tenuous position in the South, and those who possessed slaves could send a reassuring message to their suspicious neighbors. Even if they themselves violated the expected equation of blackness with slavery, they posed no general challenge to prevailing racial arrangements. Knowing how reluctantly whites tolerated them, they could distance themselves from enslaved blacks and demonstrate that they were "safe," guided primarily by the profit motive.[9] So it now was with the Healys, but their slaveholding served another purpose as well. Here was one more way to distance themselves from African Americans, one more way to proclaim that they were not black at all. Coming so soon after their declaration for whiteness by the choice of their religion, the acquisition of their father's slaves was another means of denying their blackness.

As Michael Healy had directed, his "negroes" were hired out, and it proved a profitable operation. The practice was a familiar one in the Old South; perhaps as many as 10 percent of all the slaves in the region, most of them the property of recently deceased owners, were being rented out at any given time. They were leased for the term of a year—fifty-one weeks, actually; they got a week off at Christmas—and the market for them was always good. Neighboring farmers could use additional hands, the railroads needed strong backs and arms for laying track, and slaves with special mechanical skills could command a good price. Beginning in January 1851, therefore, the forty-nine Healy slaves were hired by twenty-one different masters. Generally, an effort was made to keep family groups, or at least mothers and their small children, together. Thus, one of the executors, William

Moreland, hired the husband and wife David and Vina for $140, and a neighbor widow hired Amy and her three young children for $20. Not every slave could bring in a suitable fee, but they had to be placed somewhere: Harriet and her four children were let out for their "victuals + clothes." Altogether, the profit on these transactions was good: after a commission for the leasing agent had been deducted, the proceeds to the estate in the first year came to more than $1,450. Profitability continued thereafter, rising as high as $1,635 in 1853; by the end of the leasing arrangements in 1855, a total return of just under $5,000 had been realized.[10]

Lucrative though it was, hiring out the slaves was also a good deal of bother. One local man made a successful claim against the estate for transporting the leased chattels to their work sites and for having to spend six days chasing down and returning runaways. The local doctor earned almost $80 in 1851 on visits and medicines, and two midwives had to be paid $5 apiece for attending slave childbirths. Ultimately, the only sensible course of action was to realize the full potential of the slaves by selling them off. This process began on January 3, 1854, at the regular slave auction in Macon. Able-bodied men were highly prized by potential owners, while women were often harder to sell. True, they could produce new slaves, thereby increasing long-term capital, but in the meantime, they and their children were more likely to represent a drain on resources. The laws of supply and demand also affected the price of slaves, but the trend of 1850s was steadily upward, and the Healy estate was thus selling at a good time. A slave named Daniel, who had been appraised conservatively at $400, brought in $1,200 on the auction block. Mothers and their children were often sold together—Caroline and her three babies, one an infant, went for $1,500—but economic reality could overrule sentiment, and sometimes families were split apart. The couple Ned and Melvina, for example, went with their daughter Emily to one buyer for about $1,700 altogether, but their son Ambrose was sold to another for $1,200. When the day was done, with some of Michael Healy's "negroes" still unsold, the estate had taken in more than $30,000, a healthy 25 percent more than the appraisal of three years earlier.[11]

A second and last recourse to the slave auction was made at the beginning of January 1856, eventually adding another $3,000 to the profits, and it further underlines the ambiguity (or worse) of the slaveholding children of Michael and Eliza Healy. This group of slaves included a woman named Margaret and her four children: William, Julia, Violet, and the tellingly named Martha Ann, a child who had the same name as her deceased master's oldest daughter, a young woman who was now one of her owners. A year before, Margaret had initiated a suit against the estate for her freedom, on what grounds is unclear. At this time, however, slaves could almost never win cases of this kind: even if she could argue that Michael had promised her her freedom before his death, a circumstance that seems virtually impossible, such promises had no legal standing. Still, Hardeman and Moreland (Macarthy had withdrawn as an executor by now, unable to devote any more time to Healy's complicated business) had to retain a lawyer to go into the county court to get the suit dismissed. This was done easily enough, and immediately thereafter Margaret and her children were sold, each of them to a different master, perhaps as a form of redoubled punishment for the trouble they had caused.[12] The escape into freedom by the Healy children would not be possible for their own slaves.

But the account of the Healys' ownership of slaves has a happier, if partly mysterious, final chapter. In February 1860 the record books of the Jones County court contain the notation of a seemingly routine transaction. For the sum of $1,400, Samuel Griswold, a well-to-do planter and entrepreneur, sold some of his property to a neighbor: "to wit, a Negro woman, Nancy, of yellow complexion, also a Negro girl named Nancy, of yellow complexion, which Negroes I warrant to be slaves." Nothing would attract attention to this sale, except that these two women were sold again just four days later for the same $1,400 to "James A. Healy, of the State of Massachusetts, city of Boston." Why was Michael Healy's oldest son, well settled by then in Massachusetts, buying this slave mother and daughter, whose designation as "yellow" was a code to indicate that they were of mixed racial background? Why was he purchasing slaves at all, barely a year before the outbreak of civil war? Speculation alone must offer answers. Perhaps the older Nancy was a sister to Eliza Clark Healy, long held on a neighboring plantation, thus making her an aunt of the Healy siblings. Perhaps Nancy was even a woman by whom Michael Morris Healy had had a child, the younger Nancy, who was thus a half-sister to the others. The fragmentary evidence supports no conclusion, but we must presume that James Healy bought these two women in order to give them their freedom. What subsequently became of either one we do not know, but this final act of generosity may partially mitigate the shock we otherwise feel at the ongoing profit the Healys derived from slavery.[13]

Settlement of the estate was now nearly complete, and the proceeds were regularly sent to Hugh Healy and John Manning. This process began in 1852 and continued until October 1859. Every few months (sometimes more often), as money accumulated, the executors visited the Macon office of the Mechanics Bank of Augusta and secured a draft for transmittal to New York. Over time, at least $51,000 was transferred in this way. The number is impressive on its face, but its value at the time was even more substantial. Converting historical monetary amounts to present-day sums is always a risky business, but one historian has calculated that an antebellum dollar was worth about $15 today. That puts the proceeds from the Healy estate at the equivalent of more than three-quarters of a million contemporary dollars, a healthy capital base on which to build. Thanks to their parents' success, founded on the labor of slaves, the Healy children would be financially secure for the remainder of their lives.[14]

There were, of course, far more important things to get out of Georgia than the cash: namely, the three younger, now orphaned, Healy children. Precisely how and when this happened is not clear, for none of those persons interested in the family's welfare ever discussed them explicitly, and the probate documents are silent on the subject. Michael Healy seems to have intended to send them to New York shortly after his wife's death, but he was unable to act on this plan before his own. In July 1850, Hugh had written to his old mentor at Holy Cross, Father George Fenwick, telling him: "If you come to N.Y. be sure to call in. It is probable I will want you to make a few Christians." The closing words suggest Hugh's desire to have his younger siblings baptized as Catholics, but since the prospect was only "probable," rather than certain, they had apparently not yet arrived in the metropolis. Immediately on their father's death a month later, therefore, Josephine, Eliza, and Eugene were most likely looked after by a neighbor, perhaps Mathis White and his wife, with whom the Healy overseer's nine-year-old son, George Hornaday, was already boarding. There they could be protected—"hidden" may not be too dramatic a word—until their removal from the state.[15]

Hugh Healy himself finally returned to Jones County to retrieve his siblings sometime in the middle of 1851. Such a trip held genuine risks for him. He was still a slave in the eyes of the state of Georgia and therefore technically a runaway. On his arrival there, the tough new Fugitive Slave Law, which had been passed by Congress the very summer of his parents' deaths, might be applied to him by some enterprising neighbor. The law enshrined the presumption that all apprehended blacks were slaves, and it placed on them the burden of proof to demonstrate that they were legally free; this was something Hugh obviously could not do. In its first year of enforcement, the statute was applied to eighty-four fugitives, and only five of them managed to secure their freedom. Those were not very good odds. Free blacks were sometimes kidnapped, even from northern cities, because their abductors could make some easy money by turning them in as runaways and collecting a reward. Anyone who captured an alleged fugitive could prove the case solely on the testimony of white witnesses, who could be readily found on the promise of a percentage of the subsequent sale price. Those harboring fugitives were also subject to harsh criminal penalties, and the same sanctions applied to those who stood in the way of capture. Thus, not even the family's friends would be secure if Hugh were in the area.[16]

There is only circumstantial evidence for his brief return to his birthplace, but it is convincing. Somehow he managed to get into Georgia and back out with his younger sisters and brother. By June of 1851 the children were safely north of the Mason-Dixon line, where a priest did indeed "make a few Christians" of them: they were baptized at a New York City parish staffed by Jesuit priests on the thirteenth of that month, with Hugh and one of the priests as godparents. The following winter, the courts at home recorded John Manning as having received a transfer of money from Michael Healy's estate, not through the usual channel of a bank draft but rather directly "by the hands of Hugh C. Healy." The Jones County workman who was paid to erect a stone marker on the graves of Michael and Eliza also silently testifies to their son's last visit. No memorial had previously been erected. This was more likely the duty of a son, and the marker's completion at the end of 1851 had probably been arranged earlier that year when he had stood on the spot himself.[17] It was the final chapter in the lives of his unusual parents.

※❧

As a young man just beginning to make his way in the business world, Hugh now became the de facto parent for his siblings, some of whom were young enough to be his own children. The older members of the family were by then reasonably well provided for. Patrick had graduated from Holy Cross in the summer of 1850, and Sherwood was making steady progress in his studies there. Even now, both were heeding inner voices of religious motivation that would soon lead them to the priesthood. Young Michael was enrolled at the college in Worcester, though he shortly began to exhibit rebellious behavior, including periodic episodes of running away, that would prove worrisome to his older brothers. James was pursuing his future, and the decision he had made in that regard also provided at least a temporary answer to the question of what to do about Martha, the oldest daughter, who was twelve years old when her parents died.

During his final year at Holy Cross, after his long talk with Father Fenwick, James had decided to become a priest. Catholicism had helped resolve his racial dilemma, and he intended now to solidify that new identity forever. A young man preparing for the priesthood in nineteenth-century America had only a limited number of ways to go about it, and those of James Healy were even more circum-scribed than most. Maryland had been the traditional center of Catholicism in the United States, and the only seminaries worthy of the name were there. The largest was Saint Mary's College in Emmitsburg, just outside Baltimore, which had opened in 1809. Enrollment there, however, was out of the question. Having es-caped his heritage by moving north, he would only be asking for trouble by re-turning to a state where slavery was still legal. Even if, like Hugh, he could avoid apprehension under the Fugitive Slave Law, he faced a difficult time there. Ac-cordingly, he looked not south but rather north, to Canada. Boston's Bishop Fitz-patrick noted the decision while recording his own thoughts on the Holy Cross graduation in 1849: "two of these graduates, John Brownson, son of Orestes A. Brownson, the celebrated Catholic Reviewer, and James Healy of Georgia, declare their wish to embrace the ecclesiastical state. The Bishop," Fitzpatrick continued, speaking of himself in the third person, "sends both to the Theological Seminary of the Sulpitians [*sic*] at Montreal."[18]

Fitzpatrick knew the Seminary of Saint-Sulpice well, since he himself had been a student there almost twenty years before. His personal connection with the Healy family, now deepened considerably since his first encounter with them, had once again worked to their advantage. The Sulpician Fathers who conducted the school had been organized first in seventeenth-century France, and they took as their special mission the education of diocesan clergy in seminaries. In addition to the training in theology and rubrics that a priest would need for parish work, the Sulpicians also imparted to their pupils a spirituality that stressed regularity of practice, rigorous forms of mental prayer, and a reliance on the confessional. To prepare the aspiring priest for a life of hardship and service, they also enforced strict separation from the outside world, forbidding all contact with family and friends during the period of seminary training. James had enrolled at Montreal in September of 1849 and, besides John Brownson, he found four other Boston seminarians there.[19]

Records of James's academic performance do not survive, and in any case, sem-inary training was more a matter of slow spiritual "formation" than of intellectual progress. Truth to tell, young men could learn what they had to in far less than the time allowed them. Patrick would write Father Fenwick in 1853, urging his brother's ordination a full two years ahead of schedule: exasperated at the delay, Patrick insisted that "he is all prepared." James was willing to let matters take their normal course, however, and he even internalized the steady, traditional ap-proaches of his instructors. Writing Fenwick at the end of his first year of study, he noted that permission even to send a letter to his old patron was a departure from the normal rule and, quoting another teacher, he dutifully observed that "exceptions + exemptions are bad things." Still, he flourished at Saint-Sulpice as he had at Holy Cross, and he was promoted each year to a new rank among the so-called minor orders of the church, each one a step along the road to the priesthood itself.[20]

His placement at Montreal also clarified the next step for Martha Healy. Her arrangement with the Bolands was good enough, but she was now an adolescent and a more regular placement was needed. Because she was the oldest girl, whose upbringing might be expected to set the pattern for her two younger sisters, she was a special concern for James. While still at Holy Cross he had received a letter from her and complained to his diary that it was "very short and poorly written." Her opportunities for education were limited, however, as indeed they were for all young Catholic girls in Boston. There was no equivalent to Holy Cross, which enrolled only boys, and no prospect that one would develop. The Ursuline Sisters had been chased out of town by the nativist riot that destroyed their convent and academy in 1834. Another group of sisters, coming east from Ohio, opened a girls' school in Roxbury, a suburb of Boston, in 1850, but it was shaky and unpromising. Thus, the opening of a Canadian option for Martha presented her with a better prospect.[21]

Located near the property of the Sulpician seminary in Montreal was the motherhouse of a community of sisters known as the Congregation de Notre Dame. Distinct from the other American orders that bore the "Notre Dame" designation, this group had been founded in the earliest days of Canadian settlement by Marguerite Bourgeoys, a pioneering nun from France. By the time of her death in 1700 she presided over seven convents, maintained by forty sisters. Steady growth throughout the next 150 years had put the community in charge of an impressive network of schools for girls throughout Canada. Mostly French-speaking themselves, the sisters taught English to French Canadian girls, some of whom would eventually find work in the mills of New England, and French to American girls who sought the distinction of a refined education. Their Villa Maria motherhouse and academy in Montreal advertised itself as "renowned all over the continent as a school of high distinction." If Martha Healy, the daughter of a comfortably well-off planter, wanted an education suitable for her station, this seemed a good place to get it. There was little chance that she would be able to see her brother, securely cloistered behind the walls of Saint-Sulpice up the street, but indirect connections could be maintained. Priests from the seminary served as chaplains for both the nuns and the girls, visiting the convent and the school regularly to say mass and hear confessions.[22] In this way, the extended religious family of the Catholic church could once again shelter the Healy children.

The Notre Dame sisters were clear about their goals: they were "progressive in . . . educational ideas, and yet conservative of tradition and its prestige, distinguished, refined, and in sympathy with the type of education suited to the gentlewoman of America," their historian enthused. Their school combined attention to the usual academic subjects with dutiful religious practice, including many of the vivid and emotionally rich devotions that were beginning to characterize nineteenth-century Catholicism. In their chapel, they practiced "perpetual adoration," a custom in which at least one member of the community was engaged around the clock in prayer before the consecrated host on the altar. They also instituted the so-called forty hours devotion, an increasingly popular exercise that commemorated the precise amount of time, Saint Augustine had said, Jesus had spent in the tomb. The pupils took part in these and other devotions along with their teachers. No less a personage than the bishop of Montreal preached a retreat for them at the end of Martha's first school year, and priests from the Sulpicians offered several days of particularly intense religious instruction in both French and English each term.[23]

Together with nine other girls, most of them with Irish surnames, Martha Healy enrolled with the Notre Dame nuns in August 1850—as it happened, just a week before her father in faraway Georgia died. The normal language of instruction was French, and Martha must have had either some grounding or a special facility in this, because by the end of her first term that Christmas she placed second in her class. The curriculum included the three Rs, together with a smattering of science and "physical culture" (that is, regular exercise) unusual in Catholic girls' education at the time. She also took advantage of other opportunities: beyond the basic charges for room and board, her brother Hugh and John Manning paid for music and drawing lessons. The sisters proudly advertised that their young girls could learn to play the piano and other instruments, and these talents were sure to complement their cultivation of diction, conduct, and "la politesse." The number of students grew steadily throughout the early 1850s, requiring construction of a new dormitory for the girls. There were even some conversions to Catholicism from among the daughters of New England Protestants, precisely the eventuality that many nativists feared.[24]

The sisters intended to prepare their graduates to meet the requirements for teachers in the public schools of Quebec and elsewhere, but the nuns also hoped that many of their students would be drawn to the religious life and would join their order. Perhaps encouraged by the religious vocations of her brothers, Martha Healy felt this pull to become a member of the Notre Dame nuns. Individual motivation in such cases is difficult to reconstruct after the fact, and it is even more mysterious in this case given the total absence of surviving documentation. Martha never felt the need to explain her decision. Having been immersed in an environment that valued such things, however, she probably felt some genuine attraction for a life dedicated to the service of others. As a nun, she would also have the chance to pursue a professional career as a teacher. Few contemporary women had such promising career options, and the prospect may have had special appeal to this young woman whose financial security left her able to entertain such possibilities.[25]

At the same time, she may also have felt the racial dilemma of her family more deeply than her brothers. Her life outside the convent would otherwise be governed by marriage and children, and those could be especially problematic for a woman of mixed heritage. In choosing a husband, should she keep her background a secret? Could she do so even if she wanted to? No document or photograph testifies to Martha's complexion, so it is impossible to know the ease with which others might discover her secret, but it mattered little: even if she could disguise her own "black blood," that of her brothers would be apparent to any suitor. Moreover, because society defined blackness as internal as much as external, she would always be accounted an African American woman, eligible only for an African American husband. She and her siblings might have decided to pass over the color line from black to white, but they could not expect others, including potential spouses, to be so accepting. Thus, whatever rewards it might offer in the next world, the life of a celibate religious woman had some appeal in this one precisely because it helped Martha avoid these questions.

Accordingly, she decided early to enter the sisterhood, and her brother Patrick reported her "very happy in her choice of life." By 1853 she had enrolled as a novice, and in September of 1855 she made her first profession of vows as a member of the Congregation de Notre Dame. She was seventeen years old, young by later standards but common then, and she was to be known as Sister Saint Lucie. Perhaps unwittingly, the officers of the convent confirmed the reconstruction of the family's story when they identified the new sister as the "minor child of the late Michael M. Healy and Lady Eliza Clark, her father and mother, deceased." This was probably the first and last time anyone had ever honored Eliza Clark Healy with the title "Lady." The sisters noted Martha's "zeal and perseverance," and they accepted as genuine her desire "to pass the rest of her days in the aforesaid community, observing the rules thereof, and to be employed in the instruction of children or such other works, duties, and functions which the superiors require of her."[26]

Some practical matters were also settled as part of the profession ceremony. It was still customary, for example, for women entering Catholic sisterhoods to present their new community with a dowry that would contribute to their material support. This was a carryover from the medieval custom whereby the payment that would otherwise have gone to a woman's husband went instead to her religious order. Thus, a dowry of 250 "livres"—the currency in question is not clear; most probably it was English pounds—was promised by the Healy estate to the Notre Dame sisters, and it would be paid in two installments in 1857 and 1858. The ceremony was made official by a notarized contract, signed by the new nun, the superiors of the community, her brother James (who was present as Martha's "duly authorized guardian"), and a priest from Saint-Sulpice.[27] Martha was following the lead of her older brothers in choosing to make her own the religion that had accepted them all in spite of their background.

In becoming a sister of Notre Dame, she exchanged several old and troubling identities for a new one. Having chosen to be white, she confirmed that choice by joining an all-white religious community. It was religion, not race, that mattered there. At the same time, she had broken with the nation of her birth, one that would define her according to the slavery of her mother. Secular politics meant little to her as a nun, of course, but she separated herself even further from that country by enlisting with a group that was, legally, under the ultimate jurisdiction of the British crown. She might at some point return to the United States, but when she did, it would be as to a foreign country. Culturally, too, the break was sharp. Daily routines, prayer, and classroom instruction would be conducted largely in French, a language not natively her own. Even the convent itself was liberating as much as it was confining. Becoming a nun seemed like a loss of autonomy, and so it was: henceforth, her individual personality would be subsumed into the larger whole that was her community. At the same time, her decision was an act of taking control of her own destiny. Martha would leave behind the debilitating effects of her background and, through a career in religious life, claim instead the right to define herself.

✐

Patrick and Sherwood Healy were in the process of claiming the same power. They ended their college careers as they had begun them, with routine studies, minor infractions of discipline, and rare lapses of application. Patrick was sometimes faulted for "inattention," and Sherwood, who was given to untimely "talkative-ness," was once sent out of class "on account of his conduct." Still, both were seri-ous when they had to be and regularly placed near the top in their studies. Patrick graduated from Holy Cross in the summer of 1850. The valedictory address was given by a classmate, but Patrick delivered an "ably presented" speech on "mental philosophy." Sherwood pronounced a Spanish oration during the exercises and ranked second in his class overall. More personally, Hugh took the two of them aside and explained "their situations in life."[28] We know nothing of this conversa-tion except that cryptic phrase, which Hugh used to describe it to Father Fenwick. Perhaps it was merely a discussion of family finances. Perhaps it was something more, including an explanation of just what these two young mixed-race men might expect from white society.

Patrick had already decided that the career of a priest was for him. Unlike James, however, he sought entry not into the ranks of the parish clergy, but rather to the Jesuit order he had come to know as a student. He was, Hugh had told Fa-ther Fenwick, "resolutely determined to join your Society," and at one point he had written his father in Georgia to secure permission. The senior Michael Healy had not lived to grant his approval, but Patrick assumed it and entered the Soci-ety of Jesus in September 1850. He had some misgivings, worrying that "my irreg-ularities" might prove embarrassing to the Jesuits, and he was right to be con-cerned. In recommending the applicant, the Jesuit president of Holy Cross had taken note of the "family difficulties in the way." The "difficulties" and "irregular-ities" were canonical, deriving not from the interracial nature of his parents' union but from the fact that Michael and Eliza Healy had never legally been mar-ried. Since the Middle Ages, the law of the church had prohibited the ordination to the priesthood of boys defined as illegitimate. Originally, these statutes were a way to reinforce the requirement of clerical celibacy itself by eliminating the pos-sibility that the bastard sons of a priest could, in effect, inherit their father's busi-ness. By the nineteenth century, the canon law still presented a serious impedi-ment to the priestly plans of the Healy brothers. With the active collusion of their religious superiors, however, they were able to resolve this problem through a combination of skillful canonical analysis and covert winking at the law.[29]

James had already faced the problem when he entered in the seminary at Mon-treal a year before. "Father assured me that he and Mother were really married," he wrote anxiously to Fenwick, but he was beginning to have his doubts. Such a marriage was "certainly contrary to the laws of the state," he knew. Furthermore, "it is not at all certain that my mother was baptized," another obstacle. Worse yet, James feared that just raising the question would cause trouble, begging Fenwick "not to give the affair any chance of becoming public," though he acknowledged that "our condition is much more generally known about Boston than I had ever supposed." Even good news might turn out to be bad news: if his parents had indeed been formally married, that would solve the canonical problem, but it might also "embarrass our claim to the property"—that is, the children's right to inherit their father's estate. It might be better, James thought, if resolution of the issue could wait until "our property is once fairly and peaceably in our hands." In spite of all these concerns, Boston's Bishop John Fitzpatrick was able to offer "all necessary explanations."[30] How he did so is unclear. He may simply have ignored the problem, pretending that there was nothing amiss with the young man; or he may have been able to convince those in charge of the Canadian seminary simply to look the other way. If he, the man who would be James Healy's superintending bishop, was satisfied, they should be too.

In Patrick's case, a shrewd reading of church law by the Jesuits provided a more clever way out. In the first place, they maintained, some marriages that (for whatever reason) had never been officially sanctioned by proper authority might be considered valid if carried out in good faith: the long years Michael and Eliza Healy had spent together surely satisfied this condition. The children of such couples were entitled to all the canonical privileges available to legitimate offspring. More importantly, entry into a vowed community like the Jesuits was interpreted as "legitimizing." Because the taking of religious vows was considered an act of spiritual rebirth, it removed the impediments that a problematic natural birth otherwise placed in the path to the priesthood.[31] The active complicity of the Healys' patrons was needed to resolve the matter, but both Fitzpatrick and the Jesuit superiors clearly wanted to find a way around this problem. That such active cooperation was given, even if it required a rather loose construction of canon law, underlines the eagerness with which Catholic officials were willing to accept the unusual youngsters who had accepted them and their church.

Just as Patrick was joining the Jesuits, Sherwood too was edging toward a religious vocation. He did not return to school in the fall of 1850 for what would have been the equivalent of his sophomore year. He suffered from a persistent weakness in his eyes, and it seemed best for him to take some time off, so he moved to New York to be with Hugh. He was given a "situation" as a clerk in Manning's hardware business and remained there for two years before deciding, at the age of sixteen, to follow his brother James by enrolling in the seminary at Montreal. This he did at the beginning of September 1852. James himself had graduated by then and moved to another seminary run by the Sulpicians, this one in Paris. There, tracing yet again the route of his mentor Bishop Fitzpatrick, who had completed his own priestly studies at Paris, he would conclude his preparation for ordination. Now Sherwood was on the same path. During his time off, James noted, the younger brother's "religious sentiments" had been "altered" in a very positive direction. It was service as a parish priest the third Healy sought, and the only logical choice for the location of such a life was the diocese of Boston, under the sympathetic eye of Fitzpatrick. "I am for Boston," Sherwood concluded, "if there is any chance of my living there as a Priest." The friendly bishop could steer him too through the complicated problem of legitimacy, with Patrick noting that the prelate would help Sherwood "escape useless questions."[32]

These questions were more insistent for Sherwood because, of all the Healys, he had the darkest complexion and other features that contemporaries associated with blacks. James might arouse only vague suspicions about his background in the minds of those who met him for the first time, and Patrick was light-skinned enough that unknowing strangers would never guess that he had any "blood" in his veins other than that of white ancestors. Sherwood could not hide behind any uncertainty. His skin was dark, his short hair had the tight kinks that common understanding identified with African Americans, and his face bore the nose and lips so frequently caricatured on the minstrel stage. One of his adult passports would later describe his complexion as unambiguously "dark," in contrast to his "light" and even "fair" brothers.[33] Such descriptions were notoriously imprecise, of course: they depended entirely on what a particular passport agent saw—or thought he saw—when he looked at the applicant. The surviving photographs of Sherwood, however, confirm the conclusion that contemporaries who saw him would take him for a black man. Thus, the robes and status of the priesthood would protect him from those "useless questions," a benefit that probably reinforced his "altered" religious sentiments.

After a year of study at Montreal, Sherwood too was identified as a candidate for the Sulpician seminary in Paris. Located in the faubourg Saint-Germain, this was the "parent" to the school in Canada, and by the time of the Healy brothers' arrival there, it had been training clergy for almost two centuries. The students actually attended classes at the Sorbonne, while in their own residence they learned the chants, prayers, and other rituals they would one day direct from the altar. The life of the seminary was austere. Days began before dawn, and they were filled with private prayer and meditation, public liturgies, recitation of the priestly office, and regular examination of conscience and confession. Many American priests had studied there over the years, and the ranks of the hierarchy in the United States would come to include many of its alumni. There was as yet no seminary in Rome dedicated specifically to training American Catholic boys for the priesthood, and given its long tradition, Saint-Sulpice in Paris was most likely to assure its graduates prominent places in the American church. That Fitzpatrick was willing to send these two young men there, and to support them partially out of diocesan funds, indicates that he had already identified them for central positions in the administration of his church in Boston.[34]

Sadly, however, Sherwood's departure for Paris proved the occasion for the tragic death of Hugh, the family's de facto parent. After visiting Massachusetts to bid farewell to friends, Sherwood went to New York at the end of August 1853 and booked passage on a ship to take him abroad. On the first of September he got underway, and his brother, who apparently had some reservations about Sherwood's going so far away, went down to the docks to see him off. Hiring a rowboat to follow Sherwood's steamer out of the harbor, Hugh fell victim to a freak accident. Watching the vessel depart, he never saw another ship coming up behind him, and this one sideswiped his tiny dory, knocking him into the foul harbor water. Hugh managed to swim ashore and take himself home, but a fever quickly settled on him. Within a week he was delirious, and a priest had to be called to administer the last rites. Patrick, now the oldest sibling left in America, rushed to New York and found that Hugh only occasionally recognized him during his bedside vigil. The "excitement" of these frustrating visits, Patrick later concluded mournfully, "caused him to die sooner than he otherwise would have." During one lucid moment, Hugh confirmed the fundamental passage he and the others had undertaken. His only thought of family was not for the ties of blood but for his surrogate "Dad," as he asked repeatedly whether Father Fenwick was praying for him. On Friday the sixteenth he took a turn for the worse and was anointed a second time. By ten the next morning he was dead "without any struggle," the grieving Patrick reported.[35]

As the others learned the news, they sought their consolation in religion. From Paris James tried to convince himself that "it was good for Hugh to die young," fearing that the preoccupations of the business world might have led him "to neglect the practice of his religious duties" and to distract "his really noble mind." If that sounded a bit cold, James was nevertheless touched. The loss of this brother just two years younger than he came as "the severest stroke that ever befell me. We had grown up together," he went on, "and all our life-time had been so cordially united in our dispositions and sentiments. . . . I had thought to precede him to the other world; but I am still living. Oh, may it be for God's greater glory." Patrick was comforted that Hugh had been "highly esteemed by his friends, who were very few + select" but who unanimously found him "the most regular + exemplary young man." For his part, "Dad" Fenwick did not know where to begin in offering solace, either to himself or to the survivors. He felt the loss so intensely, he said, "that selfishness continually urges me to wish that I had never known him." Those thoughts were countered by the "sincere pleasure he has so often afforded me" and the memory of his "good + dutiful heart, . . . his gravity, and his strict integrity." Patrick arranged for his brother's burial in the cathedral cemetery in New York, not without some "painful incidents"—perhaps indicating some reluctance on the part of church officials there to admit a partially black man to a previously all-white burial ground.[36]

The might-have-beens of Hugh's death at the age of twenty-one are purely speculative but intriguing. He was the only one of the five oldest Healy siblings not to look to the Catholic church for his principal source of identity. He was determined to make his way not as a priest but as a businessman. His start on such a career was a good one, employed as he was by an established firm, run by friends of his father. He possessed a solid inheritance, and even if the care of the younger children represented a substantial draw on it, he was starting his adult life in a far better economic position than many others. New York was the ideal place for a bright young man eager to advance. The population of the cosmopolitan city was swelling at a steady pace with immigrants from all over, and his own unusual parentage was less of a disadvantage there than elsewhere. In the bustle of the metropolis, there were few who would have the time—or the temerity—for the "useless questions" that might plague Sherwood. Even if Hugh's complexion (about which there is no surviving evidence) were "dark" like that of Sherwood, he could more easily disappear into the racial and ethnic miscellany of Manhattan than he could elsewhere. Marriage and family would probably come for him, and if the experiences of his younger siblings who married is any predictor, this significant step in his life would have completed his passage into the white community. None of that was to be, however, and his premature death cut off the potential for both success and failure.

The family divided now ever more clearly into two age groups. The older ones—James, Patrick, Sherwood, and Martha—were all pursuing the religious life, and three of them were doing so out of the country. Patrick in particular worried about the toll this physical separation was taking, and he pleaded unsuccessfully with Father Fenwick that James be immediately ordained and allowed to return to America, given "the obligation he is now under." The younger children needed to be looked after. Michael, just fourteen, was at Holy Cross, though he would not last there much longer. Josephine (age eight) and Eliza (not yet seven) were sent to Montreal to the security of a school run by the Notre Dame nuns. Eugene, still a baby at barely four, remained at first with a couple in New York. This was a satisfactory arrangement in the short run, but these people were Protestants, and that worried his older brothers. "They are exceedingly kind to him," Patrick observed, but Eugene "will grow up a heathen if left in such a condition." Within the year he had been sent to Boston and entrusted to a foster family arranged for by Bishop Fitzpatrick.[37]

Between 1850 and 1853, the family had been touched several times in rapid succession by death—that of both parents and of their guardian-brother. Such losses might have proved disastrous for a less resilient group. The Healys were able to retain their stability, however, with the help of the church they had so enthusiastically joined. Here was the institution that mediated between them and the wider, potentially hostile world. In the decade that followed, as they grew into adulthood, that church was to be their true home.

CHAPTER FOUR

Priests: James, Sherwood, and Patrick

"They tell me he is everything I anticipated," Father George Fenwick wrote proudly at the beginning of 1855, "and if he be that, he has no one to compare with him."[1] The aging Jesuit was speaking of James Healy, his former pupil, who had remained at the seminary in Paris throughout the early 1850s as Bishop Fitzpatrick made plans for his return to Boston as a priest. Before he could come back, however, there was one last canonical hurdle to be surmounted. Church law prescribed that candidates for the priesthood "belonged" to the diocese where they had been born. Language in use since the Middle Ages took seminarians to be "subjects" of their home bishop, and they could go elsewhere only with his approval. In Healy's case that was the bishop of Charleston, South Carolina, in whose jurisdiction his birthplace lay. The young man needed a formal release, called an "exeat," in order to serve a different bishop. As with the problem of his illegitimacy, this impediment was removed simply by ignoring it. Fitzpatrick never asked the southern prelate for permission to adopt Healy, but rather pretended that Boston was his real home. The family's history had been amended once more. They were not from Georgia at all, the ruse proclaimed: their lives had not really begun until their arrival in the North and their baptism into the Catholic church. Accordingly, on June 10, 1854, James Healy was ordained a priest amid the grandeur of Notre Dame Cathedral in Paris while Bishop Fitzpatrick and several other visitors from America, together with his brother Sherwood, happily looked on. He said his first mass the following day, and he returned to Boston a month later.[2]

Fitzpatrick was eager to have the assistance of a bright and able young priest. The bishop superintended a diocese that covered the entire state of Massachusetts, and he had only about sixty priests altogether. Most of them did double duty, traveling from town to town, and the demands on them were always increasing. Several successive years of blighted crops in Ireland had sent streams of immigrants to Boston, and the calls on the church for religious, educational, and social welfare services were growing ever more insistent. Before 1840, the city had absorbed a small if steady flow of newcomers from Europe, averaging about 3,000 per year, a number that caused little disruption. In 1847 alone, the annual influx had jumped to more than 37,000, the vast majority of them from Ireland. Only the imagery of natural disaster—the immigrants were described as a "flood"—seemed adequate to explain what was happening. By the time Healy was ordained, Irish Catholics constituted fully one-third of Boston's entire population. New parishes opened at a frantic pace, and priests were desperately needed to staff them.[3]

Even so, Fitzpatrick had to think carefully about how to use his newest priest. Simply placing James Healy in a parish church, whether on his own or as a junior curate to a more experienced pastor, might cause as many problems as it solved. The bishop had to wonder whether white, largely immigrant parishioners would accept the ministrations of a man who, as far as they were concerned, was black. Would they take communion from his hands or tell him their sins and seek his forgiveness in the confessional? If they were not openly hostile, might they not simply avoid him, looking for their spiritual solace elsewhere? Equally in doubt was whether other priests would be willing to have such a colleague. Most personal or social contact with blacks was anathema to the majority of white Americans, and the Roman Catholic clergy were no exception: not even the demands of Christian charity would necessarily overcome a priest's reluctance—revulsion, even—to live under the same roof and eat at the same dinner table with someone he presumed to be inferior. Fitzpatrick himself accepted Father Healy and his family on equal terms, but he could not count on either his pastors or his people to be equally open-minded or accepting.[4]

Healy shared these misgivings. He was sure of his commitment to the priestly life, but he wondered whether Massachusetts or anywhere else in America was the right place for him. Even after his return to Boston, he described himself to Father Fenwick as "a poor outcast on a throne of glory which ill-becomes him." The language was formulaic, but he was as frank with Fenwick about his uneasiness as he had ever been with anyone. The "throne of glory" was a common enough metaphor for the nobility, as he saw it, of his new powers to celebrate mass and administer the sacraments, but he had more reason than many other priests to think of himself as a "poor outcast." Could he really hope for success? "If I could have been as safe elsewhere as here," he wrote just after his return, "I should have desired never to show my face in Boston," where, as he had noted, his family circumstances were "generally known" among Catholics.[5] He may or may not have meant this. Surely there was no other place in the United States where his prospects were as good, but perhaps he thought of staying in France or of returning to Montreal. As it happened, neither option had to be considered because he had a "safe" place waiting for him under the watchful eye of the man whose chance encounter with his father a decade before had made everything else possible.

Fitzpatrick eased his dilemma over what to do with Father Healy by making it more difficult. He decided not to hide Father Healy but rather to give him a visible, public position: that of his own secretary and chancellor of the diocese. Catholic church administration in the United States had grown more complex under the pressure of the rapidly increasing population, and bishops could no longer, as they had in the past, attend to all the diocesan business on their own. There were complicated financial arrangements to make, construction projects to supervise, and standardized practices to implement. Accordingly, the hierarchy had decreed that each bishop set up a chancery office "for the expedition of episcopal documents in due form." After delaying for a couple of years, Fitzpatrick now had just the man to establish and manage such an office. James Healy was to be the first chancellor of the Boston diocese, a sort of chief operating officer and alter ego to the bishop. Fitzpatrick counted on the penumbra of his own influence to cover any objections to his adviser. Skeptical clergy and laity might shake their heads in private over the appointment, but they would never dare express their doubts aloud. At the same time, absorption into routine would soon transform the exceptional Father Healy into just another priest. "I am to be his secretary," James wrote Father Fenwick, at once grateful for the "responsibility" and nervous that he might not be up to "the duties attendant upon that charge."[6] He moved into rooms in the bishop's house adjacent to Boston's Cathedral of the Holy Cross and went to work.

His first order of business was to write away for copies of the forms other dioceses used, finding those from New York the best to adopt. Much of the paperwork had to do with enforcing the church's laws concerning marriage—granting Catholics permission to marry non-Catholics, for example—and these procedures were reduced to standard forms. He established a schedule of fees that would "contribute to the support of an office every way necessary in a well regulated Diocese." He even expressed some hope that these costs, ranging from five to twenty-five dollars, would "diminish the number of requests for exemption from the laws of the Church." The professor who had warned him a few years before that "exceptions + exemptions are bad things" had found an apt pupil. He re-

*James A. Healy, 1855. Photo courtesy Archives,
Archdiocese of Boston.*

minded pastors to instruct applicants that "this tariff is not the price" in each instance: such a formulation would wrongly imply that the services of the church were for sale. Rather, these were aimed at "defraying the expenses of the chancery," with any surplus devoted to charitable purposes.[7]

Priests too were now subject to greater supervision from the bishop's office as directed by Father Healy. He instructed pastors in how to comply with state laws requiring an annual parish financial report, and he asked that a copy of this report be filed in the chancery each January. He likewise requested an annual summary of religious activity, and a form for codifying this information was distributed for priests to fill in and return. How many baptisms and marriages were there in each parish? What provision was made for the religious instruction of children? What neighboring towns, without parishes of their own, did pastors visit on a regular basis? What was the condition of church buildings and real estate? Were liturgical vestments and communion plate well maintained? The bishop and his chancellor began to exercise greater control over Catholic life in Massachusetts by regulating the flow of information about it. To handle all this business, Healy arranged to be in his office on Mondays, Wednesdays, and Fridays from nine in the morning until noon, and he promised that petitions that came in by letter—mail was delivered three times a day!—"will be attended to every day in the week, as far as practicable."[8]

The new chancellor and secretary relished his responsibilities, and for the next decade he threw himself into the work enthusiastically. He scrutinized all reports carefully and corrected irregular practices whenever he found them. A priest in Worcester, for instance, had to be encouraged to keep better track of which revenues derived from his parish in that city and which came from his service to the Catholics of the outlying towns. Healy prodded several pastors to send in the collection taken in their churches on Pentecost Sunday, a special annual offering set aside to defray the cost of educating seminarians. Lacking even the most rudimentary office help, he kept the central diocesan account books in his own hand, and he sometimes took over from Fitzpatrick the responsibility for maintaining the journal of the bishop, a kind of official diary in which parish visitations and sacramental activities were recorded. His job was not without its frustrations, including occasional "emergencies." He was in his office at the stated times, he once reminded his fellow priests a bit testily, and it was thus unreasonable of them to expect that he "should attend such matters at any other time or place. Besides the unseemly haste of such communication," he noted with the bureaucrat's dislike of "exceptions," there were "many reasons why instantaneous answers cannot be given." He categorically refused to respond to requests that came in "by express or by telegraph."[9]

As Fitzpatrick's principal aide, Healy was involved in every aspect of diocesan affairs, and he had arrived on the scene at a particularly challenging time. A new wave of nativism, the second since the 1830s, was cresting in the Bay State, and assaults on Catholics abounded. Politically, the state legislature was dominated by anti-immigrant Know-Nothings, a party named for its members' disclaimers of knowledge about its secret activities. Among its first actions was the appointment of a committee authorized to make unannounced visits to Catholic convents to expose the wickedness that, the members were certain, was going on inside. Popularly known as the "convent-smelling committee," this group quickly overplayed its hand. Several members appeared to be drunk in public, and the chairman—one Joseph Hiss, a tailor who had fled bankruptcy in central Massachusetts and settled in Boston—had allegedly occupied a hotel room with a woman of questionable virtue during the investigation of a convent in Lowell. The voters reacted against these excesses, turning the Know-Nothings out of office in 1856, but hostility toward Catholic institutions lingered. Throughout the decade, Fitzpatrick and Healy faced repeated provocation; they struggled, for instance, to secure permission for priests to visit the Catholic inmates of prisons and mental institutions. In 1859, they faced the wrath of many citizens when a brave (or perhaps just stubborn) Catholic lad set off an acrimonious dispute by refusing to read from the King James Version of the Bible in his public school classroom and was whipped by the teacher for his trouble.[10]

Father Healy found himself decidedly at the center of these disputes because Fitzpatrick's health had begun to fail. The bishop, still in his forties, presented a robust outward appearance, but he was plagued by a chronic nervous condition that his doctors diagnosed not very helpfully as "cerebral congestion"; he had probably suffered a series of minor strokes. As chancellor, Healy had to fill in the gaps left by the periodic incapacity of his superior. It was he, for example, who sent a long letter to the secretary of the navy in February 1860, protesting a policy that made it difficult for Catholic sailors at Boston's navy yard to attend Sunday mass. Healy not only compiled all the arguments in this case, but he even signed Fitzpatrick's name to the letter. With increasing frequency, the bishop left the city for quieter surroundings in a vain attempt to recover his strength, and Healy took his place. This gave him such first hand knowledge of the demands of diocesan leadership that he and another priest—half-joking, half-serious—pledged to one another "never to be bishops!"[11]

Healy's own health was never seriously jeopardized, but it was nonetheless a cause of some concern. The other Healy brothers, especially Sherwood, had suffered from headaches and eyestrain during their student years, but James had always been the strong one. He stood 5 feet, 4 1/2 inches tall, and in his prime weighed roughly 140 pounds: that put him just below average on both counts for men of his time. He escaped serious illness, though a fellow priest noted that he sometimes felt faint and had to lie down during the day. Overwork could lead to exhaustion, and when this happened he would retire for a few days to do nothing. He liked to fish, a hobby he had picked up in college, and that enforced inactivity always seemed restorative. As recovery came, he returned to his workload and to more vigorous recreation, which took the form of long walks. More than once he covered on foot the round trip between his downtown office and suburban Newton, a distance of nine miles each way.[12]

Fitzpatrick worried more about Healy's mental state than his physical condition.

"He is very subject to elation and depression of spirit," the bishop wrote, "and when in the latter frame of mind, every thing is black within and without for him and it is impossible for him to admit that there is any other color." Resort to the imagery of color was apparently unconscious, a measure of how little race had come to matter in Father Healy's case, though it perhaps carried echoes of the contemporary belief that persons of mixed heritage shared the physical weaknesses thought to be characteristic of all "hybrids." The obvious antidote to these mood swings—giving Father Healy a less responsible role in church affairs—was no solution at all, the bishop concluded, for "if he had another position, leaving him much leisure time, he would be far more unhappy." Better to keep him where he was, with activity filling the days and hours and, perhaps, reducing the opportunities for destructive introspection. "Courage" was the best medicine, and the bishop usually found that he could talk Healy out of his gloom. His own presence and reassurance would "operate a change" in Healy, Fitzpatrick said, and the results were beneficial to both of them. "I have no one who could do what he does for me," the older man concluded.[13]

From day to day, Healy had more than enough to occupy his time and attention. Besides his job as chancellor, he was also a priest serving in what was the oldest Catholic parish in the city, and as such he had to perform the normal duties of saying mass, hearing confessions, attending the sick, and burying the dead. The work of nineteenth-century American Catholic priests was both predictable and unpredictable: regularly scheduled weekly services established a routine, but unexpected demands could intervene at any time. Thus, Healy was suddenly called out one winter afternoon "to visit two young ladies, one dying and the other in full health, both of whom wish to become Catholics." Initially skeptical, he was pleased to find that their intentions were "most solid." He was responsible for training the altar boys in the cathedral, putting them through their liturgical paces and drilling them in Latin like a schoolmaster. He took an interest in the parish Sunday school, named somewhat grandly in honor of Aloysius, the pious sixteenth-century boy-saint, and he appeared often at meetings of the school's volunteer faculty to give pep talks. Perhaps the teachers might visit the homes of students who skipped their lessons, he suggested, oddly certain that this would "endear" them to the children and their parents. He could also relax with the people of his parish, joining the cathedral's choir for a sleigh ride out into the countryside just after new year's 1861.[14] Any fears that Boston's Catholics might not accept him because of his racial status quickly disappeared. Parishioners looked on him not as a black or half-black priest, but simply as a priest.

The sacraments and other ceremonies were his first order of ministerial business. He took his regular turn in the schedule of Sunday masses at the cathedral, the earliest of which was said at five o'clock in the morning. During the elaborate services of Holy Week and Easter each year, he was one of the leaders in chanting the narrative of Christ's passion. Given the increasing taste of nineteenth-century Catholics for rich forms of devotional life apart from weekly mass, he was "indefatigable" in special services, such as those addressed to the Virgin Mary during the month of May 1863. He was conscientious in preparing his sermons, and he tried to develop an oratorical technique that was at once formal and informal. "I write my sermons," he reported, "but neither read nor commit them to memory. I talk simply and to the point, follow[ing] a regular + clear plan." When one parishioner praised his delivery as "charming," he deflected attention from himself. "I wish her joy of it," he said, but his intention had not been to charm; rather, he hoped only "to work my way along, simply + humbly." Word of his effectiveness even reached his brother. "James works like a major," Patrick Healy told a friend. "He has the reputation of being the most satisfactory preacher among the clergy in B[oston]."[15]

Presiding at baptisms and marriages, two principal points of contact between ordinary Catholics and their church, was normally an important part of a priest's job, but James's other duties left him little opportunity for them. Newly ordained priests were often assigned the lion's share of the baptisms in their parish. Performing this simple ceremony accustomed them to officiating, and it also helped introduce them to their parishioners. Later, as they gained experience and came to know their people, they performed more marriages and gradually shifted their workload in that direction. Healy never really conformed to this pattern, however, probably because he was too busy doing other things. During the twelve years (1855–1866) he was in residence at the cathedral parish, he did little baptizing or marrying, though he might become involved in special cases, such as the baptism of a prominent adult convert. There were always at least three, and sometimes four, other priests in the rectory with him, and they made up the difference.[16]

The most important special demand of his years as chancellor was the question of what to do about Boston's premier Catholic church. The Cathedral of the Holy Cross, designed and built on classical lines in 1803 by no less a Boston notable than Charles Bulfinch, occupied a plot of land on Franklin Street in the heart of the city. Initially more than adequate to meet its congregation's needs, it was by the 1850s entirely too small. A papal representative touring America in 1853 had turned up his nose at it, prodding an insulted and reluctant Fitzpatrick to replace it with a "real" cathedral. As a practical matter, there was a scramble for seats at every service, a serious problem in an era when the main source of church revenue was the sale and rental of pews to specific individuals or families. One Sunday, Healy had to announce at all the masses that "trespass in the matter of pews"—that is, one parishioner occupying a seat already paid for by someone else—would not be tolerated.[17] To make matters worse, the building seemed constantly in need of expensive repairs to keep its fabric together. Finally, the surrounding neighborhood was changing dramatically. Where once there had been houses and tenements filled with immigrant churchgoers, there were now only banks, stores, and business offices, all bustling with people during the week, but mostly empty on Sundays, as the bulk of the Catholic population moved to other parts of the city.

Fitzpatrick resisted the idea of abandoning the old cathedral, sentimental attachment to which went back to the very origins of the Catholic community in New England, but there was little choice. In October 1859 he and Healy presided at a meeting of the congregation, and a decision was made to sell the property and to build a new cathedral elsewhere; a second vote the following spring confirmed the plan. In September 1860 mass was said in the building for the last time, and it proved an emotional occasion. Fitzpatrick had prepared a farewell sermon, but he was too overcome to deliver it: in his stead, Father Healy mounted the pulpit and bade the place farewell. Now there were other matters to attend to, and Healy took his usual role in expediting them. First, he arranged for the parishioners to assemble for mass every week in the Melodeon Theater several blocks away, an unlikely setting, but one that was big enough to accommodate them. Two years later, the bishop bought a former Unitarian church away from downtown in what was known as the South End, and converted it for Catholic use. At the same time, a nearby residence was purchased for the bishop, and plans were made to construct an imposing new cathedral across the street from it. In all these proceedings, James Healy was Fitzpatrick's right-hand man: he negotiated sale prices and contracts, witnessed deeds and other legal instruments, and helped convince parishioners that the changes were all for the best.[18]

Someone else of his racial background might have been tempted to hide in anonymity, but James Healy, by now sure of Fitzpatrick's backing, never retreated from public view. He even enjoyed regular contact with the leaders of Boston society, most of whom were not Catholics. Perhaps in no city in the country was there a wider gulf between immigrant newcomers and the established social order than in Boston, but by midcentury some efforts at bridging the gap were under way. Overt nativism was largely a phenomenon of the middle and lower classes, the so-called Swamp Yankees. Their social "betters," by contrast, were uncomfortable with sectarian violence, and some were even attracted to the higher cultural values they thought Catholicism represented. On a personal level, Fitzpatrick was well liked by upper crust Bostonians, those whom the poet Oliver Wendell Holmes (certainly one of them himself) called "Brahmins," gently mocking his neighbors by comparing them to the high caste of India. As a boy, Fitzpatrick had attended the Boston Latin School, one of the quintessential Brahmin institutions, with the sons of leading local families. His classmates had included the future orator Edward Everett Hale, the future historian and politician John Lothrop Motley, and Fletcher Webster, son of the great Daniel. Now, as the leader of Boston's Catholics, he moved easily in these circles, where he was known affectionately as "Bishop John."[19]

As elsewhere, Fitzpatrick's influence rubbed off on Father Healy. In 1857, for example, the young protégé sang the requiem mass at the funeral of Julia Metcalf, a convert from high church Episcopalianism who was the wife of a state supreme court justice. "The audience is almost entirely Protestant," Fitzpatrick noted with pride after the service, which had all the trappings of a state funeral. More ordinary services might also introduce Healy to "proper" Bostonians. Each year during the "watering season," for example, he traveled every other week to Nahant, a resort town north of Boston, to say mass for the Catholic servants of the "many Protestant gentlemen who with their families are spending the summer there." He got to know masters as well as servants, and both groups seemed to like what they saw in him. A slightly skeptical priest, doubting the religious open-mindedness of "the elite," worried that they were taking advantage of Healy, who was, he said sarcastically, their "favourite."[20] None of these vacationing Brahmins ever remarked on the young chancellor one way or another, and we are left to wonder what they knew or made of him. The abolitionists among them may even have relished the chance to demonstrate their racial liberality, thereby confirming their faith in the possibility of a successful multiracial society.

Healy enjoyed rubbing elbows with "the elite," for it was easy to think of himself as one of them. Skillful management of his father's estate was even then maximizing its profitability: the last of the slaves in Georgia had just been sold off, and the family's capital base was solid. In consultation with John Manning in New York, James now assumed a more active role in handling those affairs. His priestly salary was only $30 per week—the usual pay was $20, but he drew an additional stipend for his administrative duties—but all his living expenses were covered. He kept track of his family's investments and the returns on them, carefully following in the newspapers the price of securities, gold, and other commodities. He could easily meet the educational expenses of the younger children, and he also paid the room and board of his baby brother Eugene with Mr. and Mrs. Thomas Hodges, cathedral parishioners who lived not far away. The couple had become, in effect, Eugene's parents, with the wife always referred to as "Mother Hodges." Just as "Dad" Fenwick had replaced Michael Morris Healy as the family's emotional father, so now "Mother" Hodges took Eliza Clark Healy's problematic place. When Manning died just before Christmas 1859, James went by train to New York to preside at the funeral and then to take on himself the responsibility for managing the family finances.[21]

He also provided for his siblings by buying a home in the town of Newton. Situated just west of Boston, Newton was a rapidly expanding suburb, with house lots large and small carved from hilly farm and orchard land. The people attracted to the area were looking for solid middle-class respectability: they could commute to work in the city by train, but they could also return every night to greener and airier surroundings. James Healy purchased a simple wood-frame house on Waltham Street, a long road leading north out of town, in 1861, and it became his retreat from administrative demands. He continued to live in Boston, but he went to Newton at least once a week for time off. The property also became a home base for the other Healys whenever they traveled through the area. Josephine and Eliza moved in after they finished their schooling in Montreal that year, and Sherwood too would stay there occasionally after he returned from Europe. Neither the cheapest nor the most expensive property in town, the house was valued at just over $7,500, and by 1866 Father Healy had increased his holdings by purchasing another plot of land next door, appraised at more than $1,500.[22] The family had been without an identifiable "home" since their removal from Georgia. The house in Newton gave them that home at last.

James Healy was able to afford such a life, but he also plainly enjoyed living it, and an emerging sense of class identity confirmed his choices of racial and religious identity. He and his siblings had not merely become whites; they had become upper-middle-class whites. They had decided not merely to be Catholics; they had decided to be prominent and respectable Catholics. When the nuns of Martha Healy's religious order in Canada retroactively bestowed the title of "Lady" on Eliza Clark Healy, they seconded the family's own social aspirations and success. Now, the Healys had the resources to live well at home, and several of them had already traveled widely abroad. James's ordination began to accustom him to move in circles that would otherwise have been foreclosed to him and the others. Most Americans had never even seen Notre Dame in Paris, to say nothing of having that magnificent structure serve as the backdrop for a significant occasion in their own lives. Few ordinary Catholics—and fewer black or mixed-race Americans—got invited to Nahant, unless it was to do the cooking, cleaning, or some more disagreeable task; those who did make it there seldom became "favourites" of the upper-crust inhabitants. Few former slaves became suburban householders so quickly, if indeed at all. Few of his parishioners followed gold prices with as much interest as Father Healy did; they had no need to.

The acceptance the Healys found in these economic and social circles exerted a powerful attraction, and they internalized many of the attitudes and dispositions associated with those on top in society. Even as he worked among poor immigrants, James often exhibited behavior that can only be characterized as haughty. His undergraduate dismissals of classmates—"lazy," "rowdy," "loafer"—sometimes returned as outright condescension. When he went back to the college for commencement in 1865, for example, he observed that the students were "in appearance + reputation very good," but "their manners are a little uncouth." Appearance, reputation, and manners had all come to mean a great deal to him, and his sense of *amour propre* was well developed. His warning to Boston's priests that he would not hastily expedite diocesan paperwork showed a keen regard for his own dignity and position: in writing them on the subject, he even adopted use of the third person, referring to himself as "the chancellor." Traveling in Europe a few years later, he was chagrined by sanitary conditions. These might be fine for common folk—"the lower classes regard dust + dirt as a thing indifferent," he remarked coolly, "if not a blessing in disguise"—but he was certainly above all that. He and his family were distinct from "the lower classes," even if his siblings could sometimes find their older brother's self-importance a bit much to take. "Yesterday I received a very pious note from James," Patrick wrote Father Fenwick in 1856; "he is becoming very much so now-a-days."[23]

Notwithstanding such petty annoyances, the early career of "the chancellor" showed just how intimately racial, religious, and class identities had become intertwined for him and his family. Each of their acquired identities reinforced the others. Their father's wealth had provided a foundation for their metamorphoses, but, however necessary, it was not sufficient. Money might buy them respectability, but it alone could not buy whiteness. For that, they needed their concurrent embrace of the Catholic church, not merely as members but as officials. They were not ordinary parishioners in the pews; they were to be among the denomination's leaders, around whom a certain aura of status gathered. James could afford to be patronizing toward those who were "indifferent" to dust and dirt, confident that he was not one of them. Both economic and religious status confirmed their racial transformation. There were no black priests elsewhere in the United States, and there would not be for many years. By assuming leadership in this relentlessly white church, their own passage into the white world was sanctioned. To make any one of these transitions—from black to white; from "nothing" to Catholicism; from slavery to freedom; from persons who were themselves property to persons who held and enjoyed substantial property—was a difficult matter. By making all of them together, each passage lent its support to the others.

✑❤

The others might raise an eyebrow at his sometimes overbearing tone, but James was not the only Healy brother proceeding toward ordination to the priesthood and the new identity it brought. Sherwood had arrived in France in the fall of 1853, unaware for several weeks that his departure had been the occasion for Hugh's death. He enrolled in the seminary of Saint Sulpice, where, James soon reported, he was "getting along remarkably well. . . . He enters into the true spirit of a religious community." His poor eyesight was still troublesome, but he immersed himself in his studies. "He is making rapid progress," James noted, "and will probably be a very strong head for philosophy + theology."[24] Two years later, he had shown enough promise to transfer to an even more distinguished school in Rome. There, close to the administrative center of the papacy, the brightest ecclesiastical students from around the world studied canon law before returning to their home countries and, more often than not, positions of leadership. Just as James was taking up his key administrative post in Boston, Sherwood was being groomed for a similar career.

First, however, he had to face the family's by-now-familiar canonical problem. The "useless questions" about his parents, and therefore about his own legitimacy, were expected, but Fitzpatrick's willingness to evade the precision of the law was by now well established. Accordingly, in June 1854, a year before Sherwood's transfer to Rome, Boston's bishop had quietly administered the tonsure to him. This initiation rite for seminarians, consisting of a symbolic cutting of the hair, marked a young man as ready to advance to the priesthood. The timing was critical: if Sherwood arrived in Rome already with this status, his subsequent progress would not be questioned. Even the most punctilious canonist would assume that, since Sherwood had already come that far, there was no impediment to his taking the final step. James confided to Father Fenwick that he had spoken of this private ceremony to no one, and the strategy of pretending that everything about the Healy brothers was normal worked once again. What is more, life on the continent seemed to agree with the young man physically. Sherwood was "fat as butter," Patrick reported happily.[25]

In December 1858 Sherwood returned to Paris, and there, like James before him, he was ordained in the Cathedral of Notre Dame. Recording his thoughts in a commonplace book he kept at the time, Sherwood made his own the conventional understanding of what this step meant. A fundamental change had taken place in his life and, indeed, in his very being. The sacrament of holy orders, he thought, imparted a new nature and essence to its recipient. The priest did not cease to be a man, Sherwood wrote, closely echoing official Catholic theology; he was still "subject to the ills of mankind," but the "special graces" he received at ordination permitted him to "walk fearlessly" toward salvation. Moreover, priests were not only "obliged to tend thither themselves, but to direct others." That responsibility placed the priest "above every other [Christian] because he cooperates more towards the accomplishment of the end." Such an exalted position demanded humility, "sanctification," and "holiness," rather than self-congratulation.[26] Still, like his brother, Sherwood embraced the priesthood in part because it afforded him an opportunity he would otherwise not have had—to be "above" others, rather than below them.

Father Sherwood Healy was now ready to receive an assignment, but both he and Bishop Fitzpatrick were uncertain about what that should be. James was already a success in Boston, but the bishop hesitated to bring Sherwood home, no matter how well prepared he was. The young man had diligently studied the canon law, and he thus possessed specialized skills that few priests in America had. He had also exhibited a keen musical talent, devoting himself to mastering the intricacies of Gregorian chant. His uncommon knowledge and abilities would potentially put him in great demand, but he was nervous about the reception he might receive in the United States, then taking the last decisive steps toward civil war. "He feels an unwillingness," Fitzpatrick explained to a papal official, "for reasons which I cannot condemn, to return to this country." Instead, "he would like to exercise in Europe his zeal and his talents, both of which are of a high order."[27] Accordingly, Fitzpatrick determined that Sherwood should go back to Rome for further studies, which led him by 1860 to a doctorate in church law.

Just then, a new opportunity for exercising his talents was opening up. The bishops of the United States had talked for years about establishing an institution in Rome to train their best seminarians, those who, once ordained, could return to America with an instinctive loyalty to the papacy. Students would actually attend classes at some of the older universities in the Eternal City, but they would live at what was called the American College, a house on Rome's Via dell'Umilta (Humility Street) near the Pantheon. This residence was to be at once a Roman and an American place. Students there would view the church worldwide from the perspective of the center, but they would also retain their own patriotic identity: the black cassocks they wore were trimmed with red buttons and blue piping, which, together with the white of the stiff clerical collar, marked their nationality. Pope Pius IX endorsed the effort, and financial support came in from Catholic benefactors in the United States throughout the 1850s.[28] By the middle of 1859 the plans were taking final shape, and consideration turned to the appointment of a rector of the college. This was less an academic office than that of a dean of students, but the priest who served in this capacity had to be chosen carefully. He was certain to become a model for his young charges, as well as a sort of "first among equals" in the American Catholic community in Rome. Responding to a request for nominations, Fitzpatrick wrote his colleague John Hughes, the archbishop of New York, in July 1859.

The bishop of Boston had "thought and thought" on the matter, he told Hughes, but in the end he was "as much puzzled to reach a practical conclusion as I was in the beginning." He reviewed two names that others had put forward, saying that he knew neither particularly well, but then he got to the real source of his uncertainty. He had a name of his own, one he wanted to propose but knew he could not: Sherwood Healy. According to any reasonable standard, Fitzpatrick argued, Healy was "admirably qualified for the office." He had "the advantage of a most complete education, from the alphabet to theology. He went through the entire course at St. Sulpice, Paris, where he was *facile princeps* [i.e., easily first] in studies, whilst he was at the same time a model of piety, regularity, and good conduct." He was not well known among other American bishops, Fitzpatrick recognized, but that was not the reason why it was "useless to recommend him." No, there was "also another objection," the Bostonian concluded, "which, though in reason less substantial, would in fact be quite as stubborn. He has African blood and it shews [*sic*] distinctly in his exterior. This, in a large number of American youths, might lessen the respect they ought to have for the first superior in a house."[29]

Fitzpatrick was essentially thinking out loud as he wrote. He was, as ever, sympathetic to the Healy brothers, but there were limits to what he could do for them. He could promote their development as much as possible, but there were some barriers he could not overcome. The evidence on Sherwood's own face and the conclusions white Americans drew when they saw that face were "stubborn" indeed. "I have known this young priest and his history since his youth, from top to bottom," Fitzpatrick told another prelate. "His education from beginning to end was carefully done, . . . and his success responded fully to the advantages he had been given."[30] Sadly, however, this could carry him only so far. Objections to him were "in reason less substantial" than they ought to have been, but "reason" did not always triumph. In Sherwood, the presence of "African blood" was an intractable problem, precisely because it "shewed" too "distinctly." There was no hiding it, and this was almost certain to work against him. As rector, he would have to command the respect of his students, but because of his skin that respect might be undermined. Unwilling to put his young friend in that position and similarly unwilling to introduce uncertainty to the fledgling American College, Fitzpatrick could sing Sherwood Healy's praises but could not nominate him to be its leader. Sherwood himself may not even have known that his name was under discussion, but he more than likely shared Fitzpatrick's hesitancy. He had already expressed his desire, for reasons that Fitzpatrick could not condemn, never to return to America—where, after all, the bishop could offer him some shelter; how then could he be eager for a prominent American position in Rome that presented all the same dangers?

Despite his misgivings, Sherwood did eventually set sail for the United States, arriving in Boston a few days after the last service in Holy Cross cathedral in September 1860. Living temporarily with his brother at the cathedral rectory, he was soon assigned to work at an orphanage in the city's North End known as the House of the Angel Guardian. Founded in 1851 by a priest named George Foxcroft Haskins, who had been an Episcopal minister before his conversion to Catholicism, the house provided occupational training for wayward boys. Orphaned, abandoned, and truant Catholic lads had formerly been placed in the city's public House of Industry, but religious tensions often manifested themselves there. Haskins, who supported the Angel Guardian largely with his family's money, hoped that a separate facility would reduce such problems and guard against the possibility that Protestant charities would "steal" Catholic youths from their faith. The house had a population that normally hovered around one hundred. Resident houseparents supervised things on a daily basis, but Father Sherwood Healy was assigned to look after the spiritual needs of the inhabitants. He said mass and heard confessions regularly, and he provided religious instruction to the often-unwilling boys.[31] It was not a difficult assignment, and it may have been Fitzpatrick's intention to place him there while deciding on a more important and permanent ministry. For the time being, Sherwood was vastly overqualified for the job he was being asked to do, but that would change soon enough.

✍

Patrick Healy's religious initiation was longer and more complicated than that of James or Sherwood. After his graduation from college in 1850, he had traveled to Maryland to enter the Jesuit novitiate at Frederick, a town in the hilly countryside fifty miles northwest of Washington. Diocesan priests could be trained in as little as four years, but prospective members of the Society of Jesus got a rigorous preparation that lasted for more than a decade. They began as novices with two years of spiritual reflection, at the end of which they professed their first vows of poverty, chastity, and obedience. Next came an extended study of philosophy, after which they completed what was called a regency, a period usually spent teaching the younger students in Jesuit schools. Several years then went into the study of theology, in the middle of which they might at last be ordained to the priesthood. That was followed by yet another year of intensive spiritual formation, known as tertianship, and then they took their final vows and were ready for a regular assignment. Thus, Patrick Healy knew when he went to Maryland that he was starting out on a very long road.[32]

He found the Jesuit novitiate a surprisingly hospitable place—a surprise because the religious order he was joining was hardly immune to the racial attitudes permeating society at large. The Jesuits had owned slaves since their arrival in Maryland two hundred years before, and they would continue to do so elsewhere until the Civil War. Various "plantations" of the Society still relied on slave labor as much as those of secular planters. Though they tried to look after their slaves' religious welfare by baptizing them, Jesuit masters treated their chattels no better than the average owner. Nor did they hesitate to maximize the profits of slavery. In 1838, for example, the Maryland Jesuits had sold nearly three hundred slaves to several planters in Louisiana, a transaction considered controversial only because those who were Catholics might not be allowed to practice their religion with their new masters. Jesuit attitudes toward blacks in general mirrored those of other white Americans. Shortly after emancipation, one Jesuit could casually complain to another that "you cannot now tell an African from a Caucasian except by the smell."[33] In the face of such overt racism, Patrick Healy might well expect little of anything from his new religious companions.

He did, however, have several advantages, and the foremost of these was his complexion. Those who knew nothing of his family background had no reason to doubt, from looking at him, that he was anything other than a white man. His passports invariably described him as "light" or "fair" in appearance, and those perceptions, confirmed by surviving photographs, were common enough to let him get by. In contrast to Sherwood, his skin alone would not betray him, since his "African blood" did not "shew." Moreover, he had a powerful patron in Father George Fenwick. The Jesuit "Dad," whose long career commanded the respect of his confreres, recommended Patrick unreservedly, playing the role of protector for him that Bishop Fitzpatrick played for James and Sherwood. Thus, when Patrick entered the community, he came with the highest of endorsements. Father John Early, the president of Holy Cross, wrote the Jesuit superior at Georgetown College in Washington that Patrick was "a young man in every way worthy of being rec[eive]d."[34]

In the isolation of the Jesuit novitiate, Patrick followed the normal course of things, and in 1852 he pronounced his vows, a turning point marking him in Jesuit parlance as a "scholastic." After a year at a school in Philadelphia, he was then sent back to the familiar surroundings of Holy Cross College, where he was responsible for teaching a typically wide range of subjects, from English and French to algebra and bookkeeping. He was happy to be back at what was, in so many ways, home, and he expressed his satisfaction tangibly. The school's main building had been destroyed by fire, and he contributed $2,300—part of his share of his father's estate—to its reconstruction. This cemented his relationship with the Jesuits, and theirs with him: they were all part of the same family now. His work was both demanding and unrelenting. He was "very cheerful," another Jesuit said, but he was also a little "lonesome without someone who would lighten the outside work and with whom he might have a moment's chat after the labours of the day." What he really needed was a fellow scholastic for "company and assistance," but such a colleague was unavailable. He adjusted quickly enough, however, and his brother James reported that Patrick "seems to succeed admirably" and that he was "extremely well-liked by the students," notwithstanding that he was "very vigilant with regard to discipline." He was even, James thought, better looking than when he started.[35]

At the same time, Patrick experienced first-hand the unpredictability of his racial passing. Two months after arriving at the college, he wrote a long, candid letter to "Dad" Fenwick, saying he was "busy, though by no means discontented." The double negative bespoke a deeper uneasiness, apparently in response to an unpleasant encounter with some students. "Placed in a college as I am, over boys who were well acquainted either by sight or hearsay with me + my brothers," he explained, "remarks are sometimes made (though not in my hearing) which wound my very heart. You know to what I refer," he added, unwilling to commit his racial secret to paper, even with Fenwick. "The anxiety of mind caused by these is very intense," he went on, an anxiety that was redoubled because his brother Michael, now age fourteen, had entered Holy Cross as a student that fall and had suffered this "same ordeal." Such wounding jeers had not been heard from classmates during his own student days, but now that he was in a position of authority he made a more tempting target. Patrick took comfort that the "re-marks"—quite obviously racial slurs—had occurred "but once since my return hither," and he was hopeful that time would solve the problem. "I trust that all this will wear away," he said optimistically, as new students who did not know the family's story came to the school. For now, he was pessimistic: "I feel that whilst we live here with those who have known us but too well, we shall always be subject to some such degrading misfortune."[36]

Patrick's anguished complaint to Father Fenwick was as close as he or the others ever came to speaking openly about their dilemma. He himself was light-skinned enough to pass as white, and young Michael was similarly fair; if it were just the two of them, there would be no problem. But their brothers had darker complexions, and they were still known on campus, either by "sight" or "hearsay." As Bishop Fitzpatrick noted, anyone who looked at Sherwood knew that there was "African blood" in the family. The whispered conversations among the students could begin there, and the furtive thrill of talking about the Healys was perhaps redoubled by their achievements. Here were young men who were defined as black, and yet they were not behaving as blacks were supposed to. Here was a teacher, someone whom the students had to respect and obey, and yet in their eyes he was "really" a black man who, almost by definition, deserved neither respect nor obedience from whites. It takes little imagination to reconstruct their "re-marks." Patrick was probably right, however, that time was his ally. The problem would "wear away" as the students who knew his darker-skinned brothers graduated and moved on, thus burying his racial heritage further underground.

His waiting worked. In the next few years his spirits improved as the insults ceased. He became a better teacher, he thought, expanding both the range of subjects and the grade levels he taught. By 1855 he was instructing the boys in the high school division, but he also taught in the so-called grammar and poetry classes, the equivalents of the freshman and sophomore years of college. "I keep them very closely at work," he reported cheerily to a superior, relying on "the admirable system" of Jesuit education. Even if "none of them are particularly bright," his pupils were at least diligent: "a more studious set I have never taught." He also deepened his own commitment to his religious community. Acknowledging James's encouragement that he become "a real Jesuit, . . . a man of interior spirit, of deep religious feelings, a model + leader of souls to God," Patrick seconded the hope "that his wish may be verified."[37]

By 1858, his regency at Holy Cross was ending, and it was time for him to exchange the role of teacher for that of student. At the end of the summer he left the campus—as it happened, he would never be back—and went to Georgetown to begin concentrated theological studies. Almost immediately, however, his superiors decided that his intellectual talents justified sending him to Europe for a better education than he could get in America. Accordingly, he sailed for Rome that November and proceeded overland to the famed university at Louvain in Belgium, the oldest continuously operated institution of Catholic higher learning in the world. A college for Americans had been established there the previous year, and he joined its first classes, not returning to the United States until the summer of 1866.[38]

While in Europe, he finished his transformation into the "real" Jesuit he wanted to be. He got consistent spiritual direction, and he felt his interior life changing for the better. After attending a series of lectures by a French Jesuit known for his "solidity + lucidity," Patrick told a friend that the preacher "literally sacks the 'old man'—it is his favorite expression." He too was eager to exchange his old self for a new one. Speaking about religious conversion in such terms was familiar, of course, a vocabulary stretching back to the New Testament itself, but Patrick Healy had more than one "old" man he wanted to "sack." In the process, he more than once worked his way through the Spiritual Exercises of Ignatius Loyola, the Jesuits' founder. These presented a focused system of prayer and meditation in which the participant was guided by a more practiced adviser. The experience was an intense one, lasting an entire month, but Patrick drew "solid conviction" from it. "Every time I make the exercises I seem to appreciate them better," he wrote, and they confirmed his Jesuit identity. In return, he prayed that "the Society may never have reason to repent of having allowed me to be . . . one of its children," in spite of the risk that he might tarnish "its good name by my irregularities."[39]

His "irregularities" were perhaps only too obvious, but in his emerging identity as a member of the Society of Jesus, he found the "new" man to replace his old one. By September 1864, he was ready for ordination, which came at the hands of a visiting bishop from Luxembourg in the cathedral at Liege. "I will not attempt to portray in words the consolations exceeding great which have inundated my soul," he wrote to his superior at Georgetown immediately afterward, but he was certain of "the great change which God has wrought within me" and the "great calm" that had come over him: "I feel a new man." Almost all new priests talked this way, but Patrick felt the change more keenly than they. His emotions surged, he reported, when the ordination ritual came to the part that repeated Jesus's words from Saint John's gospel: "I no longer call you slaves, but my friends." The passage evoked the imagery of leaving behind slavery to sin and becoming instead a true friend of God. In Patrick Healy's case, the words also had a more literal meaning. He, after all, had actually been a slave under his country's law, even if he had never actually experienced bondage. How much more, then, could he appreciate the transition and the institution that had made it possible. After God, he said, the Catholic church had been the source of all the "favours" he had ever received, and his sense of "obligation shall ever be living and fresh in my memory." He doubted that he would ever be able to "repay" the Jesuit order for "the care it has had for me," but he pledged it all his "labour" and "devotion."[40]

Patrick Healy remained in Europe for another two years, but he had successfully joined his brothers James and Sherwood in their vocations as priests. The chain of events that had begun with their baptism as students at Holy Cross, just escaped from Georgia, had reached its logical conclusion. Their problems were by no means over—passing across the color line was still a hazardous proposition—but they had managed to erect the defenses of religion and status around themselves. Larger events might always conspire against them, however, and even then their nation was coming apart, split by the very question of what place America would have for black people. No American, of whatever race or color, was beyond the reach of that terrible swift sword.

CHAPTER FIVE

Northerners: The Healys and the Civil War

No war, we like to think, is inevitable. We resist the idea that fate alone can decree the systematic destruction of life and property. There must always be, right up to the last minute, some human agency that can forestall the tragedy. Some conflicts, such as the First World War, seem highly contingent, the product of thoughtless, avoidable blunders: if only this or that had happened differently, historians argue, the carnage might have been prevented. With the American Civil War of the years 1861–1865, by contrast, the case for inevitability seems more compelling. In the election campaign of 1858, Senator William H. Seward of New York had predicted an "irrepressible conflict" between North and South, one that would decide the matter of slavery once and for all. Even as some politicians sought to forestall Seward's prophecy, a sense of irrepressibility grew in the nation at large.[1]

Together with their fellow citizens, the Healy family was affected directly by this war, but as usual their dilemma was sharper than that of other Americans, for they incarnated the contradictions that lay at the heart of the contest. Born in the South, they now lived in the North. Born into slavery, they were now free. Born as black people and destined by law, society, and (it was thought) biology to remain so forever, they had chosen to define themselves as white. The American quandary about race found particular expression in them. Initially, of course, the war would be fought over a narrow constitutional question: could individual states, having once joined the Union, now withdraw from it? Soon enough, however, especially after President Lincoln's proclamation of freedom for slaves, it would also become a struggle for emancipation. More broadly, it was a war over the place of African Americans in the life of the United States. To that extent, the Healys were precisely what the war was about.

As the nation came apart, all Americans had to decide where their loyalties lay and to identify unequivocally the home that was worth defending. For the Healys, home was Boston, the heart of pro-Union sentiment. Their birthplace in Georgia had long since been sold and forgotten; the house James bought outside Boston was their geographic and emotional center. Even so, in an age when American regional consciousness was more potent than it is today, they remained aware that they were transplanted Southerners. As early as his student days, James carefully noted in his diary whenever he heard what he called a "Yankee term," different from the idioms of the South. He laughed, for example, when a classmate hooked a catfish in a nearby lake and called it a "pout."[2] By the time of the war, the Healys were well established among the Catholics of Boston, and it was from the perspective of that community that they followed public events.

They and their neighbors always viewed secession with contempt. The *Boston Pilot*, a newspaper for immigrants published with support from Bishop Fitzpatrick, scorned the South's rejection of "more lawful, more noble, more American means of redress" for its supposed grievances. The weekly journal quoted Andrew Jackson's succinct opinion of thirty years before that "disunion by armed force is treason." The duty of its readers, even those who had only recently arrived in America, was clear. "We Catholics have only one course to adopt, only one line to follow," it editorialized in early 1861, just as the first southern states were going their own way: "Stand by the Union; fight for the Union; die by the Union." As time went on and it became clear that the conflict would last far longer than anyone had expected, the newspaper urged enlistment to fill up the Union ranks. In 1862, for example, when a call went out for 300,000 volunteers, the paper had no doubt that this quota "will be at once filled." Intimations that recent immigrants who signed up might be rewarded with a shortened path to citizenship only reinforced the *Pilot*'s endorsement of unambiguous loyalty.[3]

Boston's Catholics wholeheartedly supported the war, but theirs was a narrow interpretation of what was at stake: preservation of the Union, not freedom for the slaves, was the goal. Abolitionist sentiment played no part in rallying Catholics to the cause. The war left unchanged traditional Catholic attitudes toward slavery in particular and blacks in general, attitudes summarized by Orestes Brownson's blithe acceptance of "the fact of Negro inferiority" in spite of the friendship between his own sons and the Healy brothers. Brownson spoke for most members of his church in asserting that the inherently "degenerate" nature of the African American was a powerful "reason why we should not seek to form one community with him," even should emancipation come. Those who entertained the chimerical idea that America could ever be a multiracial society, including abolitionists like Garrison and Wendell Phillips, were thought to be more dangerous radicals than secessionists.[4]

More seriously, in American Catholic minds the cause of abolition was always tainted with nativism, and there was some justice in that assessment. As Sherwood Healy himself had said, those "who pity the negro hate the church." Too many advocates of emancipation were Protestant ministers who had stirred anti-Catholic hostility. Too many leaders of the Republican Party, particularly those called "Black Republicans" because of their support for African American civil rights, had cut their political teeth as Know-Nothings. Foremost of these was Massachusetts's own junior senator, Henry Wilson, who, in the opinion of one Boston priest, "deserve[d] a halter and a lamp post" for his earlier anti-immigrant platform. The same observer managed to lump all the familiar enemies together when he lashed out in his diary against the "antichristian and ungodly set of misanthropists, abolitionists, Black Republicans, and Know Nothings," all of them infected with the "cursed, Puritanic, and satanic spirit of New England." The *Pilot* was more temperate but no less certain that antislavery "agitation" only prolonged the war by persuading Confederates that northern intentions really were in favor of "conquering" the South.[5] Better to keep the two issues—restoring the Union and freeing the slaves—separate than to risk losing the one in an ill-advised pursuit of the other.

The Healys' adopted home also had its racial tensions. Boston might be the seat of abolition, but it was no paradise for African Americans, who accounted for less than 2 percent of its 175,000 inhabitants. A long-standing pattern of residential segregation was only the most obvious disadvantage in a city ruled by their supposed friends. As late as the 1820s, the state legislature had seriously debated excluding free blacks from entering Massachusetts altogether. Until 1843, racial intermarriage was every bit as illegal there as it was in Georgia, and seating in railroad carriages was still allocated by color. The public schools had been segregated since the Revolution, and a court challenge in 1849 only affirmed the principle of "separate but equal" schools, a case that set a national precedent for the next hundred years. The legislature in 1855 prohibited the use of race in making student assignments, but so-called Jim Crow laws—the name itself may have originated in the Bay State—persisted. Blacks could vote, but they were not admitted to jury service until 1860. Limited progress toward equality during the war years was short-lived: many public accommodations resegregated themselves in the later 1860s.[6] Thus, Boston would probably have been a less congenial place for the Healys had they defined themselves as blacks. As it was, their religious positions secured them in the white community as they watched the progress of the conflict.

For four years, talk of the war was on everyone's lips, and James Healy was no exception. When news of the fall of Vicksburg arrived in July of 1863, for example, he thrilled to the "immense sensation," marked by the "ringing of bells + the like." When other Union victories were not greeted with sufficient enthusiasm, he worried about "apparent apathy" and hoped that war weariness would not make Northerners "desirous of settling the matter some how or any how." In March 1865, he read with interest Lincoln's majestic second inaugural address, promising "malice toward none" and "charity for all" once the war was over, and he characterized it correctly as "very short + scriptural-like." He sometimes bemoaned the havoc that the war was causing in the South, grimly following the merciless progress of General Sherman through Georgia, for instance, and shaking his head over the "destruction of property, public of course and private." Father Healy belonged to no political party, and he seems never to have voted in a national or state election. Little can be read into this: in his day, many priests registered and voted, but many others never did. Still, he read the newspapers and was a keen observer of national affairs, often bipartisan in his skepticism. He generally approved of Lincoln and his cabinet, for example, but rumors that the administration was cynically angling for Catholic votes brought a cool disapproval from him: "Not being able to mind its own business, the government is inclined to mind the business of every body else."[7]

As a priest, Healy was especially eager that Catholic interests be safeguarded during the war. He was bothered by news that Jesuit houses in Maryland might be confiscated for use as army hospitals without compensation. Reports that Georgetown and other Catholic schools in the border states had been "denounced to the government as hot-beds of secession" were troubling for the possible retribution this might bring, even though he was convinced that "they are such without doubt." When the archbishop of Cincinnati published an open letter in 1864, declaring "with his whole soul for the union and the abolition of slavery," Father Healy was nervous about yoking the two causes, but he was even more dismayed by the unpredictable public statements of John Hughes, the hot-tempered archbishop of New York. Fittingly nicknamed "Dagger John," Hughes seemed incapable of resisting a fight, sending too many fiery letters to the editors of various newspapers. After one such explosion, Healy commented that the ensuing public rancor did "no honour to His Grace of New York" and was "unworthy of him": the prelate's harangue may have "pointed the right way, but that was all."[8]

Healy's responsibilities for managing the Boston church were also redoubled now because, for much of the war, Bishop John Fitzpatrick was out of the country. The bishop had enthusiastically supported the Union cause, helping to recruit "Irish regiments" and appointing chaplains to accompany them to the front. In return, Fitzpatrick was awarded an honorary doctor of divinity degree from Harvard, the ultimate Brahmin institution, in June 1861. "This would not have been done," one crusty Yankee, Amos A. Lawrence, observed, "were it not for the loyalty shown by [Fitzpatrick] and by the Irish who have offered themselves freely for the army." All the while, however, the bishop's health continued uncertain at best, and by the spring of 1862 his doctors were recommending a voyage to Europe in the hope of reviving his strength. There may have been other motives at work, too. The Confederacy had already dispatched several Catholic bishops from the South on informal diplomatic missions to Rome and other European capitals, and the Lincoln administration hoped to counteract them with prelates of its own. Fitzpatrick, who spent much of his time abroad in Brussels, may have had this purpose in mind as much as the recovery of his physical well-being.[9] In any event, he sailed from Boston in May 1862, not to return until the fall of 1864.

In his absence, Healy was more than ever the man at the center of local church affairs. He even became a kind of religious ward boss to whom political leaders deferred in matters Catholic. In particular, he developed a close relationship with John Albion Andrew, the Republican governor of Massachusetts who had swept into office in 1860 and was as strong a Union man as one could find. Andrew relied on Healy as his clearinghouse for information about the state's Catholic soldiers. The governor solicited, and the priest gladly provided, advice on the appointment of officers for the local Irish regiments. On one occasion Healy even wrote to Archbishop Hughes in New York for assessment of a man who had lived there before the war, but more often he relayed the recommendations of Boston pastors about local officer candidates: this one was "a very worthy + steady man"; that one was risky and "his appointment would prove prejudicial to the service"; a third was "strongly recommended." He passed along a request from the bishop of Prince Edward Island for the discharge of a Canadian volunteer whose mother wanted him home, but he did not press the case. If the governor could readily do them this favor, fine, Healy wrote; "if nothing can be done, there the matter ends." Though Andrew was unable to help in that particular case, he was later useful to Healy in securing the back pay of a Boston priest who had been wounded in action.[10] Fitzpatrick stood at the center of a web of friendship and influence with the state's political leaders, and James Healy now came increasingly to occupy that position himself.

He was no less important to the common Catholic serviceman. Several soldiers at the front, who seem to have had no previous personal connection to Healy, regularly sent him their salaries to hold on their behalf. Perhaps with reason, these

men feared that they would only squander their pay if they held onto it themselves, so they turned to this trusted figure to look out for their interests. "Will you
be so kind as to keep it until I send for it?" one wrote, enclosing his enlistment
bonus. The confidence they placed in him shows once again how successfully his
identity as a priest had replaced his racial identity. These soldiers would almost
certainly not have trusted a black man with their money, but they would trust
him. Father Healy kept a careful accounting of all such funds, depositing them in
a savings bank and paying the money to wives or other family members on demand. He also periodically visited the troops at local staging areas. In June of 1861
he accompanied Fitzpatrick to the encampment of the principal Catholic regi-
ment, the Ninth Massachusetts, on one of the islands in Boston harbor. There the
bishop administered the sacrament of confirmation to more than two hundred of
the men as a kind of added spiritual protection in the battles ahead.[11]

The war did nothing to encourage Healy to reconsider the distance he had put
between himself and African Americans. If anything, it confirmed his self-
definition as white, different from them. Lincoln's momentous announcement in
July 1862 of his intention to free the slaves and the formal proclamation of emancipation six months later went entirely unremarked by this former slave. In February 1865, when Congress passed what would become the Thirteenth Amend-
ment, forever abolishing slavery, Healy noted the news without comment; in fact,
he was a little confused about constitutional law, thinking at first that the measure
had to be submitted directly to the voters for ratification. Beyond that, he was
leery of politicians who pressed too hard for racial equality, shaking his head in
amazement at the public statements of the flamboyant Massachusetts general
Benjamin Butler, who had entered the war a Democrat but was by its end a Radical Republican. Nor did Healy show much interest in the famous regiments of
black troops, mustered in at Boston and led into battle by the idealistic but inex-
perienced Robert Gould Shaw. He followed their movements in the newspapers,
and he seemed to attach some significance—perhaps it was merely irony—to reports that black troops were the first to occupy Richmond, the rebel capital.[12]
Otherwise, the struggle for black freedom had no noticeable effect on him.

As the war came to its dramatic conclusion in the first two weeks of April 1865,
Father Healy experienced the same emotional jolts as his fellow citizens. Confederate regiments surrendered one by one, and the false rumor that Jefferson Davis
had resigned and fled the country caused a brief uproar. Then, more certain news
arrived in Boston, the "glad tidings that Gen. Lee has surrendered to Gen. Grant."
Observing that the fateful meeting at Appomattox, during which the behavior of

the opposing commanders did "great honour to both," had occurred on the Sab-
bath—it was Palm Sunday, in fact—Healy commented that "all the great events of
this war have taken place on a Sunday." The celebrations that followed were rather
less edifying. "Everybody is happy. Stores, schools, + all places except rum-shops
are closed," Healy wrote, frowning at the unseemly display of jubilation. "Everybody was allowed to get drunk," he wrote. "Liquor dealers dispensed their fluids
gratis + the judges dismissed the arrested without trial." As usual, perhaps, he was
more restrained than the rabble, content with "intoxication mental + spiritual."[13]

From these euphoric heights, he was quickly plunged into the depths of shock
at the assassination of the president. Lincoln had just begun to spell out his plans
for reuniting the nation, and Healy found them "sensible," though he recognized
"the difficulties of reorganization." Then came the news of the president's murder
on Good Friday night, leaving the Boston priest "perfectly aghast at this dreadful
deed." Reports that the new president, Andrew Johnson, was not up to the task
ahead of him likewise disturbed Healy, though he was relieved to learn that the allegedly alcoholic Tennessean was "sobered by his new position." Church bells were
tolled in Boston for an hour in mourning; houses and public buildings were
draped in black. Ordinary Catholics sought their own consolations: Healy reported that the number of parishioners going to confession that Saturday afternoon was unusually large, "much beyond what could be heard." On Easter Sunday,
the Te Deum, the traditional hymn of joy usually chanted on the feast, was omit-
ted because of the national trauma. During his Easter sermon, Father Healy did not
dwell on current events, but he did make "a short allusion to the assassination."
Such a dramatic act of political violence seemed almost too much to comprehend.
"God knows what the end will be!" another Boston priest exclaimed.[14]

As the assassination drama played out over the next several weeks, Healy
looked primarily to Catholic interests, especially since several of those involved
had links to the Roman church. John Surratt, for instance, who had been recruited into the plot by John Wilkes Booth, was a Catholic; several meetings of the
conspirators had been held in the boardinghouse his mother ran in Washington.
Surratt had become disillusioned with the erratic Booth, however, and was actually in Canada at the time of the assault, but he was implicated nonetheless. Healy
likewise noted that Lewis Paine, who failed to carry out the simultaneous assassination of Secretary of State Seward, had once been a student in a Catholic school
near Baltimore. David Herold, who also participated in the attack on Seward, was
not a Catholic, Healy was relieved to learn, but he had attended Georgetown, and
Doctor Samuel Mudd, who had set the leg that Booth had broken while fleeing

the scene of the crime, had had a brother at Holy Cross. These connections, however tenuous, led Healy to fear that Catholics might be the objects of "dreadful bitterness + revenge." Historians have debated the guilt of Mudd and the Surratt family ever since, and Healy shared those doubts at the time. "The trial of the assassins shows the meanness of the court more clearly than the guilt of the murderers," he said, observing that the Surratts protested their innocence all the way to the gallows.[15]

He never questioned, however, where the war had left him and his family amid the changed American racial arrangements that came with black freedom. As Reconstruction of the Union proceeded, James Healy only stiffened his resolve to distinguish himself from African Americans, whose status became more than ever the central issue of public debate. The college student who had casually called plantation slaves "the niggers," who reproduced the white caricature of black dialect, and who laughed at the racially charged minstrel show was now more sure than ever that he was not black. By the end of 1865, Healy was openly unsympathetic toward Radical Republicans in Congress who were pressing the rights of freed slaves. In part, this reflected a generalized scorn of politics. Without abolition to "furnish material for speeches," he said, troublemakers had to take up some other cause, but what a strange cause it was. "The protection, the equalization and the super-elevation of the negro is to be made the reason of strife," Healy wrote.[16] "The negro" was evidently someone else, and any attempt at the "equalization" of that other sort of being was foolhardy. That he could characterize legislative efforts to guarantee black civil rights as "super-elevation"—the unusual word itself rings with skepticism—is a measure of how far he put himself from the objects of congressional attention. Legitimate "protection" might be one thing, but James Healy would hardly have mocked the "super-elevation" of a group that included himself and his family. Safely in the white community, Healy, like many other whites, viewed the "equalization" of blacks as a dubious political and social goal.

✑

Healy's easy identification with white Americans did not go entirely unchallenged, and throughout the war the tensions he faced were close to home. During these years, he shared his rectory with a priest who had a decidedly different outlook on public affairs. Father Hilary Tucker had been born in Perry County, Missouri, downriver from St. Louis, and was educated in Rome. Nearly a generation older than Healy, Tucker had spent his early career as an itinerant missionary in the Midwest. Drawn to New England in the 1840s to work with immigrants, he superintended parishes in Lowell, Massachusetts, and Providence, Rhode Island. By 1857, he was at the cathedral in Boston, where Bishop Fitzpatrick appointed him to the position of rector, the pastor of the parish and a kind of "first among equals" of the priests assigned there. Tucker was a man of strong opinions and grumpy moods, and he may have had a weakness for drink: entries in the very informative diary he kept sometimes trail off into an illegible scrawl. Even apart from his difficult personality, Tucker made a strange housemate for James Healy because he had the sentiments of a Copperhead, the unflattering name applied to Northerners who sympathized with the Confederacy.[17]

As Healy sympathetically followed the progress of the Union armies, Father Tucker took a more jaundiced view. He did not countenance disunion, but he was sharply critical of Northern efforts to reunite the nation by force. "This most iniquitous and despotic administration," he wrote of the government in Washington, was pursuing policies "which no civilised or barbarian nation ever did in the pagan world." His racial attitudes could be equally graphic, and though he was circumspect in public, he confided uglier opinions to the pages of his diary. He scoffed at the local regiments of black troops, whom he dismissed as "Gov. Andrew's pets." Their attempts at military formations were simply laughable, he said after watching them drill one day on Boston Common, but, descending into crude racist caricature, he concluded that "they will be invincible in battle, at least as much as skunks are, especially if [the] time be hot." The war was only having a negative effect on society, as far as he could see. "It is sad to reflect on the change for the worse to be met with everywhere in traveling," he wrote in 1864, returning to Boston by rail with a fellow priest. Their train had stopped at a military camp just outside the city, "where we were flooded with a rowdy set of white and black of all classes, men and women, most negro and mulattoes, women no doubt mostly whores, and rakes of the lowest grade." Such were the inevitable results of "this cruel and unnatural war.... The country is ruined and fast going to the dogs." Unable to tolerate the mixed-race passengers, he got off the train before it reached his stop and took a horse trolley back to his rectory instead.[18]

Given these racial opinions, all too common among white Americans in the 1860s, we may well wonder how Tucker felt about living in the same house as one of the very "mulattoes" who caused him such consternation. While others might be disposed to overlook the Healys' ambiguous racial standing, Hilary Tucker seems unlikely to have been so open-minded. Even more difficult for Tucker to accept was Fitzpatrick's decision to replace him as rector of the cathedral in the spring of 1862 with none other than James Healy. With reason, the bishop probably feared leaving a man of such volatile and contrary political opinions in charge of things during the war, especially since he himself was about to leave for his extended stay abroad. Tucker dutifully accepted his demotion, but it rankled nonetheless. He likewise deferred to Healy's authority, but he remained deeply ambivalent about this younger, partly black priest.

Tucker exhibited almost schizophrenic reactions to Healy—now including him among the priests affectionately designated as "our family," now spilling out his anger and frustration into his diary. The younger man's rapid rise under the patronage of Fitzpatrick was a persistent source of irritation. Father Healy was, Tucker thought, "not satisfied unless he has his finger into everything." He was "very ambitious, very proud," and he seemed reluctant to let the other priests of the parish take their share of the credit for anything. Even with all his other re-sponsibilities, for instance, Healy insisted on attending meetings of the parish de-votional societies. "It seems to me," Tucker wrote, "he is jealous of any other priest to do anything with the societies, with the women, lest he lose his influence." Tucker's concern that Healy was too forward with the women of the parish may have been an echo of the racist conviction that black men were too forward with white women, but the disapproval of his colleague for simply being pushy was also more general. "He does not know himself," the Missourian concluded. "He has too high an opinion of himself and his abilities, great as they certainly are."[19]

Some of Tucker's criticisms were professional disagreements rather than per-sonal animosities. Healy, he thought, tended to preach over people's heads, for in-stance. Tucker judged one Healy sermon "extraordinary and novel, . . . very able, but in my opinion too theological or above the reach of the people." It might have been a suitable instruction for theology students, but for the average parishioner it was too deep: "I fear at times that the pride of showing learning will sway or at least deeply tinge even the best." The maintenance of order in the cathedral rec-tory might also be a sore subject, and Tucker found Healy overly censorious, par-ticularly toward him. One day, after Tucker had received "one of my usual scold-ings from the chancellor"—perhaps a warning about alcohol or a reprimand for some outburst—he concluded that "Rev. Father James Healy knows me less than he thinks he does. . . . He has misjudged me and suspicioned me in things of which I am not guilty." Tucker acknowledged Healy's "kind and good intention for me," and he resolved to do better at controlling himself, but he could not help remarking that Healy "would do well to strive to know himself better, especially to do to others as he would wish them to be done by."[20] Tucker's version of the Golden Rule came out a little garbled in the heat of the moment, but it no doubt irked him that the reprimand had come from this particular source.

It was when Tucker observed Healy among his brothers and sisters that his disapproval was most vigorously expressed. The "pride of family" and the resulting "ambition of power, which is *insatiable,*" were too much to take. In Tucker's view, the family was entirely too close. In 1864, for example, the younger siblings, then living at the house in Newton, had all trooped into the city for a lingering farewell to their brother, who was leaving town for a few days on diocesan business. "Such is the nature of this family," Tucker harrumphed, "that they cannot be out of sight of each other for a day or so without thinking that the absence of one, or especially Father James, would bring about the final cataclism [*sic*] of all creation." James Healy still played the role of substitute parent, but like many parents, Tucker thought, he had his unaccountable favorites: he was, for example, "perfectly blind with regard to his brother Eugene"—barely fourteen at the time—"who deserved twenty lickings when he never got one." Overt displays of affection were particularly distasteful. Healy "does not see or feel how very silly and undignified in him it is for his sisters to be allowed, on almost every occasion when he is at home and sometimes elsewhere, to kiss and fawn on him as they do."[21] The years of separation and uncertainty had drawn the siblings closer together, but Tucker, the skeptical outsider, nonetheless disapproved of all this fawning and kissing.

Tucker could be harsh in his judgments of Healy and his family, but as time went on he could also be friendly, accepting, and even affectionate. This change of heart was not hypocritical; it grew out of the ordinary circumstances of everyday life. When Tucker was feeling ill or lost his voice, for example, Father Healy said his assigned masses for him or preached in his stead, and the older priest was always grateful. Healy's too-scholarly sermons could elicit disapproval, but sometimes they hit the mark: "Mr. Healy preached a very fine homily on the gospel of the day." The new rector might scold Tucker for his behavior, but he also actively sought his advice. "Mr. J. A. Healy asked my opinion on a very delicate matter" concerning another priest, Tucker wrote in the spring of 1864, "how he should act in the case." Tucker gave his recommendation "conscientiously," and Healy thanked him for his counsel. Healy was perhaps overzealous in attending to the parish societies, but the results were hard to argue with. His series of sermons during the special devotions to the Virgin in May 1863, Tucker said, were sure to bring "great profit."[22]

Even the tenderness of the Healy siblings for one another could win Tucker over, especially on those occasions when he himself joined the extended family circle. More than once, Tucker spent his days off at the Healy home in Newton. Tucker's own family, such as it was, remained far away: he had a brother who was also a priest, but that man had stayed in Missouri. Without near relations in

Boston, Tucker was left isolated, so the Healys welcomed him into their family, just as the city's Catholics had once welcomed them. Tucker happily joined in. Early on a May afternoon, for example, Healy spontaneously proposed a carriage ride, and Tucker reported that "I rode out to Newton with him. . . . A most delightful ride it was. We staid [*sic*] until 6 p.m." Visits to the suburbs became habitual, and other outings took off from there. One Tuesday morning in June 1865, after six o'clock mass and a quick breakfast, Tucker and Healy left the cathedral, "and then we went to the Charles river, fishing" with Josephine and Eliza Healy, ages twenty and eighteen respectively. "They caught a good string of perch," Tucker laughed; "I caught none and got well sun burnt." A year before, he had even taken an extended summer vacation with them. For two weeks they made their way along the Maine coast, going for boat rides, visiting friends, and generally relaxing. One afternoon, an impromptu carriage race was declared: "Eliza Healy and I in an open rickety buggy and a poor lame horse, Mr. Healy and Josephine in another." This companionable recreation left them all "much improved in health" and spirits, Tucker declared.[23]

These unguarded moments of friendship could lead Tucker, perhaps in spite of himself, to defend Healy, even from the racial animosity he himself occasionally shared. One day, while cataloging Healy's faults, Tucker brought himself up short and took his friend's part. "Now I hope no one will think," he wrote in his diary, as if he were speaking to someone else, "I am jealous or prejudiced against him, for I am not! I have almost always taken his part when other priests speak against him."[24] Racist remarks, like those Patrick had heard while teaching at Holy Cross, could apparently burst forth at any time, from any source—even from "other priests." But when that happened, Hilary Tucker, an improbable man for the job, might spring to Healy's defense, if only "almost" always. Tucker might have been protesting too much here, covering his own periodic hostility by denying it. Still, through his personal contacts with the Healys over an extended period, he may also have begun to feel some uneasiness with the common prejudices, unconsciously exploring the possibility that popular racial understandings—misunderstandings—needed revision.

Thus, Tucker could experience genuinely contradictory feelings toward the Healy family. Little in his background disposed him to challenge the racial assumptions of white Americans: that blacks could not be soldiers, that "mulattoes" were "of the lowest grade," almost by definition. But suddenly he was confronted not with theory but with actuality. The Healys were not the "mulattoes" he disdained in a generic sense; they were individuals he knew personally, real people and friends. Father Healy's sisters might fawn over their brother too much, but Tucker could still travel to the family home and enjoy his own leisure time with these same fun-loving girls. Presumably they might display a similar affection toward him, and he could hardly censure that. The Healys might be defined as African Americans by society at large, but to Tucker, for at least some of the time, they did not seem to be such. Part of him thought it "knew" that he should treat them as if they were black, but since they seemed most often to be white, Tucker sometimes forgot himself and his prejudices.

Their light skin may have aided this selective amnesia, but it was the Healys' association with the church that really counted in Tucker's mind. The pattern that had manifested itself early in the family's association with the Catholic community of Boston—the Christmas celebrations with priests and their families of twenty years before—had only been reinforced with time. The transition from "nothing" to a religious identity was more complete now, as the Healys had fully assumed Catholicism into their true self-definition. To Tucker, who clung to that same religious identity himself, they were thus more like him than different; he and they were, in this sense, the same. He could still periodically lash out, but the ordinary, day-to-day friendship also moved Tucker in a more tolerant direction. He could always become disagreeable, but he was also capable of heeding what Lincoln called the "better angels of our nature."

ℒ♥

The real test of the friendship between Fathers Healy and Tucker came in July 1863, when Boston, like other cities throughout the North, was disrupted by rioting, sparked by the imposition of a military draft. The Lincoln administration had resisted conscription for more than two years, relying instead on the states to meet enlistment quotas. As the war dragged on, the only way to fill the ranks seemed to be through a draft. Accordingly, in March 1863 Congress approved a complicated system, hoping to raise three-quarters of a million men for the Union forces. Draft agents in each congressional district chose inductees at random from the names of all male citizens between the ages of twenty and forty-five until a fixed allotment had been selected. Apart from medical incapacity or proof that the draftee was the sole support of a widow or an orphan, the only legal way to avoid service was to pay $300 for a substitute. The administration hoped that a large new army would bring the conflict to a close, and the timing seemed auspicious. The first lottery was conducted that summer, just as the Union armies were winning the simultaneous victories at Gettysburg and Vicksburg.[25]

From the first, however, resistance to the draft was widespread, and it was particularly keen among recent Irish Catholic immigrants. Conscription seemed fundamentally unfair to them since, if drafted, they would almost certainly have to serve. The price of hiring a substitute might just as well have been a million dollars as far as they were concerned, and some newspaper headlines ridiculed that option as nothing but a stick-up: "Three Hundred Dollars or Your Life." Father Hilary Tucker agreed with cynics who took this as proof that the conflict was a "rich man's war but a poor man's fight." He denounced the "injustice . . . in making the fine [*sic*] $300 for a substitute, equal for the rich millionaire and the poor hod-carrier."[26] That the draft law was endorsed by Massachusetts's own Senator Henry Wilson, a former Know-Nothing, confirmed Tucker's view that this was yet another plot against the Irish. Moreover, the Emancipation Proclamation of the previous January had transformed the war against secession into a war against slavery, and that hardly seemed like a cause worth dying for. Opposition to the draft simmered for months, and in the hot days of mid-July 1863, it exploded. The worst of it was in New York City, where rioters rampaged for three days, attacking policemen, burning houses and stores, and beating up well-dressed young men: "There's a $300 man!" they would cry, singling out a victim. Black citizens unlucky enough to be in the rioters' path were dragged away and summarily lynched. Pugnacious statements by Archbishop Hughes added fuel to the fire, and order was restored only by the presence of 20,000 troops.[27]

In Massachusetts the draft had begun optimistically enough. "The brilliant victories recently won by our forces," the staunchly Republican *Boston Herald* opined, "have strengthened public confidence in the ultimate and speedy success of our cause." Conscription was not discriminatory, it argued: "all classes of our citizens were included," and in one case every member of a single business firm was called up at once. The "only" ways of avoiding service were physical infirmity or possession of the ready cash, the *Herald* said in blissful oblivion, though it acknowledged that certain draftees might be "somewhat pinched" by the price of a substitute. Other observers were less sanguine about the whole business. James Healy reported hearing rumors that as many as five hundred men had escaped "to the British Provinces" (that is, to Canada) to avoid the draft. As news of unrest in other cities filtered into Boston, tensions mounted. "There is an awful riot in New York," Healy wrote; "it will be strange to me if we escape some such trouble."[28]

Popular discontent found its way to the streets of Boston's North End, a district into which Irish immigrants had been crowding for years. About noon on Tuesday, July 14, two draft agents were beaten by a crowd, whose ranks then continued to swell throughout the afternoon. By dusk, several hundred people had assembled in front of an armory on Cooper Street, in which an artillery battery and a detachment of infantry were quartered. "For a while the mob contented themselves with shouting and yelling at those inside," a newspaper reported, but soon they were tearing up paving stones and throwing them at the garrison. Next they broke through the doors, and the commander gave the order to fire. One rioter, who "appears to have been a laboring man," was killed instantly, and several adolescent boys, drawn by the thrill of it all, were also killed or wounded; at least three young women were reported among the casualties as well. Next, the crowd surged toward the market district around Faneuil Hall, apparently intent on looting hardware stores for guns and ammunition. Many store owners had posted guards to repel the invaders, but one merchant later claimed to have lost one hundred rifles and seventy-five handguns. False fire alarms were turned in, and the firemen who responded were pelted with bricks and stones. By midnight, however, the rioters were losing interest and "all was as quiet as could be expected."[29]

The next morning, word of the disturbances spread throughout the city, and at the cathedral rectory, Fathers Healy and Tucker were dismayed at what they heard. Particularly distressing were reports that Catholics made up most of the rampaging crowd and that several priests may even have played a role in inciting the violence. "It is said," Healy wrote, that two clerics, one in Cambridge, the other in Chelsea, "have spoken in church on the conscription + used words calculated to inflame the minds of their hearers." The word was out that "an Irish society" had met on the night of the riot at a Catholic church in the North End and had closed with "cheers for Jeff Davis." Even Tucker thought such rabble-rousing "most dangerous, and even criminal." Throughout the day on Wednesday, however, it seemed that a show of force by the troops had had its effect in preventing a repeat of the disorder.[30]

Had he been in the city, Bishop Fitzpatrick would have felt compelled to add his church's voice to those calling for law and order. In his absence, that responsibility fell to James Healy. He consulted with Father Robert Brady, pastor of Saint Mary's parish in the North End, and Brady spent the day moving among his people, telling them to stay off the streets. Healy also asked Father Tucker for advice, and the older man did some quick legal research on "the law concerning the militia." The two had had their differences, but in the crisis they banded together. Taking his cue from a proclamation by Mayor Frederick Lincoln, Healy drafted a letter to all parishes, urging priests "to use their utmost efforts to preserve the public peace among their congregations—to caution them not only against taking part in factious assemblies, but even against being present at them. It is clear to all of us," he concluded, "that riot is against the best interests of society and of religion." Healy was prepared to distribute this letter immediately, "but, seeing the quiet state of things, forbore to do it." Two days later, he reconsidered, however, and sent the letter out to selected parishes "in the disturbed portions of the city"; it was also published in the newspapers.[31]

By the end of the week, calm had been restored. There was still, the always pessimistic Tucker thought, "a threatening and sullen look in [the] countenances of everyone that bodes no good," but Healy was cautiously encouraged by the "most profound quiet" that had settled over the city: "I did not anticipate any trouble." Scattered disturbances continued in some of the surrounding towns, but these were short-lived. At Sunday masses on July 19, Healy's call for order was read from pulpits in the city, and it seemed to forestall further violence. The news from New York was still quite bad, and the two Boston priests were particularly distressed by the counterproductive efforts of church officials there. To Tucker, the conduct of Archbishop Hughes was entirely "inexplicable." He had published a long, angry public letter that only further inflamed passions, "a damaging document for his fame and character," Tucker concluded. "It is a great pity he will dabble so much in politics."[32]

In Boston, the trouble was over, and Mayor Lincoln publicly thanked Healy for his help in the restoration of calm. Reporting to the city council at the end of the month, the mayor singled out "as worthy of our applause the good influence exerted by Reverend Fathers Healy and Brady and others of the Roman Catholic clergy, who labored to preserve quiet among their congregations."[33] The public congratulations for Healy spoke volumes, both in what they said and in what they did not. The public-spirited "Father Healy" was no more than that: a priest with an Irish name. No published report ever alluded to his racial background, a fact that might otherwise have been thought salient to the issues surrounding the draft riots. Even in this crisis, race had ceased to be a relevant consideration.

✑❧

If James Healy was the leader of Boston's Catholics during the Civil War, he was also very much the head of his own family, and the war proved a critical time for his younger siblings. In the decade since they had left Georgia, Josephine and Eliza had grown to young womanhood. After a brief stay in New York following Hugh's rescue of them in 1851, they were sent to Montreal to the convent school of the Notre Dame nuns where their older sister Martha had studied. Like her, they acquired all the refinements the school could give them, signing up for music and art lessons in addition to the routine classes of the grammar school. They received the religious instruction of their newly acquired church. A composition book of Eliza's, written in her best penmanship, shows their work in catechism classes, studying the devotions that now wove themselves into their lives. James expressed "continual satisfaction" that the two had grown "so sweet, pious, and obedient" under the nuns' care. They returned to Boston each summer during the school vacation, going back to Canada for the start of a new academic year until they had completed the equivalent of the high school course in the fall of 1861.[34] At that point, they settled into the family home in Newton, adopted now into the extended church family that centered around their successful oldest brother.

Although Martha had prepared the way for them with the Notre Dame Sisters, by the early 1860s she was concluding that the life of a nun was not for her after all. Since her entrance into the order in 1855, she had advanced through the prescribed stages of preparation, but as the day of her final solemn vows approached, she began to have second thoughts. The critical point came in the spring of 1863. The decision to leave a community of sisters was not uncommon among her contemporaries: girls who enrolled as adolescents often thought differently about their future as they grew up, and sometimes their families too changed their minds about whether this was the right course. Withdrawing from an order did not carry the stigma of failure it would acquire later on. Accordingly, the twenty-five-year-old Martha Healy, known as Sister Saint Lucie, left the Notre Dame convent at the end of March 1863, explicitly renouncing all claims to recover the dowry paid on her entrance, and she rejoined her family in Massachusetts. As it happened, James subsequently demanded return of the dowry, which was repaid by the sisters in installments over the next year, but he was convinced that Martha had made the right decision. A year after her return to Newton he reported her "very tranquil, happy, and content."[35]

Still at home too was Eugene, the baby of the family, who turned twelve just as the Civil War began. As arranged by Bishop Fitzpatrick, he continued to live with "Mother" Hodges and her family. His older brothers doted on Eugene, often from a distance. Patrick, seeing him in 1853 (probably for the first time), had described him as "a fine looking, healthy, + intelligent little child," while James, making his baby brother's acquaintance after returning from Paris two years later, pronounced him "a most charming little fellow" who was affectionately "*my* boy."[36] The lad's early schooling had been provided for here and there, but as he grew up something better was needed. Accordingly, in the summer of 1863, James took

Eugene to Europe and enrolled him in the famous English-language seminary at Douai in France, not with the intention of pushing him toward the priesthood, but merely to give him a religiously based education while his native land was torn apart by war. After the stresses of the draft riots, James was feeling the need for some time off, and the decision to take Eugene to France gave him that opportunity. Thus, at the beginning of August 1863, the Boston *Pilot* reported that Father Healy was sailing for Europe "in order to recruit his health, which has been greatly impaired by hard labor in the services of the Catholics of New England." The newspaper also took the occasion to lavish on him an unusual editorial encomium, declaring that "few, if any, of our young clergy"—he was thirty-three—"have labored more zealously. . . . He is justly beloved by all, more particularly by the old Cathedral congregation, to whose wants he has ministered at all times and in all seasons."[37]

While in Europe that summer and fall, James pursued an ambitious itinerary. Landing first at Liverpool, he proceeded to Brussels. There he was reunited with Fitzpatrick, whose own health seemed better in spite of what he called the "small apothecary shop" of medicines he had to take daily. The bishop had also made headway in his informal diplomacy on behalf of the Union. The American ambassador to Belgium, a career diplomat named Henry Sanford, was frequently absent from his post, busy on missions to other capitals, and Fitzpatrick took over many of his duties while he was away. The bishop-turned-ambassador managed the daily business of the legation, aided traveling Americans, and even fended off an ingratiating but overeager spy who, Fitzpatrick suspected, was a double agent for the Confederacy. Now Fitzpatrick and Healy set off together for some leisurely travel, after depositing Eugene at Douai. They drifted down the Rhine before returning to Brussels, where James was joined by his brother Patrick, in from the university town of Louvain, only a few miles away. Patrick's seminary studies had been "hard, very hard," and James's arrival was a welcome surprise: "you can judge of my emotions," Patrick wrote a Jesuit friend at home.[38] By the beginning of September, with Fitzpatrick back at his diplomatic post, the two Healys set off again, together for the first time since James had left Holy Cross almost fifteen years before.

They went first to England, where they boarded a ship bound for Gibraltar and a series of stops at other ports along the Mediterranean coast. It was a version of the grand tour, and the two kept track of the historic sites they visited, the Americans they met, and the unusual sights they saw. They glimpsed the seamy side of Dickensian London: Patrick was affronted by the sight of "prostitutes" and "gin palaces in full vigor." Spain was a more agreeable place, and getting there was half the fun. Off Trafalgar, "near which was won the famous victory of Nelson," Patrick chuckled at the "Britishers" who "venerate this spot + cork up a bottle" in its honor; "we benighted Americans," he mused, "passed it in perfect sang-froid." Once ashore, he found the dress of Spanish women preferable to that of the English, though he found them a little too bold: "I think the costumes of the former much more comely," he said, "altho', it may be, more seductive." Spanish men cut a fine figure indeed: "tall, intellectual looking men, their faces bearing the impress of culture + study." The brothers moved along at no particular pace, with one evening ashore much like another: "after drinking our sherry iced, after smoking a good cigar in our room," Patrick wrote laconically, "we sallied forth for a walk." This was, perhaps literally, just what the doctor ordered for James, who seemed to recover from the run-down condition he had brought to Europe with him.[39]

On the sixth of October they parted company at Marseilles, with Patrick heading back to school by way of Paris and James proceeding round-about to Rome through Strasbourg, Genoa, Pisa, and Florence. He was armed with several letters of introduction, including one from Isaac Hecker, whose stock in Rome was high just then. Like Orestes Brownson a convert to Catholicism from the transcendentalist movement, Hecker attracted favorable attention for his newly formed group, the Paulist Fathers, who set the conversion of American Protestants as their goal. Healy was "a priest of rare talent," Hecker wrote, "full of zeal for the glory of God," and he had won "the esteem and respect" of all who knew him. With no particular business to accomplish in the Eternal City, James took in classical ruins and the art treasures of the papacy, and he won a brief audience with Pius IX, who gave him the silver religious medal all papal visitors got as a memento. In addition, Healy managed to secure an indulgenced blessing for the choir of the cathedral in Boston; this was a common enough thing, but it came with an elaborately illustrated certificate, guaranteed to impress those back home. Then he headed north again, stopping briefly in Paris before rejoining Fitzpatrick in Brussels in November. At that point, he sailed for home, landing at New York and then taking the train to Boston, where he arrived a few days before Christmas. To celebrate his safe return, Hilary Tucker noted, the priests of the cathedral opened a bottle of champagne.[40]

Eugene Healy remained at Douai for only a year. It was a long way from home, and since he felt no calling to the priesthood, the seminary was not preparing him for a career. To make matters worse, the war was having a bad effect on the exchange rate for the American dollar, and the costs of tuition, room, and board were consequently higher than expected. Family members consulted with Fitz-patrick, who thought that the "expense is more than James can bear"—the phrase acknowledged James's primacy among the siblings—and that keeping Eugene in France was "unjust towards the other children." Thus, when Fitzpatrick decided to return to Boston at the end of the summer of 1864, he brought Eugene with him. They left Brussels together and stopped over in England, where they were joined by a Belgian priest also traveling to America. The spirited Eugene might have preferred to stay and have a little fun in England. Assigned one day to guide this older priest around London, he got caught up in a cricket game and left the poor man, whose command of English was marginal, to entertain himself. With no further plans for education or work, Eugene arrived home with Fitzpatrick at the beginning of September and joined the family household in Newton.[41]

Eugene was uncertain about his future, but the remaining Healy brother was growing more sure about his. Michael Augustine Healy, born in 1839, had left Georgia shortly before his parents' deaths, and by the early 1850s he was a student at Holy Cross, where he was never as happy as the others had been. He may have experienced some of the general anxieties of younger brothers who follow in the footsteps of popular and accomplished siblings, and the contrast was only re-inforced by Patrick's return to the college in the fall of 1853 as a Jesuit scholastic. Worse, Michael was coming to understand the racial ambiguities of his fam-ily. When Patrick complained to Father Fenwick about the "remarks . . . which wound my very heart," he noted that Michael was subject to the same taunts. Singled out as black even though his complexion was extremely light, Michael felt the sting of prejudice; coming as it did in the formative years of adolescence, the pain of it may have been particularly sharp. If his adult personality is any evidence, the animosity nurtured an aggressive persona, characterized by a need to prove himself and to strike first before he could be wounded by someone else. Any at-tempt to psychoanalyze him from this historical distance is, of course, impossible. Still, his school experiences set him on a course of his own.

At first, this took the form of simple rebellion, and more than once he ran away from the college, never getting very far. By the beginning of the 1854 academic year, he was "a source of great anxiety to us," Patrick reported; "his conduct hith-erto gives us no reason to hope for a change." Sternly, James sent the fifteen-year-old to the seminary at Douai, not, as he explained to Father Fenwick, "to make a priest of him, but to give him a chance to redeem his lost time and character. . . . His conduct has not corresponded to my hopes." Running away from the French school was more difficult, but it also opened up some exotic possibilities, and

Michael took advantage of them. In the summer of 1855, he fled to England, where he felt the pull of the sea, signing on as a cabin boy on a merchant ship bound for the Far East. Revising his own story a decade later, Michael would say that this had been arranged by his parents—they had been dead for five years by then—"in order to punish me for my misconduct," but in fact the idea had been his alone. If his account can be credited, for the next several years he wandered the world: India, China, Africa, the Caribbean and the Mediterranean, England, and America. Rising through the ranks to first mate, he had a talent for the work, and his life was "comparatively easy, having never suffered actual shipwreck."[42]

By time of the Civil War he was back in Boston with a "definite determination" to continue his seaborne life in the United States Revenue Cutter Service, predecessor of the modern-day Coast Guard. The service was a civilian agency, a part of the Treasury Department, which supervised coastal trade, pursued smugglers, enforced fishing and whaling regulations, and offered emergency assistance. Enlisting in September 1863, Michael Healy applied for an officer's commission a year later. He was twenty-five years old, he said, "have been to sea for nine years, and have been three times second officer and once first officer of a brig." He had not done as well as he hoped on the written examination, but captains under whom he had served praised his ability. He was also able to marshal some important endorsements. Bishop Fitzpatrick signed a letter written for him by James Healy, saying that he had "no hesitation in expressing my conviction that he is qualified." David Bacon, the bishop of Portland, Maine, was likewise importuned to send in a recommendation, and this was particularly useful since the Secretary of the Treasury, William Pitt Fessenden, was from Maine. The political connections of the candidate's brother were also set to the task. At James's request, Governor John Andrew urged swift action on the case. "I do not know [Michael] Healy myself," the Massachusetts chief executive wrote a well-placed Republican ally in Washington, "but I am well acquainted with his brother, Revd. James A. Healy, the Secretary of the Bishop of this Diocese; and if one can argue from the qualities of a clergyman to those of a sailor, and the two brothers are alike, I should say that you would have few brighter and more capable young officers in your Revenue Marine than Healy." All the lobbying paid off, and by January 1865 Michael's appointment to the rank of third lieutenant came though.[43]

By now, it comes as no surprise to note that none of those endorsing Michael Healy's promotion within the Revenue Service ever mentioned his racial background. Some of them knew it, but others almost certainly did not. Work on the sea had long offered unusual opportunities to black Americans: aboard ship, raw ability and level-headedness in a crisis usually mattered more than skin color. Moreover, during the war the navy had been more willing to enlist black men than the reluctant army.[44] But the color line was drawn at officers, and Michael Healy had little hope for promotion to the higher ranks if he was black. His family had already established that its racial designation was not with blacks at all, but rather with whites, and the young officer's decidedly light skin permitted him to conform to that practice. For the next forty years, his racial background remained largely unknown to those—fellow officers, crewmen, and others—he encountered on the high seas.

His embrace of whiteness was further secured by his marriage to Mary Jane Roach, the daughter of Irish immigrants to Boston who were parishioners at the cathedral. The wedding ceremony, presided over by Father James Healy of course, took place at the end of January 1865, just a week after the groom's promotion to lieutenant. It was a joyous occasion: even Hilary Tucker, who attended both the marriage and the celebratory dinner afterward, declared it "a most happy and agreeable match on both sides." Precisely when the two had met is unclear, but the Roach and Healy families had probably come to know one another under the shelter of the local church. Later evidence demonstrates that Mary Jane and Michael genuinely loved each other, but from his perspective there was another issue at stake. In the choice of a white wife, Michael Healy was making a clear statement not only about his own racial identity, but also about that of his future family. The very same decision was made six months later, when Martha Healy, who had been out of the convent for two years by then, married Jeremiah Cashman, an Irish immigrant store clerk in Boston.[45] Of the eight Healy siblings, only one other (Eugene) would ever marry, also to a white woman, though only Michael and Martha would have children of their own. By choosing spouses from the white community, they completed the work of severing their connection to the racial heritage of their mother. Thus, the turbulent years of the Civil War confirmed their passage into the future—a white future.

CHAPTER SIX

The Rector: Sherwood

Neither a white future nor a white present was ever possible for Alexander Sherwood Healy. Some of his siblings could pass unnoticed in the white world, but Sherwood could not. The "African blood" of which Bishop Fitzpatrick had spoken, the blood that "shewed" distinctly enough to keep Sherwood from appointment to the American College in Rome, was equally visible to those who met him in the United States. When he walked down the street, passersby were sure that they had just seen a black man. Thus, even more than his brothers and sisters, he had to find a way to insulate himself from the disadvantages white society was eager to impose. Like them, he found his way out through religion.

By the time of the Civil War, the identity of a Catholic cleric was fully his own, and his preparation for that role had been unusually thorough. Few American priests of his day had had so rigorous an education as he. Too often, candidates for holy orders had been quickly taught the theological basics and then trained to say mass before being sent off to begin their work in the cure of souls. Even worse, America had from the beginning attracted more than a few priestly adventurers from abroad who were apparently more interested in advancing their own worldly status than in the spiritual welfare of their flocks. On becoming bishop of Baltimore in 1789, for example, John Carroll had complained about the strange "medley of clerical characters" he found at his disposal: had he known that one priest could neither read nor write and showed no interest in learning to do so, Carroll told a friend, he would never have permitted the man to be ordained.[1] Improving the quality of these "characters" had been a goal of the American hierarchy ever since.

In contrast to such unimpressive clerical parvenus, Sherwood Healy stood out. His was not the rough-and-ready preparation of other American priests, but a serious education in the traditional centers of learning in Europe. From the first, he

A. Sherwood Healy. Photo courtesy Archives,
Archdiocese of Boston.

had thrilled at the chance to succeed there, demonstrating what James called his "very strong head for philosophy + theology." Sherwood reported himself "happy, yes, very happy" in all his studies, even if his "eagerness for reading" now and then caused concern about his weak eyes. As time went on, Sherwood felt a deepening commitment to the church and to his own role in it, solemnly accepting the burden of priests to "sanctify ourselves + [to] direct others."[2] In his notebooks, he punctiliously copied out rules for conducting religious ceremonies, and he assembled quotations from devotional writers that he might one day work into his sermons. Following his ordination at Paris in December of 1858 and the additional year of doctoral study in Rome, he was one of the best-schooled American priests of his generation.

The long tradition of the church impressed him deeply, and it gave him an institution greater and older than America itself of which he could be a part.

Catholicism was a "difficult" religion but a "sublime" one, he wrote, and both characteristics reassured him that he was part of something grand indeed. He reveled in its glory, developing a keen appreciation for the church's aesthetics. While few of his countrymen worried about such things, he became a connoisseur of church music and liturgy. "Music," he said a bit pretentiously, "is preferable to the other arts." In Rome during Holy Week 1859, he made the rounds of churches, rating them like a professional critic. The psalms performed on Holy Thursday at one small chapel were "very fine," he thought, even if the other music was "not so beautiful as at St. Peter's." On Good Friday, the melodies of Palestrina were "touchingly + beautifully sung, and the ceremonies excellently executed." The hymns on Easter were moving and, he thought, "much more pleasing" than any he had heard in Paris. His musical ear perhaps attuned him to languages as well, and he was now as comfortable in Latin, French, and Italian as he was in English.[3]

How far he had come in barely fifteen years. The fugitive from the laws of Georgia, laws that defined him forever as a slave, was now a young priest who spoke several languages and enjoyed refined musical tastes. The expatriate from a nation where it was still, in many places, illegal to teach him to read and write possessed a doctoral degree. The man at risk of arrest and enslavement in parts of America was now an expert in the fine points of theology. The man who, at home, might be penalized at any time on account of his physical appearance had found a way to render that appearance less of a disability. Throughout the nineteenth and twentieth centuries, some black Americans escaped to Europe, there to discover (as W. E. B. Du Bois had) their African cultural roots.[4] Sherwood Healy used his time on the continent for precisely the opposite purpose: to separate himself even further from his African American heritage and, instead, to complete his adoption of the new cultural identity of the Catholic church.

On his understandably reluctant return to the United States in the fall of 1860, Sherwood was certainly better prepared than he needed to be for his assignment as chaplain at Boston's House of the Angel Guardian. He knew more about arcane scholarly disciplines than he could possibly use, given that his immediate task was the basic religious instruction of "wayward" boys. In a few short months, he had gone from debating scholarly theses in his doctoral exams to urging the young residents of the orphanage to learn their catechism, to say their morning prayers, and to go to mass every Sunday. Soon, however, he was playing a wider role in Boston Catholicism, thanks in part to his brother's prominence. Sherwood's musical training, for example, meant that he was always a good candidate to sing the high mass on special occasions. If James had become an alter ego for Bishop Fitzpatrick, Sherwood was sometimes the alter ego for his brother. When James sailed for his European vacation in the summer and fall of 1863, Sherwood became the acting chancellor of the diocese, moving his few personal possessions into the rectory of the Cathedral of the Holy Cross.[5] Not yet thirty years old, he was rapidly climbing the ladder of success in the church.

Because his rise had been so rapid and perhaps because his African blood did indeed "shew," he faced skeptical glances from some of his fellow priests, and none were more wary than those of the family's sometime friend and sometime critic, Father Hilary Tucker. Notwithstanding his growing affection for the Healys, Tucker's first instinct was always to find fault, and he applied this habit to Sherwood no less than he had to James. Here was a new interloper who was not deferential enough for Tucker's liking. "I was told," he complained to his diary, "by Rev. J. A. Healy when he left that I was head of the house and was to direct all matters. . . . His brother, S. Healy, whether he thinks so or not, acts as if he cared for no authority whatever. He is a proud and undiscipl[in]ed priest." Sherwood had thrown himself into his bureaucratic duties, perhaps a little too vigorously, and when he claimed that the press of business made him unavailable to help out with Saturday confessions or Sunday masses, Tucker thought this "particularly ungracious." There was a distastefully inflated sense of superiority about the young man, making him "a little censorious of the clergy" in a way that was "too sharp to be pleasant." Most of all, "Mr. S. Healy must learn more respect for older and more experienced priests than himself," and Tucker doubtless had in mind a particular "older and more experienced" man deserving of respect.[6]

White Americans were of course accustomed to deploring the least sign of assertive or "uppity" behavior on the part of blacks, and for Tucker, Sherwood's appearance reinforced a readiness to carp. Even more offensive, however, were what he took to be aristocratic airs in the young man. "He lacks humility, has too much of an opinion of himself"—Tucker had once reproached James for the same failing, using almost precisely the same words—and he seemed to think "that he is ordained priest *sub tit[ulo] patrimonii.*" Use of the obscure Latin phrase said much about Tucker's true complaint. He was citing a procedure from medieval church law that made it possible for sons of the nobility to be ordained outside the usual channels on account of their family's independent wealth. The practice was unknown in America, but Tucker thought Sherwood was behaving as if it applied to him. The Healys' financial resources were considerable, of course, and the time in Paris and Rome may indeed have cultivated patrician self-possession in Sherwood. His acceptance of the idea that his priesthood placed him "above" other

Christians might well buttress a sense of noblesse oblige. "He will insist on doing just what he pleases," Tucker concluded, "and nothing even as an accommodation or favor for a brother priest."[7]

Still, Sherwood had talents that Tucker had to recognize, and as time went on he acknowledged them, just as he had done with James. In the pulpit, Sherwood could preach a "magnificent" sermon—"the best I have heard in the cathedral in any time," Tucker enthused once in the spring of 1864. Sherwood himself said that he always tried to preach for fifteen minutes or less, except on "great festivals," and when he followed that rule, Tucker found the results "splendid." If he could only learn to check an inordinate "desire for popularity with the people," Tucker said, an "accursed propensity" that had "a hold in the minds of the Healy family," he would go far, since he was surely "able, devout, and worthy." Tucker was sympathetic toward the younger man's perpetually uncertain health, even if he found Sherwood "somewhat imaginative" in his ailments. The crusty veteran even came to enjoy his colleague's company, more than once setting off with him on walks around the city. At first writing only of "Mr. S. Healy," Tucker warmed as time went on, and the young man soon appeared in the pages of his diary as the more familiar "Sherwood."[8] Their common work and growing affinity served to break down the barriers that American racial attitudes had otherwise placed in the way of friendship.

These were the tense years at the height of the Civil War, but Sherwood showed little interest in the conflict. He kept a scrapbook of random newspaper clippings, but these offer only indirect clues about his view of public events. He saved a few reports on the progress of the Union army and on the initial caution of the Lincoln government toward the emancipation of slaves. By an odd coincidence, in 1862 he clipped the review of a performance on the Boston stage by John Wilkes Booth, long before the actor gained notoriety for other reasons. Sherwood's attention was drawn to a chart from one newspaper showing the free black population of the southern states, and he thought a discussion of compensation to slave owners important enough to add to his collection; in neither case did he annotate the clipping with any thoughts of his own. Beneath the story of a patriotic flag-raising in Boston which had featured a "fine speech" by Edward Everett, the overshadowed orator at Gettysburg, Sherwood offered this demurrer: "In a similar spirit Catholics honor + raise everywhere the *cross* + the image of Mary to protest their feelings in spite of an indifferent + unbelieving world."[9] He was as patriotic as the next person, but love of country was always less important than love of church.

Only rarely did he comment on the issues of the day, and when he did, he was no more likely to identify with African Americans than the other members of his family. He clung to the traditional Catholic moral distinction between slavery itself and the slave trade. Abolition of the latter was the "one glory" of the nineteenth century, he wrote, but he doubted the sincerity of "those in modern times who pity the negro." The distancing phrase—"the negro"—James used in discussing Reconstruction came readily to Sherwood as well. Some abolitionists had cited Catholicism as "the authoress of negro slavery," but that was a calumny he was quick to rebut: interest in the well-being of slaves was "only a pretext," Sherwood thought, for their real campaign against the church. Long before contemporary agitators had stirred up the issue, Catholics had been "at work to console & civilize the negro."[10] Despite the evidence that others might see on his own face, Sherwood had concluded that "the negro" was a category of people that did not include him.

As the war proceeded, a more suitable assignment came for this talented priest, one that would temporarily take him away from Boston. He had been denied a position at the American seminary in Rome, but when a similar institution was established closer by, he was an obvious candidate to join its faculty. For several years, the bishops of New England and the Middle Atlantic states had sought to open a theological school in their region. "The time has come," one of them wrote a colleague, "when in many Catholic families there will be aspirations for the priesthood." Accordingly, at the end of 1862 the bishops bought the land and buildings of a failed Methodist college in Troy, New York, set on a high bluff above the Hudson River, getting the place for a song. Renamed Saint Joseph's Seminary, it would prepare the sons of Catholic immigrants for work in the church and, not coincidentally, contribute to their families' concurrent rise up the social and economic scale. When it opened in October 1864 it had seventy students, but the number rose to more than a hundred by the end of the year. As the core of its faculty, four Belgian priests were dispatched by the bishop of Ghent, who had taken an unaccountable interest in America.[11]

Early on, Sherwood Healy was identified as a likely addition to the faculty. The seminary needed to have at least some Americans at the place, if only because the Belgians were slow to pick up English. Sensitive to recurring nativist accusations that theirs was an inherently foreign church, the bishops wanted domestic clergy among the school's officers, but there were few with the necessary academic credentials. Sherwood was manifestly qualified, and he had the advantage of coming from not very far away. He visited Troy in the summer of 1864—he was "very pleased with it," Father Tucker reported, "and the prospects are bright"—and concurred in the decision to send him there. His principal responsibility was to teach moral theology, but the shortage of manpower meant that he would take on other duties as well, including those of business manager. Apparently, concern that the students would not respect him, the worry that had led Fitzpatrick to resist his appointment to the seminary in Rome five years before, was less troubling now. His "African blood" was every bit as evident as it had ever been, but now he was an experienced and mature priest, better able to withstand any gibes from students.

He left Boston for Troy in September 1864. New York's Archbishop Hughes had described the place as "picturesque and beautiful," but day-to-day circumstances were far less idyllic, especially as the pleasant autumn gave way to bleak winter. One of the Belgian priests recalled later that heat was a rare commodity in the buildings and that the windows were practically useless in keeping out the harsh upstate winds. The students suffered from an alarming rate of sickness, and Sherwood himself reported that "many are hopelessly gone with consumption or some other equally fatal malady." A daily routine possibly intended to toughen them up generally had the opposite effect. Rising at 5:30 every morning, students spent time in the chapel until almost 9 before being allowed to wash and have breakfast. Discipline was always strict. Silence was enforced in the evenings, and students could not smoke, visit one another's rooms, or even speak to the kitchen help. Their mental horizons were similarly limited. All lectures were delivered in Latin, with the likely result that understanding was spotty. The library was open only three hours a day, and seminarians were warned against accumulating books, "lest they be confused by a variety of opinions." Anyone caught smuggling in a newspaper was subject to expulsion. Separation from the world, physically and intellectually, was understood to be the best training for future priests.[12]

As in most seminaries of the era, moral theology was at the heart of the curriculum, largely because it prepared graduates to hear confessions after they were ordained. Ever since a church council in the thirteenth century had set the requirement that Catholics go to confession at least once a year, this sacrament had been one of the central priestly tasks. Future priests thus had to give detailed consideration to the morality of particular actions, the distinction between so-called venial and mortal sins, and the assignment of penances for those who transgressed. Textbooks emphasized rigor in such matters, but practicality was also prized. Getting penitents used to the idea of confessing regularly—by the nineteenth century, once a month was the norm for the pious—was key, and confessors thus had to be both strict and encouraging. The teaching of this critical subject at Troy fell largely to Sherwood Healy, who also served as prefect of discipline for the seminarians: if they were to enjoin high moral standards on their parish-ioners, they had to be well grounded in such behavior themselves. In both capac-ities, he proved himself "an able theologian," a colleague remembered later, and "an interesting lecturer." His musical talents were also put to good use, and he de-voted time to instructing students in the intricacies of Gregorian chant. His eye for the niceties of church ceremonies also made him the likeliest teacher of rubrics, another important subject in an age when adherence to the precise forms for saying mass was thought the mark of a good priest.[13]

At first, the seminary prospered, in spite of the harsh living conditions; in July 1866, Sherwood proclaimed it "a great + complete success." There were also many problems. The Belgian priests maintained a studied distance from the Americans on the faculty, and the place never lost its foreign aura. The students were not al-ways the best, and the sheer effort it took to drum some learning into them could be discouraging. In the middle of the first academic year, James Healy received a letter from his brother, describing "a despondent + rather dissatisfied tone among the professors." A dissatisfied tone is probably the natural one for professors, but Sherwood's discontents were general rather than particular. Apparently, he suf-fered no insults on account of his racial background. In fact, his considerable ad-ministrative abilities were useful and valued. Even so, he was always a bit of an outsider. Most of the Belgians had never seen black people before. They marveled at the African American stevedores they saw on their arrival in New York, one of their number remembered later, and were left "wondering at the blackness of the hands that served their supper" on the steamer trip up the river to Troy.[14] Before those perceptions could affect Sherwood, however, unexpected events in Boston brought him back to that city, where he achieved a prominence few would have predicted.

✍

Less than a year after the last shots of the Civil War sounded, John Fitzpatrick, pa-tron of the Healy family for more than two decades, died. Ever since his chance meeting with Michael Morris Healy, Bishop Fitzpatrick had been the protector of these unusual siblings, the man who made possible their passage into new lives. He oversaw their education, helped them sidestep the "useless questions" about their background, and willingly bent the laws of his church for them. He arranged for the care of the younger children, even placing Martha in the household of his own sister. He lent his considerable local prestige as James and Sherwood assumed in-creasingly responsible positions in the Boston Catholic community. Tall, straight, and fleshy, Fitzpatrick presented a deceptive picture of health. The least excitement disrupted his equilibrium, and any improvement in his condition was always temporary; hopes for lasting recovery seemed continually "poor indeed," as James Healy wrote another bishop in 1864. More than once his condition was grave enough that he received the last rites of the church, a procedure understood at the time to mean that death was imminent. A brain hemorrhage on Christmas Day 1865 initiated an irreversible decline, and on February 13 of the new year, he died.[15]

His death might have changed everything for the Healy family. With their protector gone, they might have been immediately relegated to the inferior position most white Americans thought the only one blacks deserved, but that was not their fate. Before his death, Fitzpatrick had arranged for the appointment of a successor, and this new bishop continued to support and to rely on the Healys. John J. Williams had been born in Boston in 1822, the only child of immigrant parents, and his route to the priesthood had gone, like that of the Healy brothers, through Montreal and Paris. He served as pastor of several large churches in the city, peopled increasingly by refugees from famine in Ireland. No less Irish than his parishioners, Williams often seemed more of a Yankee. He was silent and serious, always frowning on idle chatter at the dinner table, and his habits were temperate and regular. In a quiet way, he was also a methodical and far-seeing planner, astutely buying up desirable property in the suburbs on which churches would be built, some of them decades after his death. Never eager to call attention to himself, he served as Boston's bishop—elevated to the title of archbishop in 1875—for forty-one years, longer than any other man before or since.[16]

At the beginning of his tenure, Williams did some routine shuffling of personnel, and in the spring of 1866 he replaced James Healy as chancellor of the diocese with another priest. It was not a demotion. James had tired of administrative duties after eleven years at them, and he was more than willing to step aside. Williams immediately appointed him pastor of Saint James's church in the heart of Boston, a post that the new bishop himself had once held. This was the largest parish in the city, growing at an astonishing rate, and designation as its pastor was both an honor and a reward for previous service. It put Healy in a visible public position: it had been Williams's stepping stone to the episcopacy and might serve the same function for him. The two men had been friends and collaborators for a decade, and Williams would later say that "we were just like two brothers." At the same time, while James Healy would now take a diminished role in managing diocesan affairs, Sherwood Healy came to occupy a more important place, emerging as confidant and aide to Williams in a way that his brother had been for

Fitzpatrick.[17] Remaining for the time being at Troy, Sherwood commuted back to Boston regularly to assist Williams on a variety of projects.

The first of these was to accompany Williams to a general meeting of the American Catholic hierarchy in the fall of 1866. The Roman church had remained unified during the war between the states, even as many Protestant denominations (notably Baptists and Methodists) divided into northern and southern branches. Still, with restoration of the Union, the Catholic bishops saw the need for a reconciling national council. For two weeks in October 1866, forty-five prelates from across the country, each accompanied by a theological adviser, gathered in Baltimore to discuss matters of common interest. Church law made each bishop more or less supreme in his own territory, but coordination had its advantages. Accordingly, the bishops adopted some uniform procedural rules, and they banned Catholic membership in "secret societies" like the Masons and the feckless Fenians, thought to be hotbeds of sedition and anti-religious agitation. More practically, they addressed the social needs of their people, committing themselves to opening hospitals, orphanages, and other social welfare institutions, especially in the crowded and dangerous cities.[18]

The most divisive item on the agenda was the question of what the church should do on behalf of the recently freed slaves. This population of nearly four million seemed ripe for what was called "evangelization"—that is, efforts to convert them to Catholicism—but many of the participants regretted having to address the issue at all. The council's final document expressed a preference that "a more gradual system of emancipation could have been adopted," ostensibly preparing the slaves "to make a better use of their freedom." Some bishops, especially those from southern states, were more waspish. "Behold . . . the desire for promoting the salvation of the blacks," the bishop of Richmond, Virginia, said sarcastically, "as if they alone were derelict and neglected." More sympathetic observers in Rome had suggested the appointment of a single bishop whose responsibility would be to supervise all work among the freed slaves, regardless of diocesan boundaries, but this idea was overwhelmingly rejected. The meeting ended with some pious language about the "new and most extensive field of charity and devotedness [which] has been opened" by emancipation, but with no specific program in place; better to trust "the zeal and prudence of the local bishops to decide what must be done," the council said. Given the opportunity, the Catholic hierarchy had failed to take any significant steps for black Americans with the coming of freedom.[19]

Neither John Williams nor Sherwood Healy took part in these discussions or challenged the disappointing outcome. Williams maintained his characteristic silence throughout, and many other northern bishops did likewise. Even John Mc-Closkey, who had succeeded the pro-Union John Hughes as archbishop of New York, said flatly that "in no way was the conscience of the bishops of the North burdened" when it came to African Americans. A prelate from Louisiana said that the freed slaves were "no business of bishops and theologians who know nothing about the negro race," and northerners like Williams deferred to that pointed judgment.[20] Sherwood Healy, who might have been presumed to know something about "the negro race," was present throughout as an adviser to Williams, but it was impossible for him to have spoken up, even if he had wanted to. The meeting's procedures permitted only bishops to address the gathering, and in any case Sherwood had his own reasons for silence. His careful aloofness from "the negro" made him no more sympathetic to these objects of "charity and devotedness" than anyone else present. He certainly had no intention of becoming a champion for former slaves. To do so would only have called attention to the aspect of his life he had worked so long to keep at a distance.

Back home by the end of the month, he and Williams never had to devote much attention to the call for charity toward blacks. The problems of freed slaves seemed far away. The *Pilot* addressed the general question with an air of detachment. In the preceding years, the newspaper had been vigorous in its early support for the war, but it became decidedly less enthusiastic after 1863. So long as the conflict was an effort to preserve the Union, the *Pilot* was strongly in favor of it; as soon as it became a war to free the slaves, ardor waned. Now, with stunning understatement, the editors acknowledged "the disabilities under which colored men have heretofore labored," but there was only so much that could be done. "The barriers of prejudice" against African Americans "are not to be shaken down in a day," an editorial concluded, urging instead a long, slow endeavor "to free our minds of prejudices." In all, the problem remained a largely theoretical one for the leaders and people of Catholic Boston. Williams ordered the Baltimore council's statement read from the city's pulpits, but thereafter he and his clergy could safely turn their attention to other matters.[21]

Sherwood went back to his teaching duties at Troy, but Williams continued to draw on him repeatedly. In November 1868, for example, Healy did most of the legwork for a meeting of Boston's priests which codified local church rules on such matters as marriage between Catholics and Protestants. He had "read all the books" on the procedures of such synods, he assured Williams, and with his usual eye for ceremony, he even suggested how the public events of the meeting should be conducted. "If you decide to have a high mass to open," he counseled his superior, "I venture to recall to you that the clergy are, in general, wretched singers"; a paid professional choir would be a good investment, he thought.[22] A year later, Williams decided that he needed the services of this capable young man more regularly, and so Healy resigned his post at the seminary and returned to Boston. His assistance was wanted now in an even more important matter: an assembly in Rome of bishops from all over the world. Sherwood returned to Boston at the end of that summer and almost immediately sailed for Europe with Williams to attend the First Vatican Council of 1869–1870.

The council was a landmark in the history of Catholicism. The age-old church had entered the nineteenth century very much on the skids. Pope Pius VI had begun it ignominiously by dying as a prisoner of Napoleon—"Give him a decent burial," the emperor is supposed to have said; "he once had an important job"—and subsequent events had steadily reduced both the territory of the Papal States and the influence of the pontiff. By the 1850s the more forceful Pius IX had come to occupy the throne of Saint Peter, and he aggressively reasserted the authority of his office, even as his power as the ruler of central Italy continued to erode. In 1854 he single-handedly proclaimed the dogma of the Immaculate Conception (the belief that Mary, like Jesus, had been conceived without original sin), in part simply to demonstrate that he could pronounce a new article of faith when he wanted to. A decade later he issued a stern "syllabus of errors," condemning as heretical such modern ideas as democracy and religious freedom. Now, "Pio Nono" had decided to ask the world's bishops to declare formally that the pope was infallible when he spoke officially on matters of faith and morals.[23]

From around the world, seven hundred bishops and their attending theologians gathered in Rome for the opening of the council in December 1869. John Williams and Sherwood Healy had arrived in the Eternal City two weeks early, after a leisurely progress through London, Paris, Munich, and Florence. Other business was discussed first, but everyone knew that the "great question" of infallibility, as Williams called it, would be the climax of the debates. Opinion was sharply divided. Some prelates, led by England's Henry Manning, were eager to give the pope what he wanted, but others held back. Without challenging papal primacy, this faction, led by Felix Dupanloup of France, thought that church doctrine was definitively articulated only when the pope acted in consultation with all the bishops; proclamation of a personal infallibility, this group thought, was at the very least "inopportune." Bishops from the United States were similarly divided: Martin Spalding of Baltimore sided with the "infallibilists," while Peter Kenrick of St.

Louis led the American "inopportunists." With his usual reserve, John Williams never expressed a public opinion on the subject, but he has usually been numbered with those who wanted to avoid defining the controversial dogma.[24]

If we can judge from Sherwood Healy's views, Williams was indeed hesitant about infallibility. Healy was discreet about the affairs of the council—strict secrecy governed its deliberations—but his own sentiments were clear. He supported the papacy wholeheartedly, and he denounced the leaders of the emerging Italian nation in uncompromising terms: Garibaldi was "a pirate," Cavour a great man "in much the same way as the Devil is great," and King Victor Emmanuel "a puppet" of the other two. Sherwood drew the line, however, at exclusive papal authority in religious matters. "The preponderance of talent is decidedly on the side of the non-definitionists," he wrote a friend in America; "the preponderance of numbers," however, was "all on the side of definition." Moreover, the pope himself was "avowedly" for it, Sherwood knew, and that was likely to carry the day. "I go with the church," he concluded, "if a definition be made." There was reluctance in his tone, and he even had to reassure his correspondent that, though some thought him "not so willing," he was resigned to accept infallibility if it came. After weeks of debate, the final vote was taken. While a violent July thunderstorm raged outside the walls of Saint Peter's Basilica, the council approved the doctrine of papal infallibility. There were only two dissenting votes (one of them, curiously, cast by the obscure bishop of Little Rock, Arkansas), though about eighty bishops had purposely absented themselves so as not to have to vote against it. Acquiescing finally to the "preponderance of numbers," Williams was among those who voted yes.[25]

The very next day, Williams left Rome for the long trip back to Boston. He was eager to get home, all the more so because in the preceding weeks Sherwood Healy had suffered a physical collapse. What James called his brother's "long martyrdom" of ill health had taken a new and alarming turn on Saint Patrick's Day 1870. Confined to his bed with what was diagnosed as typhus fever, Sherwood was unconscious for hours at a stretch. His kidneys were entirely "deranged," he wrote afterward, and the treatments were almost as hard to endure: "I thought the pain would kill me," he said of one procedure. At times, the patient could not even recite the prayers he knew by heart, and in the last week of March he was anointed with the final sacraments while those around him prepared for the end. "My death was expected every moment," he said later; "at one time they thought I was dead." By the beginning of April, however, the worst was over, and his condition slowly improved. As the spring came on, he went for carriage rides and short walks around Rome, and at the beginning of July he began the trip home, leaving Williams behind for the dramatic closing days of the council. The two joined up in Paris, and by the middle of August they were back in America.[26] His recovery would be only temporary, but in the five years left to him, Sherwood Healy moved into an even more visible position in the little world of Boston Catholicism.

✐

After slowing during the Civil War, immigration to the United States resumed with full force once peace had been restored, and few places were affected more than Boston. In 1860, the city had a population of just over 175,000, a number that would triple by century's end. As before, the Irish led the way, but they were soon joined by newcomers from Italy, Poland, Lithuania, Germany, and elsewhere. By 1895 fully one in three residents of Massachusetts had been born outside the United States. To John Williams and Sherwood Healy, the most important fact about these immigrants was that many were Catholics, demanding the services of religion. Older and smaller churches had to be replaced, and entirely new parishes had to be opened. Schools, hospitals, and orphanages had to go up practically overnight if they were to stay even with the always expanding need. When Williams assumed the leadership of Boston Catholicism in 1866, it consisted of 112 parish churches scattered the length of the state; when he died in 1907, there would be more than twice as many (244) in his jurisdiction, which had by then shrunk geographically to include only the city itself and the near suburbs. The ranks of the clergy would increase fourfold during Williams's tenure, and the number of nuns would increase by a factor of seven.[27] With barely time to think about the changes all around them, the leaders of Catholic Boston had to carry out a vast expansion of their church's institutional presence.

Sherwood Healy was at the center of these efforts, and in the fall of 1870, just after he and Williams returned from Rome, he was appointed to the position of rector of the Cathedral of the Holy Cross. Parishioners were still gathering in the temporary quarters that James Healy had arranged, but plans for a permanent home were well under way. Before his death, Bishop Fitzpatrick had purchased the land for a huge cathedral building on Washington Street in the city's South End. Immigrants were crowding into that district, and at least for a time it was managing to hold on to the emerging Catholic middle class as well. Sherwood's designation as rector, the honorific title given to pastors of the cathedral church, ensured that he would become an influential leader of that community. It also meant that his most important task would be to oversee the construction of an imposing new edifice to accommodate his congregation.

The South End was a curious and perhaps unfortunate location for what would become the largest Catholic church building in New England. Well into the nineteenth century, much of the area had been under water at high tide, and it was only gradually filled in as the city reclaimed the land. Initially a more desirable area than the crooked streets of the old colonial city, it gradually lost its cachet to the even newer and tonier Back Bay. The South End offered proximity to the center of town, but it could be a dicey neighborhood: a row of fashionable brick homes became, a few streets over, a section of rooming houses, suspicious characters, and fear of crime. Decades later, the novelist John P. Marquand captured its problem succinctly. His fictional creation, the father of a dour Brahmin named George Apley, knew instinctively that it was time to move out of the South End to a better address when he saw a neighbor venture out into the street in his shirtsleeves. A district in which shocking things of that kind might happen was obviously no place for a gentleman.[28] By siting the cathedral there, Fitzpatrick condemned his church to a largely peripheral position in the public spaces of Boston. However that may be, it now fell to Sherwood Healy to bring the construction project to a successful conclusion.

Ground was broken in June of 1866, and by the time of Sherwood's appointment as rector four years later, a great deal of progress had been made. The architect, Patrick C. Keely of Brooklyn, had become the foremost builder of Catholic churches in the country, specializing in massive Gothic piles that held throngs of worshipers and made impressive artistic, social, and even political statements. In places like Boston, where Catholics were easily caricatured as uniformly poor and hopelessly foreign, Keely's buildings deliberately stood out: the Roman church was here to stay, they seemed to proclaim. The new Holy Cross was of truly monumental proportions, "grand enough to meet our wants + to satisfy our aspirations," Sherwood said. With a floor plan of nearly 50,000 square feet, it would be almost as big as Notre Dame in Paris, and the rose window over its front door would be flanked by two square towers, each topped by a soaring spire. When complete, Healy wrote, the spires would be, "with the exception of the gilded dome of the State House, the most prominent object of view . . . for miles around." In the end, the spires were never built. Because of the sogginess of the land, the two base towers were not plumb: had the spires been added, they would have simply toppled over. Nevertheless, the cathedral fulfilled the "aspirations" of which Sherwood had spoken: he liked to point out that the taller of the towers was, at three hundred feet, a full eighty feet higher than the Bunker Hill Monument.[29]

Sherwood Healy supervised the entire project, which cost about a million and a half dollars by the time it was done. Everyday oversight of the workmen fell largely to Keely, but the new rector had to ensure a regular flow of cash so that the work, once begun, would not have to be interrupted. Pledges came in from other parishes to get the effort started, and a handful of successful Catholic business-men had been persuaded to make individual benefactions. Sherwood dipped into his own resources and pledged $1,000 for a stained glass window, depicting the Nativity, that would catch the morning sunlight over the main altar. Mass was said for the first time in an unfinished side chapel shortly after Williams's return from the Vatican Council, and a final push for money began soon afterward. To ac-complish this, Sherwood organized a massive fund-raising fair at the end of 1871. Despite some initial confusion—at the same time as one planning session, Williams had scheduled another meeting to raise money for a Catholic cemetery, "without telling me about it," the slightly annoyed Healy noted—plans for the bazaar soon fell into place.[30]

The fair opened in the half-completed shell of the cathedral at the end of Oc-tober 1871, and it ran nightly until the beginning of December. More than 6,000 people showed up the first evening, and attendance remained encouragingly high thereafter. Participants could buy religious bric-a-brac, take a chance on a piano and other items in a raffle, listen to concerts by parish choirs, and sample the of-ferings of the food and floral tables. As rector, Sherwood moved easily among the crowd, encouraging the volunteers and enjoying the fun along with everyone else, each of whom had paid 25 cents to get in. Advertising in the local newspapers had been extensive, and the event became an object of public notice and goodwill reaching beyond the city's Catholics. The *Boston Herald,* the newspaper of the Yankee Protestant middle class, ran a report on the fair's progress every other day, happily noting that "each night witnesses a large attendance of both Catholics and Protestants from all parts of the city." When it was all over, the fair had taken in a very respectable $65,000, with another $25,000 in pledges. "The Catholics of Boston have reason to congratulate themselves," Healy wrote, "in every sense." He organized an equally successful fair in the fall of 1874, and in December of the next year the new cathedral was opened for use and formally dedicated.[31]

Sherwood Healy's role in accomplishing all this put him more than ever on public display, and he never hid from that visibility. The man whose skin color had disqualified him from the narrow prominence of a Roman seminary a dozen years before now stepped into the brighter limelight of leadership in Boston's Catholic community without any ill effects. His position as rector of the cathedral exempted him from racial stereotyping and animosity. His position as a priest blocked identification of him in exclusively racial terms. Many of his contemporaries might interpret the evidence that was, literally, on his face to mean that he was forever a black man and, as such, disqualified from taking on certain roles in white society. Now, that evidence had come not to matter.

That he and Archbishop Williams saw his priestly status as more significant than his racial status is not unexpected. Both men shared the contemporary Catholic view that saw the priesthood in essentially objective and impersonal terms. In this theological understanding, ordination conveyed a transforming power, essentially extinguishing all other characteristics and replacing them with a new and more exalted reality. The priest did not cease to be human—still less was he made perfect—but he did become in effect a different kind of human, one in whom personal traits faded into insignificance. At ordination, the "old man" was decisively abandoned, and the "new man" of which Patrick Healy had spoken emerged. The act of becoming a priest was comparable to that of a seal making an impression in an unformed lump of hot wax: what mattered now was the seal, not the wax.[32] Because he bore that powerful impression, Sherwood Healy could confidently believe that he had ceased to be what others took him to be: a black man. He had been remade into another sort of creature—a priest—to which racial categories did not really apply.

More remarkable than this view of himself, however, was the extent to which his parishioners too had come to see him through a nonracial lens. He might well want to define his identity apart from race, but why did they so readily accept that definition and make it their own? Surely, as a theoretical matter, these immigrant and working-class Catholics were unlikely to challenge prevailing racial orthodoxies. As recently as 1862, their newspaper, the *Pilot,* was speaking casually of the "natural inferiority" of African Americans and proclaiming that "the negro race is happier in slavery than in freedom," as if those were propositions no sensible person could dispute. Now, a decade later, newspapers all over the country were filled with lurid reports of black state legislators in southern Reconstruction governments who made fools of themselves by assuming responsibilities of which they were, by common consent, incapable—responsibilities that properly belonged only to whites. In his own realm, Sherwood Healy was doing much the same thing, but that aroused neither comment nor censure. He was a black man who was, somehow, not a black man. When the *Boston Herald* praised "Rev. Father Healey" for the success of the cathedral fair, it might misspell his name, but it found nothing unusual to report about him. He was, simply, "Rev. Father Healey," a priest like any other.[33]

The people of Holy Cross parish lacked a sophisticated understanding of the theology of the priesthood, but on a deep emotional level they felt its effects. Unable exactly to explain why, they knew that Sherwood Healy was different by virtue of his ordination, and they therefore deferred to him as they almost certainly would not have done otherwise. His actions conditioned their reactions. When he organized committees of his white parishioners and told them what to do, they did it enthusiastically. Few of them would have accepted such supervision from someone else who had Sherwood's skin. When he circulated in the crowds of the cathedral fair, prompting all to generosity, their largesse flowed. Few of them would have parted with their hard-earned money so freely if another man with Sherwood's complexion had urged them. We cannot know the inner thoughts of the ordinary Catholics who met or saw him, of course, for none of them recorded their reactions; but their silence is itself eloquent testimony that they were overlooking his "African blood," even though it showed "distinctly."[34]

The occasions on which his people saw him also helped blind them to his racial characteristics and to make him like the other, all-white, priests they knew. The "uniform" of his calling was useful in this. Parish priests in America at the time seldom wore distinctive clothing; the shapeless, floor-length cassock and the Roman collar were still uncommon. Rather, Catholic clerics most often wore the same dark suits and neckties common to Protestant ministers and proper gentlemen of all sorts. When he appeared on the altar, however, Sherwood emerged in elaborate liturgical garments that set him apart. Flowing robes in colors that changed with the seasons of the church year underlined his priestly status, reinforcing his position as one distinct from and even "above" ordinary Christians. On such occasions, he spoke a foreign language, Latin, which few of them understood but which they associated with the ultimate concerns of salvation. His administrative responsibilities meant that he left most of the routine work of the parish to his four assistant priests: he performed only a small fraction (about one in every twenty) of the baptisms and marriages of his parishioners.[35] Still, he was the one who said mass and preached on the great occasions, the one who intoned the high mass more often than the "wretched singers" among the rest of the clergy. These roles augmented his standing and helped render the color of his skin more or less irrelevant.

Even if his own parishioners overlooked his heritage, why the wider, non-Catholic community went along with his transcendence of racial categories demands explanation. Everything we know of American attitudes about race in this period leaves us unprepared for the apparent ease with which Sherwood's complexion came not to matter. He was excused from the rules whites generally enforced on African Americans. A mere ten days after the *Boston Herald* praised "Rev. Father Healey" for the success of the cathedral fair, it reported with dismay the case of the Reverend Alexander Ellis, pastor of "the Joy Street Colored Church" on Beacon Hill. Ellis caused consternation when he had the temerity to sit at the captain's table while traveling on a ferry out of Boston, a dangerous pretension to the "social equality" of blacks which alarmed many whites. As the crew made ready to remove him to the boat's Jim Crow section, the Baptist minister backed off, recognizing that he had overstepped the boundaries of segregated public accommodations.[36] Sherwood Healy and this man, both leaders of important churches in the city, were alike in many ways, and yet the unusual position of one was tolerated in a way that the other's was not. Sherwood had never been denied service on a train or steamship, nor had he ever been ejected from a "whites-only" cabin. The church apparently mattered as much as the clergyman. By serving a white congregation, Healy could become white himself—even as Ellis, who served a black congregation, remained black in the public eye.

That Sherwood could, in effect, get away with defining himself into the white community is even more unexpected because these years saw a steady deterioration of race relations in Boston. The prewar capital of abolition had felt great optimism with emancipation, but in the next decades a harsher reality emerged. The city's black population nearly doubled in the ten years after the war, but the increase was accompanied by a reinvigorated pattern of residential segregation. African Americans were effectively shut out of certain neighborhoods and confined instead to the aging housing stock in such areas as the so-called North Slope of Beacon Hill. By 1900, one historian has maintained, Chicago was the only major northern city more strictly segregated than Boston. The constitutional extension of full legal and political rights was accompanied by the reappearance of much actual discrimination. As early as 1866, courts in Massachusetts were upholding the right of white business owners to refuse service to blacks, and soon the exclusion of black Bostonians from certain trades was well under way.[37]

Father Sherwood Healy was never a part of Boston's black community. The priest who had distanced himself from "the negro" found little time for African Americans as he went about his work in the cathedral parish. His people were white Catholic immigrants and their offspring, not the city's black residents, who were predominantly affiliated with Protestant congregations like the "Joy Street Colored Church." When he did take note of the city's black residents, Sherwood viewed them mainly in religious terms. They were simply members of non-Catholic religions whose greatest need, as far as he was concerned, was the "evangelization" to which the Baltimore Council had paid lip service. In the spring of 1872, Herbert Vaughan, an English priest who was organizing conversion efforts among former slaves in the United States, came through Boston on a speaking tour. Healy took little interest in this work, though he put Vaughan up at the cathedral rectory for a few days while the Englishman spoke in local churches, collecting a meager $200. His visit attracted slight notice from the newspapers, none of which took the occasion to comment on Vaughan's host.[38] That Healy was a sponsor of this effort attracted no more public comment than if his name had been O'Brien or Murphy, or if he had come to Boston as a famine immigrant from Ireland rather than a fugitive slave from Georgia.

So fully had Sherwood become a part of the white Catholic community that, as the new cathedral neared completion, he was ready for other duties, equally challenging and visible. Accordingly, when his brother James moved on from his post as pastor of the nearby Saint James's parish in April of 1875, Sherwood was appointed to take his place. This new assignment put him at a church in the heart of downtown Boston, one that had itself just completed an impressive new building for its congregation, which numbered an astounding 17,000 people. Overwhelmingly Irish, these parishioners would soon be joined by significant numbers of Italians and others, even as their neighborhood was also filling up with non-Catholic Greeks, Chinese, and one of Boston's first identifiable communities of Jews.[39] The area in and around Saint James's had become the principal ethnic cockpit of the city, and a man of Sherwood Healy's experience was a good choice for solidifying the Catholic presence there. Everything in his career so far promised success, and greater public recognition for him seemed inevitable.

Those developments were not to come, for in the summer of 1875 his long-standing medical troubles returned. In August he suffered several episodes of bleeding in his lungs, and he recovered a little less fully each time. Soon he was confined to the Carney Hospital, a facility operated by a community of nuns for Catholic immigrants who could not afford the services of Boston's more renowned hospitals. His brother James visited him there and found him "very low indeed," and Archbishop Williams reported "little hopes for his recovery." At ten o'clock on the morning of Thursday, October 21, he died quietly, three months shy of his fortieth birthday. "He was exceedingly well prepared" for death, Williams commented with characteristic emotional restraint: "the diocese loses an excellent priest, and St. James a devoted and well beloved pastor." A funeral mass was said that Saturday and was, a newspaper reported, "among the most impressive that have ever taken place in Boston," with 150 priests and several bishops from

New England attending. Williams "said a few words from the rail of the sanctuary, as the friends of the deceased could not control their feelings sufficiently to preach a funeral sermon." The body was taken to the chapel of a cemetery in South Boston, the oldest Catholic church building in the city, and entombed in the floor in front of the altar.[40]

Even in death Sherwood Healy's extraordinary personal circumstances went unremarked. "His brief life has been identified with the Catholic Church," the *Boston Globe* observed accurately enough, but its description of his career—birth near Macon, education at Holy Cross, studies in Rome, and the rest—offered no hint of the most obvious thing about him. He "was greatly respected by all who knew him," the paper went on, "and was a man of much ability." The grief of his family was "too great to touch," another journal quoted Williams as saying, and no other delicate subjects were touched either. The papers listed his surviving siblings in a formulaic way, but that was all.[41] The reality that had governed his entire life and career—the "African blood" that "shewed"—remained unacknowledged. In the process, that reality itself was obscured: readers who did not know him would conclude simply that an Irish Catholic priest (of which there were many) had died.

Sherwood Healy's form of passing was harder than that of his brothers and sisters, but it was no less complete. Crossing the color line was difficult, if not impossible, and knowing white eyes were supposed to be able to detect and thwart any attempt to do so. Moreover, racial passing was thought always to be surreptitious, a form of racial deception, with one's allegedly "true" identity carefully concealed. Others in the Healy family adopted that secretive strategy, masking the African blood that was theirs as much as his, but Sherwood's approach was breathtaking in its boldness. He did not conceal his African heritage, for that was impossible. Instead, he chose to hide in plain sight. By acting as if the disabilities imposed on African Americans did not apply to him, he forced others to respond in kind, and his life thus upsets our historical generalizations about race in the United States. If the unbending American rules for racial classification—"one drop" was all it took—could be applied to anyone, they should have applied to Sherwood Healy, but there were other options. In a lifelong assertion of his right to define himself, he succeeded in living by a set of rules in which race had become immaterial. Amid all the remarkable stories of his family, his may be the most remarkable of all.

CHAPTER SEVEN

The Bishop: James

During his younger brother's ascendancy, James Healy temporarily yielded center stage in Boston, but he remained an important and recognizable figure nonetheless. That he should play an influential role in the white Catholic community was normal by now, but the ease with which he did so would always be remarkable. His "African blood" did not "shew" quite so distinctly as that of Sherwood, but it showed plainly enough: those who knew either of them knew something about the background of both. Like Sherwood, however, James used his status as a priest to secure his passage across the color line. Just thirty-six years old when he stepped down as chancellor of the diocese in 1866, James rightly expected to have most of his career still ahead of him. In the ensuing years, he would rise even higher in the church that had given him that opportunity. In so doing, he moved ever farther away from the "nothing" he had once been.

In leaving his administrative post to become a pastor, he was exchanging one set of insistent responsibilities for another. Saint James's parish was more populous than the cathedral and second only to it in prominence. It was located in the South Cove section of Boston, one of the oldest continuously inhabited neighborhoods in the city. A plain brick church had been put up in the 1850s, and thereafter the place flourished. Urban parish life was always unpredictable for the clergy, whose responsibilities were just beginning with Saturday confessions and Sunday masses. Priests might be called upon at any time to exercise their ministry. Baptizing infants, for example, was a constant, often daily, occurrence. The theology of the era, according to which the unbaptized never attained heaven, and the high rate of infant mortality meant that newborns were rushed to church immediately (often the same day) for the sacrament. One year of Healy's pastorate at Saint James's saw an average of two baptisms every day. Presiding at weddings was not quite so demanding, especially since marriage was discouraged (though technically not forbidden) during certain seasons of the year, such as Advent and Lent. Even so, Healy and his curates officiated at about two hundred marriages each year. Beyond that, they could be rousted out of bed in the middle of the night to visit the dying, to offer counsel to anyone who rang the rectory's doorbell, and to administer the temperance pledge to those who were at least temporarily reformed. Saint James's also had 1,300 children enrolled in catechism classes, and in 1869 alone nearly 900 youngsters were prepared for their first communion and confirmation.[1] To be the pastor of such a parish was an honor for Healy, but the job was no sinecure.

Leaving much of the day-to-day work to his three curates, Healy applied his administrative experience to the tasks at hand. Managing Saint James's was like running a business. Income and expenses averaged about $60,000 per year, and watching the budget was a more or less constant job: several times Healy had to advance short-term loans to the parish out of his own resources. He inherited a debt of more than $90,000, and he worked to pay that off while funding routine maintenance and seeing to such improvements as the installation of an expensive new organ in 1867. Five years later, the city's burgeoning railroad system demanded the plot of land on which the church stood for expansion of its yards, and so the old building was sold and torn down, while planning for a new one began. Just as his brother Sherwood was overseeing construction of the grand new cathedral a few blocks away, James was superintending a similar project for the new Saint James's Church. Even as the parish contributed to the cause of the cathedral, it was conducting its own fund-raising efforts, realizing more than $10,000 from a fair that kicked off the effort. The new edifice went up rapidly and was dedicated in the summer of 1875.[2]

By then, James Healy was approaching the capstone of his life in the Catholic church: his appointment as bishop of Portland, Maine. For any capable and successful priest, the next logical step up the career ladder was into the ranks of the episcopacy. The American Catholic clergy was then a small enough group that a priest might know virtually all of his fellows in the immediate vicinity, and, as in any profession, their after-hours conversation often turned to speculation about who was destined for promotion. In any talk of advancement, Healy's name was always prominent. That he had, in effect, already acted as a bishop during Fitzpatrick's Civil War years abroad only improved his prospects. He was widely traveled, had friends in Rome and elsewhere in Europe, and had gained a reputation as a preacher on significant occasions. Not even his ambiguous racial status counted against him, for his long identification with the white community had resolved that ambiguity. By simply refusing to acknowledge his case as anomalous, he overcame his racial problem.

In contrast to those of a later period, the nineteenth-century procedures for filling vacancies in the Catholic hierarchy were elaborately participatory. The Vatican administrative apparatus sought advice from the priests and bishops (though not the lay people) of the country in which appointments were to be made, and these consultations were especially important in the United States. Officials in Rome often had laughably inaccurate notions of American geography and conditions; even under the best of circumstances, local input was essential. The priests in each region were periodically asked to recommend those who had the desirable traits for advancement, and local bishops were charged with maintaining a list of three names, known in Latin as a *terna*, from which Rome might choose when necessary. Soundness of doctrine was presumed, but equally valued were managerial ability and robust physical health. When vacancies occurred through death or the transfer of a bishop from one place to another, these *ternae* were consulted and selections made.

Such an occasion came in New England at the end of 1874, when the bishops of Hartford, Connecticut, and Portland, Maine, died within a month of each other. The two sees had historic roots in the Boston church, and, like the metropolitan diocese, they faced pressure from exploding immigrant populations. James Healy's name had not originally been on either list, but he quickly emerged as the leading candidate for designation to Portland. The locals there wanted a popular pastor named John Barry, a native of Maine then stationed in New Hampshire, but investigation of his background raised some troubling concerns. There were rumors that his father had had several illegitimate children by a servant girl and that one of these might be the potential bishop himself. Scandal-mongering of this sort was not uncommon: those who opposed a nominee for any reason (including personal jealousy) often resorted to the kind of whispering that could evoke caution. In this case, Rome worried that the sins of the father might be visited on the son.[3] The safer course, therefore, was to ask for a new roster of nominees, and by January 1875 Healy's name had come to the fore, most likely promoted by his longtime friend, Boston's Archbishop John Williams.

Given the possibility of scandal over Father Barry's parentage, Healy's selection was at least ironic, since his illegitimacy was, strictly speaking, a fact. Potentially more problematic was his racial status. Although Rome had by then begun to name bishops of non-European origin in Africa and other parts of the world, such an appointment in 1870s America was too bold a step. James Healy's designation

James A. Healy, 1875. Photo courtesy Archives,
Archdiocese of Boston.

as bishop was possible only because his family background was left entirely un-mentioned throughout the process. The conspiracy of silence about the Healy brothers, begun by Fitzpatrick during their seminary days, continued in full ef-fect. The secret remained secret. The data forwarded to Rome reported simply that James had been born in Georgia—about 1827, it said vaguely, making him older than he really was—and that he had become a priest in Boston. The lack of precision may have been deliberate: the Roman bureaucrats reading the report could be counted on to have only hazy notions of just exactly where Boston and Georgia were. Instead, Williams emphasized the traits he knew Rome was look-ing for. Here was a man with substantial experience, a prudent disposition, a sturdy constitution, and a solid reputation. The case was convincing, and on Feb-ruary 16, 1875, word reached America that James Healy would be the next bishop of Portland.[4]

The Catholics of Maine knew little of their new leader. One Portland newspa-per reported that he had been born in Boston—it seemed a safe assumption about a priest with an Irish name—and it rehearsed his previous assignments without elaboration. A few priests, however, knew enough of his story to be troubled by it. There were unconfirmed reports that a pastor in the town of North Whitefield, just outside Augusta, had denounced the new bishop; another story had a priest covertly warning his parishioners of the "indelicate blood" in Healy's veins. More detailed were objections registered behind the scenes by Father Eu-gene Vetromile, who was in charge of the church at Eastport, located on the far end of the Maine coast, just across a narrow strait from Canada's Campobello Is-land. Vetromile had studied in Rome, and he wrote a friend there to express his dismay over the news. Projecting his own objections onto his parishioners, he wrote that "the Catholics [in Maine] are mortified and humiliated to have a mu-latto for Bishop. The Protestants will not respect him," Vetromile continued and, referring to the two tribes of Catholic Indians in the state, "the savages look down on the blacks." Healy might be able to get away with a public position in Boston: in the cosmopolitan city such a man was less exotic, and, in any event, "the au-thority of the bishop" (i.e., Williams) helped guard Healy from slights. "But it is not that way in the woods of Maine," Vetromile concluded, where prejudice against Catholics was strong. It was too late for the decision to be undone, he knew, but he put his objections on the record anyway. Rome never responded.[5]

Vetromile's letter is noteworthy because it is one of the few surviving docu-ments that ever explicitly raised the central historical problem of Healy's life. Here was one of the rare people willing to name racial names. What we know of American attitudes at the time leads us to expect that the question of James Healy's race would be the first subject on everyone's lips—but it was not. Nowhere else does one find the word that the rules of the day prescribed for him: mulatto. Nowhere else does someone argue that, notwithstanding the decisions he himself had made, he had to be defined by race alone. Nowhere else does someone challenge his ability to use his status as a priest to cross the line from black to white. Even more telling was that those who put Healy forward continued to support his effort to ignore what might otherwise have been an ironclad disqualification. By then, it was thirty years since James Healy and his siblings had exchanged their nothingness for Catholicism, seizing a white identity with the help of religion. In becoming a bishop, he proved the completeness both of that transformation and of the acquiescence that others gave it. Healy traveled to Portland in early April 1875, and he was formally installed at the beginning of June in the Cathedral of the Immaculate Conception, which stood on a hill overlooking the city. Inclined as ever toward criticism, he complained afterward about the length of the ceremony and the "badly served" dinner that followed it.[6]

✒

Catholicism had come to northern New England with French explorers in the seventeenth century, but a stable presence for the Roman church was more recent. Not until 1855 had there been enough communicants to warrant the establishment of a diocese, which encompassed all of Maine and New Hampshire. Administratively, it was a small operation, even if it did cover a wide area of remote, mountainous interior and picturesque seashore. There were only 58 parish churches—the Boston diocese had twice as many in a much smaller territory—serving a Catholic population estimated at 80,000. Ethnically, the Irish predominated, but they were nearly equaled by French Canadians who had come over the border from Quebec and New Brunswick looking for work in the bustling Yankee mills. There were also small settlements of Penobscot and Passamaquoddy Indians, Vetromile's "savages," who had been converted by the earliest missionaries two centuries before. Relations with non-Catholics were sometimes tense. As recently as 1854, a Jesuit priest passing through Ellsworth, Maine, had been tarred, feathered, and paraded through town on a rail as a warning to anyone who tried to advance the cause of popery in the state. This "Ellsworth outrage" brought widespread condemnation, but it signaled that Catholics still might not be entirely welcome.[7]

Healy's managerial experience stood him in good stead in addressing these challenges, and he now had the added authority that came with his new position. The deference Catholics paid to their bishops meant that skeptics like Vetromile would have to keep their objections to themselves. Healy noted that he received at least one "anonymous + insulting letter" after his arrival in Maine, but public discussion of his background was always off-limits. As he had done for years, he identified only with his white Catholic congregation, walking away from his African heritage; he refused to play the part of America's first black bishop, despite later efforts to remake him as such. One account, circulated fifty years after his death, told of his hearing the confession of a Portland schoolboy, who asked forgiveness for having used the word "nigger" on the playground. The bishop pulled aside the curtain of the confessional, the story maintained, revealing his own face and asking the astonished child, "Well, son, is there anything wrong with being a nigger?"[8] It is a moving tale, but it probably never happened. The man who had casually used the insulting epithet and who had distanced himself from "the Negro" was unlikely to dramatize the need for racial tolerance by calling attention to himself. Better that he stay in the character he had long since established: someone who had put his "indelicate blood" far behind him and had moved out into the world on other terms.

With his usual energy, Healy set to the work of being bishop. In the first months, he made an extended progress through his territory, going from town to town to visit the scattered parishes of the diocese. Along the way, he got to observe firsthand the ethnic divisions that plagued many communities. Bonded by their common religion, Irish and French Canadians often found themselves at odds in local churches. Their worshiping styles and devotional emphases differed, but more divisive were questions of language and the education of children. The mass and the sacraments were conducted in Latin, of course, a language uniformly foreign to all of them, but the Canadians' desire for priests who could preach and hear confessions in French often led to open hostility. Irish priests and congregants simply could not understand why their fellow parishioners so stoutly refused to speak English. Also at issue was whether Catholic schools for Canadian children would be conducted in French, thereby preserving the language in subsequent generations. The rallying cry in many places was "la foi, la langue, la culture"—faith, language, culture—and the preservation of each seemed to depend on the preservation of all.[9]

Establishing distinct churches for Irish and French Canadian populations was the sensible solution, but there was always room for misunderstanding. Dividing congregations along ethnic lines, especially in small towns, was never as easy as it looked. Each group thought of the local parish as theirs, and for the most part they were content to let the others simply fend for themselves. Worse, the clergy, rather than promoting harmony, often kept ethnic hostilities alive. After less than a year in office, for instance, Healy had to remove a priest named Walsh from a church in Portsmouth, New Hampshire: the man's "abusive temper and tongue," directed particularly at his French-speaking parishioners, had made him what the bishop considered "a standing scandal and stumbling-block to his people."[10] The bishop himself was perfectly fluent in French, and he was sympathetic to those for whom it was a mother tongue. Still, his Irish surname often led many to conclude that his real sympathies lay on that side of the ethnic fence. These tensions would endure well beyond his quarter-century in Maine, and they are not entirely settled even today.

A far more troublesome priest absorbed much of Healy's attention during his first years as bishop. Father Jean François Ponsardin had come from France to serve the parish of Canadians at Biddeford, Maine, a tough mill town south of Portland. Dazzled by the comparative wealth of his working-class parishioners, Ponsardin let his imagination overpower his common sense, and soon he had debts on the church far beyond the ability of his people to pay, all the while investing, for his personal benefit, funds they had deposited with him for safekeeping. He was even loaning that money back to the parish, thereby double-dipping by charging a high rate of interest. Acting on complaints from the people, Healy removed Ponsardin from his position in 1877, but the volatile priest refused to go quietly, challenging the bishop's right to fire him and appealing his case to Rome. There it dragged on for four years, with charges and countercharges flying back and forth in lengthy documents submitted to the canon lawyers. In the spring of 1878, Healy traveled to Rome to defend himself against Ponsardin's more outlandish claims, an effort that took a good deal out of him. "I had a very bad night, sleepless," he told his diary on one occasion, "being occupied with thoughts of Biddeford." He even offered to resign as bishop, an idea papal officials rejected. By 1881 the technicalities of church law ran against Healy, who was forced to settle a pension on the surly Ponsardin in exchange for the man's agreement to leave Maine for the far west, where he disappeared altogether.[11]

This was not the last controversy in which Healy would be involved during his tenure, but throughout it the absence of racial insult is striking. Amid all the heated arguments, no one was tempted to bring up the bishop's "indelicate blood." Where now was Father Vetromile, smugly saying "I told you so" to his correspondents in Rome? Where were the sharp tongues of apocryphal schoolboys or their parents, shaking their heads knowingly over a bishop who met the "one-drop" test for blackness? They and others had almost certainly used the famous American epithet for such people before, so why did no one say it now? Ponsardin could be brusque—during one interview, Healy observed, the problematic priest had not even removed his hat, an act that seemed deliberately discourteous—but there was always a line that was never crossed. The dispute between the two remained a simple one between a superior and an underling, not a contest between a white man and a black man. Their contention with one another was not about race; it was merely, as Healy himself described it, a matter of "difficulties of administration."[12]

Even in tense circumstances like these, respect for Healy's spiritual office promoted a personal respect he would have been hard-pressed to win otherwise. In challenging him, his opponents passed up the chance to play the powerful trump card of race. Healy exercised his authority calmly, and by expecting acquiescence from those under him, he generally got it. His official duties, carefully recorded in his diaries, were remarkable for being unremarkable. The Ponsardin affair had been difficult, but it was the exception to an otherwise placid rule. On other occasions, when Healy removed a priest for administrative laxity or questionable finances, the offender went quietly. When the bishop demanded an accounting of local parish funds, he got it. When he regulated one priest's salary or urged another to open a parochial school, his orders were obeyed without objection.[13] Vetromile had claimed that the Catholics of Maine were "mortified and humiliated" by their "mulatto" bishop, but that was not true: they accepted him as they would any other bishop. Apparently, if race did not matter to him, it did not matter to them.

To characterize Healy's tenure as one marked only by tension would be wrong. More mundane duties filled his days, and more genuine successes were evident. The Catholic population grew sufficiently so that in 1884 a new diocese was established at Manchester, New Hampshire, giving that state its own bishop and leaving Healy in charge of Maine alone. He worked at improving the public standing of his church, and he knew how to take advantage of opportunities to demonstrate that Catholics were good citizens. In 1881, for example, his public eulogy of the assassinated President James Garfield, delivered before a large gathering at the Portland City Hall, was commended as one of the finest speeches ever delivered in the city. He joined with members of Portland's Yankee elite to win permission for priests to visit prisons and other public institutions, though the task was not without its difficulties. The superintendent of the state's reform school, eager to catch miscreants, insisted on listening in while the Catholic chaplain heard the boys' confessions, and Healy had to insist that this practice was contrary to both church and civil law. He established close ties with prominent Catholics in Maine, including James Madigan, a successful lawyer from the northern town of Houlton, and Winifred Kavanagh, the philanthropic sister of the state's first Catholic governor. He recruited religious orders to oversee new educational and charitable efforts. When he arrived in Portland, he found a single group of nuns, a number that had grown tenfold by the time of his death.[14] Running the diocese was not glamorous, but it was a job Healy worked at diligently.

Schools were a particular concern. Catholic bishops throughout the United States devoted much of their energy in the 1880s and 1890s to establishing a wide network at the elementary and secondary levels. A meeting of the national hierarchy in 1884 laid down the principle that there should be a desk in a Catholic school for every Catholic child, but that goal proved elusive. Some even questioned it as an ideal. In Boston, for instance, Healy's old friend John Williams was distinctly unenthusiastic about parochial schools, especially since Catholics were coming to dominate the public school system, in numbers of both students and teachers. With the state-run schools effectively transformed into institutions influenced by the church, even though they taught no religious doctrine, Williams saw little reason to incur the expense of a parallel school system. In Maine, Bishop Healy took a more forceful approach. "To be indifferent to the religious education of children," he told one parish as early as 1876, "is to expose them and their parents to the gravest of all dangers." He urged another pastor to "leave a school as your best legacy and surest passport to heaven." Parents "who have the purity of their children at heart cannot hesitate about where best to place them," he wrote. Parochial schools were especially important for girls, saving them from the scandalous habits too often seen among "girls upon the public highways—the bold look, the loud voice, the shocking laughter that attracts the attention of the dissolute man." Healy was even willing to consider denying communion to parents who refused to send their children to Catholic schools. His persistence paid off: the number of parochial schools in Maine grew from six at the beginning of his tenure to twenty by the end of it.[15]

To staff these schools, Healy had to rely on communities of religious women. Throughout the country, vowed sisters were the heart of the labor force that operated Catholic educational and charitable agencies. In some places, nuns outnumbered priests by factors of four or five to one: thus, although these women lacked official positions of leadership in the church, they exercised enormous

day-to-day influence over American Catholic culture. Each order of nuns specialized in a particular kind of work, some teaching school, others staffing hospitals,
still others running homes for orphans or the elderly. The Sisters of Mercy were the
largest and most important group in Maine during Healy's time there. Organized
in Pennsylvania thirty years before, the Mercy sisters had convents in half a dozen
Maine towns by the 1870s, and they taught in several parochial schools in Portland,
including those of the cathedral itself. Their superior was Mother Frances Warde,
an Irish immigrant who had the skills of a corporate executive and the personality
to match. She was nearly as strong-willed as Healy himself: the two were so much
alike that some conflict between them was probably unavoidable.[16]

One source of friction derived from the peculiarities of local church geography.
Though scattered throughout Maine, the Mercy sisters were directed from a convent in New Hampshire, and Healy thought this arrangement gave them too much
independence from his own authority. Warde understandably valued her freedom
of action, and she moved her personnel around as she, not the bishop, thought
best, leaving Healy to complain of insufficient consultation. That a woman was exercising such authority probably increased his irritation: some of her actions were
"ridiculous," he grumbled, or simply "childish." He wanted more control over the
sisters' work and, though hedged in by church laws that protected their autonomy,
he was sometimes able to maneuver around them. In 1883, for example, knowing
(as Warde did not) that the partition of the diocese was coming, he blocked the
nuns' plan to open a new convent and school in Dover, New Hampshire. When the
split came, individual sisters would be affiliated with the diocese where they were
living at the time, and he wanted to keep as many of them as possible in Maine, subject to his jurisdiction. Still, he and the sisters found ways of getting along. He
stepped in to defend communities when they were victimized by local pastors,
scolding one priest who was both the confessor and the landlord for a convent, demanding that he sever his business connection in favor of his spiritual one.[17]

With the laity, Healy exhibited the same mixture of authority and warmth.
Most ordinary Catholics did not see much of their bishop, encountering him once
or twice in their lives, if that. More immediate personalities, like their local pastor
or the sisters who ran the parish school, embodied the church. The only Catholics
who saw the bishop regularly were those who lived in the cathedral parish in Portland. There, Healy took his turn at mass on Sundays and weekdays, and he talked
with the children playing in the schoolyard. A later story told of his democratic
encouragement that reluctant parishioners take a shortcut through the rectory
grounds when coming to church; another remembered his love for the lilac trees

he had planted on the property. He was fondly called a "children's bishop," taking school groups on sleigh rides and picnics as a reward for academic success. Like most pastors, he could be stern when he had to be: he reportedly whipped one delinquent lad who hid in the priest's section of a confessional box and heard several unsuspecting parishioners recite their sins. He also kept an eye on public decorum, warning the sisters of the cathedral elementary school not to let their pupils, girls especially, run around too boisterously during recess.[18]

The small tribes of native Americans in Maine were a special object of his pastoral care. Though not subject to the same attempts to "civilize" American Indians on the western frontier, these tribes maintained an uneasy separate existence. Healy worried about them, attentive because they had been Catholics for generations. He spoke at length about their needs during a meeting in Rome with Pope Leo XIII in 1886: the pope seemed interested, and when Healy presented him a letter opener in a sheath decorated with native beadwork, Leo giddily "brandished it about like a sword." Back home, Healy encouraged the state to open schools in Old Town and Pleasant Point, towns made up almost entirely of Indians, and in 1884 he had written to Maine's governor urging that more land be set aside for tribal farming and grazing. He supported the appointment of special constables who would be responsible for "keeping *rum* out," a source of any number of problems. Most important of all, he urged respect for "the Rights of the Indians," testifying to a committee of the state legislature that the natives were not "wards of the state" but "a nation whose rights are guaranteed by treaty. . . . Is it too much for me to ask," he went on, "that this consideration should make you listen more attentively to their requests and their claims?"[19]

Concern for native peoples was starting to attract some interest from the American Catholic hierarchy as a whole. Just as the bishops had collectively endorsed the idea of working with freed slaves, so they discussed coordinating efforts on behalf of Indians at a meeting in Baltimore in 1884. Two decades of missed opportunities in the black community offered a poor basis on which to build, however, and the persistence of familiar stereotypes was a barrier to genuine progress. "Colored people do not stand very high in the scale of morality," one supposedly sympathetic bishop asserted, and it would require great effort to turn them into "honest men, chaste women, obedient, law-abiding citizens." The same applied to Indians. "Religion and civilization go hand in hand," another prelate said, never doubting what "civilization" meant. "Discard religion and you prepare the condition of the barbarian or the savage." To address these problems, the bishops mandated that a special collection be taken in all Catholic churches in the country once a year to support what came to be called the "Negro and Indian missions." They also appointed a committee, consisting of three of their number, to oversee this work and to distribute funds from the collection. Since James Healy had native Americans in his jurisdiction, he was appointed to the committee.[20]

The board was supposed to coordinate work for both native Americans and African Americans, and Healy's membership might thus have been a tacit acknowledgment of his own background—but it was not. He was on this committee not for what he knew about black Catholics, but rather for what he knew about Indian Catholics. Just as his brother Sherwood had evinced little interest in African Americans at the earlier meeting of the hierarchy, so now James exhibited a similar diffidence. He did have experience with the concerns of native Americans, however, and those were the qualifications he brought. He took a modest interest in the work. He corresponded with Maine's most powerful politician, Thomas Brackett Reed, speaker of the United States House of Representatives, on schools for Indians in western states, and he expressed an "earnest hope" that the annual collection among Catholics would "meet with deserving success." Beyond that, his commitment was marginal. He did not even take up the collection in Portland's parishes every year, and he never applied for a share of the funds to support missions for the Penobscots and Passamaquoddies of Maine: "we can get along as heretofore," he said. He never spoke at all about African Americans, and it is clear that in thinking about the "Negro and Indian missions" he always put more emphasis on the latter. He resigned from the oversight committee in 1892, telling Baltimore's Cardinal James Gibbons that "a western prelate will be more active + useful."[21] The suggestion reveals much. A bishop from the west, where most of the Indians lived, was appropriate for this program. The idea of appointing a bishop from the deep south, where most African Americans still lived, never even occurred to him.

꧁

Healy's lack of interest in the Negro and Indian missions was in keeping with his own racial attitudes, which were those of the white community. He took his opinions not from what might be called his "fellow blacks" but rather from his "fellow whites." He wished the church's missionary efforts well, but he was never optimistic about what they could ultimately accomplish. The majority of Indians "will always be children," he explained to a correspondent, and he worried that not many had "distinguished themselves by honesty, honor or morality."[22] The words could have been spoken as easily by the colleague who had found so few "honest men" and "chaste women" among African Americans. Healy's own life had not disposed him toward any dissatisfaction with the racial caricatures of white America. Instead, he had been confirmed in the belief that white, European culture—which he took to be his own—was always superior to that of other peoples.

The question of race was thrown into especially sharp relief during Healy's later years, particularly around the time of the Spanish-American War of 1898. As a new American empire emerged from that "splendid little war," political leaders spoke of the responsibility to extend the benefits of white civilization to "lesser" peoples, like Filipinos and Latin Americans. James Healy seconded the aspiration, but he was not persuaded that much improvement was possible. It was necessary "to take the races of man as they are," he told a friend, "and do our best for them according to prudence and knowledge of their gifts. Our country is entering upon the experiment of making republics and republicans of races that have no adaptability," and he thought it unlikely that the experiment would succeed, either at home or abroad. "We may promise ourselves a century of civil war before the result is attained, if ever."[23] Here was a biological understanding of race, undiluted. The "races of man," Healy thought, were "as they are," fixed by nature, and their fundamental characteristics were unchangeable. If some races, whether Indians or African Americans, were "children," they always would be. Their betters had to "do our best" for them, Healy wrote, deliberately including himself in the white American "our." No personal experience of his own life outside the traditional American racial categories encouraged Healy to challenge them. No personal experience suggested to him that one might not have to take races "as they are"—or were thought to be. Defining himself apart from the iron laws of race never led him to conclude that others might be able to do the same thing.

That Healy sustained these views throughout his adult life explains his coolness toward attempts to organize African American Catholics in the 1880s and 1890s. In those years, there were several national conventions of the white Catholic laity, and black Catholics, though far fewer in number, decided to attempt a similar program. The prime movers were Daniel Rudd, an indefatigable editor from Cincinnati who in 1884 had begun publishing a newspaper called the *American Catholic Tribune*, and his friend Robert Ruffin, a roving reporter for the paper. Former slaves and lifelong Catholics, the two enthusiastically encouraged African Americans to join their church, in spite of lukewarm support from the nation's bishops. "The Holy Roman Catholic Church offers to the oppressed Negro a material as well as spiritual refuge," Rudd editorialized, "superior to all the inducements of other organizations combined. . . . The Catholic Church alone can break the color line. Our people should help her do it."[24] To advance the cause, Rudd issued a call for a "Congress of Colored Catholics," to assemble in the nation's capital on New Year's Day 1889.

In support of their plan, Rudd and Ruffin sought endorsements from selected members of the hierarchy, particularly those they hoped might be sympathetic. One of these was James Healy. That they wrote to him at all is telling, an indication that his racial background was widely known, even if it was never discussed openly. The tiny number of black Catholics in the Portland diocese—less than three hundred by Healy's own estimate—would have otherwise ranked him low among potential backers, but the organizers hoped to interest him anyway. Healy was not entirely unfamiliar with them. He had endorsed Rudd's *Tribune*, saying that it was "devoted to the religious and temporal interests of the colored people." As always, his reference to blacks was in the third person. The paper even ran a description of the Catholic churches in Maine, a report that barely mentioned Healy by name and certainly gave no indication that he might have a personal connection to African Americans.[25] Amid a deafening silence, anyone reading the *Tribune*'s account of Bishop Healy would not conclude from those pages that he shared any common racial ground with most of its readers.

His response to the idea of a "colored congress" was predictably cool. He was "much obliged" for the invitation to attend, he told the organizers, and "I wish you all success for the convention." Then he made an acceptable, if not particularly original, excuse: "my uncertain health hinders me from accepting any invitation to distant places," he said.[26] His real reason for staying away was a continuing desire not to be identified with the racial group in question. He offered the same excuse each year between 1890 and 1893, when annual black Catholic congresses were held, each one drawing smaller numbers than the one before. By then, interest in the whole project was waning nationwide, and Healy joined the chorus of those counseling abandonment of the idea. "I confess that I have some apprehension," he told one of the organizers at the end, "about conventions which are held on such strictly racial lines." Better, he thought, to set aside such distinctions: "I trust your convention and its results will make us all realize the words of St. Paul that we are of that church where there is neither Gentile nor Jew; circumcision or uncircumcision; barbarian or Scythian, slave or free."[27]

The sentiment was appropriately noble, but it was perhaps too easy for a man who had escaped disadvantage to urge those who had not been so fortunate to pretend that racial distinctions did not matter. Most of the delegates to the black Catholic congresses had to ride to the convention cities (Washington, Cincinnati, Philadelphia, and Chicago) in Jim Crow railroad cars, and once there they had to stay in segregated hotels. These were indignities James Healy had never experienced. The *American Catholic Tribune* had said hopefully that the conventions proved that "something above politics" was the best hope for advancing "the interests of the race," but it also had to bow to reality. Besides its reports of religious news, the newspaper also ran large display ads for pistols, promising "Every Man His Own Protection." James Healy, who had never faced the terrors of the night-riding lynch mob, had felt neither the anxiety over personal safety nor the need for that kind of protection.[28] He was removed from all that because his identification was, as it had always been, religious and not racial, white and not black.

At the same time, he could assure an inquiring scholar that "there is no distinction or discrimination as to colored people in churches, schools, etc. in the Diocese of Portland." He saw no reason to put any special priority on that segment of his flock. He refused the offer of a young African American from Maryland, just embarking on seminary studies, who wanted to come to Maine after ordination to work there as a priest. The young man's request, like the endorsements sought by Rudd and Ruffin, indicates that many black Catholics knew enough of James Healy's story to look on him as "one of their own." Seminarians were normally ordained for the place where they had been born, and this man would probably not have looked to Maine unless he thought the bishop might be particularly disposed to accept him. Healy, however, would have none of it. "The number of colored people" in the Portland diocese "is so small . . . and so widely scattered that it would be idle" for the applicant to come, he wrote back. "I should advise you . . . to apply to some Southern or South Western bishop."[29] Healy never considered the possibility that a black priest might serve a white congregation, in spite of his own and his brother's experience among white parishioners in Boston. He presumed that this black seminarian would have to work in a black parish; since there were none in Maine, that was not the place for him.

Healy's success at defining himself onto the white side of the American racial dividing line was tested most directly in the 1880s with the emergence of a Catholic priest who did identify with the African American community. Augustus Tolton had been born into slavery in rural Missouri in the 1850s, and he won his freedom as a child when his mother escaped with him across the Mississippi River at the start of the Civil War. Encouraged by local priests, Tolton was eventually enrolled in a seminary in Rome, where he was ordained in 1886. He had originally hoped to take up work as a missionary in Africa, but instead he returned to the United States and became the pastor of a parish in Quincy, Illinois. Encountering hostility, more from fellow priests than from his white parishioners, he moved to a church in Chicago and frequently undertook speaking tours around the country to raise money for the support of his African American congregation. In the summer of 1892 he visited New England.[30]

Newspaper coverage of Tolton's public activities in Boston stands in sharp contrast to that accorded James and Sherwood Healy, and it demonstrates their success at becoming white. Race was the one topic never mentioned in speaking of the Healys, but it was precisely what made Tolton newsworthy. Boston's dailies ignored his appearance in the city, but the *Pilot*, the paper for the city's Irish Catholics, offered an account of a public lecture by Tolton, "the first American negro raised to the priesthood." Daniel Rudd's *American Catholic Tribune* ran a fuller report, including a vivid description of Tolton in the pulpit of the Cathedral of the Holy Cross. That magnificent edifice, completed a few years before by Sherwood Healy, was graced by "an offspring of the children of Africa," the *Tribune* said, as if that had never happened before. Even more remarkable was the respect accorded Tolton. It was amazing, the *Tribune* reported, to walk along the street with Father Tolton: why, even "white gentlemen raise their hats to him as readily and as reverently as they do to other priests." That a white man might raise his hat in respect to a black man was increasingly unthinkable in an America sinking ever deeper into legal and customary segregation. Tolton earned that respect, however, not because of who he was, but rather because of what he was: as a priest, he could at least partially overcome the liability of being a black man. Then and later, Tolton was consistently identified as "the only Colored priest in the country."[31]

It was true: Tolton was the "only colored priest" in America. Neither James Healy nor his brothers had ever aspired to that title. They had worked long and hard to avoid designation as "colored," and their contemporaries, white and black, accepted that decision. Like Tolton, James Healy had had the improbable experience of meeting white men who raised their hats to him, as they almost certainly would not have done were he not a priest. Unlike Tolton, however, he had abandoned any connection to blackness, and the descriptions of Tolton confirmed that decision. To say, as the *Pilot* did, that Tolton was "the first American negro" ordained to the Catholic priesthood was to say that James Healy, who had been ordained thirty years before him, was not a "negro." To say, as the *Catholic Tribune* had in 1889, that "there is but one (Colored) Catholic priest in this country, Rev. Augustus Tolton" was to say that there were no others.[32] To say that Tolton was a black man was to say that James Healy was not.

✑❧

The anomalies of Healy's racial position might have encouraged him to maintain a deliberately low public profile—was there not always a possibility that someone might expose his "indelicate blood"?—but throughout his career the opposite was the case. His position as a bishop gave him a confidence that he never hesitated to use. He was unwilling to take the lead in the American hierarchy's efforts on behalf of the "Negro and Indian missions," but on other issues he was not so demure. In particular, he emerged as a national figure in the disputes of the 1880s between some leaders of the Catholic church and the growing ranks of organized labor.

As American workers began to join forces in defense of their interests, some priests and bishops looked on union organizing with suspicion. Modern labor unions were a new phenomenon, and Catholic leaders had no clear way of thinking about them. There had been no such things in the experience of the church before, and the apparent analogs were disturbing. The most successful, the Knights of Labor, had been founded in Philadelphia in 1869, and, like many early unions, it adopted elaborate and quasi-religious ceremonials. Were these substitutes for true religion, some wondered, or new incarnations of familiar opponents of the church? Many saw in them a latter-day version of the Masons, considered an all-purpose exemplar of anti-Catholicism, while others thought unions were fronts for socialism. The archbishop of Cincinnati denounced them in 1872 as agents of "Internationalism"—that is, the Socialist International, so threatening to peace and good order in Europe. This was an especially potent fear in Catholic minds after the radical Paris Commune of the year before, which had briefly seized the French capital and "martyred" its archbishop. Insofar as socialism was grounded in materialist philosophy, unions were also likely to be "anti-supernatural," another bishop said, inherently at odds with the church and its mission. Outbreaks of labor violence did not help matters, leading some churchmen to equate unions with civil disorder and ultimately with revolution.[33]

Perhaps worst of all from the hierarchy's perspective was the secrecy enveloping union activities. With the odds against them so steep, most unions guarded their plans closely, lest owners infiltrate their ranks with spies and ringers. Strictly speaking, even the very existence of a union was supposed to be kept secret from those outside it, and most used coded symbols and signs, both to build solidarity and to keep specific job actions from leaking to enemies. The Knights of Labor in particular employed an intricate system of ciphered messages and hand signals, and members were sworn to guard these with their very lives. This only aroused the suspicion of Catholic leaders further: what did organizers mean that these secrets could be divulged to no one? Could Catholic unionists not even talk about them to their priests in confession? That possibility challenged the very authority of the church, replacing its requirements with those of the union, and that was obviously unacceptable. The bishops had seen "secret societies" before—early versions of the later-innocuous Ancient Order of Hibernians had been denounced as such—and they lumped unions into the same category.[34] Better that Catholics steer clear of labor organizations altogether, trusting the church and its demands for economic justice, than sign on to a movement that raised so many cautions.

Some bishops sought accommodation between their church and organized labor, but James Healy held the line in opposition. Maine had enough paper mills, textile factories, and other light industries so that many in his flock wanted to unionize, but he disapproved. That the leader of a working-class church should seem to come down on the side of the bosses was incongruous, but for him it was entirely in character. Financially secure, he had long since come to look on himself as part of the propertied class in America. More specifically, he was one of those troubled by the problem of union secrecy. He had already condemned the Hibernians, the Odd Fellows, and some temperance organizations on this ground, and he was even suspicious of the Grand Army of the Republic, an association of Civil War veterans. As debate continued, he remained unpersuaded by reassurances that union members could indeed discuss their activities fully with their confessors. Such declarations were a "subterfuge," he thought, and this deceit only made "more plain the character" of groups like the Knights of Labor. Taking as his precedent a statement by several Canadian bishops who had denounced the Knights in that country, he was blunt with anyone who sought a sympathetic hearing for the union. "The Knights of Labor are condemned," he told an inquiring Catholic from the town of Lewiston in 1885. "Have nothing to do with them."[35]

Union officials knew they had to overcome this kind of opposition if they were to make any headway among Catholic workers, and the head of Knights of Labor set himself to that task. Terence Powderly, the son of Irish immigrants born in the coal country of Pennsylvania, became president of the Knights in 1879, assuming the grand (and, to bishops' ears, very Masonic) title of "General Master Workman." A Catholic, Powderly seemed the ideal person to solve the problem, and he met with churchmen around the country to explain the union's work and to allay their fears. The task was not easy. "Some of the best men I ever knew were Catholic priests," he wrote later in his memoirs, after abandoning Catholicism because of its continued resistance, but "some of the most vindictive, revengeful, arrogant, and intolerant men I ever met were [also] Catholic priests and bishops." Among the latter group, he almost certainly included James Healy, with whom he had a very unpleasant exchange in the spring of 1885.[36]

Powderly was in Maine to lecture and organize, and sympathetic Knights all along his route told him that they were stymied by their bishop's opposition. Deciding to face the problem head-on, the labor leader asked Healy for a personal interview. "I will be pleased to explain everything in connection with the workings of the Knights of Labor to you," he said obligingly, and he even ticked off some of his arguments in advance. The organization had "no affiliation with any communistic or socialistic order," he said, and he was even sure that he could explain the secrecy problem to the bishop's satisfaction.[37] Sadly, his hopes for accommodation were quickly dashed. Healy described their meeting as calm and amicable. "After hearing his account of the [Knights]," the bishop wrote, "I showed him the [Canadian] writ of condemnation." Then, he urged Powderly to modify the union's practices "so as not to be in conflict with the laws of the church. This Mr. Powderly promised to do, [though] I have never heard that he did so." The labor leader's account of the meeting was quite different. He was peremptorily summoned to the bishop's residence, he remembered later, and then made to wait for nearly two hours. Once face to face, Healy began by cross-examining him. "Are you a Catholic?" Healy demanded summarily. When Powderly said that he was, Healy told him that as such he had no right to speak in "my state without my permission." Powderly could not believe what he was hearing, and after Healy had said "my state" several times, the Master Workman exploded. "I became indignant," he recalled, "and told him that there were a few people in the state of Maine who did not belong to him, that human slavery had been abolished, and that it was a piece of presumption on his part to assume that Maine was all his."[38] With that, the interview abruptly ended.

The language of this exchange was highly charged, and Powderly later had second thoughts about it. "Perhaps I should not have said that," he noted from the cooler distance of years, "but I feel that the provocation was sufficient, . . . and I have no apology to offer." Even so, any reference to slavery in the presence of James Healy came dangerously close to impertinence. It is not clear, however, that Powderly entirely knew what he was saying. So fully had the bishop suppressed all reference to his background that Powderly may not have been aware of it. Instead, his reference to slavery was apparently intended as a sarcastic deflation of someone with too grand an opinion of himself. What bothered the union leader was the peremptory nature of Healy's claim that Maine and its people somehow belonged to him, as if he were some feudal baron or warlord. "I do not acknowledge your right," he told Healy, "or the right of any other man, no matter what his religion or position in society may be, to question me for doing that which I have a right to do under the laws of my country."[39] Far from alluding to Healy's "indelicate blood," Powderly was simply turning on this prelate the same scorn he had used so often in facing down self-important captains of industry who challenged his right to organize "their" workers. Even in confrontation, Healy managed to elude the question of race.

With nothing resolved, the Knights of Labor continued to organize, though Healy's opposition limited membership in Maine. He repeated his denunciations of the union, once in July 1884 and again in February 1885, and he has been described by one historian as "easily the foremost episcopal opponent" of the group in the United States. Soon, however, more moderate views prevailed. Cardinal James Gibbons of Baltimore, the leading Catholic bishop in the country, was openly sympathetic to unions, and he sought to win recognition for the rights of labor. Aware that official disfavor had contributed to defections from the church by the working class in Europe, Gibbons wanted to avoid a similar disaster in America. Lobbying behind the scenes, he succeeded in 1891 at influencing the text of a papal letter, called Rerum Novarum (Of New Things), in which Leo XIII endorsed the universal right of workers to form unions and to secure a living wage. James Healy remained unsympathetic to the very end. He described himself as one of the few bishops in America who actually "*desired*"—he underlined the word in a letter to a Roman official—the condemnation of the Knights and other unions, but he dutifully accepted the Vatican's resolution of the issue once it came.[40]

His stance on the labor question positioned Healy squarely in the conservative wing of the Catholic hierarchy. Throughout his years in Portland, unanimity among America's bishops gave way to ongoing conflict, and two self-conscious factions formed. One of them, called "Americanists," was led by Gibbons and John Ireland, the hyperkinetic archbishop of Saint Paul, Minnesota, who sought reconciliation between their church and the larger American culture. They embraced such notions as religious freedom and the separation of church and state, and they even thought these offered a model for other countries to emulate. They welcomed the idea of a distinctly American expression of Catholicism in which separate Catholic institutions, like parochial schools, were unnecessary. The opposing group, led by New York's Archbishop Michael Corrigan, came to be known as "ultramontanes" because, like their conservative counterparts in Europe, they looked "over the mountains" to Rome as the source of all authority. Intensely loyal to the pope and the Vatican bureaucracy, they saw America as a "Protestant country," always potentially hostile to Catholicism. The tension between the two groups played itself out in the last decades of the nineteenth century, with the conservatives eventually gaining the upper hand as the new century opened.[41]

Healy's sympathies were wholeheartedly with the ultramontanes. In 1893, he told a Roman friend that the bishops of the United States were no longer "a solid phalanx," but were divided by a differing "appreciation of the sprit of the American people." Gibbons and Ireland were too optimistic about the prospect for rapprochement between church and state, he thought; their naive hopes had "no foundation." On the question of Catholic schools in particular, he found the Americanists' position simply indefensible, "a total misapprehension . . . of our position versus the Protestant sentiment and the public school educators," eager to "steal" Catholic children from their faith. Abandoning the goal of separate parochial schools would do "incalculable evil," Healy said. He reported that he himself lost nearly a fifth of the students in his cathedral's school because of this Americanist "confusion," and that a pastor who had just built a new school said that he would not have bothered if such ideas persisted.[42]

Healy was also wary of the new enthusiasm for the recently deceased Isaac Hecker. As a young man in the 1840s, Hecker had moved in the Transcendentalist circles of Emerson and Thoreau, even spending time at the utopian community of Brook Farm outside Boston. Later, he converted to Catholicism, became a priest, and founded the Paulist Fathers. Hecker was convinced of the compatibility between Catholicism and American culture, and he emphasized the ability of individual believers to know and do what was right in religion, apart from hierarchical direction. After his death in 1888, Hecker became a controversial figure—praised by liberal Americanists as an ideal to be emulated, condemned by conservative ultramontanes for being more American than Catholic. Healy, who had known Hecker from his student days, took the conservative side, as he explained to a biographer of the Paulist founder. Hecker's "spirit, his love of liberty if you please, led him more than once into words and ways that made his devoted friends tremble." Hecker had been sincere, Healy had no doubt, but "his views will not escape without blame." The bishop was thus pleased when Leo XIII condemned such opinions in 1899, concluding that the rejection of liberalism in church affairs was "very necessary."[43]

ℒ❧

Healy's conservatism on issues was rooted in a deeply conservative personality. Privately, he was fastidious and even a bit fussy: his complaint about the "badly served" dinner that followed his installation in Portland was entirely in character. A few years later, while traveling through Europe, he was repelled by the general uncleanliness of the continent. Everywhere, "houses + churches looked as if the bugs + fleas, having once entered, would remain undisturbed from generation to generation," he wrote in a small travel diary he kept as he went along. Lack of cleanliness was a familiar complaint from Americans traveling in Europe, but what he saw was more disturbing to him because it had even invaded churches. In Naples, he said mass in a church whose beautiful and "remarkable" altar was ruined by its "tawdry vestments and dirty linens." Things were not much better in Rome. He disliked kneeling on the cold marble floors of churches there, but standing could be a blessing in disguise, since one was "liable to kneel where someone has expectorated the moment before."[44]

Throughout adulthood, he found it easy to criticize anything he considered common or undignified. Stopping in Paris to visit the world exposition in 1878, he applied the same haughty rigor he had once directed toward the noisy minstrel show of his college days. The American exhibit was "a poor affair," he said, with "no taste in the arrangement." Even so, it was better than the Irish offering, which featured nothing but "specimens of whiskey!!! God save the mark." That he needed three exclamation points to express his displeasure showed the intensity of his offense at anything that fell short of perfect respectability. He judged art the same way, quickly tiring of what he called "the Italian school of sacred pictures." Besides their "unnecessary nudities," they had "too much of flesh and blood—too much of animal nature—too little of spiritualized expression." One might admire such paintings, but "seldom or never pray" before them, and for him that was more important. German religious art was preferable, since it had "no mixture of the earthy and earthly man."[45] We must be wary of modern-day psychologizing, but we can perhaps hear in these words an echo of his personal dilemmas. One whose own body was anomalous for his countrymen in racial terms might well want to de-emphasize the "flesh and blood" of the "earthy and earthly man," preferring instead a "spiritualized expression."

His personality was influenced as much by his sense of social class as his racial status. The comfortable economic circumstances in which he had lived since the death of his parents only got better during his years as a bishop. He never profited personally from his office, but he had the resources to travel extensively, and he did so without hesitation. During his twenty-five years in Portland, he went to Rome and other destinations in Europe on four separate occasions; he also traveled across the American continent to California and back four times. He did not go in an unnecessarily grand style, but neither did he have to scrimp. He could linger in side trips and visit places few Maine Catholics, and even fewer African Americans, would ever see. He rode the just-opened London subway—a "curious sensation," he thought, "to be burrowing away under the houses + streets"—and he visited Blarney Castle in Ireland, passing up the chance to kiss its famous stone, though he did merrily poke it with his umbrella. Without lording it over others, he could nonetheless take quiet satisfaction in how high he had risen. Returning frequently to his theme of the dirtiness of much of what he saw, he remarked that of course "the lower classes" were untroubled by it, but things that "the brutal multitude" accepted were unacceptable to him.[46] Far out of mind was his own birth as a slave, the lowest of "the lower classes."

Healy's formidable personality was framed by the fundamentally religious understanding of his identity. His self-image was first and foremost that of a Catholic bishop, and he saw everything through that lens. The Catholic theology of his day asserted that the Roman church was the only "true" one, and he never doubted the inferiority of other forms of Christianity. Crossing the Atlantic at the beginning of 1886, he found pleasant company aboard ship with several upper-class Americans, taking turns around the deck with the ladies and joining the gentlemen for games of whist. Privately, he pitied them, non-Catholics all. Could one imagine "anything more hollow, unreal, and disjointed than the belief of the average Protestant," he mused, "not holding firmly to any principle, not believing without hesitation in anything"? By definition, they were clinging to "the merest shred of Christianity," he thought. At home, he firmly resisted any overt interdenominational cooperation. He refused the request of an Episcopalian minister in Portland to work together for stricter enforcement of the state's liquor laws, citing a recent papal instruction that Catholics avoid any meeting "where they make part of a ministerial assembly," a ban that "came none too soon."[47]

Like that of many of his contemporaries, Healy's Catholicism was always proper, even puritanical. Religion and morality were practically synonymous for him, and he could be easily shocked at minor breaches of decorum. The three exclamation points he expended over the Irish whiskey measured his usual reaction. Once, traveling through Genoa, he was appalled by a lively "Masquerade Ball!!!—on Sunday night, the first Sunday of Lent," when penitential devotions and self-denial were more appropriate. Likewise, he was shocked to see a soldier in Italy "coming out of church with a cigar in his mouth." He applied similar standards at home. Preferring voluntary abstinence to legal prohibition, he spoke frequently on alcohol's ill effects. He commended one of his priests, for example, who had refused absolution in the confessional to shopkeepers and tavern owners who sold liquor on Sundays, and he praised even small progress in the public recognition of religious duties. That Portland was growing more likely to observe Christmas "by a cessation from ordinary labour" was a source of genuine satisfaction.[48]

If his religion was often expressed in these simple ways, it was nonetheless genuine. From the time of his baptism until his death he remained committed to the church that he had chosen and that had, in return, chosen him. Some churchmen, caught up in their own advancement, come to believe more in the institution than in the underlying theological impulses, but Healy never succumbed to that temptation. Throughout his life, he could be deeply moved by religious experience. Revisiting his old seminary in Paris after three decades, tears came to his eyes. The sight of "the altar at which he had said his first Mass," he wrote, speaking of himself in the third person, "was almost overwhelming." Stirred by more than nostalgia, he thought the "plain and bare" chapel "beautiful indeed" for the spiritual comfort available there. He was similarly awed by Saint Peter's Basilica in Rome, even though the hub-bub of tourists made it hard for him to pray. He was greatly affected by Lourdes, where only twenty years before a peasant girl named Bernadette Soubirous had reported seeing the Virgin Mary. He was sure of the validity of the "startling + innumerable miracles" that had taken place at the spot, and he judged the apparitions "authentic + undoubted."[49] The depth of any religious sentiments are difficult to measure, especially more than a century after the fact, but those of James Healy seem themselves "authentic + undoubted."

To the very end, however, religion played a dual role for him. It had given him his new identity, but it also functioned as a way of putting an older identity behind him. He was not the "only colored priest" in America—Augustus Tolton was—and the ease with which he looked on black people as other than himself never diminished. When he traveled the world, it was as a white American. Aboard a steamship leaving New York on the first leg of a trip to California in 1889, for example, he spoke with mild condescension to his steward, "an old colored man, a smiling Catholic." Crossing the isthmus of Panama a week later, he noted the composition of the local population, "the blacks predominating"; their faces were "dark, even very black," and he shuddered to think what might happen "if all had guns." Once in California, his identification with white America never wavered. San Rafael, which he had visited once before, was now full of "Chinamen," with the result that it had "lost its charm." During all his travels his passport had consistently specified his own skin as "dark," but that did not change his identification with the white community.[50]

James Healy's quarter-century in Portland thus confirmed his earlier pattern of using his religious standing to silence questions about his racial standing and to cross over into white America. He had rendered his supposed disability irrelevant. The people of Maine, Catholic and Protestant alike, were not, as Father Vetromile had predicted, "mortified" by him; instead, they embraced him as their own and as one of their own. "The good bishop enjoys the esteem and respect of the community without distinction of creed," a Portland newspaper editorialized in 1900 on the celebration of his twenty-fifth anniversary in the city. "His executive ability, his good sense and clear understanding," were widely appreciated, another newspaper said, and he was universally "respected by Protestants."[51] That neither editorialist felt it necessary or appropriate to bring up the delicate subject of race is a measure of how inconsequential he had made that subject. He had not succeeded in erasing the color line—that had never been his desire—but he was able to live on the white side of that line.

CHAPTER EIGHT

The President: Patrick

No less than his brothers, Patrick Healy needed to escape the confinement of the American system of racial classification. His particular anxieties were intensified by the lightness of his skin. Whereas Sherwood had been obviously African American in appearance and James's face might also betray his origins, Patrick had coloring and features that were European. On the street, his brothers were readily identifiable as black, but Patrick appeared to be white. When passport agents described his complexion as "fair" or "light," they corroborated the common perception: he was what most Americans thought a white man looked like. And yet, the one-drop test for racial identity was becoming ever more strict during his lifetime. The definitions of who was white and who was black were increasingly rigid, imposing a standard for whiteness Patrick would never be able to meet. He carried the fateful one drop, and that was supposed to be that: since his "blood" was black, so was he. He was foreclosed, it was thought, from moving in circles where men of color simply did not belong. If he hoped to slip that trap, he needed a sharp break with his past. His journey took him away from the home that the others had found in New England, but it also opened new possibilities to him.

The need to separate himself from his darker-skinned brothers had been apparent on his return to Holy Cross College at the age of nineteen for his brief stint of teaching there. When he complained in the fall of 1853 to his "Dad," Father George Fenwick, of the "remarks . . . which wound my very heart," he had felt the sting of being treated like a black man even though he neither looked nor felt like one. He realized that he would be free from this "affliction" of racial taunting only if he could remove himself from the rest of his family. His students sneered at him, he knew, because they were "well acquainted either by sight or hearsay with me + my brothers." It was a kind of racial guilt by association: so long as he tarried "with those who have known us but too well," he would "always be subject to some such degrading misfortune."[1] He needed an enforced forgetting of who he was, and he advanced that process by going away to live among those who were not "well acquainted" with him and his family. His first years as a Jesuit in Maryland and Europe added distance to the protection of time, and the strategy worked. When he returned to the United States, Patrick Healy had an identity of his own, that of a white Jesuit priest.

When he and James parted company in Marseilles after their tour of the continent in the summer of 1863, they would not see each other again for three years. James returned to his career in America, and Patrick went back to the university at Louvain in Belgium to complete his studies. He was glad to have had the time with his brother, but the trip left him with a melancholy he was hard put to explain. "Is it fatigue? Is it reaction? Is it homesickness?" he wondered. The last was surely part of what was bothering him. After a decade apart from his immediate family, he had relished James's company, appreciating "the strength of family ties, the delicacy of feeling which they engender." Perhaps recalling his own boyhood uprooting from Georgia, he even added an aside condemning "the neglect of the family circle + the sad necessity of our age: the boarding school." Still, he knew that he could not be physically close to his family, and he sought relief in "the tramways of daily routine," the "monotonous regularity" of study, work, and prayer. With "patience," he thought, "all will come right." He had one goal: "I want to become a good Jesuit, and I am bound to become one."[2]

Among the priests of the Roman Catholic church, Jesuits stood out for their intensity. Organized by the Basque Ignatius Loyola, a former soldier, they were often identified as the "shock troops" of the church, and the reputation was not entirely undeserved. Members took a special (and frequently misunderstood) vow to go wherever they were sent by their superiors or by the pope, and this sometimes aroused the suspicion of outsiders, Catholic and non-Catholic alike. Officially designated "the Society of Jesus"—frequently clipped to "the Society"—they had a single-minded devotion to their work and a fierce sense of comradeship: fellow Jesuits were always referred to as "ours." The order had even been disbanded for a time out of fear that it was too powerful, but after its restoration in 1814, it made teaching the core of its distinctive mission. The Society had an important presence in Catholic America from the beginning, as many of the earliest missionaries were either Jesuits or former Jesuits. All were expected to keep a close watch on their own spiritual development, a self-examination reinforced through a system of annual retreats. These periods of withdrawal from routine activity might last for a few days or for as long as a month, and they took as their guide the Spiritual Exercises of

Ignatius. Those pursuing the exercises followed a guided program of meditation and reflection, all the while encouraged to see themselves as collaborating personally with God's plans.[3]

Patrick Healy adopted this spiritual approach as his own, and he got into the habit of monitoring his thoughts and behavior. He may or may not have been the most introspective of the Healy brothers, but he is the one for whom the most evidence of self-assessment survives. His reflections were often formulaic, repeating the cadences of spiritual directors. Thus, he could scold himself for "want of faith, of religious earnestness"; he could indict his excessive "levity"; he could question his worthiness, persisting only so as not to be "recalcitrant." The reader of these words today may account them a species of false modesty in one so purposeful about his life. Notwithstanding the stylized language, the expectations of the Jesuits had become fully his own as his "sense of my obligations" deepened. "I redoubt the priesthood very much," he wrote, using the unusual word in its older meaning to express his awe and respect; he had a "solid conviction" that it was the right thing for him to do with his life.[4]

Sentiments of that kind pulled him into the priesthood, but this was also a way to put old ambiguities behind him, just as it was for his brothers. The "degrading" insults were reminders of the racial labeling that would dog him forever if he did not secure another identity. His first impulse might be aggression: he confessed to "thoughts of conceit" and an occasional "manner + tone of controversy." These were forms of self-defense, striking out first before "remarks" were made by others. At the same time, he harbored deeper insecurities, making him sensitive lest others "laugh at my expense." By assuming the priestly mantle he could eliminate these swings between combativeness and docility. Most important of all, becoming a priest could quiet the greatest fear whites had about black and mixed-race Americans: that they would perpetuate racial confusion through their children. No portion of the color line was policed more carefully than that which condemned intermarriage. The priesthood foreclosed the possibility of marriage and children, and Patrick thus signaled his intention not to challenge prevailing racial conventions any more than he already had. Like his brothers, he would accept celibacy. Whatever its (no doubt sincere) religious motivation, this offered reassurance that he would play no part in furthering racial confusion. His becoming white was countenanced because he agreed that the process would go no further. He had admired the "tall, intellectual looking" priests he had seen in Spain, "their faces bearing the impress of culture + study."[5] A face suggesting culture and study was obviously preferable to one that suggested racial subversion. This was the face he would present to the world.

His ordination to the priesthood came in due course in September 1864. It was then that he felt the emotional power of the scriptural quotation, "I no longer call you slaves, but my friends." Becoming a priest was not, however, the last act of a Jesuit's preparation, as it was for diocesan clergy like James and Sherwood. Instead, Patrick stayed at Louvain—a plan for studies in Germany fell through— earning an advanced degree in theology. This left him, like Sherwood, much better educated than the average American Catholic priest, and so, after he had worked for another year in a French parish church, his Jesuit superiors decided that it was time for him to return to America to teach at Georgetown University. He sailed for home at the end of the summer in 1866, and upon his arrival he was honored at a private dinner in Boston, hosted by his brothers. Even the often grumpy Father Hilary Tucker was impressed on meeting this member of the family for the first time. "He has been absent for 8 years," Tucker wrote, "and gone through all the colleges and universities. . . . We had a good time in honor of Father Patrick Healy, S.J., a star of the Society and of the church, as is to be hoped!" From there the rising star went to Washington to take up his new duties.[6]

Georgetown was the oldest institution of higher learning in the country operated under Catholic auspices, and it was the traditional center for American Jesuits. Opened shortly after the American Revolution, it concentrated as much on secular as on religious learning. It was called a "university," but it actually combined the programs of a modern high school with those of an undergraduate college, though it also maintained semi-independent law and medical schools. Another division prepared future Jesuits, and it was to this work that Healy was assigned in the fall of 1866, apparently in an effort to work him slowly into the life of the school. His "African blood" did not "shew" as Sherwood's did, but his "irregularities" were not unknown to the Jesuits. They accepted and endorsed his self-definition as a white priest like themselves, but they had to be careful nonetheless, because Georgetown had a distinctly Southern flavor. Students from below the Mason-Dixon Line had traditionally predominated, and during the Civil War the college was correctly reputed to be a nest of rebel sympathizers. With the reopening of classes after the war, fully a third of the all-male student body came from the states of the old Confederacy; several students had been officers in the secessionist armed forces.[7] For Patrick Healy, technically a former slave, to take a prominent place in such an institution was possible, but it had to be done cautiously. Settling him first within the family of Jesuits before exposing him more widely to the general student population was a good idea.

The leaders of Georgetown were also acutely conscious of where they were. Washington was in the process of being transformed from a fair-sized but not very interesting Southern town into a bustling cosmopolitan city. A population of about 60,000 in 1860 had exploded to 110,000 a decade later, and it had been nearly twice that high during the war itself. As the general population grew, so too did the black segment of it. African Americans constituted only one in every six Washingtonians at the start of the war, but by 1870 they numbered one in three of the city's residents. Freed and escaped slaves had been flooding into town, a safe haven between two slaveholding states, seceded Virginia and tenuously loyal Maryland. The slave trade had been outlawed there since the Compromise of 1850, and the institution itself was abolished in the first year of the conflict; all runaways physically in the city were expressly declared free in 1862. For many blacks, this was the best place to get a first taste of freedom.[8]

Administered directly by Congress, then firmly controlled by Radical Republicans, the District of Columbia became a test case for sweeping social change in the aftermath of the rebellion. The public schools were integrated, and black voting rights were endorsed (over significant white opposition) in 1867. The word "white" was removed from the city charter, and local directories abandoned the practice of identifying inhabitants by race. Public accommodations were similarly opened to people of color, and for a time at least white resistance was minimal. One new law levied a fine of $20 on theater owners who refused admission to black patrons, for instance, and only a single complaint of this kind was reported. Black strength at the polls was soon measurable: in 1868, one African American was elected to the fourteen-member board of aldermen and another to the twenty-one-seat common council. A black community that was well defined, self-conscious, and middle class emerged, and Washington came to be identified as the "capital of the colored aristocracy." Entry into such professions as law, medicine, teaching, and government clerkships was rapid for some, and many had reason to hope that the city foretold a new day in American race relations. Skin color had not ceased to matter—those with lighter complexions often found social and economic position easier to achieve than others—but advancement seemed unexpectedly possible in a city where slavery was still a recent memory.[9]

For the moment, such an environment might be hospitable for a man of Healy's background, but he could not test the racial tolerance of the day by acknowledging his African American heritage, either on campus or off. Georgetown's connections with the local black community were virtually nonexistent, and the school's faculty were often just as unsympathetic as other whites with the tenor of the times. "All our public men here," the university's treasurer wrote shortly before Patrick Healy's arrival on campus, "have got the nigger on the brain," adding with an insult he probably thought clever that there was "very little brain on the nigger. . . . In what year of our Lord will this nigger question be settled?" An only slightly more benign Jesuit expressed amazement at the public lecture by a professor—"a colored man!"—from Howard University: "Fred Douglass will have more rivals every year," he snorted.[10] The persistence of such casual but entrenched racism meant that Patrick Healy could never disclose his background, even if he had wanted to.

More generally, the university kept its distance from the rest of the capital. The city of Georgetown had long been a separate municipality, not incorporated into Washington proper until 1871, and the school was similarly in and out of the life of the District. Professors were rarely seen in local society. Eager to overcome the stigma of disloyalty during the war, the faculty made a point of inviting Union war heroes to campus, and many came, including Generals Grant and Sherman, the latter of whom had a son (eventually a Jesuit himself) enrolled there. Otherwise, discussion of public affairs was usually off-limits. Even though there were no legal barriers to priests voting, for example, Jesuit superiors forbade their men to do so, hoping to calm fears of undue priestly influence at the ballot box. At the same time, students were discouraged from venturing downtown too frequently, lest they succumb to temptations that could be more closely regulated on the campus, which occupied a high promontory above the Potomac River.[11]

Precisely because Georgetown was cut off from its setting, Patrick Healy could ease into his work without much notice. He said mass occasionally at the nearby Visitation Convent, an important center of the small Catholic social circle in Washington. It was there that he met Julia Gardiner Tyler, the widow of President John Tyler, who turned to him for instruction in Catholic doctrine. After several months, she expressed her desire to convert to the Roman church and was baptized. So strong had their bond grown that she asked Healy to be her godfather, a role he gladly accepted. This proper Virginia lady would almost certainly never have asked him to fulfill this role if she had had any doubts about his racial background.[12] Closer to home, he also became more involved in the affairs of the college. Enrollments were growing, though the number of students could still fluctuate between three hundred and about half that. Even so, a halting expansion was underway. Some non-Catholic parents were sending their sons to Georgetown, "partly for the greater security of their morals," one observer claimed, "partly on account of the more thorough, or at least better grounded, course of instruction" than that available elsewhere. Evolution of that program brought Patrick his first promotion. The college had always been a simple operation administratively, but by 1868 the need for greater control demanded reorganization. Accordingly, the position of "prefect of studies," a sort of academic dean, was created, distinct from the office of president. A year later, after the first prefect, an older Jesuit, was killed in a storm at sea, Patrick Healy was appointed to take his place.[13]

The students at Georgetown, unlike their earlier counterparts at Holy Cross, knew only Patrick, not the rest of his family, and the new dean was thus spared the "affliction" of "remarks." He had been right all along: time and distance did indeed solve his problem. To students, most of them Southerners, he was simply "Father Healy," to whom they deferred as they would to any other priest. They might know that he had brothers who were priests in Boston, but that only reinforced their perceptions of him. A priest with an Irish name and family in Boston was readily positioned among the racial and ethnic classifications of the day. Stories occasionally circulated that Father Healy had some "Spanish blood," a conveniently vague description that was not unknown among Irish Americans, but this probably counted in his favor. Suggesting descent from the supposed survivors of the wreck of the Spanish Armada off Ireland in the sixteenth century, by then hailed as Catholic heroes in the struggle against Protestant England, Spanish ancestry was a romantic, even aristocratic trait. Otherwise, the students had no clue about Healy's real genealogy. Stephen Mallory, a student from Florida, spoke for all of them. In his senior year, young Mallory took a philosophy course with Father Healy and remembered him later as "a finished scholar, a remarkable linguist, and the clearest thinker and expounder of his thoughts that I ever met."[14] Such words of praise would have been unthinkable for Mallory, who happened to be the son of the former Confederate Secretary of the Navy, had he known that Healy's blood was not of Spanish, but of a very different provenance.

After becoming dean, Healy's career advanced swiftly. Jesuit custom limited the length of time any man could serve as president of one of their schools. Regular rotation in office was seen as a positive thing, though a president might return after a term or two away. Georgetown was now facing this kind of transition, one that was complicated by the advancing age, ill health, and other perceived deficiencies of several possible candidates. The likeliest nominee was thought, at fifty-six, to be too old, even though, one Jesuit said confidentially, he would at least have "an outstanding man as his assistant, Father Healy." The same commentator went so far as to say that he "would have much preferred" Healy as president, "except for the problem related to his background"—the last phrase an indication that the other Jesuits knew Patrick's life story, even if their students did not. As the search dragged on, however, one name kept coming up. "Clearly Healy is best

Patrick F. Healy, S.J. Photo courtesy Archives,
Georgetown University.

qualified," the head of the Maryland Jesuits wrote, "despite the difficulty that perhaps can be brought up about him." In the end, circumstances intervened. Georgetown's president died suddenly on May 23, 1873, and the board of directors met the next day to appoint Healy to fill his place. Jesuit officials in Rome later confirmed the appointment and made it permanent.[15] At the age of thirty-nine, Patrick Healy assumed the presidency of what was then the largest Catholic college in the United States.

In doing so, he completed his triumph over his lifelong "difficulty." His background had first been reduced to only "perhaps" an impediment, and then it was no impediment at all. Racism among Jesuits was still strong, and it would endure: an oral tradition reports that some Jesuit houses were unwilling to receive Patrick Healy when he traveled because, they thought, no one else would later be willing to sleep in the bed he had used.[16] In spite of all that, his confreres saw him as "ours," and his "outstanding" ability was sufficient to overcome the "problem." The details of his ancestry could be kept quiet, and they were eventually forgotten. His light complexion would not betray him if others agreed to guard his secret. His designation as president of a college in Reconstruction Washington might have been a bold statement by the institution's leaders; it might have been the brave herald of a new multiracial America. But it was not that. It was instead an endorsement of his whiteness, a sanctioning of his decision to defy—firmly, if quietly—the conventions that assigned him to a racial place he did not want.

❧

At the beginning, neither Healy nor his superiors in the Jesuits had grand plans for his presidency. Simply keeping the school afloat set the immediate agenda. Enrollment in the undergraduate program continued to fluctuate, touching bottom at less than 170 in the academic year of 1873–1874. Attracting and holding students was difficult, given the school's traditionally Southern base. With the region's economy decimated by the war, fewer parents had the resources to invest in the higher education of their sons. Moreover, some members of the faculty were beginning to question the curriculum, still focused primarily on the classics, wondering whether this was the sort of program the times demanded. The institutional coherence of the place was also uncertain. The medical and law "departments," which together enrolled about 120, operated as virtually autonomous schools; they were not even located on the campus. Finally, disaster might strike at any time, threatening to undo whatever progress was made. Two months before Patrick's appointment to the presidency, fire had destroyed part of an old classroom building, raising questions about the safety of the entire complex.

If he had been intended, like most of his predecessors, merely to be a manager of problems as they came up, the new president instead took a more active role. "He never allowed precedents to stand in the way of development," an acquaintance would later say. Healy turned first to the curriculum, an area of concern across American higher education in the last quarter of the nineteenth century. The passage of the Morrill Act in 1862, setting aside grants of land for the establishment of public colleges, had initiated a reconsideration of just what a "university" was, and courses of study were changing everywhere in response to the perceived needs of modern life. Mathematics and the sciences got new emphasis, as college presidents and faculties began to conclude that the traditional stress on philosophy, theology, and literature was inadequate. Patrick Healy followed these discussions and experimented with taking Georgetown in new academic directions.[17]

The teaching in Jesuit colleges was still grounded in the *ratio studiorum* that Patrick and his brothers had themselves pursued as students. This program began with three years of "rudiments" and then moved up through "poetry," "rhetoric," and "philosophy," the respective equivalents of the sophomore, junior, and senior years. At each level the Latin and Greek classics were prescribed, learned through student composition and recitation. In class, there were "disputations," oral arguments defending or challenging assigned propositions, most of them drawn from scholastic philosophy. Exams were given at regular intervals, with numerical grades read out at monthly assemblies and prizes awarded. Healy never abandoned this approach, but he introduced an alternative in 1875. Designated the "scientific course," this program emphasized math, chemistry, and physics. Students had to present "specimens," reproducing experiments that they explained as they went along, and they were eligible to receive the Bachelor of Science degree rather than the traditional Bachelor of Arts. A later president praised it as "a system which, while retaining the spirit of the 'Ratio Studiorum,' agreed more closely with the curricula of the best non-Catholic colleges than had previously been the case." The reform began optimistically, but little really changed: only thirty-three students enrolled in it during its ten years of availability, and only seven actually took the B.S. degree. In 1886, after Healy's term was over, the program was abandoned.[18]

Healy had more success at reining in the independence of the law and medical schools. Professional education was still uncommon: most lawyers learned their trade by "reading" the law with an established attorney, and would-be doctors gained more of their competence from apprenticeships than from formal study. As these approaches began to change elsewhere, Georgetown likewise took some tentative steps. A law curriculum, originally a substitute for undergraduate study rather than a supplement to it, had taken shape in 1870, and several local doctors had been overseeing a "proprietary" medical school (meaning that they ran it for their own financial profit) since the 1850s. The law department did reasonably well, attracting students from the Washington area and a growing number of former undergraduates. In 1879, a decision to drop the tuition from $80 to $50 per year helped expand the student body from 28 to 48, and soon there were more than 160 law students. Medical department enrollments were similarly good, though they had fallen off from more than a hundred in the immediate aftermath of the Civil War.[19] In both cases, however, the specialized schools were only tenuously connected to Georgetown, and Patrick Healy sought to tie them more directly to their parent institution.

Reform of the medical school came first. Breaking with the tradition of earlier presidents (who kept their distance), Healy attended the opening of classes there in the fall of 1874 and gave an address that damned with faint praise. Medicine had changed so dramatically in recent years, he said, that "more is expected of the candidate for a [medical] degree than ever before." Long discussions followed, but the solution seemed clear. Within a year and a half the entire faculty had voluntarily resigned to make way for reorganization. Some were immediately reappointed, but they were now more clearly a part of the larger university that was Georgetown. The separate medical trustees were disbanded, and President Healy was acknowledged as the final authority. Stricter standards for admission and graduation were adopted, and specialized courses were introduced. The full cycle of instruction was extended from two years to three, and the medical school year expanded from five months to eight. Clinical internships were mandated, and strict written examinations replaced the informal oral variety. Writing from Massachusetts, Harvard University's President Charles W. Eliot, who was attempting the same reforms at his own medical school, congratulated Healy in 1878 for his "stand in behalf of a proper system of medical education" and for abandoning "the old and disgraceful methods."[20]

Healy also succeeded at overhauling his law department, and this was more important, since Georgetown faced competition from several other law schools in Washington. Alert to market pressures, Healy joined the law faculty in trying to improve the school's reputation by raising its standards. Written examinations were required in all classes to ensure their rigor, and such practical experiences as moot court were also introduced. Changing standards for admission to the bar supported these reforms. The District of Columbia bar association was now demanding three years of explicit legal education before aspirants could practice, and Georgetown was a good place to get that preparation, especially for those from around the country who came to Washington hoping for a career in government. Moreover, Healy worked to tie the law school more closely to the rest of the university. He himself taught a course in legal ethics, and he explored the possibility of constructing a law building on the campus. Though that was financially impossible until well after his presidency, the law school was a singular success when he left office. By 1890 it was larger even than the undergraduate school, enrolling more than 250 students.[21]

In the college division, Healy's plans for change depended on improving the quality of the faculty. As in most colleges of the day, it was teaching rather than research that counted: ability in the classroom was much more important than creativity in the laboratory or a distinguished publishing record. The Georgetown faculty was never very big during this period. There were twenty-five instructors during his first year as president, but only nine were assigned to the undergraduate program, with the remainder teaching the lower grades. Most of them were Jesuits, juggled from subject to subject as needed. This made for flexibility, but it meant that subject matter was not always in the hands of those who had mastered it themselves. An instructor might teach English grammar and French one year, only to find himself teaching algebra and chemistry the next. Expanded offerings in the sciences put even more pressure on the faculty, who often knew little about these disciplines. To address that problem, Healy began sending his teachers to other schools for advanced training: several younger Jesuits, for example, were enrolled in a summer program at Harvard for a concentrated course in mathematics. Lay faculty filled some of the gaps, but the resulting financial strain worked against this as a general solution. All the lay teachers on campus had to be let go in the early 1880s because the school was simply unable to pay them, and it would take the better part of a century before non-Jesuit teachers came to pre dominate.[22]

It was in recasting the student body that Patrick Healy had his most lasting effect. In particular, he transformed the university from one that attracted students mainly from well-to-do Southern families to one with a broader base. The largest percentage of students—always at least one-third—were from the immediate Washington vicinity, but among those from "away," the transition was dramatic. In the 1870s, about 32 percent of the students came from Southern states, with only about 20 percent from the Northeast. In the next decade, Southerners were halved to only 16 percent of the student population, with Northeasterners jumping past them to more than 25 percent. The numbers for particular states were even more dramatic. Louisiana, for example, sent twenty-eight boys in the 1870s, but only seven in the 1880s; students from Georgia and Alabama all but disappeared.[23] Some change would have happened regardless of who was president. The South's economic infrastructure had been shattered by the war, and college was becoming a luxury. Concurrently, an aspiring Catholic middle class in the cities of the North was looking to education as a means for personal and family advancement. There was a steady decline of non-Catholic students, and the feel of the school was more Irish and Catholic, even in little things. By 1880, for instance, Saint Patrick's Day had become an official school holiday.

The transformation of the student body was also part of a deliberate policy by Patrick Healy. Astute enough to know that the old regional base could no longer support the school, he shifted resources to where they might have more effect.

Financial aid to students, for example, had never been very generous, but even so it was redirected. In the 1880s, not a single student from a Southern state was given any relief from his tuition bill. Of those from the old Confederacy who did enroll during this period, only a fraction (about 7 percent) actually stayed long enough to receive their undergraduate degrees, while the expansion of the American Catholic community elsewhere helped fill the void.[24] Georgetown's changed geographic focus may also have had a personal meaning for Healy. Though he never spoke of it, the shift away from the South looks, at least in part, like a kind of lingering but effective revenge. By changing his school's orientation toward the North, he could point it in the direction that he and his family had faced. For one last time, he could turn his back on the place that had defined him, at his birth, not as a person but as property.

The change in student demographics heightened the isolation of Georgetown from its surroundings, and that separation worked to President Healy's advantage. His "difficulty" had been overcome on campus, but if it were exposed publicly there would probably be disastrous consequences. All his plans for the school would collapse if word got out that Georgetown had a black man—or at least a man defined as black—as its president. In fact, the need to guard his secret was growing more urgent, for the earlier optimism about race relations in the nation's capital was giving way to a harsher reality. Employment of African Americans in the government declined sharply after 1876, and blacks were steered into jobs on the lower end of the wage scale. Residential segregation was more rigorously enforced, and this was accompanied by a clearer pattern of segregated schools. Transportation and other public accommodations were increasingly restricted. Bars, for example, continued to serve an integrated clientele, but more genteel restaurants began routinely to deny service to black patrons. What one historian called a "withering of hope" for the city's black community was well under way.[25] Patrick Healy had to continue his practice of keeping a safe distance from that community, living in the enclosed, white, religious world of his university.

His work there came to focus increasingly on a physical reconstruction of the campus. His brothers James and Sherwood had distinguished themselves as builders of churches in Boston, and Patrick too would leave a stone legacy. Georgetown's small huddle of buildings was plainly inadequate for the great national university he wanted it to be, and thus Healy embarked on an ambitious plan. There had been talk of relocating the school elsewhere in the District of Columbia or even out in the Maryland countryside, but he committed to rebuilding where they were. He brought in two local architects who had just won the commission to erect an elegant new home for the Library of Congress, and they drew up plans for a building of classrooms, laboratories, and a library. The structure would make an impressive statement on the emerging Washington skyline. Five stories high, surmounted by turrets and two towers, the Romanesque stone building offered a sharp contrast to the relentlessly Federal architecture of the rest of the city. Just as Sherwood Healy had wanted to build a cathedral that reminded Yankee Boston that Catholics were there to stay, so Patrick wanted Washingtonians who looked up at the new Georgetown to know that it had turned toward the future.[26]

Some of his fellow Jesuits were reportedly "astonished" by the scale of his plans, but Healy presided over the start of construction and helped lay the cornerstone in December 1877. Work proceeded steadily, but he could not have chosen a less auspicious time to undertake such a project. Depression and panic earlier in the decade had left the college in a very precarious financial condition. Without an endowment or a tradition of fund-raising from alumni, Georgetown had suffered a serious blow when it lost more than $30,000 in the failure of a Baltimore bank four years before. Borrowing was essential, and this Healy did in several installments as the cost of construction grew frighteningly close to half a million dollars. A few outlying Jesuit properties were sold off to provide a little revenue, but the whole effort was still a gamble: a cooler financial head would probably never have undertaken it. Happily, luck was with him. The shell of the structure was complete within two years, and Healy continued to watch the workmen carefully, fired by what an alumnus praised as "close attention to the minutest details." The inside was complete enough for the opening of classes in the fall of 1881, though it was not until the school's centennial in 1889 that the last details had been attended to.[27]

Beyond the vision to conceive of them in the first place, these grand plans mostly needed money, and that was in short supply. The general public considered all Catholic institutions fabulously wealthy, Healy explained to his sometime correspondent, President Eliot of Harvard, but that was not the case. "With the exception of $25,000 given by Congress in real estate, for which we have paid taxes since '42, and about $11,000 presented at intervals with the onus of a scholarship attached, we have no endowment whatever," he lamented. "What we have achieved has been the result of economy and the vow of poverty" taken by the Jesuit faculty, whose salaries could be diverted to general operating expenses. In an attempt to improve this poor outlook, Healy embarked on what would be the school's first real fund-raising campaign. The original plan had been to send another Jesuit on a tour across the country, visiting scattered alumni and appealing to Catholic generosity. At the last minute, his superiors decided that Healy should go too. He understood the importance of the trip, but the abruptness of the command troubled him. On Thanksgiving Day, 1878, he was told that he would be leaving for California that Saturday. "I felt almost shocked at the idea," he wrote in his diary. "The voyage would be agreeable at any time, because it implies rest, variety, and possible profit in many ways to me and to the College," he acknowledged. "But to go at a day's notice, to leave all—teachers, boys, friends, building, debts, and all—was it not a confession of the little space I held in the great work of which I was the reputed chief? My very vanity revolted against the proposition."[28]

He had a point, but he was being oversensitive. He could do far more for Georgetown by raising an endowment than by staying behind to supervise the construction workers. What is more, the trip would thrust him into the eye of an even wider public. He would leave behind the safe and familiar world of the campus, where the question of his race had long since been neutralized. Now he was moving onto a national stage, becoming a roving ambassador for Georgetown and meeting all sorts of people, from whom he was soliciting money. The assignment was thus an expression of confidence in him by his Jesuit superiors, not a relegation to a "little space." If the school's directors were willing to put its future so visibly in his hands, he had indeed succeeded in his long work of self-transformation. He and his traveling companion, Father Joseph O'Hagan, took a train from Washington to New York City, and on November 30 they boarded a ship bound for California. Once there, they hoped that a concentration of successful alumni would get their fund-raising effort off to a good start.

The two old friends proceeded down the east coast and landed at Panama ten days later for the overland trek across the isthmus in those days before the canal. The mild ocean air and the easy shipboard pace offered welcome rest. Crossing the narrow land mass to the Pacific side, Healy was keen to observe this unfamiliar world, and what he saw confirmed his perceptions of himself. He was struck by the appearance of the people he saw, adopting the language his brothers had used to set himself apart. "The negroes," he wrote, specifying a category that obviously did not include himself, "are intelligent and mostly able to read and write." These capabilities seemed to surprise him, but he also noted that too many of these "negroes" were "rather lazy," invoking the common white stereotype. His own status was happily reinforced a week later as his ship touched in at Mazatlán on the Mexican coast. There, he was befriended by a chatty American sea captain who, Patrick said, "detected my Irish accent."[29] The jocular words speak volumes. Michael Morris Healy probably retained the brogue of his homeland, but his children almost certainly did not. Patrick Healy had spoken his first words in Georgia, and his education had been in Massachusetts, Maryland, and Europe; as an adult, he was fluent in Latin, French, Italian, and German as well as English. Precisely what kind of speaking accent emerged from that cosmopolitan mix cannot now be reconstructed, but it is unlikely to have been rightly characterized as "Irish." No, this self-description was an expression of Patrick's hopes; this was how he wanted to be heard. To be sure, being Irish in nineteenth-century America was not without its problems, but for Patrick Healy it was surely better than the alternative.

Interrupted by the sudden illness and death of Father O'Hagan, Healy continued the journey, arriving at San Francisco two days after Christmas 1878. The vista of the Golden Gate was "much over-rated," he sniffed, though he conceded that the place had the potential, in time, to become "the third or second city in the world." Settling in at a church that the Jesuits ran there, he began to look up Georgetown grads. He got an early pledge of $10,000 from a member of the class of 1869, a newly rich mining tycoon, but that only fueled expectations that could not be realized. "There is a story going the rounds of your having rec[eive]d $100,000," a fellow Jesuit wrote him excitedly from Washington, but nothing close to that was either in hand or likely to be. Healy met some alumni of the medical school who were "doing very well here," but he could only get small gifts out of them, and several sizable pledges went unfulfilled.[30] He left San Francisco at the end of July 1879, making his way back across the country by train. Everywhere he stopped, the response to his fund-raising appeals never matched his hopes. Worse, the restorative benefits of the sea voyage were gone by now, and he became simply exhausted. He was back at Georgetown by the beginning of September, but he soon retreated to Maine for a month of real vacation with his brother James.

For the next few years, Patrick Healy retained the title of president of the school, but he spent more and more time away from it. His health deteriorated, and he suffered fainting spells, aches in his joints, and general weakness.[31] He was also dispirited by not raising more money, though he should have been happier than he was. In the final accounting, he had brought in about $60,000, far less than he wanted, but it was still an achievement for a school with "no endowment whatever." Even so, the gap between hope and reality spoke to him of failure. At the beginning of February 1882 he asked permission to resign as president, and the board acceded to his request. "My work is done," he would later tell a colleague; "you and younger men are to carry it on." His diaries and correspondence from this period suggest that he nursed an extended disappointment over his efforts, but that was too harsh a judgment. Georgetown had been almost entirely remade under his stewardship. When the student newspaper praised him, saying that "no president ever did more to put the college upon a broad and firm basis," it had a better appreciation of his work than he did. He would later be identified as the "second founder" of the school, and that honorific was more deserved than such titles often are.[32] When, several years afterward, the structure he put up began to be called the Healy Building in his honor, the school recognized his tenure as its decisive modern turning point.

✒

After his resignation, Patrick Healy lingered for nearly thirty years in what seems a long twilight. Those decades had little of the drama or demands of his earlier career. At first, he spent a few years traveling the globe, usually with members of his own family. Then, he settled into the quiet routine of a parish priest, and these duties seemed to agree with him, both temperamentally and physically. For Jesuits, parish work was always secondary to the more important task of teaching. Still, the order had charge of a sprinkling of churches around the country, and it was in them that Patrick spent the last third of his life.

Travel had always been appealing to him, and it was further justified now by the need to recoup the energy he had expended during his presidency. After several months with James in Portland, the two brothers took a jaunt to Bermuda in the early spring of 1883. No sooner had they returned than Patrick received a letter from their younger brother Michael, then stationed with the U.S. Revenue Cutter Service in San Francisco. Michael had risen steadily through the ranks of the service, and he was now assigned to the fleet that patrolled the icy waters around Alaska. He had just been given command of his own ship, and he invited Patrick to join him on his regular summer tour of the northern latitudes. The voyage was to be a family reunion of sorts, since Michael's wife, Mary Jane, and their twelve-year-old son, Fred, would also be along. Patrick first thought himself "in no condition to stand the rough ride across the continent, much less to undertake a long cruise in the upper waters of the Pacific," but soon he yielded to the temptation. Arriving again in California, he provisioned himself with several new sets of underwear and "a pair of good stout shoes" before setting sail aboard the cutter *Corwin* on May 23, 1883.[33]

Even as they got under way, he still had some doubts. The *Corwin* was "confined, [with] provisions + coal on deck, no place to walk + many attendant inconveniences." Gradually, though, the landlubber became enchanted. They proceeded north through the Bering Strait, and, without much ceremony, Patrick was "admitted to the Arctic Club," whose one requirement for membership was "that you pass the Circle. This we did in the silence of a smooth sea and the blaze of the most brilliant sunset I have ever seen." There were other firsts too. On July 12, they put in to take on fresh water at Plover Bay in Siberia, and Patrick noted ornately that "for the first time I stepped upon the continent of Asia and entered the realms of his Imperial Majesty, the Czar." He said mass aboard ship and, ashore, he did the same before groups of curious natives. These religious duties often conflicted with the routines of the vessel. One morning, he was just putting on his vestments when the alarm bell rang for a fire drill. The ship's steward came rushing into the cabin, only to be struck dumb by the sight of a priest dressed in the elaborate robes of his church: "he came to a stop mighty quick, you bet," young Fred Healy laughed in his diary. For his own part, Father Healy was undeterred. "I was anxious to say mass within the Arctic Circle," he said, happy that he could do so on the feast of Saint Ignatius Loyola, a special Jesuit day, "the very day I should have chosen of all others."[34]

The journey gave him the chance to observe peoples he had never seen before, and they helped validate his sense of who he was. Like most Americans who traveled in Alaska, Patrick Healy drew a sharp and simple distinction between "natives" and "white men." In Sitka, for example, "a straggling village falling to decay," he saw that the natives all lived on a "ranch," separated from "the white town" by a stockade. White men often took native women as "concubines," he noted disapprovingly, and the offspring of these temporary matches were everywhere. He wrote sympathetically of one "little half-breed," desperately poor, with sad eyes and a "reproachful" look. He discerned in her "instincts toward something better," thinking that "in proper dress" she would be pretty, but that was all the empathy he could muster. His condescension seemed harmless enough, and it recurred whenever he met with "the better class of natives or rather creoles."[35] Still, his benign observations had a deeper meaning. His easy way with the conventional racial language of white America left no doubt that he himself was one with that America. Long out of memory was the possibility that he himself might be characterized as a "half-breed" or a "creole."

The *Corwin's* voyage was comparatively uneventful, and the time went by pleasantly. References to ill health completely disappeared from Patrick's diary. Basking again in the warmth of the family circle he had rediscovered on his travels with James, he and his nephew Fred became the best of pals. They played cards for hours on end, explored on shore with the ship's dog, Roxie, and shot ducks from the deck. At the end of the summer, the cutter turned south, and they were back in San Francisco by the beginning of October. For the next year, Patrick lived at the Jesuit residence of Saint Ignatius College (the future University of San Francisco), taking his turn at saying mass in the church attached to the school. He also traveled about in California, going down to Los Angeles and San Diego for a time, making a tourist visit to the mission at Santa Barbara, and looking in on another Jesuit college at Santa Clara.[36] There always seemed to be enough to keep him busy, but he had fallen into a kind of working retirement by the time of his fiftieth birthday in February 1884.

As one year gave way to another, his life became that of an ordinary parish priest. He stayed at the cathedral rectory in Portland with his brother for several years; then, it was on to a Jesuit parish in Providence, Rhode Island, and finally to a church in New York City. He occasionally took on special assignments, including participation as one of the American delegates to a meeting of Jesuits from around the world, held in Spain in 1892 and 1893. That excitement aside, his was a calm and even dull existence, marked only by the minor ups and downs in the lives of his parishioners. He sat in the confessional box for hours, sometimes all afternoon and evening. On one day in Providence, he heard the confessions of seventy-three penitents in the afternoon and then came back to hear a hundred more after supper. Occasionally this was "interesting," he thought; sometimes it was just "ponderous." He embraced the parish routine, pacing the rectory yard while reading his breviary, leading rosary devotions, and blessing the throats of parishioners on the feast of Saint Blaise. Where once he had been a stern master of his students, he became mellow with age. Watching the playing schoolchildren of the parish in Manhattan, he sentimentally found them "full of life + jollity." He often remembered his years as a college president—once, he complained when an annual directory ran the advertisement for Georgetown in a "diminished" place—but that was all in the past.[37] He slipped, unresisting, into old age.

This last third of his life seems now, as it may have seemed to him, anticlimactic. The big plans and big efforts of the past occupied him no longer. From the perspective of more than a century, however, it is his remaking of Georgetown that stands out, the more so because he was the one who had done it. Too many were ready to declare someone like him incapable of such a thing, because they defined him as a black man. His skin was light, to be sure, but white America was increasingly insistent that complexion mattered less than the inner, unchangeable racial essence carried in the blood. No matter what he looked like, Patrick Healy could never meet that challenge. And yet he did. He knew, better than most, the disadvantages from which he could not escape were he not to be a white American. Early on, he had heard the "remarks which wound," and with an appropriate sense of his own abilities, he resolved never to hear them again. His adult life was the fulfillment of that resolution.

CHAPTER NINE

Sisters: Martha, Josephine, and Eliza

Until now, the story of the Healy family has largely been that of the brothers, and this is not, perhaps, surprising. Throughout the nineteenth century, men rather than women were thought to do the things of which history properly took notice. Women had their own sphere, the conventional wisdom went, one that restricted them to the private world of home and family. More recently, historians have appreciated the importance of women's activities, in matters large and small, and the need to examine that work if we hope to understand the past. So it must be with the women of the Healy family. On the surface, there seems little to tell. Two of them spent their adult years behind the sheltering walls of convents; the other lived quietly as a housewife in the Boston suburbs. Seldom, if ever, did they attract public notice. Like their brothers, however, Martha, Josephine, and the younger Eliza Healy had to find a way to transcend the conventions that assigned them to a prescribed racial place.

Because they were women, theirs was a double disadvantage. It minimizes none of the difficulties of interracial males to say that interracial females had even fewer opportunities to escape racial confinement. Men could at least try to establish careers as the focus of their identity; with luck they might, as the Healy brothers did, find a place in institutions that helped secure passage into white America. By demonstrating that they shared common values of hard work and striving, interracial males might undercut their contemporaries' facile caricatures of what "mulattoes" were like. Women had fewer opportunities of this kind, and they were thus more likely to be bound by stereotypes. Education was limited and most professional positions beyond reach, so women found it more difficult than their husbands or brothers to win prestige and influence. Interracial women were caught in a cruel logic. Constrained on account of their race, they had fewer chances to prove themselves as individuals. Limited because they were women, they had fewer chances to escape into the public roles of men.

It would be fruitless now to attempt a description of the psychology of Martha, Josephine, and Eliza Healy, or to speculate on how they addressed these dilemmas. Were they alive today, we would want to ask them many things. How did their understanding, as women, of their racial identity differ from that of their brothers? Was it significant, for instance, that it was their mother and not their father who had been black? Did this make it easier for the sons in the family to see themselves as white, and correspondingly harder for the daughters to do so? To what extent did the Healy sisters feel special tensions as they considered the prospect of having children themselves? In popular accounts, anxiety over potential children was thought to be especially intense for interracial women: what if the child of a light-skinned mother were to have a dark skin or other tell-tale characteristics? Would that not expose the "lie" of passing?[1] For better or worse, all these questions about the Healy sisters are beyond the scope of the available evidence. Instead, we must simply follow the trajectories of their lives as members of this remarkable family.

More than once, Martha Healy, the oldest girl and fifth in birth order of the siblings, had led the way for her two younger sisters. Sent north while her parents were still alive, she followed James, Hugh, Patrick, and Sherwood to Massachusetts and found a home among the Catholics of Boston. At six she was baptized, just a month after her brothers had been initiated into the church in 1844. Boarding with the relatives of Bishop Fitzpatrick and with other Catholic families, Martha likewise entered the protective religious circle in which her racial heritage became irrelevant. Josephine and Eliza would retrace her steps after Hugh rescued them from Georgia in 1851. Then Martha led the way again, enrolling at the age of twelve in the Villa Maria school of the Notre Dame sisters in Montreal; later, Josephine and Eliza would receive their early schooling at the same academy. Martha also opened to them the possibility of becoming nuns by entering the Notre Dame order in 1853. Though she left the sisterhood a decade later, her time in the convent suggested that religion might provide the women of her family with a refuge from racial dilemmas, just as it had the men.

Martha returned to Massachusetts in the spring of 1863, and she once again settled into the familiar and accepting society of Catholic Boston. Because James, now the bishop's right-hand man, was a leader of that community, her position in it was all the more secure. No wonder he could report her to be "happy and content." She moved into the house James had bought in suburban Newton, and, given the family's financial independence, she could afford to be simply "at home." Social contacts were numerous, and soon Martha had met Jeremiah Cashman, whom she married on July 25, 1865; at twenty-seven, she was two years younger than her husband.[2]

Little is known of Cashman. Their marriage record, which identifies James and Sherwood as the official witnesses to the wedding, says simply that the groom had been born in Ireland. Most likely, he had come to Boston as a boy with other famine immigrants in the 1840s. There were several interconnected Cashman families in the cathedral parish in Boston, and he probably settled down among those near or distant relations. Given that James Healy was the rector of the parish, it is a permissible speculation that the couple met at some church function or other. We must assume that Jeremiah knew of his wife's background—as always, Sherwood gave away the family secret—but he embodied the indifference with which Boston's Catholics had come to regard the Healys. He was willing to marry a woman whose racial status would have dissuaded someone else, a woman who, by the standards of the day, was a "mulatto" and therefore off-limits as a life-long partner. There are no surviving photographs of Martha, so we cannot judge her complexion or tell whether she had any of the physical characteristics whites associated with African Americans; most probably she did not.[3] That his wife had "black blood" in her veins was immaterial to Jeremiah; indeed, by marrying her he assisted her identification with white America. She was able to live as a white woman, and he would help her do so.

The newlyweds rented a house on Canton Street in Boston's busy South End, not very far from the new cathedral church, construction of which Sherwood would shortly begin. Jeremiah worked as a salesman for a dealer in trunks and leather goods, and he and Martha started a family. Births came in regular succession, but as so often then, the deaths of those babies might quickly follow. The Cashmans lost their first two children, a boy and a girl, in 1867 and 1868. By 1869, their fortunes changed, and the daughter born on February 25 of that year would live into old age.[4] Eventually, five more children would be born, and three of these (two girls and one boy) would also survive to adulthood. Official records at the time were beginning to classify newborns by race: town clerks in Massachusetts often specified babies who were "other than white," but these children were never given that distinguishing label. Without fanfare or display, Martha Healy Cashman had definitively settled the matter of race for her children.

The growing family moved several times to larger rented quarters. Jeremiah was also advancing to better, more stable sales jobs, and by 1876 he and Martha were able to buy a home of their own in the Jamaica Plain section of Boston. "J.P.," as it was called, offered many of the advantages of the "streetcar suburbs" then emerging outside of town, including new construction, modern household amenities, open space, and lots of grass and trees. It was a suitable address for upwardly mobile young families. Shortly after their last child was born in 1879, the Cashmans continued their progress by moving into a newly built house in Newton, not far from the home James Healy had owned for twenty years but had, by that time, sold.[5] Unlike many immigrants who were attempting to climb out of the working class into low-level white-collar jobs, Jeremiah Cashman seems never to have slipped back down the social and economic ladder, and he and his family lived comfortably. Martha Healy Cashman never worked outside the home, as seemed proper for a woman of her emerging status.

Even so, the size of the family and the demands on Jeremiah's salary sometimes created tension, particularly between Martha and her oldest brother. James had long been accustomed to acting as substitute father for his siblings, and his scoldings had run particularly in Martha's direction since his college complaint about her penmanship in a "very short and poorly written" letter. From a distance, he continued now to keep a sharp eye on her family's finances. Once, under pressure of their first house, Martha and Jeremiah found themselves with cash-flow problems, and James stepped in with a temporary loan, never letting them forget that he had done so. "A little later the family will, like Oliver Twist, call for more," he complained to his attorney. He set up a fund for the education of the children; for a time he even enrolled the girls in parochial schools near him in Portland, though he did not think that this gesture was sufficiently appreciated. If Martha was unhappy with it, he told her once, she could take them home, "and when you do you will all be poorer than you are now."[6] We should not read too much into these petty disputes, common enough in many families. James could sometimes be itchy, but he also doted on the children, proudly noting their progress in school, keeping tabs on their health, and making arrangements in his will for a long-term trust in their behalf. He might occasionally be an officious brother to Martha, but he was a loving uncle to her children.

Of the rest of Martha Healy Cashman's life there is little that can be said. Her daily activities were many, as were those of most housewives of her time. The routine tasks of the home were both demanding and unremitting: doing the laundry was still a job that could take the better part of an entire day, and the persistent chores of preparing meals, sewing, and cleaning filled almost every moment.[7] As she saw to all these duties, she left virtually nothing in the way of documentary evidence. Like other women of her era, she was excluded from the ballot box, so her name appears on no roster of voters. No letters of Martha survive among the papers of the other family members, and only rarely is she mentioned in one of their diaries; she herself apparently never kept a journal. These gaps in the record are disappointing but not unexpected. She was absorbed in the concerns of daily middle-class life: caring for children, keeping house, getting to know the neighbors, seldom venturing very far from home. Her children grew, and the family expanded into subsequent generations: that was her legacy, no less than the buildings left behind by her brothers and sisters.

For its being inconspicuous, however, her life was still extraordinary, since the transit she made across the color line was done alone, without the intervening institution of the church, so essential to the others. Her siblings had had a transitional option between black and white: they confirmed their resolve to be white by choosing first to be priests and nuns. Martha, by contrast, faced only the stark either-or of color, and her choice was one that America's racial rules were not supposed to permit. Moreover, her case runs counter to the experience of other mixed-race Americans at the time. In the decades after the Civil War, the one-drop rule was solidifying more firmly than ever, and anyone with that one drop was presumed to be numbered irrevocably among black Americans. She managed to move in the opposite direction, situating herself, her children, and her grandchildren in the world of white America, their black roots forgotten. Martha Healy Cashman had prepared the way for that amnesia by crossing the color line decisively. By the 1950s, her great-grandchildren would have to be taken aside by their parents and told the unexpected news that there was remote "black blood" in the family.[8]

Many details about the middle of the three Healy sisters are obscure, owing largely to her early death. From what we do know, however, she followed the family pattern of using religion to escape from racial ambiguities. Given the names Amanda Josephine at her birth in January 1845, she was called Josephine or, within the immediate family, Josie. Just five years old when, within months, she lost first her mother and then her father, she probably retained little memory of either of them by the time she was an adult. Taken to New York City, she, Eliza, and baby Eugene were baptized there in June 1851. After Hugh's tragic death two years later, other arrangements had to be made, and the family's first thought was for religious schooling.

With the beginning of the academic year in 1853, Josephine and Eliza entered the elementary school of the Notre Dame sisters in Montreal where Martha had studied. There they were almost literally surrounded by family: James was a student at the seminary located nearby, and Martha had entered the Notre Dame convent that summer. The four probably did not see each other very much—seminarians and young nuns were kept strictly cut off from the outside world and from family contacts—but they were more or less together under the care of the same benevolent church. Josephine and Eliza followed the usual course of study, though James also paid for music lessons in addition to the regular expenses for room and board. By the time they left the school in the summer of 1861, they were, James was pleased to observe, "sweet, pious, and obedient," virtues he valued both as a brother and, by then, as a priest. They might have stayed a little longer but, as Sherwood later told the superior of the convent, "our unhappy war" convinced the family that the girls were better off at home.[9]

Home was the house in Newton, where Josephine and Eliza settled in. Together, they constituted the household of Father James Healy and, after his return from Troy, Father Sherwood Healy as well. The young women ran this household, maintaining the distinction, increasingly important to middle-class Americans, between the private sphere of the home and the public sphere of society. They helped look after the young Eugene, who was already exhibiting some of the rebellious behavior about which the family would worry for the rest of his life. The two sisters cooked, cleaned, and gardened, and they entertained the other Boston priests who spent the occasional day off at the Healy home. They were openly devoted to their brothers, and it was this "silly and undignified" affection that had elicited the disapproval of Hilary Tucker.[10]

Foreign travel was also possible for Josephine and her sister. In 1868, James took them on a five-month cruise of the Mediterranean, a trip that testifies both to the family's aspirations and to its ability to fulfill them: few children of Irish immigrants and even fewer children of slaves enjoyed such opportunities. More prosperous American families, however, had come to think of a European grand tour as the last act of their daughters' girlhood, a chance to see something of the world before settling down. The Healy sisters left Boston right after New Year's with Father James, Mrs. Thomas Hodges ("Mother" to Eugene), and their sister-in-law, Mary Jane, who had married Lieutenant Michael Healy of the Revenue Cutter Service three years before. The midwinter Atlantic crossing was rough, and more than once their beds were awash and their luggage soaked; seasickness plagued all, though the "always kind" sailors offered what comfort they could. Eventually, they got their reward. Sailing past Athens at the beginning of February, they thrilled at the sight of the Parthenon through binoculars. They spent balmy evenings on deck, reading Shakespeare aloud and engaging the captain, "a Universalist in religion," in friendly philosophical conversations. Once at Smyrna in

Turkey, a popular stop for American tourists, they were wide-eyed at the exotic surroundings, touring ancient ruins and attending "a mass according to the Greek rite." Any doubts about their status were dispelled as they were received "hospitably" by the local archbishop and other notables.[11]

The return voyage included a layover of six weeks in Sicily and southern Italy. They went to the opera several times—once, it was Verdi's *La Traviata*—and they took in all the usual landmarks and museums. James had been to most of these places before, so he served as the knowing tour guide, pointing out improvements since his last visit. Only the turmoil of Italian nationalism clouded their pleasure. The traditional processions of March 19, San Giuseppe's Day, for instance, had been converted into blasphemous celebrations of Garibaldi (whose first name was Giuseppe), and this dismayed the Americans, who probably understood little of the politics of it all. "We are edified by the numbers found at mass," one of the travelers wrote, "but were horrified and disgusted at hearing two Italian shopkeepers call the pope a devil and wish his throat was cut." For the most part, however, the mood was light, with the women taking advantage of James's "unsuspicious" nature by playing April Fool's Day jokes on him.[12] By the middle of May, they were home again, with happy memories and the tacit reassurance that their unpromising family origins were now in the distant, unremembered past.

By the early 1870s, with both formal education and the finishing school of foreign travel behind her, Josephine Healy was ready to make some decisions about the rest of her life. The example of her older sister Martha presented marriage as a possibility, and there is no reason to suppose that Josephine had flatly ruled out family life for herself. The stronger example, however, came from her brothers, who were achieving success and even distinction in their religious vocations. Becoming priests had made so many things possible for them, and she thus understood that a life in the church could have its rewards. Through a process of thought that we cannot now reconstruct—and most probably with the prompting of her priestly brothers—Josephine decided to become a nun.

A friend would later identify the Smyrna trip as the turning point in making her decision. While they were on the high seas, this account went, a violent storm came up, threatening imminent shipwreck. In the midst of the tempest, Josephine all at once "understood seriously the importance of assuring the health and well-being of her soul"; safely back home, she resolved to enter a convent. The dramatic tale had surely been embellished over the years. Stories of sudden religious conversion, often amid raging storms, were commonplace from Saint Paul to Luther, and Josephine's decision was probably more gradual than she and others remembered afterward. She also had to decide which group of religious women to join. The nineteenth century had seen a proliferation of Catholic sisterhoods in America. New orders were founded while older ones redefined their mission, most of them de-emphasizing quiet prayer apart from the world in favor of more active involvement in works of charity and education. In Boston alone, by the 1870s there were more than two hundred sisters in half a dozen different groups, each one specializing in its own activity.[13]

More seriously, Josephine's racial status might impede her plans to become a nun. Like her siblings, she herself had consciously passed over into the white community, but others might understand her position differently. Her complexion was "dark," in the opinion of the agent who issued her passport for the Smyrna trip; perhaps, like Sherwood's, it was dark enough to disclose the family secret, but since there are no photographs of her, we cannot judge for ourselves. Her brothers had managed to sidestep this issue in becoming priests, but she might not be so fortunate. Racial consciousness had only intensified since the end of the Civil War, and all-white communities of nuns might not be so willing to take on someone of her background. She had no special patron, no one already in a religious order to smooth her way and bend the rules, as Bishop Fitzpatrick had done for James and Sherwood or as Father Fenwick had done for Patrick. She gave no thought to joining the Sisters of the Holy Family in New Orleans or the Oblate Sisters of Providence in Baltimore, the two orders of black Catholic nuns in the United States. Not only were they far away, but they also represented an identification with the black community that she rejected. Instead, Josephine looked closer to home, to a white religious order, the Sisters of the Good Shepherd.[14]

First organized in France in the seventeenth century, the Good Shepherd sisters had come to America in the 1840s, and soon they had establishments in several major cities. Their work was with prostitutes and unwed mothers, social offenders whose alleged depravity often excluded them from other charities. The Good Shepherd nuns maintained asylums for these women during pregnancy and for their children after birth; the sisters also trained them in useful skills they could take into the respectable workforce. The nuns even accepted vocations as sisters, known popularly as Magdalens after the reformed woman of the gospels, from among their clients, though the numbers in this auxiliary branch of the community were small. Controversial in many quarters—to some, helping "fallen women" seemed to condone the behavior that had gotten them into trouble in the first place—the sisters prided themselves on being "true mothers" to those they helped, and they pioneered many of the psychological approaches to social work of a later era. A House of the Good Shepherd had opened in Boston in 1867, and with the active support of the clergy, it expanded rapidly; eventually, it accommodated a residential population of four hundred women and children. James Healy was a member of its board of directors, and he helped raise $11,000 for construction of a new home in 1873. Perhaps it was through this familiarity that his own sister settled on the Good Shepherd nuns as the community in which to pursue her religious life.[15]

Earlier that year, Josephine had entered the convent as a postulant. Communities of sisters required that candidates move through a prescribed series of steps before final acceptance. Postulants were at the first level of this process, and they devoted themselves to prayer, study, and reflection on whether the religious life was really for them. They were introduced to the group's work and spiritual outlook, and they were scrutinized by the order's officers. If successful, a young woman was advanced to the rank of novice, where she went through several more years of formation before taking her final vows as a member. No records survive of Josephine Healy's postulancy, so we know only that she left the convent of the Good Shepherd sisters after three months. On its face, there was nothing particularly unusual in this hasty departure: almost twice as many young women entered religious life as persevered in it. Since postulants were young, many of them returned to the world as their judgment matured. Josephine Healy's leaving, however, may have had another dimension. One story assigned blame for it to the Good Shepherd superior in Boston, an aristocratic Kentuckian who, it was said, was unwilling to accept this applicant because of her racial ancestry.[16] The explanation is both plausible and not. Predominantly white American sisterhoods did not routinely accept black women until nearly a century later, so Josephine's exclusion on these grounds is entirely possible. At the same time, she was no ordinary young woman. Her brothers were two of Boston's most prominent Catholic priests (one of them a member of the house's board), and if anything this might have made her an object of competition among local religious communities. Whatever the dynamics in this case, Josephine left the Good Shepherd sisters and sought her vocation elsewhere.

She did so by retracing her steps to Montreal to seek advice from the Notre Dame sisters with whom she had spent her school years. In those familiar surroundings, the sisters introduced her to a priest who had a reputation for wise counsel in such matters. His English was poor, however, and her own command of French still too rocky for so important a discussion, so he sent her to a more fluent colleague. This priest was encouraging and, according to a later account, then and there "she determined not to return to her family." The order she chose was the Religious Hospitallers of Saint Joseph, and she entered its large complex of buildings, known as the Hotel Dieu, on November 21, 1873. This group was also French in origin, and its first sisters had come to Canada with the earliest settlers. As their name implied, they specialized in nursing, and they staffed institutions for the sick poor throughout eastern Canada. The largest of these was the Hotel Dieu itself, the only hospital in Montreal until the 1820s and one that was pioneering such innovations as sterile operating theaters, a medical and surgical college, and even private rooms for patients. After a short stay at another convent of the Hospitallers in New Brunswick, Josephine Healy returned to Montreal, where she would live for the remaining years of her short life.[17]

In many ways, this was the oddest possible choice for any American woman seeking life as a sister, for the Hotel Dieu had a controversial history, not in Canada but in the United States. Few Americans had ever been there, but many thought they knew it, and only too well. In the 1830s, amid rising anti-Catholicism, a grisly image of the Hotel Dieu had taken hold in the American popular imagination. A young woman with the too-apt name of Maria Monk appeared on the lecture circuit, claiming that she had been held against her will in the place, and she thrilled audiences with lurid tales of what went on inside. Secret passageways, she reported, permitted lecherous priests to sneak into the cloister and have their way with pious young sisters, and the babies born of these passions were first strangled and then buried in the cellar. In January 1836 Monk's story (ghost-written for her by several Protestant ministers) appeared in book form under the title *Awful Disclosures of the Hotel Dieu Nunnery*, and it was an immediate sensation; eventually it sold more copies than any other book published before the Civil War except *Uncle Tom's Cabin*. Thinly disguised pornography, it offered detailed, if fanciful, floor plans of the convent showing trap doors, a "priests' gaming and feasting room," and just enough "secret compartments" and "unknown" chambers to make it all seem real. The nativist fervor had died down long before Josephine Healy's entry, but the Hotel Dieu still had a reputation to live down.[18]

Ignoring all that, Josephine was happy with her decision. Religious vocations for women were often described in language that emphasized the similarities with marriage, and that is how she saw her calling. She "betrothed her heart" to God, one of her fellow sisters wrote, and when in December 1875 she professed her final vows, the ceremony was understood as a kind of wedding. "She was not everything that she wanted to present to the Divine Spouse," a narrative of the ceremony said, using the conventional language of such occasions, but still she "offered completely her own will, an immolation which for her was no small thing." Her brother James, by now the bishop of Portland, had even traveled to Montreal, in effect to give away the bride. Josephine had to struggle against "her natural independence," an officer of the sisters wrote later, an independence that derived partly from her relatively comfortable circumstances. The sisters made oblique reference to her parents, "distinguished both by their social position and their wealth," a description that suggests that the nuns either did not know the whole story or were complicit in covering it up.[19] No less than her brothers, she would now be effectively married to the Catholic church.

From the scanty evidence of her time at the Hotel Dieu, she entered fully into the routines of the convent and the hospital. If outsiders thought that nuns led peaceful lives of contemplation, her experience presents another picture. Once, she wrote a cheerful letter to her brother Patrick at Georgetown, enthusiastically describing her "mode of life." All the sisters rose at about five in the morning and spent an hour in prayer and meditation. Then it was on to the "service of the poor," the patients in the wards, bringing them breakfast, making up the beds, and doing other chores. Only then did the nuns take their own breakfast, followed by mass and recitation of the prayers of the day. By the middle of the morning they were back attending the patients. The afternoon was spent in much the same fashion, alternating the work of nursing with brief periods of communal prayer. At noon and again in the evening, they had the chance for "recreation," which consisted of walking around the grounds in groups of two or three. By nine o'clock they were in bed, resting in anticipation of similar rigors the next day.[20] Their duties were decidedly unglamorous, and it would be decades before many of the Hospitallers got formal nursing instruction and later still before any of them were trained as physicians. Even so, with several hundred patients to care for, the demands on them were constant.

At the beginning, Sister Josephine Healy seemed destined to follow this unremarkable routine for years, though she and others may have thought that the family's administrative talents were hers as well. She was one "on whom we based our very best hopes," a member of the order wrote after her death, and that may have portended a larger role for her. Such a course did not materialize, for within two years her health began to give out. The precise nature of her ailments is unclear, but some of Sherwood's frailty apparently troubled Josephine as well. By May 1879, James was informed that his sister was "beyond hope of recovery," and several times in the next few weeks he was summoned from Portland to attend what was presumed to be her deathbed. Death finally came for her on Wednesday,

July 23 of that year, and he arrived the next morning to preside over her funeral and interment in the crypt that held the bodies of the other sisters of her community. She was only thirty-four years old.[21]

Speculation alone must suffice for what Josephine's life might have been. Had she lived to a normal old age, she could well have advanced within her community. She may not have risen to the top of the Hotel Dieu itself, but there were other opportunities in the growing network of hospitals opened by the sisters in the next half-century throughout Quebec, Ontario, and New Brunswick. Had she lived another three or four decades, Josephine too might have manifested the drive that marked her siblings. As it was, she died young but no less accomplished, for she had achieved the hardest goal of all. Born legally into slavery, exposed to the threat of actual enslavement by her parents' deaths, she grew into a life untouched by those dangers. She had managed to reinvent herself. When her religious sisters remembered her family as "distinguished both by their social position and their wealth," they confirmed the Healys' rewritten memory. Her parents had indeed been wealthy, but "distinguished" was never a word that could be applied to her mother's social position without irony. In her own way, Josephine Healy had contributed to the work of recasting the family's history.

❧

The mother for whom she was named had died when Eliza Healy was barely three years old; soon her father too was dead. She almost certainly carried no recollection of either of them into adulthood. Eliza's early years were spent largely in tandem with Josephine, and the landmarks in Josie's early life—the rescue from Georgia, the schooling in Montreal, the adolescent years in Newton, the Smyrna trip—were similarly important to Eliza. Seldom in these early years do the two girls stand out distinctly from one another. A school notebook of Eliza's from 1859 and 1860 survives, but it offers little sense of her as an individual. Begun when she was twelve, the slim volume allowed her to practice her penmanship and her catechism lessons at the same time. Every week she copied out an essay on a religious subject, concluding each with a short prayer. Such exercises no doubt helped her become the "sweet, pious, and obedient" child her brother James later praised.[22]

This practice in devotion may have disposed Eliza from an early age toward a vocation as a nun. By the early 1870s, as Josephine was entering the Hotel Dieu, Eliza too returned to Montreal, and after consulting some former teachers among the Congregation de Notre Dame, she decided to join their community. She knew them well, having boarded with them as a student and observed their work at close hand. Her sister Martha's years as a Notre Dame novice may also have encouraged Eliza to see these sisters as extensions of her own family. As with Josephine, we cannot capture Eliza's thinking about the possibility of marriage and motherhood, but by April 1874 she had ruled them out. Just six months after Josephine joined the sisters at the Hotel Dieu, Eliza entered the Notre Dame convent, located nearby in the district of Montreal known appropriately enough as "Monklands." A bit homesick at first, she had had "a pretty hard struggle" leaving Boston, Josie wrote to Patrick at Georgetown, but she was firm in her resolve. Two years later, in July 1876, having been given the name "Sister Saint Mary Magdalen" by her superiors, Eliza made her formal declaration of vows, signed the necessary legal papers, and began her life as a nun.[23]

Religion was, in effect, the Healy family business by this time, but even so, Eliza's choice, like Josephine's, was more radical than that of their brothers. The two girls had decided not merely to forswear the secular world in general; they also separated themselves from the land of their birth and moved to what was, after all, a foreign country. They did not have to give up their United States citizenship, but they were implicitly turning their backs on their own country. Hereafter, their affiliation with the larger international community of Catholic religious women counted for more than national loyalty. From then on, Eliza's daily affairs were conducted largely in French, the vernacular tongue of the Congregation de Notre Dame. Many anglophone women from "south of the border" were joining this community, and they were welcomed: as the sisters opened new schools throughout eastern Canada and the United States, they needed nuns who were bilingual. Still, French rather than English was now Eliza's first language, and that represented a sharper break than her brothers had made with the nation that had defined them all, at birth, as slaves. She was not deliberately emulating those slaves who had once escaped to Canada for freedom, but like them, she put her past behind her.

If her decision was a turn away from the past, it was also a turn toward opportunities within the order that had become perhaps the most important community of Catholic sisters in Canada. The Congregation de Notre Dame had been in Quebec since the seventeenth century; two hundred years later, its influence across the country was expanding geometrically. Numbering only 80 sisters in 1830, there were more than 1,200 by the end of the century. Equally impressive was their expansion of services. Always committed to staffing schools for girls, the sisters were in increasing demand: during Eliza's years with them, they would open a hundred new academies, thereby tripling in size. The sisters' prestige was likewise growing. At a time when educational opportunities for women were still limited, the nuns offered what one contemporary called "the most complete education that persons of better quality could desire," and their schools attracted young women from the leading families in French Canada. They may even, their most recent historian argues, have played a role in the development of feminism in Canada because of the self-confident, independent values they inculcated.[24] Eliza Healy had joined no confined community of demure nuns. Rather, this was a group that placed demands on all its members, eager to identify those who could contribute to its ongoing success.

As with all the Healys, we must wonder what her companions knew about Sister Saint Mary Magdalen and her background. Some knowledge of the family may have survived among the older nuns who had known her as a girl, but the healing passage of time that Patrick had experienced now worked to the advantage of Eliza as well. Her origins had become helpfully obscure. "She belonged to a family of rich planters from Texas," her death notice would say years later. Her precise birthplace—Texas? Georgia? Where, to these Canadian sisters, was either of those places?—apparently mattered less than the family's wealth. Her physical characteristics were unremarkable, though since her image was never captured by a camera, there is uncertainty. In contrast to Josephine, whose complexion was described as "dark," Eliza had "light" skin, a passport agent thought. Thus, those who met her for the first time probably had little reason to suspect anything out of the ordinary. More important, she came to the convent with powerful endorsements. "She did not lack," the later memory of her continued, "for protectors among the high clergy" of the United States, including Boston's Archbishop Williams. The sisters probably knew little of him directly, but someone who came as the protégé of an archbishop was sure to be welcome. The religious vocations of her siblings were also known, and they too served as strong testimonials for her.[25]

Having professed her vows in the summer of 1876, Sister Saint Mary Magdalen was ready to embark on a career in teaching. Catholic schools in Canada had always been numerous, especially in Quebec and, to a lesser degree, in Ontario and the Maritimes as well, and sisters were set to work almost immediately. Notre Dame nuns were better prepared for this work than those of other religious orders. Their Villa Maria in Montreal was similar to the "normal schools" then emerging on both sides of the border, offering formal courses of teacher training. These lasted only a year or two, and thus a nun barely out of her teens might soon find herself in charge of a packed classroom of students not much younger than she. In such circumstances, she relied mostly on a standardized curriculum and on instructional techniques learned from more experienced teachers. Her position as a sister enhanced her authority, and that command was reinforced by her distinctive garb. Dressed in a black habit and a peaked bonnet that covered all of her head except the face, with a large rosary draped from her belt, a Notre Dame sister was an imposing figure to her students. With so little of the face exposed, it was difficult even to know how old a sister was, and the younger ones profited from that indeterminacy in keeping order. Eliza Healy was older than most—she was thirty years old when she began teaching, whereas others in the order might be barely twenty—but she too relied on the status that came with her choice of vocation.

Her first assignment was in Brockville, Ontario, a town about a hundred miles up the Saint Lawrence River from Montreal. There had been a parish elementary school there since the 1850s, and the Notre Dame sisters took charge of it in 1878; in August of that year, Sister Saint Mary Magdalen was sent to it with two more experienced nuns. The accommodations were "far from satisfactory," according to the sisters' understated report, and the equipment "most inadequate." Hasty partitions marking off classrooms were put up in an old building, and the nuns borrowed some spelling and other textbooks from the local public school. Since there was no place for them to live, the parish priest moved out of his rectory into a boardinghouse, and the sisters took up residence in his stead. Brockville was a predominantly non-Catholic town, and many of its inhabitants were curious about "our strange manner of living," one sister said, so Eliza and her companions set out to make friends. At the end of the regular school day, they offered music lessons and needlework classes for the girls of the town, regardless of religious affiliation. Besides building goodwill, this also helped make ends meet: sisters often conducted such after-school programs for the income they generated. Eliza left Brockville after only three years, but by then the place had begun to thrive. Soon, the parish constructed a handsome new school building, and eventually the sisters, hired originally to teach only the girls of the parish, began to teach the boys as well.[26]

Sisters were regularly reassigned by their superiors, especially in their first years. Change always came at the end of the summer: a sister might be preparing to resume classes, only to get word that she was off to somewhere else, more or less immediately. Such transfers became the pattern for Sister Saint Mary Magdalen during the next few years. From Brockville, she went first to the booming town of Sherbrooke in Quebec, one of the largest English-speaking settlements in the province, located just north of the border with Vermont. There, amid the scenic "conifers and maples" noted (perhaps with some dismay) by the community's chronicler, the Notre Dame sisters presided over an expanding empire: an acad emy they had run for thirty years was overcrowded, and Sister Saint Mary Magdalen was part of a contingent sent to open a second school. Then, in 1886, she returned to Montreal, teaching successively in three different parish schools, followed by a year in Ottawa, the national capital.[27] In all cases, her language skills proved helpful. The population of Irish immigrants was growing in Canada, and many of the children in Catholic schools needed to take their lessons in English. Sister Saint Mary Magdalen was able to work with these children, and this gave her a chance to demonstrate her many abilities.

Those skills, and perhaps her ties to the "high clergy," contributed to her advancement. In fact, since her brother James was now a bishop, her association with that "high" clergyman was proving useful. As early as 1880, Eliza was dispatched to Portland with another nun to talk to him about opening a school in the mill town of Lewiston. As James's sometimes strained relations with the Sisters of Mercy had shown, discussions of this kind could be tense. Bishops wanted to exert as much control as possible over the sisters' work, while the nuns wanted to maintain their autonomy. In this case, the superiors of the Notre Dame order hoped to smooth their way in Maine by involving the bishop's own sister, and their plan seemed to work. "Prospects favourable," James said after their first meeting. Normally, he was a tough bargainer on such occasions, but he proved more tractable here, and an agreement was struck to bring in the sisters at the start of the next school year. "A competent number of English-speaking nuns" would be available, he was assured, and he even hoped that Eliza "may be of the number," but that possibility did not play out. The leadership in Montreal prudently decided that it was best not to place the sister too close to the brother, and this was probably wise: within two months, Bishop Healy was complaining about the superior at Lewiston, while Eliza returned to her classrooms in Canada.[28]

By 1895, after more than twenty years in the community, Sister Saint Mary Magdalen was ready for promotion. Religious orders such as hers had an elaborate system of administration, arranged in hierarchical layers. At the top, a superior general and a governing council at the motherhouse in Montreal were elected to fixed terms and exercised general supervisory authority. Each local convent had its own leadership, appointed by the superior general and charged with responsibility in more immediate matters. The superior of each convent had to pay the bills of the place, usually without assistance from headquarters, and this often took some doing. Sisters received a small salary from the parish—almost always insufficient to cover expenses—income that was applied to common needs, since the individual nuns had all taken vows of personal poverty. Schools charged tuition, but because most students came from poor and working-class families, there were natural limits on these fees. Local superiors always had to watch their budgets closely, while maintaining the property and keeping enrollments above the break-even point. Not every sister was cut out for the job, but whenever one showed managerial skills, she was appointed to the rank of local superior. This would usually be in a smaller establishment at first and, if successful there, she moved on to larger and more demanding positions.[29]

Eliza Healy's later career proceeded in this way, beginning in 1895 with her appointment as the superior of a convent and school in Huntingdon, Quebec. Located in a tight angle of land formed by the Saint Lawrence River and the New York border, Huntingdon was not really near anyplace, but the tiny farming settlement had had a Catholic parish and school since 1862 in a town where, the order's historian noted, "Protestantism reigned as master." Managing such an operation had its challenges, but this was a small enough world that a new superior might safely learn her duties on the job. The mundane tasks of Sister Saint Mary Magdalen's two years at Huntingdon remain undocumented. She probably felt the daily pressure of uncertain finances, and worked to build good relations with the people of the region, those local "masters" who went to a different church. As far as we can determine, she was a success: she even helped secure Huntingdon for the future, talking her brother James into contributing to a fund for its maintenance, a prospect that may not have been far from the minds of her superiors in sending her there in the first place.[30]

Having proved herself, she returned to Montreal in 1897, spending a year as superior of a school in the middle of the city. This was one of the showcases of the Notre Dame sisters, an academy that commanded the loyalty and affection of generations of alumnae. That the order's leadership showed no hesitation in giving her this prominent position mirrored the ease with which her brothers' patrons had advanced them. Eliza had long since overcome any disadvantage on account of her origins; she had put behind her any thought that her racial heritage might disqualify her from leadership. If her birth into slavery was remembered anywhere in the order by then, this appointment signaled that it was immaterial. Next, she returned to the Villa Maria motherhouse and spent several years teaching in the normal school there. This interlude was probably a welcome one, exchanging the cares of business for the ideals of the classroom.[31]

Capable women were always in demand, however, and in the fall of 1902 she was hastily sent to Chicago to address a growing crisis there. For twenty years, the sisters had had charge of the school at Notre Dame parish, a church of French Canadians in a city where other ethnic groups were far more numerous. For a while, the school flourished, with more than five hundred pupils, but by the time Sister Saint Mary Magdalen went there, the forces of urban change were taking their toll. The French-speaking population was moving out of the neighborhood on the West Side, replaced by Italian immigrants for whom the sisters could do little. The French Canadians were "drowned" by these newcomers, their chronicler said, a verb that indicates that this was not a happy experience in a parish that had traditionally been "theirs." No amount of experience could turn back the tide, and Eliza left after only a year of struggle; a decade later, the Notre Dame sisters withdrew from the parish altogether, leaving the school in charge of an order of Italian-speaking nuns.[32]

In the fall of 1903, at the age of fifty-six, Eliza Healy took up her most important position, becoming superior of an academy in St. Albans, Vermont. St. Albans (pronounced "Snawlbins" by the locals) was a railroad town on the shores of Lake Champlain about thirty miles above Burlington. It had garnered national attention only twice. In October 1864, a Confederate "raid"—actually, a string of bank robberies by Southern sympathizers—had permitted the town to claim distinction as the site of the northernmost battle of the Civil War; a few years later, a band of Irish American Fenians had gathered there with the plainly crazy intention of bringing down the British Empire by invading Canada. Life had been more tranquil since, but the town's religious history was interesting. There were a number of conversions into the Catholic church, led by the rector of the local Episcopal parish, who even became a Catholic priest after the death of his wife. Joining him in what one observer called (perhaps ironically) an "epidemic" of conversions were most of the members of his Episcopal congregation, including the family of the town's most prominent citizen, Bradley Barlow. In 1870, the Catholics bought a house just off Main Street and opened it as a school, christening it "Villa Barlow" in honor of its benefactor. The Notre Dame sisters arrived to teach that winter, and they remained in charge at the time of Eliza Healy's appointment just over thirty years later.[33]

Her assignment was to put the place on an even footing. Several debts remained outstanding, though the mortgage holders were generally lenient. Enrollments fluctuated annually, and these needed stabilizing. During Eliza's first years there, as many as 280 pupils—boys and girls in the lower grades; girls only in the higher—were under instruction, but with just nine sisters it was necessary to hire lay teachers as well. By 1910, she set a cap of 230 students, and this proved sustainable thereafter. The students came mainly from town, but there were some accommodations for boarders from farther afield. Besides elementary and secondary instruction, there were evening classes for young adult women and afternoon catechism lessons for parish children who went to the local public school. As usual, Eliza also had to meet the occasional emergency that came with managing property. The school was located at the foot of a long hill, for example, and the spring thaws periodically sent water rushing into the cellar. Her students later remembered her as strict, but that alone hardly distinguished her from other sisters. Some traits were particularly her own. Colleagues described her as "a model superior, the perfect mistress of a house." She knew how to balance exactness in academics and discipline with a concern for such matters as a healthy diet and regular exercise for sisters and students alike.[34]

The daily routines of Eliza Healy at St. Albans had little in the way of grand historical significance, but in them we can observe a professional career that was rare for women of her era. Countless details had to be attended to: replacing the convent floors, buying laboratory equipment for the science classes, worrying over the fuel bill, responding to an influenza outbreak. Sometimes there were tensions with the local pastor. Just before Christmas 1909, the school put on its annual holiday concert, "the proceeds of which are always claimed by Father O'Sullivan," one of the sisters wrote with evident disapproval. More often, relations with the local clergy were happier: the pastor sponsored summer outings on Lake Champlain, and when he died, the sisters' grief was genuine. Sister Saint Mary Magdalen encouraged extracurricular activities, always showing up at school plays (scenes from Shakespeare were the usual offerings), formal teas in which the girls could show off their manners, and on one occasion "a Basket Ball match" against students from the town public school (who defeated the Villa Barlow team by the score of 7 to 6). She was occasionally called away to Montreal, New York, and elsewhere to consult with leaders of the Notre Dame order on various matters. At home she was noted for her willingness to pitch in with any work that needed doing, menial or otherwise, and for giving in to only one indulgence: puttering in the garden and orchard behind the convent.[35] When she left Vermont in the fall of 1918 for a Notre Dame convent and school on Staten Island in New York, she was prepared for a peaceful retirement there.

Taken together, Eliza and her own sisters, Martha and Josephine, had earned the right to expect historical appreciation and maybe even admiration. While their brothers had overcome one of society's great disabilities, they had overcome two. Martha's passage into the white community through marriage had been quiet and private, but it was no less impressive for that; indeed, her life was extraordinary precisely for being so ordinary. All around her, the rules for determining who was black were hardening, rules intended to keep people like her in a subordinate position. She ignored those rules but suffered no consequences. She defined herself into the white community, and that identity was carried on by subsequent generations, including the reluctant Bessie Cunningham, who had feared investigation of the family in the 1950s. Without fanfare, Martha Healy Cashman accomplished the very thing that the American consensus about race was supposed to preclude. If even a suburban housewife, a woman without the assistance of powerful institutions, could defy society in so critical a matter as this, anything might be possible. Perhaps the all-important distinctions of race really meant nothing at all.

Josephine and Eliza Healy exhibited more evident parallels to their brothers, for like them they used their religious identity to replace a problematic racial identity. For these two, the Catholic church, that unlikely ally of their brothers, also provided a way out. Moreover, the convent gave Josephine and Eliza the chance for career and success, together sufficient to set racial ambiguity aside. With Josephine, early death cut off the prospect for advancement of the kind her siblings had. Given their drive, however, it may be an allowable speculation that she too would have achieved prominence. With Eliza, there is no need to speculate, for her adult life was, in its way, a typical American success story. Born into uncertainty, she achieved many things in the work she had chosen. That choice was unusual and its opportunities unexpected: outsiders probably thought the convent confining, both a literal and a figurative retreat from the world. Yet, it was her place of liberation. There, Eliza had a career equal to that of her brothers James, Sherwood, Patrick, and (in a different sphere) Michael. Against powerful odds, all three of these women were able to seize control over their own lives and destinies.

CHAPTER TEN

The Captain: Michael

"I am not much of a Christian," Michael Augustine Healy told a friend in 1893; "don't know as I care to be an over zealous one, but I respect everyone's motives and beliefs, though their methods and ways of thinking may be different from mine."[1] In thus declining to be identified by religion, he was not explicitly contrasting himself with his brothers and sisters, but he might just as well have. They were priests and nuns, after all, and he might indeed seem "not much" of a Christian by comparison. In fact, he was probably understating his own religious disposition: he remained what was called a "practical Catholic" his entire life, observing the demands of his church as regularly as he could. It was nonetheless true that he was not defined by religion as his siblings were. He never considered the priestly vocation that came so readily to his brothers, striking out instead on a very different course.

Perhaps, however, he was not so unlike the rest of them. His native ability and drive brought him to the top of his profession just as surely as they had risen to the top of theirs. He too passed over a color line that was supposed to restrict him to a lesser place in American society. Early on, he had felt the insecurities of being an interracial child in a country where such people were dangerous aberrations. He had been present with Patrick in the 1850s when both were on the receiving end of "remarks" from his fellow students. When he ran away to sea a few years later, he distanced himself from those insults. By the time he secured an officer's commission in the Revenue Cutter Service in 1865, his racial status had been settled. Aided by his light complexion, he entered fully into the world of white America, and as his career took him thousands of miles away from the darker Sherwood and James, his racial secret remained secret. It had to be that way. A firm grasp on whiteness was essential, for although the institution sheltering his siblings was willing to overlook their racial transformation, the institution he had joined was not so forgiving. His choice of career made him an exception in the Healy family, but he also confirmed its racial rule.

A life on the sea made sense from a number of perspectives. His successful early experiences on commercial vessels—never shipwrecked, as he had pointed out— had developed his aptitude for the work. More important, he had entered a world in which the rules of race were looser than they were on land. African Americans had long sailed on deep waters, especially in the fishing and whaling fleets, and there they developed both a sense of their own community and a degree of integration with the white world. Life as a sailor imparted what one scholar has called an "occupational identity": a black man's abilities as a mariner, whatever his rank, overrode his position in the American racial order. Even so, Michael's "true" racial identity might block his advancement. None of the political friends of his brother James who had supported his promotion had mentioned this dangerous subject, and that silence had to be maintained. As Michael rose through the ranks, the political realities of American society were changing, to his possible detriment. The doors of opportunity that had cracked open in the immediate aftermath of the war were everywhere slamming shut. Discriminatory attitudes were being "nationalized," and the confinement of black and mixed-race Americans to inferior positions was becoming ever more rigorous.[2] If Michael Healy was to make his way in the Revenue Cutter Service (RCS), it had to be as a white man.

Several important changes were just then coming to the agency that was eventually renamed the Coast Guard. The work was much as it had been since the service was established in 1790: patrolling coastal waterways, collecting customs duties, intercepting smugglers, and assisting commercial ships that met with accident or disaster. In all, there were about three dozen steam and sail cutters, most of them on the Atlantic and Pacific coasts but with a sizable contingent still on the Great Lakes. For all that, the service did not enjoy a good reputation. In contrast to the Navy, it was often dismissed as a "pleasure fleet," and the ridicule was not completely groundless. Shore-bound customs inspectors regularly demanded that revenue cutters shuttle them around, often with friends and relations aboard. Officers were appointed with the help of political connections—as, indeed, Mike Healy had been, though often with far less experience at sea. All this changed in the early 1870s with the appointment of a new head of the service. Sumner Kimball, originally from Maine, began an overhaul that bolstered both the image and the reality of his department. He weeded out deadwood: as many as one-third of the captains and other officers were let go immediately, and stricter physical and seamanship examinations were instituted, with merit the firm basis for promotion. Older vessels were sold off and newer ones commissioned, ships that could be managed by smaller, more efficient crews. Together, these reforms created a congenial atmosphere for ambitious young officers like Healy.[3]

His early career was unremarkable. A normal tour of duty was two years, and he spent that period on a succession of vessels in ports of the East Coast: Newport, New Bedford, New York City. The work was seldom adventurous, but it was steady. Off Rhode Island in 1871, for instance, he participated in the seizure of five thousand illegal "segars" smuggled in from the Caribbean, and a few weeks later he organized removal of a sunken vessel blocking a shipping channel. A first lieutenant by then, he periodically took the helm of the ship, gaining command experience. These early assignments also permitted him to visit now and then with his family in Boston, including his wife, Mary Jane, who remained there. Their only child, Frederick Aloysius Healy, was born in October 1870, and the proud father saw the baby as often as his duties permitted. Lieutenant Healy sometimes went to RCS headquarters in Washington, where he could visit his brother Patrick at Georgetown.[4] The early rebelliousness that had so worried James and Patrick was gone, and Michael's energy was instead channeled into the responsibilities of work.

The assignment he got in the summer of 1874 dropped Michael Healy into the very different surroundings where he would spend the rest of his life. In July of that year he was ordered to join the crew of the cutter *Richard Rush,* based in San Francisco, a part of the small revenue service fleet that patrolled the waters off Alaska. The United States had purchased the vast land from the Russian czar in 1867, and few Americans had much of an idea about what to do with the place. An army post at Sitka, far from the bulk of the territory, was the only governmental presence, and after it was abandoned in 1877, a single customs collector was the sole official in more than half a million square miles. Institutions of civil government were entirely absent—as an afterthought, Congress passed legislation twenty years later applying to Alaska the laws of Oregon, then the nearest state— and settlement was fitful and slow. An informal census in 1880 counted a population of perhaps 33,000, of whom less than 500 were settlers from "below." The frontier in the continental United States was gradually filling up during these years, but Alaska was still very much an open, unsettled territory.[5]

The Revenue Cutter Service filled the vacuum created by the neglect of other agencies. Overnight, it became the only force for law and order in Alaska. The real power there was the Alaska Commercial Company, a diversified business formed to exploit untapped natural riches, and the revenue cutters often found themselves supporting the company's many interests. The American whaling fleet had

Mary Jane Roach Healy. Photo courtesy Thomas Riley.

been in the treacherous waters of the Arctic Ocean for decades, and whalers were particular objects of the service's supervision and assistance. Illegal seal hunting was common in the Bering Sea, and revenue ships tried to restrain its abuses as well. Basic exploring and mapping also had to be done. One cutter was immediately assigned to Sitka, and other vessels from the RCS Pacific fleet were increasingly drawn into this work, their routines taking them farther and farther north each year. Their resources were always inadequate to the task—even when as many as three vessels could be assigned to Alaska duty, the huge distances thwarted effective law enforcement—but the officers and crews of the revenue ships represented the American presence as no other institution did.[6] Relocating with Mary Jane and young Fred to San Francisco as his home port, Michael Healy took up this work, first on the *Rush* and later aboard its sister ship, the *Thomas Corwin*.

The mission of the revenue cutters may be described in a few words: they sailed around looking for trouble—that is, the trouble into which others had fallen. In the summer of 1880, for instance, the *Corwin*, with Lieutenant Healy aboard, set out to find the *Jeannette*, a missing exploration ship that had gotten stuck in the ice almost immediately upon arriving in the Arctic. The *Corwin* went out after it but got caught in the severe floes for a time itself, never reaching the explorers, who abandoned their ship to the elements. Along the way, the *Corwin* managed to gather important ethnographic data on Alaska's native peoples. It also began to document the overharvesting of the seal population, thereby contributing to a growing consensus for stricter controls on that trade. In other years, it would pick a spot at the mouth of a river and anchor offshore. Then it sent small parties upstream in launches, beginning the massive task of drawing reliable maps of the coastline and the interior. "This is a miserable country to cruise about in," Healy wrote after one such mission, "miserably surveyed and full of hidden rocks + reefs not down [on] the charts."[7] His work helped fill those voids.

In the summer of 1881, when Healy was still a first lieutenant, he was given command of the *Rush* for its annual cruise. Captains were not always available, and putting lieutenants in charge allowed the service to test their readiness for promotion. That August Healy took the usual route up the coast from San Francisco before striking out across the open seas for the RCS base on Unalaska Island, almost dead center in the long half-moon of the Aleutian chain. That leg of the trip took just ten days, Healy proudly reported, beating the best time ever made by the *Corwin*. From there his ship inspected the seal islands in the Bering Sea and Strait, monitored commercial and whaling ships, and noted the increasing impact of Americans on the area's resources. He observed the effect that white adventurers were having on the Inuit and Aleut natives, and for the most part it was not good. The introduction of alcohol, especially a potent and hideous concoction known as "quass," was distressing. The natives drank it "to an alarming extent," Healy reported, often "for months at a time," spending all the money they earned, "neglecting children and becoming totally and wholly depraved through its use." He was also eager to show off his seamanship, making detailed recommendations for outfitting RCS ships and crews with all the zeal of a rookie. "I am young in command," he admitted to a superior, "and hope you will not think that I am making too many suggestions."[8] His work impressed the service, and at that point his promotion became more or less inevitable. In March 1883 it came, and he was advanced to the rank of captain, with the *Corwin* now his own.

After two decades, he had risen to the top. For the next three years under his command, the *Corwin* did the prosaic work of the Arctic. So strict was Captain Healy in enforcing the rules against liquor trafficking that, he noted with pride, the *Corwin* was known among the natives as the "no-whiskey ship." Even more

Captain Michael A. Healy. Photo courtesy
National Archives and Records Administration.

important were its explorations in 1884 and 1885. While Healy remained anchored at Hotham Inlet, just north of the Arctic Circle, a party led by Lieutenant John C. Cantwell went hundreds of miles upstream along the Kowak and Noatak Rivers in search of a possible overland route to Alaska's north shore. No such passage was identified, but the two expeditions surveyed widely and brought back useful observations on the geology and wildlife of the interior. There were the usual rescues to be done: returning to California in the fall of 1884, the *Corwin* carried nearly one hundred passengers (mostly men from stranded whaling ships) in addition to its own crew. Healy was eager to spread word of this work, preparing reports to Congress that brought the revenue service's exertions to the attention of the public. "I desire to express the satisfaction I feel," he wrote, "in being able to be of service to citizens who have interests in these Arctic seas."[9]

Healy's growing prominence in Alaska came to seem normal, but all his success depended on maintaining anonymity amid publicity. No one could be allowed to know that he contradicted the logic of American racial categories, for exposure

risked all. White American attitudes toward blacks' place in society were hardening, and that place surely did not include the command of a ship. How could a
black man be permitted routinely to give orders to white men, who were, after all,
superior to him by definition? However much African Americans had found work
and even equality with whites in the commercial fleet, there was still a low ceiling
above which they could not rise on government ships. All government agencies,
including the Revenue Cutter Service, were increasingly inhospitable places. At
West Point in 1880, for example, a black cadet from South Carolina was tied up
and beaten by his classmates, in spite of the light complexion that had kept his secret for a while. The victim was even twice convicted of staging the whole incident
himself and was dismissed from the academy.[10] In such a context, Michael Healy
could have no future in the revenue service were his racial origins to become
known. Of course, there were blacks and even Asians aboard revenue cutters, but
they were the cooks and cabin boys. Healy's higher aspirations depended on his
remaining distinct from them; he had to be ranked with whites.

   To do so, Mike Healy relied on the habits of long years to secure his position in
the white community. His fair complexion and his Irish surname, his white wife
and child, and his apparently white brother Patrick—all three went along on his
maiden voyage as a captain in 1883—confirmed that he was white and not black.
Even the language he spoke reinforced this identity. Virtually everyone in Alaska
presumed that there were only two kinds of people there: natives and "white
men." True, there were some "half-breeds," as Patrick and others had noted, but
they were simply another kind of native. Captain Healy adopted this same language, and he left no doubt about where he belonged. To an official in Washington, for example, he described the hazards faced by isolated parties of "white
men," whom he casually designated as "our people." The clarity of that position
he even passed on to his son. During the cruise of 1883, the thirteen-year-old Fred
Healy went ashore on a remote island with his father, who carved the lad's name
into a rock. That night, Fred proudly boasted in his diary that his was "the only
white boy's name that has ever been there."[11] No less than his siblings, the Michael
Healy born into slavery half a century before had left one racial category behind
and successfully assumed a different one. Anything he hoped to accomplish
would have been impossible otherwise.

ℒ❧

In April 1886, after three years as a captain, Healy had what might be considered a
second marriage, this time to a ship. The *Bear* had been built in Scotland as a
whaler, but it was purchased by the U.S. Navy in 1884 for use in a rescue mission

Fred Healy. Photo courtesy Thomas Riley.

off Greenland. Having proved its suitability for northern duty, the Navy trans-
ferred it to the Revenue Cutter Service the next year, and it sailed from New York
to San Francisco to replace the *Corwin* as the mainstay of the RCS Alaska fleet. It
was big (nearly 200 feet long), heavy (700 tons), tough (hard oak with iron sheath-
ing), and fast (8 knots under sail, 10 with steam). Healy, by now one of the most
experienced navigators in the north, first thought it too much for work there: its
draft, he feared, was so deep that ships carrying contraband might elude it by staying in shallow water. Once in command, he changed his mind. Midway through
his maiden cruise, he proclaimed it "very efficient and serviceable," concluding
that "for ice work" it was "undoubtedly the best vessel in the Arctic Ocean." In no
time, the *Bear* became the most famous ship in the revenue service.[12]

Between 1886 and 1896, the routine of the *Bear*'s captain and crew of nine officers and forty men was the same every year. After wintering in San Francisco Bay
(usually berthed at Oakland), they set sail about the first of May, working their
way up the coast to a refueling station at Port Townsend, Washington, before
turning northwest to Unalaska. Then they sailed north to the Pribilof Islands

(Saint George and Saint Paul) and past the larger Saint Matthew and Saint Law-rence Islands, through the Bering Strait. By then they were above the Arctic Circle, clinging to the shoreline as they went around Point Hope to the very top of Alaska, where the whaling fleet was active. Heading east, they made for Point Barrow, the northernmost tip of land, but not always making it that far if the ice was heavy. Under the best of circumstances, the polar pack was never more than about ten miles offshore, even in July and August, leaving a very narrow chan-nel in which to operate. Good seamanship was essential, especially in the fogs that drifted in for days on end. "No one unaccustomed to Arctic navigation can fully appreciate the importance of extreme watchfulness, care, and judgment," Healy wrote. "The general contour of the land is unchanged for many miles," and it was difficult "to establish the identity of certain points and thus the position of the vessel." Healy might sometimes sail west in search of the lost or stranded, touch-ing at various points in Siberia and as far northwest as the icebound Wrangel Island. By the middle of summer, the floes began to get heavy, and the *Bear* had to break for home if it hoped not to be stuck for the winter. Repeating its stops at the various islands, it usually left Unalaska in early November, arriving in Cali-fornia by the end of the month.[13]

Much of the *Bear*'s attention was devoted to protecting the region's natural re-sources, especially the seal population. In the face of rising demand for fur, the seals were threatened with extinction, especially in the waters around the Pribilof Islands, the breeding areas to which animals from all over the Pacific returned during the summer months. Whereas the natives had killed seals by the simple (if brutal) method of rounding them up and clubbing them, Americans and Rus-sians adopted a more prodigal approach. Particularly destructive was pelagic seal-ing—that is, hunting them on the open seas. A ship steered into a swimming herd, and every available man aboard fired into it with rifles or shotguns. Those seals that were killed outright almost immediately sank to the bottom, irretriev-able, while the wounded swam away and died later. Only a small percentage of those killed was recovered for skinning and sale. Worse, the toll on females had a multiplier effect: when a seal mother died, so too did any pups she was carrying at the time, together with live pups ashore, who took food only from their own mother. The death of every female that was shot thus resulted in the deaths of at least three others, according to one estimate. In the thirty years after American ac-quisition of Alaska, almost 100,000 seals were destroyed annually. To avert im-pending ecological disaster, RCS ships were under standing orders "not merely to obstruct but to prevent the taking of seals in the Bering Sea."[14]

The *Bear* set to this assignment with vigor. The Pribilofs were sparsely inhabited—less than three hundred people on both islands—but their craggy coasts
meant that scofflaws might lurk anywhere. Often, a crewman was put ashore for
weeks at a time to intercept poachers, who simply waited for the cutter to leave before starting their hunt. On the open ocean, whenever Healy spied a ship thought
to be taking seals, he pulled alongside, trained his cannons on it, and sent two
armed officers aboard. In August of 1893, for instance, a party boarded the British
schooner *Ada,* out of Shanghai, and found more than 1,800 skins. The *Bear's*
coxswain was put in command of the lawbreaker, and he sailed it down to Sitka,
where the skins were impounded and the captain fined. Piecemeal efforts, however, could not dent the illegal business. The distances alone—the islands were
sixty miles apart and nearly two hundred miles from Unalaska—meant that illegal hunters had vast stretches of ocean in which to operate. There were other difficulties too. British ships complained, rightly enough, that these were international waters, and it was not until pelagic hunts were outlawed by treaty that the
problem was seriously addressed. It was very nearly too late: between 1875 and
1890, the seal population was diminished by almost 80 percent, and it has never
entirely recovered.[15]

Of even more pressing concern to the *Bear* was the American whaling fleet. By
then, the business of hunting the ocean's giants for their oil, which had many
commercial uses, was at the end of a long decline toward extinction. In 1880, for
example, American ships took just 34,000 barrels of whale oil, down from more
than 140,000 barrels twenty years before; whereas there were 125 whaling ships in
1885, there would be only 40 by the turn of the century. Still, the trade hung on,
though ships had to venture ever farther from their home ports, mostly on the
East Coast of the United States, in search of their prey. Alaskan waters were the
primary hunting grounds, and the *Bear* had to be constantly on the lookout for
whalers caught in the thickening ice, especially as the summer advanced. The
lucky ones simply drifted in the floes for a while before freeing themselves; the less
fortunate were caught fast, and it was then just a matter of time before the ice
crushed the ship to pieces. Because these vessels had American owners and
crews—often including significant numbers of African American and Cape
Verdean sailors from places like New Bedford, Massachusetts—the Revenue
Cutter Service offered whatever assistance it could.[16]

The logbooks of the *Bear* are full of encounters with the whaling fleet. In 1886,
Healy's first year aboard, the exceptionally cold summer had trapped fourteen
whalers "all fast in the ice" as far south as the Pribilofs. The *Bear* itself was some-

times caught too, but its size and weight enabled it to escape, usually after a day or two of "backing and going ahead"—simple language that understated the hard labor this represented for the cutter's men. They towed the ice-bound ships to clear water when they could, and they took the crews back to land if the whalers had to be abandoned. Often the *Bear's* men assisted in repairs, now helping to replace a propeller, now loaning an anchor to a ship that had lost its own. Dramatic rescues were commonplace. In June 1894, for example, Healy had no sooner arrived at Unalaska when word came in that the *James Allen* had gone down off the outer Aleutians. Its captain and six of his men had rowed a lifeboat 130 miles across the open sea in search of aid for ten others whom they had had to leave behind. The *Bear* set out at once and found nine survivors. "They were all in a weak and emaciated condition," Healy reported, "and their bodies covered with sores and vermin." The cutter's doctor took quick preventive measures. "Their clothes were thrown overboard as soon as possible as a sanitary precaution," Healy continued, "and hair cuts, hot baths, and dry clean clothes were given them." Then they were put aboard a ship bound for San Francisco, though most were probably back at whaling within a few months.[17]

These acts of rescue and assistance earned Mike Healy a wide public prominence, and he came to symbolize the commitment of the revenue service to help anyone in distress in Alaska. "The Arctic ice never closes for the winter until Capt. Healy has said his good-bye" and left for home, the *New York Times* reported in 1895. West Coast newspapers delighted in covering his escapades, numbering him among "the bravest and kindest officers in the national service." Mary Jane Healy, who often went along on his summer cruises, kept a scrapbook of press clippings, lovingly documenting the publicity. "I assure you," she told her diary on one occasion, "it delighted me much to see so much respect paid to my husband." The captain himself was uninterested in fame. "As to a wish for notoriety," he wrote a friend, "I don't care a rap"—an expression he had probably cleaned up a bit before putting it on paper. More important to him was the good name of the *Bear:* "professional pride would be dead if I was indifferent to the record of my vessel." Either way, his distinction grew. The owners of whaling ships commended him as "beyond all praise," calling him "the right man in the right place at every critical time."[18] The praise was no less genuine for its exuberance—and, of course, none of it ever made reference to his race or background, matters unknown to those who lauded him.

Healy was equally famous among the native peoples of Alaska, and justly so, for he was as ready to assist Inuits and Aleuts as his "own" people. "White men in this country . . . seem to think that the law was not intended to apply to them, only to

Indians," he wrote on one occasion, adding dryly: "I try to convince them other-wise." He was "always kind" to natives, his brother Patrick had observed while aboard the *Corwin* in 1883, "and thus makes them think well of Govt. ships." Kind-ness was not the only motive. Healy offered supplies to isolated villages, and he distributed presents to natives who had taken in shipwrecked whalemen and helped them survive until the *Bear* could come to retrieve them. One village was lavishly rewarded with 800 pounds of bread, 250 pounds of flour, and 40 pounds of pork in gratitude for looking after a stranded man for two years. Healy also helped local leaders with their own problems. In July of 1893 he landed at a settle-ment that was terrorized by "a native named Nanoogah, whose reputation among the people here is that of a bully and who is reported to have murdered another native some years since." Village leaders were at a loss for what to do about the man's "aggressiveness and thieving and general cussedness," but Captain Healy knew just the thing. "I confined him in single irons"—that is, handcuffed him to a stanchion on the *Bear*'s deck—"for two days as a warning to others of his kind. . . . My action may seem arbitrary," he acknowledged, "but it is the only remedy," and it was effective: thereafter Nanoogah behaved himself.[19]

Two particular problems of law enforcement among Alaska's natives occupied much of Healy's attention: liquor and guns. Whiskey had been a problem from the very beginning, and Healy had seen what might happen when those unused to the stuff fell so completely under its spell. In one village, he was shocked to discover that there were no children, "reproduction having entirely ceased through drunk-enness." He was convinced that the introduction of liquor derived solely from "the white man's greed for gain," and its ill effects were only too apparent. Total prohibition was the law in Alaska, and the revenue service had to enforce it, how-ever imperfectly. Every year, the *Bear* destroyed stashes and broke up stills. On one occasion, Healy "found 5 gal. keg whiskey in storehouse and let it run out"; on an-other, his men discovered twenty gallons in a whaler's forecastle, the captain protesting ignorance about how it had got there as it was thrown overboard; on yet another, a cache of gin was destroyed in a native village. The danger was just as Healy had observed early on: the native appetite for intoxicants was so "alarm-ing" that "if they are not stopped in their downward course [, they] will become in a few years a race of decrepit paupers on the government."[20] Paternalism of this kind was common among Americans in Alaska, and Healy shared it fully. He him-self would later come to grief over demon drink, and that turmoil would give ret-rospective irony to his crusades against liquor; for now, he carried out his re-sponsibility as fully as he could.

American officials were also eager to keep firearms, particularly breech-loading rifles, out of native hands. Whites feared that the normally docile natives might become aggressive if they had modern weapons, and Healy was not deaf to this concern. "It is true," he reported, that "the natives are, during the presence of the vessel in their midst, gentle and peaceful; but I believe they would not hesitate to take advantage of a small number of white men" whenever possible. Thus, he seized guns and ammunition all the time: seven rifles here, eight thousand cartridges there. Still, even as he enforced this policy, he disagreed with it. Keeping rifles from the Inuits not only put them at a disadvantage with irresponsible whites; it also made routine hunting unnecessarily difficult. "Anyone at all familiar with the use of arms knows how difficult it is to charge a muzzle loading gun," the only kind natives were permitted to use, especially "in cold weather," Healy pointed out. Yet, Inuits were "obliged by law to depend upon this weapon for their principal means of obtaining food and clothing where game has been largely decreased by the very people who forbid them the use of modern arms." The injustice of it all angered Healy, and he argued unsuccessfully for a repeal of the ban: "I believe that no good argument can be adduced for keeping these weapons out of their lawful reach."[21] So long as that was the law, however, he continued to seize the illegal guns whenever he found them.

Healy's sympathies with natives never undermined his sense of the distinction between them and "white men" such as himself. His observations about the peoples of the polar regions were always filtered through his sense of the distinction between the civilized and the uncivilized. Inuits had many characteristics he found trying. "They are the most persistent beggars I have ever seen," he said irritably, "and they never eat their own food as long as they can beg that of the white man." Too frequently, they interrupted important work. "Every vessel cruising in the Arctic is visited by the natives, and inflicted with their presence. They often remain twenty-four or even forty-eight hours at a time on board." Tolerance of native pestering was unavoidable, since Americans in the Arctic often had to rely on their assistance, but that did not make the cultural interaction any smoother. Even the captain's family shared these opinions. Fred Healy proclaimed that the natives were "the dirtiest people I ever saw," and his mother too fell readily into the language of comfortable superiority. Mary Jane thought that whites had to "care for these people as they would for so many children," and Mike agreed. These natives were more tractable than the Indians of the continental states, he observed, and "with proper fostering care on the part of the government they may become fully civilized" and accustomed to "our methods of living."[22] Had they all been closer to the civilization they praised, the captain and his family might have faced resistance to their own inclusion in "our methods of living." Instead, the simple distinction between native and white in Alaska worked to their benefit.

For all his impatience with "primitive" habits, Michael Healy was genuinely interested in Alaska's people, and he demonstrated this through an unusual project. The onrush of white settlers had disrupted the stable economic and social patterns of centuries, as the stocks of wildlife were steadily depleted. Maintaining even a meager standard of living was difficult in many villages, and the decline was increasingly apparent every year. A reliable source of food had to be found, and Healy and others hit independently on the solution of introducing domesticated reindeer into the territory. During expeditions into the interior, revenue service officers had noted an abundance of lichens and tundra vegetation that could support herds, and this held out the prospect of native self-sufficiency. The reindeer reproduced quickly, and herders could use their meat for food and their skins for clothing. Moreover, deer had advantages over dogsleds as a means of transportation, since they ate whatever they found along the trail, eliminating the need to carry provisions for them, as one had to do with dogs. Healy also knew from his stops on the Siberian side of the Bering Strait that the natives there had herded reindeer for generations. Why not introduce the same practice on the American side? Precisely who had first come up with the idea was the subject of later dispute, but Healy cared little for that: "if the thing succeeds, I will be amply repaid," he wrote. By 1890, a plan was taking shape, with Healy and the *Bear* at the center of it.[23]

In this work, Healy found a formidable ally in a man named Sheldon Jackson. A Presbyterian minister from New York, Jackson was a short, near-sighted dynamo who, after long missionary years in the Rocky Mountains, had come to Alaska in 1884. Well-connected in Washington, he was a close friend of President Benjamin Harrison, a devout Presbyterian layman, and Jackson used his powerful acquaintances to good effect, securing appointment as superintendent of public education for the territory. In personality, he and Healy were about as different as they could be —the one serious and intense, the other with the flamboyant rough edges of a career seaman; the one addressed respectfully as "Doctor Jackson," the other known far and wide as "Hell-Roaring Mike." Nevertheless, they became fast friends. Every year, Jackson was usually aboard the *Bear*, moving around the region on his various duties and joining the extended Healy family. "I think the Captain has come to the conclusion that to have a minister on board is a great advantage," a teasing Mary Jane wrote Jackson after his debarking on one trip, "for we have had, since we parted from you, only a succession of storms."[24]

During the winter of 1890–1891, as the *Bear* sat at the dock in Oakland, Healy and Jackson laid their plans. Unsuccessful at securing a government appropriation, Jackson managed to come up with enough private money to get the project under way; for his part, Healy mapped a strategy for buying an initial reindeer herd from the Siberians. "You know how slow and uncertain the natives are to deal with," he told his collaborator; "everything will have to be experimental." The next summer, the *Bear* went north as usual, and by the middle of July it was anchored at a village of Siberian Tchuktchi natives. Healy, Jackson, and Lieutenant David Jarvis ("without doubt the most reliable officer I have ever had," Healy said of him) went ashore to bargain, but they encountered immediate resistance. The Tchuktchis were willing to sell as much meat as the Americans wanted, but their shamans had warned against selling live reindeer for transport across the water. At this point, Healy's reputation saved the day. A herdsman named Koharra, whose son had once been treated for gangrene by the doctor of the *Corwin* when Healy was in command, intervened as middleman on his friend's behalf. Koharra proposed that he buy the deer from the herders and then sell them to Healy; thus, if any spiritual harm came of the transaction, it would fall on him rather than the village. This proved acceptable, and five animals—"beautiful creatures and gentle as lambs," Mary Jane Healy thought—were cut off from the herd and taken aboard the waiting *Bear*.[25]

For the next several years, this transaction was repeated over and over, and the importation of reindeer into Alaska became a regular part of the *Bear*'s work. It was no mean feat. After purchase, the animals were brought down to the water's edge and their legs hobbled. Herders and crewmen then joined forces to lift the struggling critters one by one into a launch, which ferried them out to the ship waiting offshore. At that point, sturdy bands were passed under the animal's stomach, and it was winched aboard and deposited in a temporary pen in the hold. The smell alone must have been fearsome, essentially converting the cutter into a floating barn. Then they sailed east for a couple of days to the Alaskan shore, where the whole business was replicated in reverse. Young deer took to the trip very badly, and many died along the way, apparently from seasickness. The area around Teller and Port Clarence, settlements on the Seward Peninsula, proved best for offloading, and this became the center of the project. Young Inuits were recruited near each "reindeer station" and put under the charge of white instructors, who were recruited and maintained by the revenue service.

This aspect of the project gave Mike Healy the opportunity to do something for his younger brother. Eugene Healy was the baby of the family, born in 1849, barely a year before his parents' deaths. In this clan of achievers, Eugene always stood out as a slacker. Little is known about him, except that he was a lifelong worry to his brothers and sisters. He never completed much schooling, and he drifted from job to job, sometimes as a "commercial traveler," an occupation with an unsavory reputation. More than once, he borrowed money from his siblings to pay off debts (perhaps from gambling), and sometimes he found himself on the wrong side of the law. Once, in 1876, James had gone to Boston on business, only to find Eugene in jail for some unspecified misdemeanor. There, the inmate felt his brother's cold displeasure. "Found that his liberation was possible," James wrote, indicating that he could be bailed out, "but left him there until repentance should come." Apparently, it never did. Eugene tried his luck in the west, venturing to Utah for a while, but soon he was back in Portland, trading on James's name. After trying to help him find a job, the bishop gave up. "I have thought over your coming," James wrote him formally in 1884. "I can only say that, if on my return to Portland from a journey I find you here, I shall be compelled to publish a disclaimer of any connection or responsibility. Furthermore, I request you not to come near the house or institutions of your brother, James Augustine Healy, Bishop of Portland."[26]

Perhaps recalling his own early rebellions, Mike Healy was more sympathetic, and in 1893 he tried to secure an appointment for his brother at the reindeer and rescue station at Point Barrow, the very top of the Alaska mainland. Eugene had been "unlucky of late," the captain wrote to Washington, understating the case, but he was "as honest as the sun [and] a thorough gentleman." The young man had put in an application for the post, but the best he could offer for qualification was to say that he was a good bookkeeper: "I am competent to render a strict and accurate account for any and all property that may be placed under my charge." In the end, someone with better political connections claimed the job, and Mike Healy backed off, telling his superiors that he did not want to push, given the "delicacy" of the case.[27] Eugene continued his spotty career in Boston and New York, and he eventually disappeared from the lives of the rest of the family.

Meanwhile, Mike Healy took pride in the reindeer project. From a total of only twelve animals brought over the first year, the deer multiplied. In 1893, for example, the *Bear* made five trips back and forth between the continents, importing as many as 175 animals. By then, Healy was ready to proclaim the work a modest success. "The experience of two years has demonstrated beyond a doubt that the purchase in Siberia and the transportation to Alaska of domestic deer is possible, feasible, and practicable," he reported. "The deer, when once landed on our side, grow more vigorously and thrive better in Alaska than in Siberia." The herds prospered, though uncertain congressional support in later years meant that the project was not, in the end, as successful as Healy and Jackson had hoped. Still, they had devoted enormous amounts of time and energy to the work of improving the lot of Alaska's people.[28]

❧

Without anyone realizing that he did not meet the accepted definition of the term, Michael Healy had easily become the most famous "white man" in Alaska. His comings and goings were always good ink for the newspapers. In the far north, he was "a good deal more distinguished," the *New York Sun* reported in 1894, "than any president of the United States or any potentate of Europe." Ask anyone in the Arctic, the paper went on, "Who is the greatest man in America?" and the answer would invariably be "Why, Mike Healy." Once, an "innocent" from the effete east saw Healy on the street and asked who he was; "he's the United States," came the succinct, and essentially accurate, reply. His reputation for vigorous law enforcement was widely praised. "There is no government official so well known along the shores of the Alaskan peninsula and the Arctic Ocean as Captain M. A. Healy," a San Francisco merchant captain wrote to Washington. "By the law abiding people he is greatly respected and admired. . . . To the law disturbing people Captain Healy's name is a terror, for they well know his word is law and he is never known to fail in executing the warning which he gives to that class."[29] After ten years in the Arctic, however, Healy's career was drawing to an abrupt and unhappy climax.

His troubles derived in part from his personality. His was an aggressive, nononsense approach to everything, and he had a quick and violent temper: "my Irish disposition," he called it. Those traits won him as many enemies as admirers. "I have made no small number of evil wishers," he told the head of the revenue service in 1893. "I never return home without the chance of a suit in court." Another man might worry about such things, but not Healy: "I do not care," he said in his typically plainspoken way. If he could be peremptory with lawbreakers, he could also be brusque with his own crew. On any other ship, the *Bear*'s green doctor wrote in 1889, "you are not afraid to laugh and look pleasant, while here you are afraid to do anything for fear of getting a blowing up." A captain's power was virtually unlimited. "No landsman could have dreamed," Herman Melville had written in his novella *Benito Cereno,* that in the ship's commander "was lodged a dictatorship beyond which, while at sea, there was no earthly appeal." So much authority transformed a man "into a block, or rather into a loaded cannon, which, until there is call for thunder, has nothing to say."[30]

Healy was just such a loaded cannon, quick to respond to any provocation. The *Bear*'s logbooks are filled with examples of his swift justice: "At 6:00, confined Bowen and Fitzpatrick, seamen, in single irons for drunkenness. Confined T. Gibbons, fireman, in double irons [that is, shackles on his ankles as well as his wrists] for insolence to an officer, and for using threatening language." Even minor disturbances might arouse his wrath. On one occasion, with his wife aboard, a fight broke out between two seamen during dinner. "You can imagine how provoked the Captain was," she wrote to Sheldon Jackson, who had probably witnessed these outbursts himself. Though theirs was a lasting and affectionate marriage— Mary Jane was "blue" whenever apart from him, she said—Healy could even turn his temper on those closest to him. By the end of the cruise of the *Corwin* in 1883, with Mary Jane, Fred, and Patrick Healy as passengers, relations among them were strained. Patrick learned to steer a wide course around his brother, who was sometimes "exceedingly unpleasant." Moodiness might throw Michael "back upon himself and his grievances," the Jesuit noted, "much to the discomfort of others." Safely returned to port, Patrick witnessed several explosions between husband and wife, including one occasion when Michael stormed away from home for four days before returning to beg forgiveness. "I hope all may go better now," Patrick wrote optimistically.[31]

Exacerbating Mike Healy's temper was a weakness for liquor that apparently lasted his entire life. The clinical notion of alcoholism was unknown at the time, but this may indeed have been his condition. Strong drink had long been a part of the seafaring life, of course, and it remained so in Healy's day. "We have a fair crew but terrible drinkers," he said of the men on the *Bear* one year, "and it has been h—l controlling them. If I discharged one for drunkenness I would have to discharge all." Still, spirits had their uses aboard ship: the appropriately named "grog" helped keep otherwise unruly sailors docile during long and tedious voyages. Healy himself more than once succumbed to its numbing consolations as a way of forgetting the "grievances" (perhaps a memory of the youthful "remarks") that Patrick had mentioned. The only blemish on his otherwise spotless service record was a reprimand for drunkenness in 1871, when he was a first lieutenant based in Newport, Rhode Island. The details of the incident are obscure, but his punishment was the embarrassment of standing on the cutter's deck in front of the entire crew while the rebuke was read aloud. The sentence could have been worse: Patrick Healy seems to have called on some political friends in Washington to use their influence in staving off a more serious penalty.[32]

Since then, Michael's backsliding with drink had been regular, though not frequent. On one trip, the ship's doctor said that he had to send "three decanters of *medicine*" to the captain's cabin, and that Healy's tongue was often "so thick that it would hardly work." The doctor was a pious Methodist, repelled by any consumption of alcohol and inclined to overstate its abuse, but Healy himself recognized his problem. During his years with the *Bear*, he took the temperance pledge at least twice. "I honor your frankness and admire your friendship," he wrote in 1890 to Captain Leonard Shepard, the commander of the Revenue Cutter Service and a fellow veteran of Alaska duty, "and pledge to you by all I hold most sacred that while I live never to touch intoxicants of any kind or description. . . . You can in future rely upon me as being strictly *teetotal*." Like many well-intentioned drinkers, Healy was not always able to keep his promise, and his personality could change markedly when he weakened. "I never knew a man whose wits and tongue sharpen so under liquor," Patrick noted after one of his brother's benders.[33] Eventually, these lapses gave the captain's enemies the opening they needed.

In March 1890, the matter came to public notice, as Healy was tried before a court-martial in San Francisco. The charges against him stemmed from an incident in the Arctic the previous summer. The *Bear* had aided an American whale ship, the *Estella*, whose men were refusing to work and threatening mutiny. Healy seized the ringleaders and subjected them to a punishment known as tricing. It was a brutal and agonizing procedure. The offender's arms were handcuffed behind his back and a hook run through the connecting links; he was then hoisted up by the wrists until only his toes touched the surface of the deck. Hanging in that position was blindingly painful, and if the man succumbed to the impulse to put his feet down on the deck for relief, his arms were bent even further back and the pain redoubled. Permanent damage to the shoulders was almost inevitable. One of the *Estella* mutineers was subjected to this punishment twice—once for five minutes, the second time for fifteen—and two others hung in midair for fifteen minutes apiece; another fainted at the prospect that he too might be triced. "It is not a customary treatment," Healy acknowledged later, "except on frontier places." In San Francisco, he pointed out, a policeman could simply haul a troublemaker off to jail, but in Alaska there were neither policemen nor jails, and summary justice was the only kind. "We are empowered by Congress to suppress mutinies," he said coolly: "I thought I was doing my duty."[34]

He had a point, but it was a technical one. Tricing was indeed still permissible according to the rules of the revenue service, but its use had become practically unknown. Healy was within his authority in resorting to it, but it was rare enough to raise questions nonetheless. Compounding the objection, however, was the charge that he had been drunk at the time and, indeed, that he had been drunk repeatedly throughout the entire voyage. One witness testified that Healy had swaggered up to the offenders, sneering at one, "You are very tricky, Alfred," before ordering the punishment with a sly grin: all this seemed to imply that the captain was not in full possession of himself. Several temperance organizations quickly seized the opportunity to make an example of Healy. "I feel very deeply in regard to this matter," an officer of the Women's Christian Temperance Union in San Francisco wrote to officials in Washington, "as it is a test case. If Captain Healy is removed, it will be a check on drunkenness and cruelty in the future." Anti-alcohol crusaders even organized a public protest meeting to denounce Healy, a gathering that featured fiery condemnations—he had assumed "as much power as a Russian Czar!" one speaker thundered—and doleful appearances by his ostentatiously contrite victims.[35]

Healy successfully rebutted the accusation that he had been drunk during his encounter with the *Estella*'s crew. He was helped by the testimony of Lieutenant Albert Buhner, second in command aboard the *Bear*, who had been with Healy long enough to tell "when he touches only one glass." The captain had been "perfectly sober," Buhner said; "otherwise I should not have obeyed any orders. That is understood." Asked whether Healy had been "unfit to transact business," Buhner answered with a firm "No, sir." The three judges found the charge of drunkenness "wholly unsustained," and they also acquitted Healy of exceeding his authority. He had used "every reasonable effort" in the case, and the mutineers had responded "only with insulting language." The court also accepted Healy's argument about the need for speedy justice—"it is evident that discipline must be enforced in these far off seas"—but they did recommend that tricing be officially banned in the revenue service thereafter, as indeed it was. Finally, the court gave the acquitted defendant a general endorsement: "The testimony goes to show that Captain Healy has been a particularly intelligent, zealous, and efficient officer in the discharge of his difficult and perilous duties in the Arctic; that he is humane and kind to his men, and to shipwrecked sailors and unfortunates." Healy was understandably relieved, but the trial had taken its toll. He had suffered "a great deal" by it, he admitted a month later, "more pained at being accused of dereliction of duty than all my other troubles."[36]

Six years later he was less fortunate, and this time the case against him was stronger, not least because it was pressed by his own men. The *Bear*'s cruise in the summer of 1895 seemed entirely normal. They had left California as usual at the end of April, and followed the regular route north. The ice was particularly heavy, so they never made it to Barrow, concentrating instead on other duties. There were half a dozen trips to the Siberian coast, and in July they transported more than a hundred reindeer (a record number for any single month) to the station at Port Clarence. By the time they got back home in November, however, it was evident that there had been trouble all along. Three junior officers—First Lieutenant Howard Emery, Second Lieutenant George Daniels, and Assistant Engineer Levin Jones—brought a damning indictment, charges in which they were joined by Professor Benjamin Sharp of the Academy of Natural Sciences in Philadelphia, who had been aboard collecting geological specimens. The picture they painted of life on the *Bear* was sufficient to empanel a court-martial of four RCS captains at the beginning of January 1896 and to bring Healy before the public again as a man on trial.[37]

The case centered on accusations of repeated, incapacitating intoxication. Healy had been drunk several times on the open sea, the accusers said, thereby endangering the cutter and its crew. Twice he had been drunk in public at Unalaska, and on one of these occasions he had had "a disgraceful altercation with a civilian." The other time, a British ship, H.M.S. *Pheasant,* had invited the *Bear*'s officers aboard for a reciprocal social visit; Healy drank so much, witnesses said, that as he staggered back to his own ship he fell off the dock into the harbor in full uniform, "to the great mortification of officers." The trouble continued after the *Bear* had returned to San Francisco. At about 8 o'clock on the morning of November 28—it was Thanksgiving Day—Healy came aboard from home. Lieutenant Daniels said that he was obviously drunk and spoiling for a fight. For no reason, the junior man went on, the captain first insulted him and then spat in his face; after Daniels reported the incident to Lieutenant Emery, Healy violently called him a liar and had to be restrained. Emery telegraphed Washington, and the captain was suspended pending investigation. His trial began in mid-January 1896 and ran for six weeks, hearing fifty-eight witnesses and compiling nearly a thousand pages of testimony.[38]

The prosecution had little trouble demonstrating that Healy had indeed failed to live up to his vow to be "strictly teetotal," and his own explanations were unsatisfactory. As to falling off the dock at Unalaska, for example, he claimed merely to have tripped: "I knew what I was about, I could walk," though he admitted that "I had taken a drink or two, I could not tell exactly how many." His chief defender, as before, was Lieutenant Buhner, but even that testimony seemed only to support the charges. "He is a drinking man, and so am I," Buhner acknowledged; "we all drink." In that context, the lieutenant's insistence that "I never knew him to be drunk" was less convincing, especially when he admitted to seeing "a few indications," such as bloodshot eyes, of Healy's condition on the fateful Thanksgiving morning. A picture of nearly constant hostility between Healy and his junior officers also emerged. He was a tough captain of the old school, and this rankled some of his men. Healy's attorney suggested repeatedly that the accusers were part of a cabal out to get him, and the defendant concurred. "I play no favorites," Healy said. "I go up there to do my duty, . . . and I expect every officer to do the same." If that made him harsh, so be it: "I do not phrase my words with an 'if you please.'" Sure of himself, he sometimes felt that the men were conspiring against him. "I understood that different officers had been named to watch my movements," he said, "and to note them down in a book. I knew that, . . . and consequently I was a little bit mad."[39]

The trial ended in early March, and the judges ruled quickly. There were nineteen counts against him, and Healy was found guilty of sixteen; he was not guilty of two more, and another was "not proved." The punishment was to be terrible indeed: "that the accused officer, Capt. Michael A. Healy, United States Revenue Cutter Service, be dismissed the Service." Shocked, his friends and relatives immediately began an appeal. "I deeply sympathize with you in your troubles," Sheldon Jackson wrote Mary Jane Healy from Washington; "I had already been to the Treasury Department in the Captain's behalf." From his parish in New York City, Patrick Healy rushed to Georgetown and tried to interest friends of the college in his brother's case. Bishop James Healy contacted the all-powerful Speaker of the House, Thomas Brackett Reed, seeking reversal or clemency. Apparently at Reed's prompting, several congressmen and senators urged a review of the entire proceeding. In the end, it was Mike Healy's own reputation that saved him. After reviewing the case, the judges affirmed that though no circumstances could properly mitigate the punishment, they were willing to relent. Healy's age (fifty-eight), his years as an officer (thirty-one), and his "creditable and valuable service" had earned him some consideration. Accordingly, instead of being cashiered, he was suspended from active duty for four years and placed in the indeterminate status of "waiting orders." His name was dropped to the bottom of the list of RCS captains, and he was subjected to a final humiliation: his condemnation would be read out at a full muster on every ship in the fleet. In June 1896, the sentence was carried out and the case closed.[40] He had managed to survive, but just barely.

He remained in the limbo of "waiting orders" for the prescribed period, occupying his time with occasional work at the office of the Alaska Commercial Company in San Francisco. He stayed away from liquor, taking seriously the court's threat that "if again found guilty of the excessive use of intoxicants during the term of this sentence or thereafter, whether afloat or on shore," he would be summarily discharged. In 1900, he won partial redemption, but it was short-lived. That spring, he was given command of a new ship, the *McCulloch*, which he took to Alaska in the summer. To be back on duty was thrilling, but the memory of happier times depressed him. Sailing between Unalaska and Seattle in the middle of July, he snapped and suffered an extended psychotic episode: "melancholia with suicidal tendency," the medical report said. After speaking sharply to a female passenger, he was tied up by the officers and confined, raving, to his cabin. There, he managed to break the crystal of his watch and made an unsuccessful but messy attempt to slash his wrists. Put ashore, he spent three months in a hospital in Washington state, where he at last came to his senses. His career was spiraling to its end. He was given nominal command of cutters in San Francisco, but his only responsibility was to supervise repairs in dry dock; he took two final cruises to Alaska in 1902 and 1903, and then he retired after forty years in the service.[41]

Healy's last years are perhaps more interesting for what did not happen than for what did. At no time during any of these proceedings and all the publicity surrounding them was mention made of his racial background. No one ever referred to his origins during any of the heated shipboard confrontations. No mutineer or disgruntled junior officer ever used a racial epithet to insult him. His antagonists were certainly not shy. One of the men on the *Estella* had dismissed him aloud as a "son of a bitch"; another derided him as a "bucko skipper," using the contemptuous word common seamen applied to brutal commanders. During the ill-fated voyage of the *Bear* in 1895, Professor Sharp, the geologist passenger, had hotly told Healy to his face that he was nothing but "a God damned Irishman." Another RCS officer, apparently sympathetic to the political nativism of the period, told Healy that he had "no place as an officer of the U.S. government" because he was a Catholic.[42]

The silence of these voices on the matter of Healy's race is powerful evidence that they knew nothing about it. They assumed he was a white man, no less than they. Would they have called him a goddamned *Irishman*, when another word would have been far more demeaning? Would they not have called him a *black* son of a bitch, had they only known that they might? Was there not a more telling disqualification from the service than Healy's religion? Where was the observer eager to point out that trouble, and even madness, was the only thing to expect when a black man stepped beyond his natural "place" and tried to do a white man's job, like commanding a ship? Where was the indignation—elsewhere in the country, it meant swift and certain lynching—at a black man who raised his hand against a white man? It is probably true that people are most honest when they are calling someone else a name; in the middle of an insult, we seldom stop to choose our words, and so it was here. Michael Healy's angry adversaries were blurting out the worst things they could think of in the heat of the moment, and their slurs had nothing to do with race. Their silence on the subject of his race shows that they knew nothing about it.

In missing those opportunities, they unwittingly demonstrated how successful he had been in crossing over the color line. Just as his siblings had done, he had succeeded in re-creating himself. In spite of the pseudoscience and popular prejudice that defined as black anyone with the telling one drop of black blood, Mike Healy had made himself into a white man. In that way, the defeats of his final years may have yielded some personal victory after all.

CHAPTER ELEVEN

The Ends

In life, the Healy family touched every corner of North America. From Boston to San Francisco, from hot and humid Georgia to frozen and forbidding Alaska, from Washington to Montreal, their story played out all across the continent as that of few families did. The geography of death was equally wide-ranging, but its timing was more concentrated. Three of the siblings—Hugh, Sherwood, and Josephine—had died young, at twenty-one, thirty-nine, and thirty-four, respectively. The others lived into old age and died in succession during the first two decades of the new century.

James, the oldest, was first. As the 1890s went along, his pace slowed, but he remained active. He relied on others more and more for "active administration," his term for the paperwork that always needed doing. He indulged the nostalgia of an old man, recalling younger days and revisiting scenes of happy memories. Each year, he wrote his former classmate Henry Brownson to mark the anniversary of their baptism together five decades before. Of that occasion's participants, he reminded Brownson, only three were still alive: the two of them and his brother Patrick. "Passing years do not wipe out the recollection of that day," James wrote fondly, "nor of those who stood with me." More than once he visited Holy Cross College, grown now into a thriving institution. In June 1899, the fiftieth anniversary of his own graduation, he attended commencement exercises, accepting the students' congratulations as alma mater's oldest living alumnus.[1]

A year later, in June 1900, celebration of his twenty-fifth anniversary in Portland brought him public acclaim. Hundreds of civic and religious dignitaries crowded the pews of his cathedral, and there was both an elaborate banquet for them and a more democratic reception for the general public. One local newspaper commended "his executive ability, his good sense and clear understanding"; another extolled him as "a man who would have made his way in any profession, but his life work was to be devoted to higher things." As bishop, he richly deserved "the esteem and respect of the community without distinction of creed."[2] His racial background, entirely unmentioned in reports of the anniversary, mattered no more—if it ever had. He was not a black man or a "mulatto," but rather a Catholic bishop and a community leader.

The rest of that summer was normal, as he visited parishes across Maine and administered confirmation to schoolchildren. One morning, he drove in a carriage to Biddeford to inspect a new church that was being built there. Returning home, he went to bed immediately after dinner, complaining of indigestion. Two days later, a crisis set in, and he fell unconscious. About noon on Sunday, August 5, 1900, he roused enough to ask a priest of the household to administer the last rites. "When he had received them," his brother Patrick wrote, describing the scene as it was later described to him, "with a pleased look, he closed his eyes and never reopened them."[3] Within the hour, he was dead at the age of seventy. He was buried that Thursday, his cortege followed by thousands of ordinary citizens who trailed the procession to the cemetery in South Portland on trolley cars. The Catholic custom of the time compelled humility in death, and so no eulogy was preached. When, a few weeks later, a large Celtic cross was erected at the grave according to his instructions, James Healy was making a final statement about who he had been: an Irish Catholic. That was all.

Captain Michael Healy died four years later. He had put off retiring from the Revenue Cutter Service for as long as he could. Stepping down was difficult for him, as indeed it was for anyone in his position. The service had no pension system: when an officer retired, he gave up his only source of income. More to the point, Mike Healy was a man with few ideas about what to do with himself on shore. His life had been governed for fifty years by the seasonal and tidal rhythms of the sea; dry land was always a bit alien to him. He was not the sort for whom one would expect a long and peaceful retirement.

He could take some consolation in the maturity that had come to his son, Fred. The young man had been schooled back east at Georgetown, thanks to his uncle Patrick, and he found work through the family's many contacts in California. For a while, Fred even read the law in the office of Barclay Henly, the attorney who had defended his father during the court-martial proceedings. First, though, a youthful rebellion had to be worked out, and in June 1896, just after his father's trial, Fred's own turmoil hit the front pages of the newspapers. After several nights of carousing in San Francisco's Tenderloin district, the young man awoke one morning to discover that he was married to a woman who, a report said, "had held her own with him in drinking for a week." When the news reached Patrick Healy in New York, he exclaimed in dismay: "What next?" Happily, everyone involved sobered up, the marriage was annulled, and Fred sailed off to the South Pacific. There he found himself, enlisting in the army in the Philippines at the outbreak of the Spanish-American War. More important, his mother told Sheldon Jackson with evident relief, "he never drinks, which is a marvel to his companions." After the war he stayed in the Philippines for a while, and then he spent a few years in business in Hawaii. Eventually he made his way back to California, where he married (for real this time) and had a family.[4]

Meanwhile, Mike Healy eased toward retirement and death. His last cruise to Alaska in the summer of 1903 as captain of the *Thetis* had been entirely uneventful. There were the usual demands of law enforcement, but his troubles had left him skittish. On one occasion, the master of a commercial vessel asked him to shackle and confine several seamen who were contemplating mutiny or desertion. "I refused to do so," Healy reported, "referring him to the U.S. attorney on shore, and informing him that I would uphold the legal decision of whatever nature it might be." A decade earlier, he would not have hesitated so. By that September he was back home, and less than a year later, on August 30, 1904, he died, a month before he would have turned sixty-five. Short, carefully worded obituaries, discreetly omitting any reference to his rocky final years, were published around the country: "Noted For His Bravery," one headline said, capturing well enough the essence of his career.[5] Burial followed in the Holy Cross Cemetery in Colma, California, just south of San Francisco; Mary Jane would join him there when she died in 1907, and so too would Fred, still a young man at his death in 1912. On the gravestone was a simple legend, summarizing Michael's life as he no doubt would have wanted to remember it: "M. A. Healy, Capt. U.S.R.C.S."

⌇❧

Throughout these later years, it was Patrick Healy who kept the family together figuratively. The siblings all corresponded with him, and he sent the news of each along to the others. Like many people without children themselves, he became intrigued by genealogy, trying to reconstruct the Healy clan in Ireland and trace collateral lines in America. He never attempted to investigate the family of his mother, realizing that that would be impossible and perhaps not wanting to know too much about it. Routine parish duties occupied his time, first in New York City and then at a church in downtown Philadelphia. At the end of 1908, he returned to Georgetown to live in retirement. He followed the news of the day, occasionally confiding political opinions to his diary—he seems to have been a Teddy Roosevelt Republican—but mostly content to watch the world from his window. His health was generally good, with occasional ups and downs. He had suffered some kind of seizure in 1903, but recovery was swift, and he never mentioned a relapse.[6]

Death came for Patrick Healy on January 10, 1910, six weeks shy of his seventy-sixth birthday. He was "a venerable and holy Jesuit," a confrere wrote, "whose life work, spent in the cause of the 'Old College,' was so productive of results that the ever-sweeping winds of time will not carry off on their speeding wings the memory of his career." Neither the melodramatic language nor the mixed metaphor obscured all he had done as Georgetown's president three decades earlier, remaking the school and rebuilding the campus. The rest of his family went unnamed in the obituary, but the characteristic Healy drive was noted by a general reference to Patrick's siblings, "all of whom, like himself, gained distinctions in their chosen walks of life."[7] When he had stepped down as president, he feared that his term had been an unfulfilled failure, but the intervening years had proved that judgment wrong.

Half a century later, the long-suppressed knowledge of his racial background was revealed. In the 1950s, as the civil rights movement gathered energy and many Catholics took a new interest in the African American community, Patrick Healy was rediscovered and hailed as the "Negro President" of Georgetown.[8] How the times had changed. The very aspect of his life that he had had to conceal was now celebrated. At his death, however, none of that could yet be spoken of, and the details of his background were buried with him in the small priests' graveyard on campus. The headstone gave only his name and the three dates that mattered in the life of any Jesuit: his birth, his death, and the date he had entered the order.

$\mathcal{L}$❤

The elusive Eugene Healy was sixty-five when he died in March of 1914. "No one seems to know anything about him," a friend of Patrick's had written. After Michael's unsuccessful attempt to secure him a government job in Alaska, Eugene had fallen back into his pattern of shuttling from one low-level sales position to another. Boston became his home as much as any place was, and he moved through a succession of rented apartments in the South End and Roxbury neighborhoods. He would sometimes disappear from the listings in the city directory for a few years, only to reemerge later at a different address. He apparently had no contact

with the rest of the family after the early 1890s. At some point he married, but neither wife nor children were identified as survivors. He had none of the accom-
plishments of his siblings, except one. By then, death certificates in Massachusetts
included a space where the recording clerk specified the color of the deceased. That
space was filled in with a simple "W."[9] Eugene Healy had been a white man.

Only the two sisters remained now. When Eliza Healy left St. Albans, Vermont,
her order sent her to Staten Island, New York. The nuns had opened an academy
there at the turn of the century, and within a few years it had more than 250 students in a large, new high school building. This success encouraged the sisters to
think about expanding it into a small college for women. Sister Saint Mary Magdalen was assigned there in the fall of 1918, not in an active capacity, but merely as
a wise elder who might offer helpful advice. She stayed less than a year before de-
teriorating health forced her to retire to Montreal, where her career had begun.
On September 13, 1919, after a brief stay in the convent's infirmary, she died at sev-
enty-two. Buried first on the grounds of the Villa Maria school, her body was later
removed to the sisters' vault in the Cote des Neiges cemetery on Mont Royal itself
in the heart of the city.[10]

The self-conscious humility of religious sisters in her era has covered Eliza
Healy no less than the hard Canadian earth. No individual's personality was supposed to stand out; the work of the community always took precedence.
Throughout this period, for example, devotional manuals written by nuns routinely identified the author simply as "A Sister." Portraits of nuns were rare, and
sadly, if there ever were photographs of Sister Saint Mary Magdalen, none survive
today. We must therefore view her through the lens of her work and recognize the
active role she played with the Notre Dame sisters. The order provided educational opportunities that were difficult for young women to find elsewhere, and
Eliza Healy was one of those who made this possible. What the community had
given her—advancement beyond circumscribed conditions, a career equal in responsibility to those of her brothers—she in turn gave to more than one generation of students. Beyond that, she used the home the sisters had offered her to
achieve a more radical social goal, crossing a line that was thought to admit no
passage. For all the meekness she embraced, it was a stunning accomplishment.

The generation of the Healy siblings came to a close with the death of eighty-two-
year-old Martha Healy Cashman eight months later. Martha had continued to live

quietly as a suburban housewife while her children grew and married. Her only son moved to Connecticut sometime in the 1890s and was thereafter lost to family connections. Her three daughters married men from the Boston area and began families of their own. After the death of her husband, Jeremiah, in 1908, Martha moved to Watertown, Massachusetts, to live with her oldest daughter, Agnes, now Mrs. Thomas Gallagher. The two others, Mary Josephine Overton and Elizabeth ("Bessie") Cunningham, lived nearby. Of Martha's old age we know even less than of her early life, but it was probably spent surrounded by her family, growing now with a steady line of grandchildren. When Agnes summoned the doctor in the early morning hours of May 18, 1920, after her mother had suffered a stroke, she provided the information for the death certificate. Martha Cashman had been born at Macon, Georgia; her parents were Michael Healy, born in Ireland, and Eliza Clark Healy, also born in Macon. Just as important were the answers to the three "personal and statistical particulars" that the form demanded: "Female; Widowed; White."[11]

✒

The century-long saga of the Healys may seem a typical American success story; many families have a version of it. An immigrant arrives on the frontier, becomes wealthy through hard work and good luck, and hands on to the next generation a host of new opportunities. Not all families have such uniformly and spectacularly successful children as the Healys, but more than a few have gone from obscurity to prominence in a single leap. To say, however, that the Healys were just another example of a recognizable pattern is to be deliberately perverse, for they were anything but that. Given what we know—or think we know—about the rules governing race in America, their successes should never have come at all. Their violations of law and custom began early, with Michael Morris and Eliza Clark Healy. No legal marriage was possible for them, separated as they were by race and status; to attempt such a thing was to invite fines or jail for all concerned, and so they validated the marriage themselves by two decades of life together. Michael's white neighbors would probably not have condemned him if he had simply kept Eliza as a concubine while being married to a white woman and having a "real" family, as many of them did. But he was genuinely committed to her and she to him; their offspring were the only children of the family, heirs and not slaves. These multiple infractions should have blocked any achievements from the very beginning, but they did not. The parents demonstrated what kind of material prosperity was attainable in a young America, but their story conforms to the national archetype only if we overlook the fundamental challenges it presented to their society.

The anomalies of the Healy family stand out in even sharper relief among the children. Other sons and daughters faced many hurdles, but those before the Healys were higher, for they had begun their lives as slaves. "Chattels" was the word that legally applied to them, classifying them with livestock and other forms of movable goods. They were not really persons; they were property—things— and the laws of Georgia were designed to hold them in that condition. After escaping to the North, they were technically runaways, and we must not underestimate the abiding uncertainty of that designation. We can now only imagine the anguish of the eighteen-year-old Hugh Healy in 1850, just starting out in business in New York City, having to contemplate a return to Georgia to rescue his orphaned siblings just as the Fugitive Slave Law was taking effect. He was the very sort of person the law had in mind: a slave escaped into freedom. If captured, he might be quickly sold into a slavery he had never actually known, but he had to risk that terrible possibility to save his baby sisters and brother from a similar fate. The absence of direct evidence obscures the details of this rescue, perhaps the most dramatic single incident in the entire story of the family. Even so, both his dilemma and his bravery in facing it compel our attention across the years.

Above all, of course, it was the matter of race that remained problematic. Even more decisive than the color of their skin—which, as we have seen, varied considerably from one to another—was the meaning assigned to their blood. They had the fateful "one drop" that was all their society needed to identify their inner essence and to assign them a fixed, inferior place. Biology was supposed to be destiny for them: their blood defined them as African Americans. White opinion about such people was nearly unanimous. The United States Supreme Court had put the matter succinctly in its Dred Scott decision of 1857, a year when the Healy siblings ranged in age from eight to twenty-seven: blacks possessed "no rights which a white man was bound to respect," the court said. Civil war had nullified that judgment, but the underlying assumptions remained in place. Once slaves, the Healys were now simply former slaves, entitled to legal personhood, perhaps, but certainly not to equality. After hopeful experiments in the 1860s and 1870s, their society intensified its means for sustaining their liabilities. The worst of these occurred in the South, where the vote was systematically restricted and violent methods of control became commonplace: lynching, for example, occurred at the rate of two or three per week between 1890 and 1917, one historian estimates.[12] The North was more subtle but no less effective in blocking freedom's promise. Even Boston, home to the Healys, had firm, if largely unwritten, rules governing black life. The local black minister who had been ejected from the whites-only cabin of a ship in 1871, just as Sherwood Healy was building his new cathedral, knew how tentative social equality might be.

Like all of us, the Healys came to see their lives as normal, but doing so required that they ignore much of what was happening around them. James, for example, became bishop of Portland in 1875. The next year, the Supreme Court declared that voting was not a "necessary attribute" of citizenship, paving the way for widespread black disfranchisement; a year after that, federal troops began to withdraw from the South, and attention to civil rights laws came to an end. Patrick went across the country and back raising money for Georgetown in 1878. Three years later, Tennessee passed a new law segregating railroad cars that became the model for Jim Crow statutes elsewhere. Eliza became the superior of a Notre Dame convent for the first time in 1895. A year before, Congress had repealed the Enforcement Act, thereby giving a freer hand to the revitalized Ku Klux Klan. Captain Michael Healy reached the pinnacle of his career in 1896. That spring, while he was awaiting the verdict in his own trial, another verdict came in: the Supreme Court decided the case of *Plessy v Ferguson,* making "separate but equal" the law of the land. In such a context, the lives of these siblings must be understood as anything but ordinary.

Their position was even more complicated than all this suggests, however, for they fell into what was, for Americans, the strangest racial category of all. Today, we rightly avoid use of the word "mulatto." Although it seems to offer a convenient characterization, its origins give it an inescapably pejorative connotation. A Spanish diminutive for "mule," it is doubly offensive, for it both compares a human being to an animal (an often difficult animal, at that) and diminishes further by resorting to the condescending way in which adults speak to children. Contemporaries of the Healys used the word, sure that only mixed-race persons such as they were more dangerous than "full-blooded" blacks. Slavery, segregation, and discrimination depended in the first instance on the ability to enforce distinctions based on complexion: it was essential to know, just by looking, who was black and who was white. Biracial people were threatening because they challenged the clarity of that understanding, and therefore it was all the more important for society to prevent them from perpetrating racial deception. Even if some individuals did not "look black," the theory went, that was what they were because that was what their blood made them. If those who were "really" black, according to the rules, could get away with "pretending" to be white, where would the erosion of racial boundaries end? Was it possible that the distinction between black and white, which seemed to count for everything, actually counted for nothing?

Individually and collectively, the Healy family managed to slip these many constraints. They refused to accept the preemptive definitions of who and what they were, deliberately deciding to be something else. Whereas society was prepared to identify them exclusively with the blackness, however attenuated, of their mother, they chose to identify with the whiteness of their father. They were not blacks or "mulattoes"; they were whites. For Sherwood and James, even with their dark complexions, "the Negro" was always someone else. For the light-skinned Patrick and Michael, "Irish" was the right way to describe their accent or their disposition. For Martha and Eugene, whose features we know only from what others said of them, "white" was the word that applied in death as in life. They had all passed over the color line, a line that everyone in their society was certain could not be crossed.

How was such a thing possible? Just as important, why did so many white Americans assist the Healys in their systematic violation of the prevailing racial code? Their allies were improbable ones. Foremost among these was the Catholic church, as unexpected a home for them as any. Given their origins, these siblings, like many other people on the frontier, might just as easily never have joined any church, let alone that one. Moreover, Catholicism was hardly known for its opposition to slavery. The standing social order, including the ownership of some people by others, went unquestioned. Together with most other American Christians before the Civil War, Catholics emphasized those features of their tradition that counseled docility rather than resistance. Saint Paul's injunction, "Slaves, be obedient to your masters" (Colossians 3:22), got more emphasis than the apostle's equally strong assertion that there was neither "Jew nor Greek, slave nor free" in Christ (Galatians 3:28). Even so, James Healy spoke for most of the family when he expressed his gratitude for their transition from "nothing" to Catholic.

The church was unprepared to be a racial co-conspirator with the Healys, but that is what it became. Bishop John Fitzpatrick first offered a way out by inviting Michael Morris Healy to send his sons to Holy Cross College. Later, he assisted James and Sherwood directly by bending the rules to get them into the priesthood and by promoting them within his administration. Father George Fenwick, descended from an old slaveholding Maryland family, became the boys' teacher and mentor, later smoothing Patrick's way among the Jesuits. The unnamed Canadian nuns who taught Martha, Josephine, and Eliza made them welcome and offered the three girls a double escape from the restrictions of race and from those of gender. Another denomination, perhaps especially one normally associated with African Americans, might not have been so helpful, but Catholicism offered

ironic advantages. Its status as a minority and slightly suspect faith in America enhanced its capacity to assist these representatives of another minority. The Roman
church was to a large extent separated—even self-separating—from the rest of
American society: it had its own distinct systems of preparation, activity, and reward, all operating largely out of sight from nonmembers. For that very reason, it
was a useful intermediary for the Healys in a way that other, more mainstream
institutions were not.

The Revenue Cutter Service played the same role for young Michael. Like the
church, it was a little world of its own. A man might enter it and proceed through
its precisely defined ranks without much notice. Seamanship and ability mattered
most, and they were the principal foundations of identity. Just as his brothers and
sisters took on new selves when they became priests and nuns, so Michael became
a new person once he was an officer in the service. That he achieved his rank in remote Alaska, far from the rest of the country, helped him further, though he was
still wise enough never to risk identification with black America. It was essential
that he be numbered securely among the "white men" of the northern frontier, and
his success was confirmed when even those who cursed him missed their chance to
call him racial names. The separated life of the service was his ally in that transition
just as surely as the separated institution of the church helped his siblings.

The Healys' passage across the color line was no doubt grounded in their parents' economic success. None of their escapes from the manifold disabilities of
their background would have been possible if they had not inherited substantial
material resources. Their father had managed to bequeath his wealth to his children. The moral ambiguities of that wealth, built as it was on the profits from slavery, never diminished, but the Healys learned to ignore them. The siblings enjoyed the prolonged adolescence of schooling, and they could afford homes in the
suburbs and vacations in Europe. They cultivated the bearing and the tastes of the
well-to-do because they were genuinely of that class. James's conservative social
outlook, especially his suspicion of labor unions, was natural enough under the
circumstances. Blacks and persons of mixed race were most often found at the
bottom of the American economic scale, and so the Healys' wealth helped mag-
nify the distance between themselves and such people. Their wealth confirmed
their whiteness.

The ways in which they defined themselves as sexual beings also assisted them
in living outside the usual boundaries. They each had to confront the most powerful taboo of all in American race relations, that against interracial sexuality. The
ease with which Patrick, traveling in the Arctic, spoke disparagingly of "half-

breeds" shows how fully the white American misgivings about "amalgamation" were shared. The three Healys who married all chose white spouses, and that seemed to settle the racial case: white spouses meant that they were white. For the others, religious vocations allowed them to sidestep the problem altogether. To be a Catholic priest or nun meant, of course, to embrace celibacy. By publicly renouncing active sexuality, the Healys could reassure the white community on a very important matter: regardless of what their parents had done, they themselves would not repeat the forbidden sexuality across racial lines. That five of the surviving eight made this choice for celibacy (and a sixth, Martha, had been willing to do so) is a strikingly consistent pattern. For the Healy brothers, chastity was doubly important, for it helped calm the stereotypical white fears of sexually aggressive black males. For the Healy sisters, it opened doors to professional careers even as it closed those to motherhood.

To note the success with which the Healys passed into the white community is to tell only half the story. Their own desire to elude the one-drop rule and its demand that they be African Americans is entirely understandable; not to do so, if they were able, invited a world of trouble. The tolerance and acceptance they won so unanimously from whites is harder to explain. Over and over, they induced a form of color blindness in those who met them. Parishioners did not see black priests when James and Sherwood said mass; they saw priests. Students did not see a black professor when they studied with Patrick; they saw, as one of them said, a brilliant thinker and an able teacher. Schoolgirls did not see a black sister when they sat in Eliza's classroom; they saw a teacher who evoked the usual sentiments of awe and affection. Crewmen and adventurers who cringed before Michael's authority did not see a black captain; they saw a captain. As individuals, the Healys might be appealing or not, sympathetic or not. Terence Powderly found James imperious as the two argued about unions, but the labor leader never indicated that the bishop's racial background had anything to do with it. Mutinous seamen might think Mike a son of a bitch, and they might even say so out loud, but it was his harsh command that elicited the epithet, not his race. Outward appearance turned out not to be everything: public presentation and even performance were as important as genealogy. If they behaved as whites did, they could be whites too. Passing was thought to be possible only in secret, but the Healys demonstrated that it might also be done in public.

This substantial achievement depended on an ongoing refusal to associate in any way with the heritage of their mother. By their lives, the Healys directly challenged the received notions of race, but they accepted them all the same. So long as they signaled that they were exceptions to the definitions of who was white and who was black, they could continue to live in the white world. If they had emphasized the blackness that came to them from their mother, they would have been more dangerous to their white neighbors. If they showed any desire to extend their own racial self-definition to "the Negro" at large, they would have been too radical for whites to accept, and their own exceptional privileges would have been in jeopardy. Like the free black slaveholders—they were such themselves for a time—they had to reassure whites that they were safe: their racial transgressions would extend no further. Thus, the Healys at once undercut the American racial system, and they acknowledged its force; they undermined the one-drop rule, and they were trapped by it.

A century and more later, their choice of whiteness over blackness seems, at some deep emotional level, wrong. Passing remains for us both a controversial word and a suspect idea, though for different reasons than in their day. Then, it implied deception, mocking society's rules by concealing one's allegedly "true" nature. Today, it suggests a lack of pride, a willingness to feel shame about oneself when no shame is warranted. It seems wrong, too, that we should claim blackness for them when they did not, to praise them as the first black bishop or president or captain or religious superior when they wanted no such honor. But to ask this family to fulfill the expectations of a society very different from their own is anachronistic. Faced with their dilemmas and their times, can we say that we would have done things differently, that we would have been bolder? Faced with the powerful forces of oppression that were all around them, would we too not have taken advantage of whatever escape fortune provided?

From the complicated moral terrain of their lives, the Healys speak to an America still struggling with the same quandaries. When W. E. B. Du Bois predicted, in 1900, that the problem of the twentieth century would be the problem of the color line, he was surely prophetic, but we know now that more than a single century will be needed to resolve that problem. As we try, we should note that the Healys' experience is becoming more common. Sociologists tell us that ours is a time when ethnic lines are increasingly unclear. By the year 2050, more or less, the statisticians predict, the United States will be a nation in which no one race (as that term has traditionally been defined) will constitute a majority of the population. The rate of intermarriage—not limited to that across the lines of black and white—continues to increase. Unusual then, the Healys now seem the forerunners of a reality becoming ever more real. Perhaps, then, the lesson they offer is in how individuals can take into their own hands the question of who they are. They refused to conform to society's preconceptions, and with the help of many allies, they managed to escape and to get on with their lives on their own terms.

Without doubt, they offer a powerful and enduring challenge to our notions of what, if anything, "race" is. They refute the persistent idea that groups of people carry immutable traits, transmitted in the blood from one generation to another: "Blacks are like this"; "Asians are like that"—the Healy family puts the lie to such facile generalizations. The physical characteristics often equated with racial identity—skin color, facial features, hair, and so on—continue to matter, affecting what others see or think they see. But such traits mean only as much as we permit them to mean. To the extent that white Americans stopped seeing black people when they looked at the Healys, they subverted the basis for racial differentiation and discrimination. Perhaps we too might break the grip of such ideas.

Of course, not all African Americans in the nineteenth century could pass as the Healys did. Today, fewer would want to and, we might even say, few should. Denying a part of what any of us is seems a betrayal. Still, there may be some hope in what they did. They showed that it was possible to escape the prison house of race. To be sure, simply ignoring the problems of disadvantage will make none of them go away. But we can resolve, as they did, to press on regardless—literally, regard-less. It was not easy for them, and it is no easier today, to challenge the stark American polarity of black and white. It may not even be possible on the larger, societal scale. Any progress, however, toward a society in which all people are valued and none are minimized surely begins with an understanding of the many ways in which individuals and families make sense of their lives, even in the most adverse circumstances. In that, the Healys have much to teach us.

NOTES

Abbreviations

AABO   Archives, Archdiocese of Boston; Boston, Massachusetts

ACHC   Archives, College of the Holy Cross; Worcester, Massachusetts

ACM   Archives, Commonwealth of Massachusetts; Boston, Massachusetts

ACND   Archives, Congregation de Notre Dame; Montreal, Quebec

ADP   Archives, Diocese of Portland; Portland, Maine

AGU   Archives, Georgetown University; Washington, D.C.

AMJP   Archives, Maryland Jesuit Province in AGU

APF   Archives, Sacred Congregation de Propaganda Fide; Rome

ARHSJ Archives, Religious Hospitallers of St. Joseph; Montreal, Quebec

ASH   Alexander Sherwood Healy

AUND   Archives, University of Notre Dame; South Bend, Indiana

GDAH   Georgia Department of Archives and History; Atlanta, Georgia

HCH   Hugh Clark Healy

JAH   James Augustine Healy

MAH   Michael Augustine Healy

MJH   Mary Jane Healy

NARA   National Archives and Records Administration; Washington, D.C.

PFH   Patrick Francis Healy

RCS   United States Revenue Cutter Service

Prologue

1. Elizabeth Cunningham to Albert Foley, March 1, 1951, Foley Papers, box 7, Josephite Archives, Baltimore.
2. Foley to "Carol and Bo," July 18, 1951, ibid.
3. Peter Guilday to Thomas O'Donnell, June 20, 1942, Foley Papers, box 3; see also Coleman Knot to O'Donnell, April 21, 1942, ibid.
4. Albert S. Foley, *Bishop Healy: Beloved Outcaste* (New York: Farrar, Straus, and Young, 1954).

5. Gunnar Myrdal, *An American Dilemma: The Negro Problem and Modern Democracy* (New York: Harper, 1944).

6. See, for example, Joel Williamson, *New People: Miscegenation and Mulattoes in the United States* (New York: Free Press, 1980); Martha Hodes, *White Women, Black Men: Illicit Sex in the Nineteenth-Century South* (New Haven: Yale University Press, 1997); and Matthew Frye Jacobson, *Whiteness of a Different Color: European Immigrants and the Alchemy of Race* (Cambridge: Harvard University Press, 1998).

1. Parents: Michael and Eliza

1. On the removal of the native American tribes and the land lottery system, see Absalom Chappell, *Miscellanies of Georgia, Historical, Biographical, Descriptive* (Atlanta: J. F. Meegan, 1874), Part 2:25–27; E. Merton Coulter, *Georgia: A Short History* (Chapel Hill: University of North Carolina Press, 1960), 219–229; and James C. Bonner, *A History of Georgia Agriculture, 1732–1860* (Athens: University of Georgia Press, 1964), 38–39.

2. Michael Healy's naturalization oath, April 3, 1818, is in Deed Book K (1818–1819): 144, Jones County Courthouse, Gray, Georgia.

3. See Patrick Healy's genealogical notes, May 23 and September 18, 1884, PFH Diaries, ACHC. The other family traditions are recorded in Foley, *Beloved Outcaste*, 3–5, and Albert S. Foley, *Dream of an Outcaste: Patrick F. Healy* (Tuscaloosa, Ala.: Portals Press, 1989), 1–3.

4. Frederick Law Olmsted, *A Journey in the Seaboard Slave States* (New York: Dix and Edwards, 1856), 538; Adiel Sherwood, *A Gazetteer of Georgia* (Macon, Ga.: S. Boykin, 1860), 183–184; Basil Hall, *Travels in North America* (1829), quoted in Mills Lane, ed., *The Rambler in Georgia* (Savannah: Beehive Press, 1990), 79.

5. On cotton production in Georgia, see Bonner, *Georgia Agriculture*, 51–63; Joseph P. Reidy, *From Slavery to Agrarian Capitalism in the Cotton Plantation South: Central Georgia, 1800–1880* (Chapel Hill: University of North Carolina Press, 1992); and James H. Stone, "Economic Conditions in Macon, Georgia, in the 1830s," *Georgia Historical Quarterly* 54 (Summer 1970): 217–218. The graphic description of cotton land is in Margaret Mitchell, *Gone With the Wind* (New York: Macmillan, 1936), 10.

6. For a first-hand account of cotton farming, see John Brown, *Slave Life in Georgia: A Narrative of the Life, Sufferings, and Escape of John Brown, a Fugitive Slave, Now in England* (London: W. M. Watts, 1855), 171–179.

7. On the debate over the introduction of slavery, see Coulter, *Georgia: Short History*, 57–68, and Winthrop D. Jordan, *White Over Black: American Attitudes toward the Negro, 1550–1812* (Chapel Hill: University of North Carolina Press, 1968), 262–264.

8. Slave populations, 1790–1860, for the South are compiled in Appendix 1, Table A of Ira Berlin, *Slaves without Masters: The Free Negro in the Antebellum South* (New York: Pantheon, 1974), 396–397. For an expression of the climatic theory, see Chappell, *Miscellanies of Georgia,* Part 2:4. As late as 1928, a historian was still advancing this idea with a straight face, asserting that the climate of central Georgia "was unhealthy for the whites, but not so for the Negroes"; see Ralph B. Flanders, "Two Plantations and a County of Antebellum Georgia," *Georgia Historical Quarterly* 12 (March 1928): 4.

9. Statistics on slave ownership have been compiled from the manuscript schedules of the slave census that was part of the federal census of 1850, microfilm copies of which are in the GDAH. See also Reidy, *From Slavery to Agrarian Capitalism*, 249; Donnie D. Bellamy, "Macon, Georgia, 1823–1860: A Study in Urban Slavery," *Phylon* 45 (December 1984): 298–310; and the excerpt from James Silk Buckingham's *The Slave States of America* (London, 1842), quoted in Lane, ed., *Rambler in Georgia*, 151–152.

10. On the rumors of slave revolts in Jones County, see John Campbell Butler, *Historical Record of Macon and Central Georgia* (Macon: J. W. Burke, 1879), 103–105, 122.

11. The most comprehensive study of this whole subject is Thomas D. Morris's *Southern Slavery and the Law, 1619–1860* (Chapel Hill: University of North Carolina Press, 1996). On the law of slavery in Georgia, see also Jordan, *White Over Black*, 124–126, 169–170; Berlin, *Slaves without Masters*, 139–140; W. McDowell Rogers, "Free Negro Legislation in Georgia before 1865," *Georgia Historical Quarterly* 16 (January 1932): 27–37; and Ralph B. Flanders, "The Free Negro in Ante-Bellum Georgia," *North Carolina Historical Review* 9 (July 1932): 250–272.

12. On the founding and early history of Macon, see Coulter, *Georgia: A Short History*, 222–225; Stone, "Economic Conditions in Macon"; and William T. Jenkins, "Ante Bellum Macon and Bibb County, Georgia" (Ph.D. diss., University of Georgia, 1966).

13. For early descriptions of Macon, see George White, *Statistics of the State of Georgia* (Savannah: W. T. Williams, 1849), 108–112; Sherwood, *Gazetteer of Georgia*, 30–32; and Butler, *Historical Record of Macon*, 115, 142, and 184. The development of the city's infrastructure is described in Jenkins, "Ante Bellum Macon," 82–187.

14. The U.S. Census, Agricultural Production (Jones County), 1850, microfilm copy in GDAH, lists the acreage and value of all property owners in the county. Sale of the Healy estate in December 1850 is recorded in Jones County Superior Court, Book R: 390–391, microfilm copy in GDAH. For some of Healy's success in the land lottery, see Jones County Court of Ordinary, Land Lottery Index, microfilm in GDAH.

15. Healy's 1825 recovery against Peter Gill and John Stillwell is in Jones County Inferior Court Minutes (1824–1827): 251–254, GDAH. Other instances of debt collection are in the record books of Jones County Superior Court Minutes, 1826–1846, GDAH.

16. For Healy's slave holdings, see the federal slave censuses of 1830 and 1850, GDAH; for Hornaday and his son, see the 1850 census of free inhabitants of Jones County, also in GDAH. The names and valuations of the slaves are included in the inventory of Healy's estate, September 20, 1850, which is in the Jones County Court of Ordinary, Inventories, etc., M:393; the sale of the slaves is recorded in the Jones County Court of Ordinary, Inventories, etc., P:5–6 and Q:268–269, GDAH.

17. Detailed inventories of Healy's property are given in the U.S. Census of Agricultural Production, 1850 (Jones County), GDAH, and in the records of the inventory and sale of his estate: Jones County Court of Ordinary, Inventories, etc., M:392–394 and N:16–26, GDAH.

18. Healy's books are itemized by title in the records of the sale of his estate on December 3 and 16, 1850, Jones County Court of Ordinary, Inventories, etc., N:16–26, GDAH. For the context of reading and book ownership in rural America, see Richard D. Brown, *Knowledge Is Power: The Diffusion of Information in Early America, 1700–1865* (New York: Oxford University Press, 1989), 132–159.

19. Albert S. Foley provides conflicting and unsubstantiated accounts of the origins of Eliza Healy in his two works on the family: *Beloved Outcaste*, 7–8, and *Dream of an Outcaste*, 4–5. Foley's works,

published twenty years apart, were based on extensive research, but they have neither footnotes nor bibliography, and it is thus difficult to verify much of the evidence. In the former, he says that Eliza was Griswold's daughter; in the latter, she is Smith's daughter and is even related to Ellen Craft, the famous runaway of the 1850s, a conclusion without foundation. See also Carolyn White Williams, *History of Jones County, Georgia, for One Hundred Years, Specifically 1807–1907* (Macon, Ga.: J. W. Burke, 1957), 72–74. There were several white Clark families in Jones County, and one of these may have formerly owned Eliza or her parents.

20. The classic studies of white American perceptions of race are Jordan, *White Over Black*; George M. Fredrickson, *The Black Image in the White Mind: The Debate on Afro-American Character and Destiny, 1817–1914* (New York: Harper and Row, 1971); and Thomas F. Gossett, *Race: The History of an Idea in America* (New York: Schocken Books, 1965). For a comparative study, see Carl Degler, *Neither Black nor White: Slavery and Race Relations in Brazil and the United States* (New York: Macmillan, 1971).

21. The best study of American attitudes toward interracial sexuality is Martha Hodes's *White Women, Black Men*. See also Jordan, *White Over Black*, 145–147 and 469–470; Catherine Clinton, *The Plantation Mistress: Woman's World in the Old South* (New York: Pantheon, 1982), 204–214; John D'Emilio and Estelle B. Freedman, *Intimate Matters: A History of Sexuality in America* (New York: Harper and Row, 1988), 101–104; and Peggy Pascoe, "Race, Gender, and Intercultural Relations," *Frontiers* 12 (Summer 1991): 5–18.

22. On the law of slavery and race in Georgia, see Rogers, "Free Negro Legislation," 27–37, and David H. Fowler, *Northern Attitudes towards Interracial Marriage* (New York: Garland, 1987), 10–11 and 61–62.

23. On the principle that children would take their mother's condition, see Morris, *Southern Slavery and the Law*, 21–29. For the general problems of interracial sexuality and marriage, see James Hugo Johnson, *Race Relations in Virginia and Miscegenation in the South, 1776–1860* (Amherst: University of Massachusetts Press, 1970), 165–190; Edmund S. Morgan, *American Slavery, American Freedom: The Ordeal of Colonial Virginia* (New York: Norton, 1975), 333–336; and Williamson, *New People*, 7.

24. The literature on slave women and slave families has been growing impressively in recent years. See, for example, Herbert G. Gutman, *The Black Family in Slavery and Freedom, 1750–1925* (New York: Pantheon Books, 1976), esp. 61–75; Clinton, *Plantation Mistress*; Deborah Gray White, *Ar'n't I a Woman? Female Slaves in the Plantation South* (New York: Norton, 1985); and Darlene Clark Hine, "'In the Kingdom of Culture': Black Women and the Intersection of Race, Gender, and Class," in *Lure and Loathing: Essays on Race, Identity, and the Ambivalence of Assimilation*, ed. Gerald Early (New York: Allen Lane, 1993), 337–351.

25. Elizabeth Fox Genovese, *Within the Plantation Household: Black and White Women of the Old South* (Chapel Hill: University of North Carolina Press, 1988), 146–156.

26. Foley, *Beloved Outcaste*, 8, and *Dream of an Outcaste*, 4; see also Michael Healy's will, dated February 28, 1845, with a codicil of July 6, 1847, in Jones County Will Book C: 412–416, copy in GDAH. On the legal issues in marriages of this kind, see Morris, *Southern Slavery and the Law*, 46, and Harvey M. Applebaum, "Miscegenation Statutes: A Constitutional and Social Problem," *Georgetown Law Journal* 53 (1964): 49–91.

27. Michael P. Johnson and James L. Roark, *Black Masters: A Free Family of Color in the Old South*

(New York: Norton, 1984); Berlin, *Slaves without Masters*, 247–248. For a measurement of the extent of this phenomenon, see Carter G. Woodson, *Free Negro Owners of Slaves in the United States in 1830* (New York: Negro Universities Press, 1968; orig. pub. 1924).

28. The remarkable story of Nathan and Susan Hunt Sayre, which has many parallels to that of Michael and Eliza Healy, has been told by Adele Logan Alexander, *Ambiguous Lives: Free Women of Color in Rural Georgia, 1789–1879* (Fayetteville: University of Arkansas Press, 1991); see esp. 62–95. Unlike the Healy family, subsequent generations of the Hunts generally identified themselves as black rather than white. See also Hodes, *White Women, Black Men*, esp. ch. 3, and Thomas E. Buckley, "Unfixing Race: Class, Power, and Identity in an Interracial Family," *Virginia Magazine of History and Biography* 102 (July 1994): 349–380. The problem of reconciling general racial theory with exceptional individual cases is also examined in Walter Johnson, "The Slave Trade, the White Slave, and the Politics of Racial Determination in the 1850s," *Journal of American History* 87 (June 2000): 13–38.

29. Foley, in *Beloved Outcaste*, 9–10, and *Dream of an Outcaste*, 6, tells of the incident with the neighbors and the dogs; this story was repeated to me by Kate Henry, a Macon local historian, during a telephone conversation on July 28, 1994. On the "Healy storm," see Williams, *History of Jones County*, 73. For mention of the daguerreotype, see JAH Diary, March 14 and April 9, 1849, JAH Papers, ACHC. For the effect of physical isolation on these issues, see Mark R. Schultz, "Interracial Kinship Ties and the Emergence of a Rural Black Middle Class: Hancock County, Georgia, 1865–1920," in *Georgia in Black and White: Explorations in the Race Relations of a Southern State, 1865–1950*, ed. John C. Inscoe (Athens: University of Georgia Press, 1994), 141–172.

30. On these two prominent local figures, see Butler, *Historical Record of Macon*, 301–302, 304. Adiel Sherwood also published an early gazetteer of Georgia; see above, note 4. On slave naming practices, see Gutman, *Black Family*, 190, and Eugene D. Genovese, *Roll, Jordan, Roll: The World the Slaves Made* (New York: Vintage, 1974), 443–450.

31. The fullest study of mixed-race Americans is Williamson's *New People*. See also Winthrop D. Jordan, "American Chiaroscuro: The Status and Definition of Mulattoes in the British Colonies," *William and Mary Quarterly* 3d ser., 19 (April 1962): 183–200; Robert Brent Toplin, "Between Black and White: Attitudes toward Southern Mulattoes, 1830–1861," *Journal of Southern History* 45 (May 1979): 185–200; John G. Mencke, "Mulattoes and Race Mixture: American Attitudes and Images from Reconstruction to World War I" (Ph.D. diss., University of North Carolina, 1976); Leonard R. Lempel, "The Mulatto in United States Race Relations: Changing Status and Attitudes, 1800–1940" (Ph.D. diss., Syracuse University, 1979); and Patricia Morton, "From Invisible Man to 'New People': The Recent Discovery of American Mulattoes," *Phylon* 46 (June 1985): 106–122. On the interracial classifications of other countries, see Degler's *Neither Black nor White*. For a glossary of the complicated language of interracial identification, see Salme Pekkala et al., "Some Words and Terms Designating, or Relating to, Racially Mixed Persons or Groups," in *Race: Individual and Collective Behavior*, ed. Edgar T. Thompson and Everett C. Hughes (Glencoe, Ill.: Free Press, 1958), 52–57.

32. For a general discussion of the phenomenon of passing, see Williamson, *New People*, 101–106, and Paul R. Spickard, *Mixed Blood: Intermarriage and Ethnic Identity in Twentieth-Century America* (Madison: University of Wisconsin Press, 1989), 335–336. Jordan, *White Over Black*, 171–174, discusses a case from colonial South Carolina in which whites confronted the confusions of racial

determination and passing. There are a number of scientific studies (some good, some bad) of the complexion of persons of interracial background; see the classic Caroline Bond Day, *A Study of Some Negro-White Families in the United States* (Cambridge, Mass.: Peabody Museum, 1932), and Pierre L. Van den Berghe and Peter Frost, "Skin Color Preference, Sexual Dimorphism, and Sexual Selection: A Case of Gene Culture Co-Evolution?" *Ethnic and Racial Studies* 9 (January 1986): 87–113. There is a more popular treatment of some of these issues in Kathy Russell et al., *The Color Complex: The Politics of Skin Color among African Americans* (New York: Harcourt Brace Jovanovich, 1992).

33. See the discussion of these legal problems in Alexander, *Ambiguous Lives*, 91–95.

2. Brothers: James, Hugh, Patrick, and Sherwood

1. On Michael Healy's efforts to find safety for his children, see Foley, *Beloved Outcaste*, 10–12 and 17–19; on Manning, see Foley, *Beloved Outcaste*, 42–44, and Bishop's Journal, December 25, 1859, AABO.

2. On Quaker antislavery, see Jordan, *White Over Black*, 271–276. Foley's work is the only source for the enrollment of the boys in the Quaker schools; I have been unable to locate independent documentary evidence for it. For general background, see Charles U. Lowell, *The Quakers in Flushing, 1657–1937* (Flushing, N.Y.: Case, 1937).

3. New Orleans Diary, March 10, 1885, JAH Papers, ACHC. On the social and psychological adjustments of interracial children, see several of the essays in Maria P. P. Root, ed., *Racially Mixed People in America* (Newbury Park, Calif.: Sage, 1992).

4. The encounter between Healy and Fitzpatrick is described in Foley, *Beloved Outcaste*, 18–19, and *Dream of an Outcaste*, 12–14, and in Thomas H. O'Connor, *Fitzpatrick's Boston, 1846–1866: John Bernard Fitzpatrick, Third Bishop of Boston* (Boston: Northeastern University Press, 1984), 63–64. There is no direct evidence for this story, but it is entirely plausible: Healy apparently traveled to New York at least once each year, and Fitzpatrick was indeed returning from Washington at this time.

5. Jeremiah J. O'Connell, *Catholicity in the Carolinas and Georgia* (New York: Sadlier, 1879), 42–45, 502–518, and 594–596; Butler, *Historical Record of Macon*, 323–325; Fussell Chalker, "Irish Catholics in the Building of the Ocmulgee and Flint Railroad," *Georgia Historical Quarterly* 54 (Winter 1970): 507–516. For comments on the early Catholic population of Macon, see Mission Chronicles, December 21–28, 1856, Paulist Fathers Archives, Washington, D.C. The low level of religious practice among the pre-Famine Irish is described in Emmet Larkin, "The Devotional Revolution in Ireland, 1850–1875," *American Historical Review* 77 (June 1972): 625–652.

6. For the early history of Catholicism in New England, see Robert Howard Lord et al., *History of the Archdiocese of Boston in the Various Stages of Its Development, 1604–1943* (Boston: Pilot Publishing, 1944), esp. vols. 1–2, and Thomas H. O'Connor, *Boston Catholics: A History of the Church and Its People* (Boston: Northeastern University Press, 1998), esp. chs. 1–2. The classic study of anti-Catholicism in this period is Ray Allen Billington's *The Protestant Crusade, 1800–1860: A Study of the Origins of American Nativism* (New York: Macmillan, 1938).

7. Thomas Mulledy prospectus, ca. 1843–1845, Early College Records, 1:7B, ACHC. The foundation and early years of the school are described in Anthony J. Kuzniewski, *Thy Honored Name: A His-*

tory of the College of the Holy Cross, 1843–1994 (Washington, D.C.: Georgetown University Press, 1999), esp. ch. 1; see also Walter J. Meagher and William J. Grattan, *The Spires of Fenwick: A History of the College of the Holy Cross, 1843–1963* (New York: Vantage, 1966), chs. 1–2.

8. On this disposition among southerners toward northern education, see Grady McWhiney, *Cracker Culture: Celtic Ways in the Old South* (Tuscaloosa: University of Alabama Press, 1988), 199–200.

9. JAH Diary, June 28 and August 14, 1849, JAH Papers, ACHC; Farren to "Father + Mother," October 6, 1851, Early College Records, 3:5, ACHC; William Brownson to Orestes Brownson, April 1, 1847, Brownson Papers, AUND. Early enrollments are charted in Kuzniewski, *Thy Honored Name*, 48.

10. JAH Diary, December 10 and 18, 1848, January 14 and March 2, 1849, JAH Papers, ACHC; "College of the holy X [*sic*] Report," February 25, 1846, photocopy in ACHC.

11. JAH Diary, December 15, 1848; February 10, 13, and 19, March 19, and July 12, 1849, JAH Papers, ACHC; Early College Records, 1:8, 1:13, 2:8A, and 3:1, ACHC.

12. See, for example, JAH Diary, March 30 and August 18, 1849, JAH Papers, ACHC. Student life and discipline at Holy Cross in this period is described in Meagher and Grattan, *Spires of Fenwick*, 159–163.

13. "Annotated List of Students of College of Holy Cross, 1848," JAH Diary, JAH Papers, ACHC.

14. Baptismal record, November 18, 1844, Thomas Mulledy Papers, 1:2, ACHC; confirmation record, June 21, 1845, Episcopal Register, AABO. Religious exercises at Holy Cross in this period are described in Kuzniewski, *Thy Honored Name*, 61–62, and in Meagher and Grattan, *Spires of Fenwick*, 65–67. The college record-keeper had moved Michael Healy from Jones County into Macon, but he was close enough.

15. JAH Diary, December 15 and 21, 1848, and August 15, 1849, JAH Papers, ACHC; PFH to Fenwick, December 24, 1856, AMJP, 75:34, AGU; JAH to Fenwick, January 1, 1854, AMJP, 75:15, AGU.

16. See Albert J. Raboteau, *Slave Religion: The "Invisible Institution" in the Antebellum South* (New York: Oxford University Press, 1978).

17. For a discussion of nineteenth-century hostility toward Catholicism, see, in addition to Billington's *Protestant Crusade*, Jenny Franchot's *Roads to Rome: The Antebellum Protestant Encounter with Catholicism* (Berkeley: University of California Press, 1994). On the struggle to gain a state charter for Holy Cross, see Kuzniewski, *Thy Honored Name*, 70–76, and Meagher and Grattan, *Spires of Fenwick*, 51–55 and 103–105. Because this charter was not granted until 1865, the Healy brothers and other students of their era technically received their degrees from Georgetown University in Washington, D.C., which was also run by the Jesuit order.

18. For studies of Catholic attitudes toward slavery, see the older work by Madeleine Hooke Rice, *American Catholic Opinion in the Slavery Controversy* (New York: Columbia University Press, 1944); her discussion of England's views is found on pages 65–70. See also the more recent Randall M. Miller, "Slaves and Southern Catholicism," in *Masters and Slaves in the House of the Lord: Race and Religion in the American South, 1740–1870,* ed. John B. Boles (Lexington: University Press of Kentucky, 1988), 127–152. Hughes's opinion is quoted in Walter G. Sharrow, "John Hughes and a Catholic Response to Slavery in Antebellum America," *Journal of Negro History* 57 (July 1972): 255–256. On Jesuit slave ownership, see Thomas R. Murphy, "'Negroes of Ours': Jesuit Slaveholding in Maryland, 1717–1838" (Ph.D. diss., University of Connecticut, 1998).

19. On Kenrick, see Rice, *American Catholic Opinion*, 70–71; on Spalding, see David Spalding,

"Martin John Spalding's 'Dissertation on the American Civil War,'" *Catholic Historical Review* 52 (April 1966): 66–85. For Brownson's views, see "Abolition and Negro Equality," *Brownson's Quarterly Review*, National Series, 1 (April 1864): 186–209. The failure of Catholicism to meet the needs of African Americans, which persisted long after emancipation, is discussed in Cyprian Davis, *The History of Black Catholics in the United States* (New York: Crossroad, 1990).

20. On the changes in nineteenth-century Catholicism, see Derek Holmes, *The Triumph of the Holy See: A Short History of the Papacy in the Nineteenth Century* (London: Burns and Oates, 1978). For the sense of Catholic certainty, see James Hennesey, *American Catholics: A History of the Roman Catholic Community in the United States* (New York: Oxford University Press, 1981), 221–222.

21. See Paul Gilroy, *The Black Atlantic: Modernity and Double Consciousness* (Cambridge: Harvard University Press, 1993), esp. 17–19, and W. E. B. Du Bois, *The Autobiography of W. E. B. Du Bois: A Soliloquy on Viewing My Life from Its Last Decade* (New York: International Publishers, 1968), 108.

22. JAH Diary, February 21 and March 5, 1849, JAH Papers, ACHC. For another instance of his use of the word "niggers," see the diary for April 19, 1849. On the uses and connotations of this word, see Eugene D. Genovese, *Roll, Jordan, Roll*, 436–438, and Willard B. Gatewood, *Aristocrats of Color: The Black Elite, 1880–1920* (Bloomington: University of Indiana Press, 1990), 190. The word's history is traced usefully in the *Random House Dictionary of American Slang* (New York: Random House, 1997), 2:656–661, and in the *Dictionary of American Regional English* (Cambridge, Mass.: Belknap Press, 1996), 3:788–791.

23. JAH Diary, July 26, 1849, JAH Papers, ACHC. The history and racial meanings of the American minstrel show have received considerable attention in recent years. See Robert C. Toll, *Blacking Up: The Minstrel Show in Nineteenth-Century America* (New York: Oxford University Press, 1974), and Eric Lott, *Love and Theft: Blackface Minstrelsy and the American Working Class* (New York: Oxford University Press, 1993).

24. ASH, "The Church + Negro Slavery," Commonplace Book, no date, ASH Papers, AABO; JAH Diary, June 12 and August 19, 1849, JAH Papers, ACHC.

25. JAH Diary, December 8, 10, and 29, 1848, January 1, February 11, June 11, August 4 and 5, 1849, JAH Papers, ACHC; PFH to Paresce, September 5, 1864, AMJP, 75:10, AGU; JAH to Fenwick, January 1, 1854, AMJP, 75:15, AGU; ASH, "On the Creed," ASH Papers, 1:3, ACHC; entry of June 4, 1860, Commonplace Book, ASH Papers, AABO.

26. JAH Diary, December 25, 1848, JAH Papers, ACHC. On Martha's boarding with the Bolands, see the entries in the diary for January 17 and July 5, 1849; her baptism on December 29, 1844, is recorded in Cathedral of the Holy Cross, Baptisms, 1844–1850, AABO.

27. JAH Diary, January 4, 18, and 26, 1849, JAH Papers, ACHC. For examples of the use of "Dad" with Fenwick, see HCH to Fenwick, July 6, 1850, AMJP, 71:13, AGU; JAH to Fenwick, June 10, 1850, AMJP, 71:14, AGU; and PFH to Fenwick, October 2, 1853, AMJP, 74:1, AGU. On Fenwick, the "giant" of the first years of Holy Cross, see Kuzniewski, *Thy Honored Name*, 53.

28. JAH Diary, December 15, 1848, January 17, March 14, April 9, and May 18, 1849, JAH Papers, ACHC.

29. James's description of the commencement is in his diary, July 26, 1849, JAH Papers, ACHC; emphasis added. His commencement address is in JAH Papers, 1:1, ACHC. There are two unsigned accounts of the ceremony, one of them possibly written by him, in the *Boston Pilot*, August 4, 1849. The commencement is also described in Meagher and Grattan, *Spires of Fenwick*, 74–77.

3. Orphans: Hugh, Martha, and the Younger Children

1. Michael Healy's land and slave holdings have already been described above, chapter 1. Cotton prices during this period are charted in Butler, *Historical Record of Macon*, 159–178. On the antebellum climax of Georgia agriculture, see Reidy, *From Slavery to Agrarian Capitalism*, 38–39, and Willard Range, *A Century of Georgia Agriculture, 1850–1950* (Athens: University of Georgia Press, 1954), 3–31.

2. The problems of drawing up wills in such cases are discussed in Morris, *Southern Slavery and the Law*, 376–379, and in Ralph B. Flanders, *Plantation Slavery in Georgia* (Chapel Hill: University of North Carolina Press, 1933), 249. Hodes, *White Women, Black Men*, 96–122, highlights the particular vulnerability of interracial children on the death of their owner-fathers. For other cases of the treatment of slave children in the wills of their fathers, see Alexander, *Ambiguous Lives*, 91–95.

3. Michael Healy's will, dated February 28, 1845, and the codicil to it, dated July 6, 1847, are both in Jones County, Will Book C: 412–416, a microfilm copy of which is in GDAH.

4. JAH Diary, July 25, 1849, JAH Papers, ACHC. The reference to his father's being "on" apparently refers to one of Michael Healy's regular visits to the North.

5. The daguerreotype of his mother that James had "recognised" has disappeared, though a story circulated a century later that the adult James Healy kept a picture of her in his bedroom, discreetly hidden under a veil; see Smith to O'Donnell, May 8, 1942, Foley Papers, Josephite Archives, Baltimore. This story probably has the accuracy of most third-hand accounts.

6. HCH to Fenwick, July 6, 1850, AMJP 71:13, AGU. The extreme weather in Georgia that summer is mentioned in Butler, *Historical Record of Macon*, 192. Payment for the enclosure of the graves is noted in Jones County Court of Ordinary, Inventories etc., N: 283, copy in GDAH. The earlier biographer of the Healys, Albert S. Foley, erected a stone marker and plaque at the gravesite in June 1975.

7. The will was admitted and the executors approved on September 9, 1850; see Jones County Court of Ordinary, Minutes (1837–1857), 318, copy in GDAH. The appraisal of the estate and other activities are outlined in Jones County Court of Ordinary, Inventories etc., M: 392–394 and N: 48–49, copies in GDAH. The sale of the land is recorded in Jones County, Deed Book R: 390–391, copy in GDAH.

8. Compare the appraisal of the estate with the returns from the sales: Jones County Court of Ordinary, Inventories etc., M: 392–394 and N:116–26, copies in GDAH.

9. Woodson, *Free Negro Owners of Slaves*, 3–4. For case studies of black slaveowners, see Johnson and Roark, *Black Masters*, and Alexander, *Ambiguous Lives*. See also Frederick Douglass, *My Bondage and My Freedom* (New York: Miller, Orton, and Mulligan, 1855), 72.

10. The accounts for the slave hiring in 1851 are in Jones County Court of Ordinary, Inventories, etc., N: 282–283, copy in GDAH; those for 1852 and 1853 are in O: 249–250, and P: 1, respectively. On the practice in general, see Genovese, *Roll, Jordan, Roll*, 390–392, and Clement Eaton, "Slave Hiring in the Upper South: A Step toward Freedom," *Mississippi Valley Historical Review* 46 (March 1960): 663–678. The hiring of slaves was a very complicated legal matter; see Morris, *Southern Slavery and the Law*, 132–158.

11. The expenses of caring for the hired slaves are detailed in Jones County Court of Ordinary, Inventories, etc., N: 284–285, copies in GDAH. The account of the first slave sale is at P: 5–6.

12. The suit and subsequent sale of Margaret and her children are accounted for in Jones County Court of Ordinary, Inventories, etc., Q: 268–269 and 440, copies in GDAH.

13. The two sales, February 16 and 20, 1860, are recorded in Jones County Superior Court, Deeds and Mortgages, Book S (1853–1869): 369–370, copy in GDAH. The intermediary "straw" in the transaction was identified as Charles Macarthy, presumably a relative of Robert Macarthy, one of the executors of Michael Healy's will. Foley, *Beloved Outcaste*, 15–16, speculates that Nancy was Eliza Clark Healy's sister, citing a Jones County oral tradition to support this conclusion.

14. For the transfer of the cash to New York, see Jones County Court of Ordinary, Inventories etc., N: 282–288; O: 250–259; P: 1–7 and 550–557; Q: 268–273 and 438–446; R: 426–428; S: 416–419; and U: 573–574; copies in GDAH. For the conversion of historical dollars to contemporary sums, see John J. McCusker, "How Much Is That in Real Money? A Historical Price Index for Use as a Deflator of Money Values in the Economy of the United States," *Proceedings of the American Antiquarian Society* 101 (1994): 297–373; see also Scott Derks, ed., *The Value of a Dollar: Prices and Incomes in the United States, 1860–1989* (Detroit: Gale, 1994). The final details of settling the estate are recorded in Jones County Court of Ordinary, Minutes 1854–1860, pp. 346–347, 423, copies in GDAH.

15. HCH to Fenwick, July 6, 1850, AMJP 71:13, AGU. The proximity of Mathis and Cynthia White to the Healy property and their boarding of young Hornaday are apparent in the manuscript schedule of the 1850 federal census for Jones County, p. 203, a copy of which is in GDAH. The census came through the area precisely at the time of Michael Healy's death, and census takers did their work by traveling around the appointed territory, writing down the inhabitants' names one after another as they encountered them. Healy's was the 345th household visited; the Whites were number 347, indicating that they lived nearby.

16. On the law and its application, see Stanley W. Campbell, *The Slave Catchers: Enforcement of the Fugitive Slave Law, 1850–1860* (Chapel Hill: University of North Carolina Press, 1970); James M. McPherson, *Battle Cry of Freedom: The Civil War Era* (New York: Oxford University Press, 1988), 78–86; Gary Collison, *Shadrach Minkins: From Fugitive Slave to Citizen* (Cambridge: Harvard University Press, 1997), esp. 51–54 and 75–90; and Peter P. Hinks, "'Frequently Plunged into Slavery': Free Blacks and Kidnapping in Antebellum Boston," *Historical Journal of Massachusetts* 20 (Winter 1992): 16–31.

17. Baptismal record, June 13, 1851, Saint Francis Xavier church, New York, New York. In later years, Patrick Healy visited the church and copied the baptismal information about his siblings into the endpapers of his diary for 1900, PFH Papers 1:4, AGU. The receipt from Manning, dated January 24, 1852, and the account of enclosing the graves, January 12, 1852, are in Jones County Court of Ordinary, Inventories etc., N: 283–286, copies in GDAH.

18. Bishop's Journal, September 18, 1849, AABO. On Catholic theological education, see Joseph M. White, *The Diocesan Seminary in the United States: A History from the 1780s to the Present* (Notre Dame, Ind.: University of Notre Dame Press, 1989).

19. Fitzpatrick visited "his" students in October of that year and expressed "much satisfaction" with the arrangements; Bishop's Journal, October 4, 1849, AABO. On the Sulpicians generally, see Christopher J. Kauffman, *Tradition and Transformation in Catholic Culture: The Priests of Saint Sulpice in the United States from 1791 to the Present* (New York: Macmillan, 1988).

20. PFH to Fenwick, October 2, 1853, AMJP 74:1, AGU; JAH to Fenwick, June 10, 1850, AMJP 71:14, AGU.

21. JAH Diary, February 27, 1849, JAH Papers, ACHC. No thought was given to placing Martha with one

of the religious orders that educated African American girls: see Diane Batts Morrow, "Outsiders Within: The Oblate Sisters of Providence in Church and Society," *U.S. Catholic Historian* 15, no. 2 (Spring 1997): 35–54.

22. On the sisters and their work, see Sister Saint Ignatius Doyle, *Marguerite Bourgeoys and Her Congregation* (Gardenvale, Quebec: Garden City Press, 1940), and *Histoire de la Congregation de Notre-Dame de Montreal*, 10 vols. (Montreal: Congregation de Notre Dame, 1941–1969). The strong ties between the sisters and the Sulpician priests are described in the *Histoire*, 10:79–100.

23. Martha's financial accounts are in the records of the "Pensionnat de la Maison Mere," ACND. On the educational and devotional life of the school, see Doyle, *Marguerite Bourgeoys*, 265, and *Histoire de la Congregation de Notre Dame*, 9:22–23, 26, 37–39, and 52.

24. Doyle, *Marguerite Bourgeoys*, 266; *Histoire de la Congregation de Notre Dame*, 9:54 and 126–134; 10:230.

25. On the role of the sisters in opening professional opportunities for women, see Marta Danylewycz, *Taking the Veil: An Alternative to Marriage, Motherhood, and Spinsterhood in Quebec, 1840–1920* (Toronto: McClelland and Stewart, 1987).

26. The profession document (original in French), dated September 13, 1855, is in ACND. Patrick's comment on his sister's vocation is in PFH to Fenwick, October 2, 1853, AMJP 74:1, AGU.

27. Profession document, September 13, 1855, ACND.

28. JAH Diary, February 5 and March 19, 1849, JAH Papers, ACHC; *Boston Pilot*, August 3, 1850. On Hugh's brief explanation of "their situations," see HCH to Fenwick, July 6, 1850, AMJP 71:13, AGU.

29. HCH to Fenwick, July 6, 1850, AMJP 71:13, AGU; PFH to Paresce, October 1864, AMJP 77:10, AGU; Early to Brocard, September 9, 1850, AMJP 71:10, AGU. Useful in understanding the complicated church law here is James A. Brundage, *Law, Sex, and Christian Society in Medieval Europe* (Chicago: University of Chicago Press, 1987), 216–223.

30. JAH to Fenwick, April 10, 1851, AMJP 72:5, AGU; see also JAH to Fenwick, June 10, 1850, AMJP 71:14, AGU. On Fitzpatrick's role, see O'Connor, *Fitzpatrick's Boston*, 155–156.

31. See Gilbert J. McDevitt, *Legitimacy and Legitimation: An Historical Synopsis and Commentary* (Washington, D.C.: Catholic University of America, 1941), 34–44 and 56–58, and James I. O'Connor, *Dispensations from Irregularities to Holy Orders* (West Baden Springs, Ind.: West Baden College, 1952).

32. HCH to Fenwick, July 6, 1850, AMJP 71:13, AGU; JAH to Fenwick, January 1, 1854, AMJP 74:15, AGU; ASH to PFH, March 10, 1854, AMJP 74:15, AGU; PFH to Fenwick, March 7, 1854, AMJP 74:15, AGU.

33. Compare Sherwood's passport (#3071, dated September 18, 1869), with those of Patrick (#10914, dated September 30, 1858; and #3762, dated December 19, 1885), all in Department of State Passport Records, National Archives microfilm # M-1371, roll 3, frames 125 and 535, and roll 5, frame 112.

34. On the origins and structure of Saint-Sulpice, Paris, see Kauffman, *Tradition and Transformation*, 8–25, and White, *Diocesan Seminary in the United States*, 87. Fitzpatrick's experience there is described in O'Connor, *Fitzpatrick's Boston*, 12–25.

35. PFH to Fenwick, October 2, 1853, AMJP 74:1, AGU. The death is described in detail in Foley, *Dream of an Outcaste*, 44–47.

36. JAH to Fenwick, January 1 and September 7, 1854, AMJP 74:15, AGU; PFH to Fenwick, October 2, 1853, AMJP 74:1, AGU; Fenwick to PFH, September 28, 1853, PFH Papers 2:2, AGU.

37. The placement of the younger children is discussed in two letters, dated just before and just after

Hugh's death: JAH to HCH, August 14, 1853, and PFH to Fenwick, October 2, 1853, both in AMJP 74:1, AGU. Fenwick apparently agreed that James should return immediately, but this could not be arranged; see Fenwick to PFH, March 21, 1854, PFH Papers 2:2, AGU.

4. Priests: James, Sherwood, and Patrick

1. Fenwick to PFH, no date but early 1855, PFH Papers 2:2, AGU.

2. The "exeat" problem is discussed in JAH to Fenwick, June 10, 1850, AMJP 71:14, AGU. On Healy's ordination, see Foley, *Beloved Outcaste*, 52–53.

3. The classic study of Boston's population in this period is Oscar Handlin's *Boston's Immigrants: A Study in Acculturation*, revised and enlarged edition (New York: Atheneum, 1997; orig. pub.1941); see esp. ch. 2. For other statistical measures of Irish immigration, see Thomas H. O'Connor, "The Irish in New England," *New England Historical and Genealogical Register* 139 (July 1985): 187–195. For the impact of this immigration on the church, see O'Connor, *Boston Catholics*, 79–88.

4. For the long-standing reluctance to accept African Americans as priests, see Stephen J. Ochs, *Desegregating the Altar: The Josephites and the Struggle for Black Priests, 1871–1960* (Baton Rouge: Louisiana State University Press, 1990).

5. JAH to Fenwick, March 22, 1855, AMJP 74:15, AGU; JAH to Fenwick, April 10, 1851, AMJP 72:5, AGU.

6. JAH to Fenwick, December 22, 1854, AMJP 74:15, AGU; JAH to priests, June 24, 1855, Chancery Circulars 1:3, AABO.

7. JAH to priests, June 24 and September [no day], 1855, Chancery Circulars 1:3, AABO; JAH to Fenwick, June 10, 1850, AMJP 71:14, AGU.

8. JAH to priests, June 24 and September [no day], 1855, Chancery Circulars 1:3, AABO. For his scrutiny of local church affairs, see the copies of the parish annual reports in AABO.

9. Power to JAH, January 18, 1864, JAH Papers 1:42, AABO; JAH to priests, May 1860 and September 1855, Chancery Circulars 1:3, AABO.

10. For a review of these events, see O'Connor, *Fitzpatrick's Boston*, chs. 6–7; Lord et al., *History of the Archdiocese of Boston*, 2:648–703; and John R. Mulkern, *The Know-Nothing Party in Massachusetts: The Rise and Fall of a People's Movement* (Boston: Northeastern University Press, 1990).

11. Fitzpatrick to Tonsey, February 9, 1860, Fitzpatrick Letterbook, AABO; Hilary Tucker Diary, May 2, 1864, AABO. Fitzpatrick's health is discussed in O'Connor, *Fitzpatrick's Boston*, 154–155 and 181–184.

12. For physical descriptions of Healy, see his passports: # 11166 (July 31, 1863), #4040 (December 22, 1877), and #3727 (December 14, 1885), all in Department of State Passport Records, National Archives microfilm # M-1371. For comments on his health and recreation, see Hilary Tucker Diary, February 15, 1863, March 15 and May 10, 1864, AABO.

13. Fitzpatrick to PFH, June 16, 1864, Varia 3-306, AGU. On popular notions of "hybrid" weakness, see Williamson, *New People*, 94–95, Gossett, *Race*, 47–51, and Fredrickson, *Black Image*, 117–124.

14. Bishop's Journal, April 7, 1860, January 14, 1861, and February 15, 1865, AABO; entries of September 21, 1862, March 23, 1863, and June 4, 1865, Saint Aloysius School Records, AABO.

15. His regular parochial duties are consistently recorded in Bishop's Journal, AABO, during these years. His participation in May devotions is noted in Hilary Tucker Diary, May 31, 1863, AABO. The comments on his preaching style are in JAH to Fenwick, March 22, 1855, and PFH to O'Callaghan,

December 1856, AMJP 74:15 and 75:35, respectively, AGU. ACHC has an extensive collection of JAH's sermons, covering the entire period of his priestly career.

16. His sacramental activity is recorded in the baptismal and marriage registers of the Cathedral of the Holy Cross, now in AABO. Throughout his years, Healy seldom performed more than 10 percent of the total for either sacrament. The normal pattern of pastoral activity for a nineteenth-century priest is described in James M. O'Toole, *Militant and Triumphant: William Henry O'Connell and the Catholic Church in Boston, 1859–1944* (Notre Dame, Ind.: University of Notre Dame Press, 1992), 20–23, and in Robert E. Sullivan, "Beneficial Relations: Toward a Social History of the Diocesan Priests of Boston, 1875–1944," in *Catholic Boston: Studies in Religion and Community, 1870–1970*, ed. Robert E. Sullivan and James M. O'Toole (Boston: Archdiocese of Boston, 1985), 235–237.

17. Compare Healy's own description of the success of this announcement, in the Bishop's Journal, AABO, with that in the Hilary Tucker Diary, AABO, both entries of July 12, 1863.

18. Bishop's Journal, October 4, 1859, May 15 and September 16, 1860, AABO; see also the contract between JAH and Muller, September 3, 1862, JAH Papers 1:37, AABO. Fitzpatrick's farewell sermon, read by Healy, is in *Pilot*, September 22, 1860. On the sale of the old cathedral and the move to a new one, see Lord et al., *History of the Archdiocese of Boston*, 2:470–473, and 3:48–55. The best description of the largely unfulfilled promise of the South End district of Boston is still William Dean Howells's novel, *The Rise of Silas Lapham* (Boston: Houghton Mifflin, 1884).

19. The personal connections between the leaders of Boston society and the bishop are described in O'Connor, *Fitzpatrick's Boston*, 8–9 and 59–60; on the appeal of Catholicism to elite American Protestants in this period, see Franchot, *Roads to Rome*.

20. Bishop's Journal, August 17, 1856, March 5, 1857, and August 12, 1860, AABO; Hilary Tucker Diary, July 3, 1862, AABO.

21. See the account book, covering the period 1860–1866, in JAH Papers, AABO, for the tracking of family investments, income, and expenses. For his interest in the price of gold and securities, see, for example, Bishop's Journal, February 16 and 20, 1865, AABO. On the death of Manning, see Bishop's Journal, December 15, 1859, and January 1, 1860, AABO.

22. The ownership of the house and property may be traced in the town reports, 1862–1867, in the Special Collections Department, Newton City Library, Newton, Massachusetts. Healy sold the property about 1868, but other members of the family moved back to Newton in the 1880s.

23. JAH Student Diary endpapers, ACHC; Bishop's Journal, April 27, 1865, AABO; JAH to priests, September 1855, Chancery Circulars 1:3, AABO; JAH European Diary, April 15, 1878, JAH Papers 3:3, ACHC; PFH to Fenwick, December 24, 1856, AMJP 75:34, AGU.

24. JAH to Fenwick, January 1, 1854, AMJP 74:15, AGU.

25. PFH to Fenwick, March 7, 1854, AMJP 74:15, AGU.

26. ASH Commonplace Book, June 19, 1859, AABO. Sherwood may have been paraphrasing a sermon he either heard or delivered at the time. See also his dialog, "Conversation with M," December 15, 1859, in the Commonplace Book. On this understanding of the nature of the priesthood, see Sullivan, "Beneficial Relations," 201–238.

27. Fitzpatrick to Bedini, July 5, 1859, Congressi: America Centrale 8:895, APF.

28. For a history of this institution, see Robert F. McNamara, *The American College in Rome* (Rochester, N.Y.: Christopher, 1956).

29. Fitzpatrick to Hughes, July 10, 1859, Hughes Papers A-9, Archives, Archdiocese of New York; there is also a copy of this letter in AABO.

30. Fitzpatrick to Bedini, July 5, 1859, Congressi: America Centrale 8:895, APF.

31. See, for example, the notation of Sherwood's work in preparing the residents for confirmation, Episcopal Register, August 19, 1862, AABO. On the foundation and early years of the House of the Angel Guardian, see Peter C. Holleran, *Boston's Wayward Children: Social Services for Homeless Children, 1830–1930* (Boston: Northeastern University Press, 1994), 80–91.

32. His official entry into the Society is recorded in the House Diary, September 17, 1850, AMJP 112:3, AGU. The formation of prospective candidates is discussed in Joseph de Guibert, *The Jesuits: Their Spiritual Doctrine and Practice*, trans. William J. Young (Chicago: Institute of Jesuit Sources, 1964).

33. Young to Lancaster, January 22, 1866, AMJP 19:3, AGU. Jesuit attitudes toward slavery and race are considered extensively in Murphy, "'Negroes of Ours'"; see also Rice, *American Catholic Opinion*, 47–51, and Robert Emmett Curran, "'Splendid Poverty': Jesuit Slaveholding in Maryland, 1805–1838," in *Catholics in the Old South: Essays on Church and Culture*, ed. Randall M. Miller and Jon L. Wakelyn (Macon, Ga.: Mercer University Press, 1983), 125–146. Sale of the Maryland slaves had been superintended by Father Thomas Mulledy, an early president of Holy Cross College, whom Michael Morris Healy had named in his will as a back-up guardian for his children.

34. Early to Brocard, September 9, 1850, AMJP 71:10, AGU. See also Patrick Healy's passports, #10914 (October 30, 1858) and #3762 (December 19, 1885), Department of State Passport Records, National Archives microfilm #M-1371.

35. O'Flanagan to Stonestreet, November 4, 1853, and JAH to Fenwick, December 22, 1854, both in AMJP 74:15, AGU. Patrick's contribution to the school's rebuilding, the largest donation received at the time, is described in Kuzniewski, *Thy Honored Name*, 92–94.

36. PFH to Fenwick, November 23, 1853, AMJP 74:1, AGU.

37. PFH to Stonestreet, December 24, 1856, AMJP 75:34, AGU.

38. These years are described in Foley, *Dream of an Outcaste*, 73–87.

39. PFH to Paresce, September 28 and October [no day], 1864, both in AMJP 77:10, AGU.

40. PFH to Paresce, September 5, 1864, AMJP 77:10, AGU. The quote from scripture is John 15:15.

5. Northerners: The Healys and the Civil War

1. Still the best general treatment of the coming of the Civil War is David M. Potter's *The Impending Crisis, 1848–1861*, ed. Don E. Fehrenbacher (New York: Harper and Row, 1976); on Seward's "irrepressible conflict" speech and its impact, see James M. McPherson, *Battle Cry of Freedom: The Civil War Era* (New York: Oxford University Press, 1988), 198, and David Herbert Donald, *Lincoln* (New York: Simon and Schuster, 1995), 208–209.

2. JAH Diary, August 18, 1849, JAH Papers, ACHC.

3. *Pilot*, January 12, 1861, July 12 and 19, 1862.

4. Orestes Brownson, "Abolition and Negro Equality," *Brownson's Quarterly Review*, National Series, 1 (April 1864): 196 and 207. Some historians have recently argued that Irish immigrants escaped classification with blacks by demonstrating their loyalty to white supremacy; see Alexander Saxton, *The Rise and Fall of the White Republic: Class Politics and Mass Culture in Nineteenth-Century America* (London: Verso, 1990); David R. Roediger, *The Wages of Whiteness: Race and the Making*

of the American Working Class (London: Verso, 1991); and Noel Ignatiev, *How the Irish Became White* (New York: Routledge, 1995).

5. "The Church + Negro Slavery," Commonplace Book, no date, ASH Papers, AABO; Hilary Tucker Diary, July 4, 1862, and July 17, 1863, AABO; *Pilot*, July 12, 1862. On the connections between abolitionism and nativism, see William E. Gienapp, "Nativism and the Creation of a Republican Majority in the North before the Civil War," *Journal of American History* 72 (December 1985): 529–559; Gienapp, *The Origins of the Republican Party, 1852–1856* (New York: Oxford University Press, 1987); and Mulkern, *Know-Nothing Party in Massachusetts*. International Catholic opinion on abolition was much the same as it was in America; on this, see Anthony B. Lalli and Thomas H. O'Connor, "Roman Views of the American Civil War," *Catholic Historical Review* 57 (April 1971): 21–41.

6. On conditions for African Americans in Massachusetts, see James O. Horton and Lois E. Horton, *Black Bostonians: Family Life and Community Struggle in the Antebellum North* (New York: Holmes and Meier, 1979); Carol Buchalter Stapp, *Afro-Americans in Antebellum Boston: An Analysis of Probate Records* (New York: Garland, 1993); George A. Levesque, *Black Boston: African American Life and Culture in Urban America, 1750–1860* (New York: Garland, 1994); Thomas H. O'Connor, *Civil War Boston: Home Front and Battlefield* (Boston: Northeastern University Press, 1997); and the classic John Daniels, *In Freedom's Birthplace: A Study of the Boston Negroes* (Boston: Houghton Mifflin, 1914). On specific aspects of segregation, see Louis Ruchames, "Jim Crow Railroads in Massachusetts," *American Quarterly* 8 (Spring 1956): 61–75; Louis Ruchames, "Race, Marriage, and Abolition in Massachusetts," *Journal of Negro History* 40 (July 1955): 250–273; Leon F. Litwack, *North of Slavery: The Negro in the Free States, 1790–1860* (Chicago: University of Chicago Press, 1961), 68–74 and 104–111; and Leonard W. Levy and Harlan B. Phillips, "The *Roberts* Case: Source of the 'Separate but Equal' Doctrine," *American Historical Review* 56 (April 1951): 510–518.

7. Bishop's Journal, July 6 and 7, 1863, March 9, 1864, March 5 and 18, 1865, April 17, 1865, and May 9, 1865, AABO. Voter registration records for Boston are fragmentary for this period, but I have been unable to locate any evidence of Healy's registration among those that are preserved in the Boston City Archives, Boston. At least one other priest of the cathedral parish was registered, but he did not vote in the election of 1864; see Hilary Tucker Diary, November 8 and 10, 1864, AABO.

8. Bishop's Journal, July 1, 3, 16, and 20, 1863, February 4, 1864, AABO. On Hughes, see Richard Shaw, *Dagger John: The Unquiet Life and Times of Archbishop John Hughes of New York* (New York: Paulist Press, 1977).

9. Amos A. Lawrence Diary, June 20, 1861, Lawrence Papers, Massachusetts Historical Society, Boston. On the unofficial diplomacy, see O'Connor, *Fitzpatrick's Boston*, 191–213.

10. See the letters JAH to Governor Andrew, October 11, 22, and 28, 1861, April 11, 1862, and February 4, 1864, Executive Office Correspondence, vol. 32, ACM. See also the letter of Fitzpatrick to Andrew, March 3, 1862, in the same collection, vol. 18.

11. On the practice of holding money in trust for soldiers, see Scully to JAH, June 12, 1862, JAH Papers 1:43, AABO; Nolan to JAH, July 28, 1862 and December 25, 1864, JAH Papers 1:40, AABO; and Cusick to JAH, December 14, 1863, JAH Papers 1:14, AABO. On the services for the Ninth Massachusetts, see entry of June 20, 1861, Episcopal Register, AABO.

12. Bishop's Journal, February 1 and 5, 1865, April 4 and 5, 1865, AABO.

13. Bishop's Journal, February 22, 1865, March 18, 1865, April 4, 10, and 11, 1865, AABO.

14. Bishop's Journal, April 12, 15, 16, 17, and 19, 1865, AABO; Hilary Tucker Diary, June 1, 1865, AABO.

15. Bishop's Journal, April 15, 20, and 28, 1865, May 28, 1865, AABO. The best recent account of the plot to murder the president is in Donald, *Lincoln*, 575–599.

16. Bishop's Journal, December 4, 1865, AABO.

17. On Tucker and his relations with Healy, see James Hitchcock, "Race, Religion, and Rebellion: Hilary Tucker and the Civil War," *Catholic Historical Review* 80 (July 1994): 497–517, and Foley, *Beloved Outcaste*, 72–91.

18. Hilary Tucker Diary, June [mislabeled "July"] 1, 1863, and April 7, 1864, AABO.

19. Hilary Tucker Diary, May 1, 1863, and September 18, 1864, AABO.

20. Hilary Tucker Diary, January 23 and 31, 1864, September 17, 1865, AABO.

21. Hilary Tucker Diary, May 1, 1863, August 16, 1864, and August 5, 1865, AABO.

22. Hilary Tucker Diary, July 13, 1862, May 31, 1863, June 14, 1863, and March 28, 1864, AABO.

23. Hilary Tucker Diary, May 31–July 1, 1863, June 20, 1865, AABO.

24. Hilary Tucker Diary, May 1, 1863, AABO.

25. For a full description and analysis of the draft, see James W. Geary, *We Need Men: The Union Draft in the Civil War* (Dekalb: Northern Illinois University Press, 1991); Eugene C. Murdock, *One Million Men: The Civil War Draft in the North* (Madison: State Historical Society of Wisconsin, 1971); and McPherson, *Battle Cry of Freedom*, 600–611.

26. Hilary Tucker Diary, July 17, 1863, AABO.

27. On this subject generally, see Adrian Cook, *The Armies of the Streets: The New York City Draft Riots of 1863* (Lexington: University Press of Kentucky, 1974), and Iver Bernstein, *The New York City Draft Riots: Their Significance for American Society and Politics in the Age of the Civil War* (New York: Oxford University Press, 1990). See also Peter Quinn's fine novel, *Banished Children of Eve* (New York: Viking Penquin, 1994).

28. There are conflicting reports of the riot in all the Boston newspapers of the period; see, for example, *Boston Herald*, July 10–14, 1863. For Healy's chronicle of events, see Bishop's Journal, July 10–13, 1863, AABO. For an overview, see William F. Hanna, "The Boston Draft Riot," *Civil War History* 36 (September 1990): 262–273.

29. Detailed accounts of the riot are given in the *Pilot*, July 25, 1863; *Boston Daily Advertiser*, July 15–16, 1863; and *Boston Daily Courier*, July 15–17, 1863.

30. Bishop's Journal, July 14–15, 1863, AABO; Hilary Tucker Diary, July 14,1863, AABO.

31. Bishop's Journal, July 14, 15, and 18, 1863, AABO; Hilary Tucker Diary, July 14 and 16, 1863, AABO; Healy's letter is reproduced in *Pilot*, July 25, 1863.

32. Bishop's Journal, July 19, 1863, AABO; Hilary Tucker Diary, July 17, 1863, AABO.

33. Mayor Lincoln's report on the riot and its suppression is in the *Boston Herald*, July 24, 1863.

34. The girls' years at Montreal can be traced in the enrollment and financial records of the Pensionnat de Saint-Jean and the Villa Marie school, 1855–1861, ACND. Eliza's composition book is in JAH Papers, ADP. James's satisfaction is expressed in his letter to "Reverende Soeur," February 16, 1864, ACND.

35. Document dated March 28, 1863, signed "Mary Anne Martha Magdalena Healy, Sister Saint Lucie," ACND. On the refunding of the dowry, see the letters to the sisters by ASH (December 9, 1863) and JAH (February 1, 1864), ACND.

36. PFH to Fenwick, October 2, 1853, AMJP 74:1, AGU; JAH to Fenwick, March 22, 1855, AMJP 74:15, AGU. On the general plans for the care of the younger siblings, see the letter of JAH to HCH, August 14, 1853, AMJP 74:1, AGU: this letter was written from Paris, and Hugh died before receiving it.

37. *Pilot*, August 15, 1863. On JAH's departure, see also Hilary Tucker Diary, August 5, 1863, AABO.

38. PFH to Paresce, August 26, 1863, AMJP 77:10, AGU. On Fitzpatrick's diplomatic work in Belgium, see O'Connor, *Fitzpatrick's Boston*, 206–207. The travels of the Healy brothers are described in Foley, *Beloved Outcaste*, 82–91.

39. PFH European Diary, September 3, 14, 15, and October 1, 1863, PFH Papers 1:1, ACHC.

40. Hecker to Propaganda Fide, August 17, 1863, Congressi: America Centrale 20:354, and JAH to Level, November 17, 1863, Congressi: America Centrale 20:493–494, both APF; Hilary Tucker Diary, December 20, 1863, AABO. In his account of James's time in Rome (*Beloved Outcaste*, 86–89), Foley quotes without attribution from a JAH diary that I have been unable to identify or locate.

41. Fitzpatrick to PFH, August 8, 1864, Varia 3:306, AGU; Hilary Tucker Diary, September 2, 1864, AABO. For the anecdote about Eugene in England, see Henry Gabriels, *Historical Sketch of St. Joseph's Provincial Seminary, Troy, N.Y.* (New York: U.S. Catholic Historical Society, 1905), 43.

42. Michael Healy's embellished and probably revisionist narrative of his early years at sea is in his letter to Captain Stephen Cornell, January 18, 1865, Revenue Cutter Service Applications, Records of the U.S. Coast Guard (RG 26), Box 12, NARA. The concerns of Patrick and James are in PFH to Fenwick, December 11, 1854, and JAH to Fenwick, December 22, 1854, AMJP 74:15, AGU.

43. See the several letters of endorsement in the Revenue Cutter Service Application Files, Records of the U.S. Coast Guard (RG 26), Box 12, National Archives: Fitzpatrick to Fessenden, October 15, 1864; Bacon to Fessenden, December 20, 1864; Thompson endorsement, October 17, 1864; Andrew to Harrington, November 19, 1864. For the work of the service in this period, see Stephen H. Evans, *The United States Coast Guard, 1790–1915, with a Postscript, 1915–1950* (Annapolis: United States Naval Institute, 1949).

44. On the opportunities available to blacks in seafaring, see Martha S. Putney, *Black Sailors: Afro-American Merchant Seamen and Whalemen Prior to the Civil War* (New York: Greenwood Press, 1987); W. Jeffrey Bolster, "'To Feel Like a Man': Black Seamen in the Northern States, 1800–1860," *Journal of American History* 76 (March 1990): 1173–1199; W. Jeffrey Bolster, *Black Jacks: African American Seamen in the Age of Sail* (Cambridge: Harvard University Press, 1997); and David L. Valuska, *The African American in the Union Navy, 1861–1865* (New York: Garland, 1993).

45. The marriage of Michael and Mary Jane Roach Healy is noted in Bishop's Journal, January 31, 1865, AABO, and Hilary Tucker Diary, January 31, 1865, AABO. The marriage of Martha Healy and Jeremiah Cashman, July 25, 1865, is recorded in the marriage registers of Saint Mary's parish, Waltham, AABO.

6. The Rector: Sherwood

1. Carroll to Grassi, July 24, 1815, in *John Carroll Papers*, ed. Thomas O'Brien Hanley (Notre Dame, Ind.: University of Notre Dame Press, 1976), 3:349.

2. JAH to Fenwick, January 1, 1854, and ASH to PFH, March 10, 1854, both in AMJP 74:15, AGU; ASH Commonplace Book, June 19, 1859, AABO.

3. ASH Commonplace Book, April 21–24, June 4, June 19, and August 11, 1859, AABO.

4. On the redefining cultural experience of other American blacks in Europe, see Gilroy, *Black Atlantic*, esp. 17–19.

5. ASH Commonplace Book, December 19, 1860, AABO; Episcopal Register, August 19, 1862, and August 5, 1863, AABO.

6. Hilary Tucker Diary, August 15, 20, and 21, 1863, AABO.

7. Hilary Tucker Diary, August 15 and 16, 1863, AABO.

8. Hilary Tucker Diary, June 4, August 15, August 16, and December 20, 1863; March 27 and April 24, 1864, AABO; ASH Commonplace Book, May 22, 1859, AABO.

9. The clippings, most of them unidentified and undated, occupy the last hundred pages of the ASH Commonplace Book, AABO.

10. ASH, "The Church + Negro Slavery," ASH Papers 1:2, ACHC.

11. See Thomas J. Shelley, "'Good Work in Its Day': St. Joseph's Provincial Seminary, Troy, New York," *Revue d'Histoire Ecclesiastique* 88 (April–June 1993): 416–438, and Arthur J. Scanlan, *St. Joseph's Seminary, Dunwoodie, New York, 1896–1921* (New York: U.S. Catholic Historical Society, 1922), 25–62. Boston's Bishop John Fitzpatrick, having spent two years in and around Brussels during the Civil War, may have had a role in convincing his Belgian colleague to provide the faculty for the school.

12. Shelley, "'Good Work in Its Day,'" 424–428; Sherwood's description of conditions at the school is quoted here, 426. See also Gabriels, *Historical Sketch of St. Joseph's*, 48–49. Concerns over Sherwood's own health are expressed in Hilary Tucker Diary, February 12 and 14, 1864, AABO.

13. Gabriels, *Historical Sketch of St. Joseph's*, 69–70. On the importance of moral theology in American Catholic seminaries, see White, *Diocesan Seminary in the United States*, 139–140.

14. Gabriels, *Historical Sketch of St. Joseph's*, 45. For James's comments on Sherwood's discouraging reports, see Bishop's Journal, March 10, 1865, AABO. Sherwood's more optimistic assessment is in Hilary Tucker Diary, July 3, 1866, AABO.

15. JAH to McFarland, December 22, 1864, Diocese of Hartford Collection, AUND. On Fitzpatrick's illnesses and death, see O'Connor, *Fitzpatrick's Boston*, 227–239.

16. Williams is now something of a forgotten man in Boston history. For his long career, see the often unsympathetic account in Lord et al., *History of the Archdiocese of Boston*, 3:3–437, and the better treatment in O'Connor, *Boston Catholics*, chs. 4–5. Donna Merwick, *Boston Priests, 1848–1910: A Study of Social and Intellectual Change* (Cambridge: Harvard University Press, 1973), considers important aspects of his tenure, but this work is marred by many errors. Merwick misstates the origins of the Healy brothers and confounds several of them into a single person (pp. 83–87).

17. Foley, *Beloved Outcaste*, 109–124, characterized these shifts in local church administration as a case of "brother rivals brother," but the implication of tension between James and Sherwood Healy is unwarranted. Williams is quoted in William L. Lucey, *The Catholic Church in Maine* (Francestown, N.H.: Marshall Jones, 1957), 215.

18. On the work of this gathering, see James Hennesey, "The Baltimore Council of 1866: An American Syllabus," *Records of the American Catholic Historical Society of Philadelphia* 76 (1965): 165–172.

19. On the failures of the Baltimore council, see Davis, *Black Catholics*, 116–122, and Edward J. Misch, *The American Bishops and the Negro from the Civil War to the Third Plenary Council of Baltimore (1865–1884)* (Rome: Patrizio Graziani, 1968). The council's statement on freed slaves is quoted in ibid., 37; John McGill, the bishop of Richmond, is quoted in Davis, *Black Catholics*, 119–120.

20. McCloskey is quoted in Hennesey, *American Catholics*, 161; Bishop Auguste Martin of Natchitoches, Louisiana, is quoted in Davis, *Black Catholics*, 27.

21. "Our Duties to the Freedman," *Pilot*, November 17, 1866. Father Tucker read the statement without comment at the cathedral; see Hilary Tucker Diary, November 11, 1866, AABO. In the 1880s, un-

der the editorship of John Boyle O'Reilly, the *Pilot* became a more outspoken advocate for black civil rights; for this, see Mark R. Schneider, *Boston Confronts Jim Crow, 1890–1920* (Boston: Northeastern University Press, 1997), ch. 6.

22. See ASH's letters to Williams about the synod, October 25, 27, and 29, 1868, Williams Papers 2:31, AABO.

23. The literature on the changes in worldwide Catholicism in this period is enormous. For useful overviews, see Roger Aubert et al., *The Church in the Age of Liberalism*, trans. Peter Becker (New York: Crossroad, 1981), and Holmes, *Triumph of the Holy See*. See also the insightful discussion in Eamon Duffy, *Saints and Sinners: A History of the Popes* (New Haven: Yale University Press, 1997), ch. 5.

24. The contentious disputes within the American hierarchy are fully examined in James Hennesey, *The First Council of the Vatican: The American Experience* (New York: Herder and Herder, 1963). The diary that Williams kept during this period, now in the Williams Papers 5:41a, AABO, is maddeningly silent on the proceedings of the council and his view of them.

25. ASH to Edwards, April 30, 1870, James F. Edwards Collection, AUND; Williams Diary, July 13–18, 1870, Williams Papers 5:41a, AABO. For Sherwood's comments on Italian politics, see his undated lecture, "Italian Affairs," ASH Papers 1:1, ACHC.

26. After recovering, Sherwood described as much as he could remember of his illness in ASH to Edwards, April 30, 1870, James F. Edwards Collection, AUND. Williams's concern for his friend is evident in Williams Diary, March 18–April 19, 1870, Williams Papers 5:41a, AABO; there are also transcripts of several now-destroyed letters of Williams's in Mother Augustine Tuckerman, "Life of Archbishop Williams," 217–222, AABO. For earlier concerns about Sherwood's health, see Bishop's Journal, September 5–10, 1865, AABO, and Hilary Tucker Diary, November 29–December 4, 1863, AABO.

27. For the dimensions of demographic change in Massachusetts in the second half of the nineteenth century, see Richard W. Wilkie and Jack Tager, eds., *Historical Atlas of Massachusetts* (Amherst: University of Massachusetts Press, 1991), esp. 34–37 and the statistical summaries on pages 140–144. For the Catholic population, compare the annual statistical reports in the Catholic directories for this period (titles and publishers vary), AABO.

28. On the changing fortunes of the South End, see Lawrence W. Kennedy, *Planning the City upon a Hill: Boston since 1630* (Amherst: University of Massachusetts Press, 1992), 56–60. See also Marquand's roman à clef, *The Late George Apley* (Boston: Little, Brown, 1937).

29. On the construction of the cathedral, see Lord et al., *History of the Archdiocese of Boston*, 3:48–55. Sherwood Healy wrote a brief history of the building in an ephemeral newspaper called *The Cathedral*. No original copies of this survive, but there is a typescript in AABO. Sherwood's reference to his "aspirations" for the building were expressed in an untitled, undated address (headed "Gentlemen") in ASH Papers 1:2, ACHC.

30. Healy kept a scrapbook, now in AABO, of circular letters, financial accounts, memos to himself, and newspaper reports of the fair.

31. See the reports in the *Boston Herald*, October 24–December 5, 1871; Sherwood's "congratulations" were expressed in his report on the fair, dated January 10, 1872, a copy of which is in the scrapbook, AABO. For a report on the dedication of the cathedral, see *Pilot*, December 18, 1875.

32. For a useful discussion of the nineteenth-century theology of the priesthood, see Sullivan, "Beneficial Relations," 217–219.

33. See, for example, *Boston Herald*, November 13, 1871. The *Pilot's* assertion of the supposed happiness of blacks in slavery appeared in its issue of May 31, 1862.

34. Hodes, in *White Women, Black Men*, 120–121, suggests the importance of "self-presentation" in influencing local white reactions to interracial individuals.

35. The baptismal and marriage registers of the Holy Cross cathedral parish, now in AABO, chart Sherwood Healy's sacramental activity. During the four years of his rectorship, he never performed more than 6.3 percent of the baptisms and never more than 6.4 percent of the marriages (both in 1873).

36. Ellis's case is reported in the *Boston Herald*, November 23, 1871. Clergymen and other prominent blacks had long been singled out for particularly strict enforcement of Jim Crow laws; see James Oliver Horton and Lois E. Horton, *In Hope of Liberty: Culture, Community, and Protest among Northern Free Blacks, 1700–1860* (New York: Oxford University Press, 1997), 171 and 204. See also Nell Irwin Painter, "'Social Equality,' Miscegenation, Labor, and Power," in *The Evolution of Southern Culture*, ed. Numan V. Bartley (Athens: University of Georgia Press, 1988), 47–67.

37. Conditions for African Americans in Boston after the Civil War are described in John Daniels's classic *In Freedom's Birthplace: A Study of Boston Negroes* (Boston: Houghton Mifflin, 1914) and in Elizabeth Pleck's more recent *Black Migration and Poverty: Boston, 1865–1900* (New York: Academic Press, 1979). On a slightly later period, see Schneider, *Boston Confronts Jim Crow*. For useful background, see also Horton and Horton, *Black Bostonians*; James Oliver Horton, "Shades of Color: The Mulatto in Three Antebellum Northern Communities," in *Free People of Color: Inside the African American Community*, ed. James Oliver Horton (Washington, D.C.: Smithsonian Institution Press, 1993), 122–144; and George A. Levesque, *Black Boston: African American Life and Culture in Urban America, 1750–1860* (New York: Garland, 1994).

38. The *Boston Globe*, May 27, 1872, included a brief notice about Vaughan's speaking tour amid reports of religious news from several denominations. See also Bishop's Journal, May 11, 1872, AABO, and *Pilot*, May 18, 1872.

39. Lord et al., *History of the Archdiocese of Boston*, 3:240–241.

40. Sherwood's last illness and death are recorded in Episcopal Register, AABO, September 16–October 23, 1875, and in Episcopal Diary, August 21–October 23, 1875, ADP.

41. See especially the long obituaries in the *Boston Globe*, October 22, 1875, and *Pilot*, October 30, 1875. See also the perfunctory death notice, similar to that accorded all American Catholic priests, in *Sadlier's Catholic Directory, Almanac, and Ordo, 1876* (New York: Sadlier, 1876), 59.

7. The Bishop: James

1. Sacramental activity at Saint James's has been tabulated from its baptismal and marriage registers, 1866–1875, now in AABO; see also the reports of the church, 1867–1875, in Parish Annual Reports 1:6, AABO.

2. Parish Annual Reports 1:6, AABO; loans to the parish from the Healy family resources are noted in the report of 1872. See also Lord et al., *History of the Archdiocese of Boston*, 3:240–241.

3. All the documentation for the Portland appointment is in APF: Scritture nelle Congregazione Generale, 1004:201–218.

4. The summary of Healy's life and career is in Scritture nelle Congregazione Generale, 1004:207 and

218, APF. The general Roman unfamiliarity with America is confirmed in these documents: in listing the languages in which Healy was fluent, for instance, the summary felt it necessary to point out that his own vernacular was English. For announcements of his appointment, see *Boston Evening Transcript*, February 16, 1875, and *Boston Globe*, February 17, 1875.

5. Vetromile to Franchi, February 19, 1875, Congressi, America Centrale, 26 (1875): 461–462, APF. On the denunciation by the pastor of North Whitefield, see Lucey, *Catholic Church in Maine*, 216–217; on the matter of "indelicate blood," see the unsubstantiated story in Foley, *Beloved Outcaste*, 127–128. The misstatement of Healy's origins appeared in *Portland Eastern Argus*, February 17, 1875.

6. Episcopal Diary, June 2, 1875, ADP.

7. For a description of the Portland diocese, see *Sadlier's Catholic Directory, 1875* (New York: Sadlier, 1875), 298–301; anti-Catholic hostility in Maine is described in Lucey, *Catholic Church in Maine*, 118–143, and Lord et al., *History of the Archdiocese of Boston*, 2:672–678.

8. Foley, *Beloved Outcaste*, 144–145. Foley, writing in the 1950s, was attempting to reconstruct Healy as a black Catholic hero. Foley may have derived this story from an oral tradition in Portland, or he may simply have made it up. Healy's reference to the "insulting letter" is in Episcopal Diary, April 22, 1875, ADP.

9. The literature on this kind of tension is large. For a case study, see Michael J. Guignard, *La Foi, La Langue, La Culture: The Franco-Americans of Biddeford, Maine* (Biddeford: Privately printed, 1982).

10. JAH to McMaster, April 7, 1876, McMaster Collection, AUND.

11. Ponsardin's case is summarized in Lucey, *Catholic Church in Maine*, 224–225, and Foley, *Beloved Outcaste*, 153–168. Acrimonious disputes between bishops and priests were not uncommon in this period; see Robert Trisco, "Bishops and Their Priests in the United States," *The Catholic Priest in the United States: Historical Investigations*, ed. John Tracy Ellis (Collegeville, Minn.: Saint John's University Press, 1971), 111–292. Healy's distress over the case is apparent in his European Diary, April 2, 1878, JAH Papers 3:4, ACHC, and in his correspondence with Archbishop Williams, Williams Papers 2:30, AABO.

12. Episcopal Diary, September 18, 1878, ADP. His complaint about Ponsardin's hat is in Episcopal Diary, October 16, 1877, ADP.

13. For examples of the more normal run of administrative duties during Healy's years in Maine, see Episcopal Diary, April 14 and September 21, 1876, and December 12, 1879, ADP.

14. On various aspects of Healy's tenure, see Lucey, *Catholic Church in Maine*, 221–222, 229–230, and 238–240. On the division of the diocese in 1884, see Wilfred H. Paradis, *Upon This Granite: Catholicism in New Hampshire, 1647–1997* (Portsmouth: Peter Randall, 1998), 105–107. The Garfield eulogy was noted in all of Healy's obituaries as a high point in his career; see, for example, *Boston Globe*, August 6, 1900.

15. JAH to Saint Dominic's Congregation, Portland, September 1, 1876, JAH Papers, ADP; JAH to Brady, February 17, 1883, Letterbooks, ADP. For the growth of schools, compare the listings in *Sadlier's Catholic Directory, 1875*, 298–301, with those in *Wiltzius' Catholic Directory, 1900* (Milwaukee: Wiltzius, 1900), 449–453. On Catholic schools generally, see Jay P. Dolan, *The American Catholic Experience: A History from Colonial Times to the Present* (New York: Doubleday), 262–293. For developments in Boston, see James W. Sanders, "Boston Catholics and the School Question, 1825–1907," in *From Common School to Magnet School: Selected Essays in the History of Boston Schools*, ed. James W. Fraser et al. (Boston: Boston Public Library, 1979), 43–75.

16. Healy's relations with the Sisters of Mercy are described in Lucey, *Catholic Church in Maine*, 187–201; Sister Mary Eulalia Herron, "The Work of the Sisters of Mercy in the New England States: Diocese of Portland, 1858–1921; Diocese of Manchester, 1884–1921," *Records of the American Catholic Historical Society* 35 (March 1924): 57–100; and Kathleen Healy, *Frances Warde: American Founder of the Sisters of Mercy* (New York: Seabury, 1973), 393–451. On the work of religious sisters generally, see Carol K. Coburn and Martha Smith, *Spirited Lives: How Nuns Shaped Catholic Culture and American Life, 1836–1920* (Chapel Hill: University of North Carolina Press, 1999).

17. Episcopal Diary, November 13 and 21, 1875; January 1 and 12, 1876, ADP; JAH to Lambert, February 8, 1883, Letterbooks, ADP.

18. JAH to Sister Eulalia, October 26, 1885, Letterbooks, ADP. On his pastoral activity, see Foley, *Beloved Outcaste*, 141–152. Present-day parishioners have repeated for me stories about Healy told by their parents and grandparents. These are almost equally divided between those who say that his racial background was well known and those who say that it was not.

19. JAH to Robie, October 16 and December 31, 1884, and JAH to Horrigan, January 25, 1887, Letterbooks, ADP. On the discussion of Indian affairs with the pope, see European Diary, February 8, 1886, JAH Papers 3:9, ACHC.

20. On this effort, see Davis, *Black Catholics*, 132–136, and Misch, *American Bishops and the Negro*. See also the address by Bishop William Gross, "The Missions for the Colored People" (pp. 71–74), and the sermon by Archbishop Charles Seghers, "Indian Missions" (pp. 114–119), in *A History of the Third Plenary Council of Baltimore, November 9–December 7, 1884* (Baltimore, 1885).

21. JAH to Marty, November 30, 1885, and JAH to Reed, October 31, 1889, Letterbooks, ADP; JAH to Gibbons, January 25, 1888, and January 29, 1892, Letterbooks, ADP. On the irregular contributions from the Portland diocese, see *St. Joseph's Advocate, 5th Year* (October 1887): 298–299, a copy of which is in Josephite Archives, Baltimore.

22. JAH to Chamberlain, January 9, 1899, Letterbooks, ADP.

23. JAH to Chamberlain, January 9, 1899, Letterbooks, ADP. For the impact of international expansion on American racial attitudes, see Matthew Frye Jacobson, *Barbarian Virtues: The United States Encounters Foreign Peoples at Home and Abroad, 1876–1917* (New York: Hill and Wang, 2000).

24. *American Catholic Tribune*, January 3 and 10, 1891; on Rudd and the black Catholic congresses, see Davis, *Black Catholics*, 163–194.

25. *American Catholic Tribune*, May 11, 1889; for his endorsements of the newspaper, see JAH to Ruffin, October 25, 1888, and JAH to Valle, May 6, 1889, Letterbooks, ADP.

26. JAH to Blackstone, December 17, 1888, Letterbooks, ADP. His appeal to health was convenient but insincere: six weeks after refusing to attend the meeting in Washington, he set out on a two-month trip to California and back. See also Albert S. Foley, "Bishop Healy and the Colored Catholic Congress," *Interracial Review* 28 (May 1954): 79–80.

27. JAH to Stecker, September 23, 1892, quoted in Foley, "Healy and the Colored Catholic Congress," 80.

28. *American Catholic Tribune*, May 11, 1889, and March 14, 1891.

29. JAH to Wood, January 31, 1893, and JAH to Reed, May 9, 1890, Letterbooks, ADP.

30. For Tolton's career, see Davis, *Black Catholics*, 152–162; see also Ochs, *Desegregating the Altar*.

31. *Pilot*, June 11, 1892; *American Catholic Tribune*, March 11, 1887; April 20, 1889; October 12, 1889; June 18 and 25, 1892.

32. *American Catholic Tribune*, April 20, 1889.

33. On the early opposition to unions generally from the hierarchy, see Henry Browne, *The Catholic*

Church and the Knights of Labor (Washington, D.C.: Catholic University of America Press, 1949), 1 33; see also Kevin Kenny, *Making Sense of the Molly Maguires* (New York: Oxford University Press, 1998).

34. Fergus Macdonald, *The Catholic Church and the Secret Societies in the United States* (New York: U.S. Catholic Historical Society, 1946).

35. JAH to Lamoureux, August 27, 1885, Letterbooks, ADP. His undated public letters denouncing the Hibernians and other organizations are in JAH Papers, ADP; see also Macdonald, *Secret Societies*, 122–123. For a general discussion of this topic, see Charles A. Scontras, *Two Decades of Organized Labor and Labor Politics in Maine, 1880–1900* (Orono: University of Maine, 1962), esp. ch. 3.

36. Terence V. Powderly, *The Path I Trod*, ed. Harry J. Carman, et al. (New York: Columbia University Press, 1940), 371–372. Powderly recalls the meeting with Healy as having taken place in 1884, but contemporary documentation shows it to have been in 1885.

37. Powderly to JAH, May 18, 1885, JAH Papers, ADP.

38. JAH to Mazella, March 15, 1887, Letterbooks, ADP; Powderly's version of the interview is in *The Path I Trod*, 345–347.

39. Powderly, *The Path I Trod*, 346–347.

40. JAH to Mazella, March 15, 1887, Letterbooks, ADP. On Gibbons's role in Rerum Novarum, see John Tracy Ellis, *The Life of James Cardinal Gibbons, Archbishop of Baltimore, 1834–1921* (Milwaukee: Bruce, 1952), 1:486–546. On Healy's role in limiting membership of the Knights in Maine, see Scontras, *Two Decades of Organized Labor in Maine*, 49–51; see also Browne, *Catholic Church and the Knights of Labor*, 128.

41. For general histories of this factionalism, see Gerald P. Fogarty, *The Vatican and the American Hierarchy from 1870 to 1965* (Wilmington, Del.: Michael Glazier, 1985), esp. chs. 3–7; see also R. Scott Appleby, *"Church and Age Unite!" The Modernist Impulse in American Catholicism* (Notre Dame, Ind.: University of Notre Dame Press, 1992). On the eventual triumph of the ultramontanes, see O'Toole, *Militant and Triumphant*, esp. ch. 3.

42. JAH to Mazella, January 5, 1893; JAH to Gibbons, January 12, 1893; and JAH to Corrigan, December 11, 1892; all in Letterbooks, ADP.

43. JAH to Elliott, December 1 and 10, 1890; JAH to Ledochowski, February 22, 1897; all in Letterbooks, ADP; see also Episcopal Diary, February 26 and March 6, 1899, ADP. On Hecker generally, see David J. O'Brien, *Isaac Hecker: An American Catholic* (New York: Paulist Press, 1992).

44. European Diary, March 4, April 11, and April 20, 1878, JAH Papers, ACHC.

45. European Diary, March 12 and 14, May 20 and 26, 1878, JAH Papers, ACHC.

46. European Diary, April 15, June 3, and June 10, 1878, JAH Papers, ACHC; European Diary, January 10, 1886, JAH Papers, ACHC.

47. European Diary, January 10, 1886, JAH Papers, ACHC; Episcopal Diary, October 27, 1895, ADP.

48. European Diary, March 10, 1878, JAH Papers, ACHC; Episcopal Diary, December 25, 1883, ADP; JAH to Looney, October 27, 1885, Letterbooks, ADP.

49. European Diary, February 22, March 1–4, and March 23, 1878, JAH Papers, ACHC.

50. California Diary, February 20, 27, and 28, 1889, JAH Papers, ACHC; California Diary, June 23, 1891, JAH Papers, ACHC. See the physical descriptions on several of James's passports, all of which are in Department of State Passport Records, National Archives Microfilm Publication M-1371: #11166 (1863); #35057 (1867); #4040 (1877); #3727 (1885); and #1077 (1898).

51. *Portland Evening Express*, June 5, 1900; *Portland Eastern Argus*, June 6, 1900.

8. The President: Patrick

1. PFH to Fenwick, November 23, 1853, AMJP 74:1, AGU.

2. PFH Diary, October 12, 1863, PFH Papers 1:1, ACHC; PFH to Paresce, September 28, 1864, AMJP 77:10, AGU.

3. On the origins and early history of the Jesuits, see John W. O'Malley, *The First Jesuits* (Cambridge: Harvard University Press, 1993); see also John W. O'Malley et al., *Jesuit Spirituality: A Now and Future Resource* (Chicago: Loyola University Press, 1990), and Robert Emmett Curran, *American Jesuit Spirituality: The Maryland Tradition, 1634–1900* (New York: Paulist Press, 1988).

4. Retreat Notes, September 1860, and Retreat Notes, January 26, 1868, both in PFH Papers 1:6, AGU; PFH to Paresce, October (?) 1864, AMJP 77:10, AGU.

5. Retreat Notes, September 1860, PFH Papers 1:6, AGU; PFH European Diary, October 1, 1863, PFH Papers 1:1, ACHC.

6. Hilary Tucker Diary, September 10, 1866, AABO. Patrick's reaction to his ordination, discussed in chapter 4 above, is described in PFH to Paresce, September 5, 1864, AMJP 77:10, AGU. On Patrick's final years of preparation, see Foley, *Dream of an Outcaste*, 86–87.

7. Curran, in *Bicentennial History of Georgetown*, 248–251, describes the condition of the school after the war; see also his tabulations of student enrollments, 398 and 422–427.

8. For the changes in Washington during and after the war, see Constance McLaughlin Green, *The Secret City: A History of Race Relations in the Nation's Capital* (Princeton: Princeton University Press, 1967), 55–90. See also James Oliver Horton and Lois E. Horton, "Race, Occupation, and Literacy in Reconstruction Washington, D.C.," in *Free People of Color*, ed. Horton, 185–197.

9. Green, *Secret City*, 91–118; Gatewood, *Aristocrats of Color*, 39–68.

10. Young to Lancaster, January 22, 1866, AMJP 19:3, AGU; Georgetown House Diary, December 28, 1874, AGU.

11. On Georgetown's relationship to the life of Washington, see Green, *Secret City*, 108; Curran, *Bicentennial History of Georgetown*, 250 and 303–330; and William W. Warner, *At Peace with All Their Neighbors: Catholics and Catholicism in the National Capital, 1787–1860* (Washington, D.C.: Georgetown University Press, 1994), esp. 15–32.

12. On this unusual connection, see Theodore C. DeLaney, "Julia Gardiner Tyler: A Nineteenth-Century Southern Woman" (Ph.D. diss., College of William and Mary, 1995), 262–270. There are about a dozen letters from Healy to Mrs. Tyler, some of them addressed "Dear God-Child," in the Gardiner-Tyler Family Papers, Archives and Manuscripts Department, Yale University Library, New Haven, Connecticut.

13. See the contemporary description, "Georgetown College," *Woodstock Letters* 1 (1872): 156–163.

14. Mallory is quoted in "Letters from Famous Old Boys," *Georgetown College Journal* 35 (December 1906): 117. See also "Our Ex-President," *Georgetown College Journal* 10 (March 1882): 71–72.

15. Georgetown House Diary, May 23, 1873, AGU; Beckx to Keller, August 17, 1874, AMJP 120:9, AGU. The search for a new president is described in Curran, *Bicentennial History of Georgetown*, 280; Curran also quotes from some of the correspondence surrounding this case, the originals of which are all in the Archives of Generalate of the Society of Jesus in Rome.

16. This story was relayed to me by the Jesuit historian James Hennesey in a personal letter of December 12, 1993.

17. Curran, *Bicentennial History of Georgetown*, 281; "Our Ex-President," *Georgetown College Journal*

10 (March 1882): 71. On the changes in the content of American higher education in this period, see Frederick Rudolph, *Curriculum: A History of the American Undergraduate Course of Study since 1636* (San Francisco: Jossey-Bass, 1977), esp. ch. 4, and George Marsden, *The Soul of the American University: From Protestant Establishment to Established Nonbelief* (New York: Oxford University Press, 1994), esp. part 2.

18. Healy's efforts at curricular reform are described in Curran, *Bicentennial History of Georgetown*, 294–298. For a contemporary assessment, see J. Havens Richards, "An Explanation in Reply to Some Recent Strictures," *Woodstock Letters* 26 (1897): 146–153. On the changing content of Catholic higher education generally during this period, see Rudolph, *Curriculum*, 170–172.

19. Curran, *Bicentennial History of Georgetown*, 398.

20. Eliot to PFH, April 22, 1878, Medical School Files (1874–1879), AGU; Georgetown House Diary, March 24, 1876, AGU. Healy's efforts to reform the medical school are described in Curran, *Bicentennial History of Georgetown*, 308–315.

21. Curran, *Bicentennial History of Georgetown*, 315–319.

22. The range of teaching responsibilities is evident from the descriptions of Georgetown that appear in *Catalogus Provinciae Marylandiae Societatis Jesu* (title and imprints vary), 1873–1882. See also Curran, *Bicentennial History of Georgetown*, 290–291.

23. See Tables 10.1 (pp. 422–423) and 11.1 (pp. 426–427) in Curran, *Bicentennial History of Georgetown*.

24. See the entire discussion of student demographics in Curran, *Bicentennial History of Georgetown*, 291–294. The school's expanding national reputation is discussed in Foley, *Dream of an Outcaste*, 152–168.

25. On the start of the long decline for African Americans in Washington during this period, see Green, *Secret City*, 119–154, and Constance McLaughlin Green, *Washington: Capital City, 1879–1950* (Princeton: Princeton University Press, 1963), 101–131.

26. For a description of the building and its construction, see Hardy George, "Georgetown University's Healy Building," *Journal of the Society of Architectural Historians* 31 (October 1972): 208–216.

27. Georgetown House Diary, November 15, 1877, AGU; see also William Dennis, "Rev. Patrick F. Healy, S.J.: An Attempt at an Appreciation," *Georgetown College Journal* 41 (January 1913): 226. The construction and finances of the school in this period are described in Curran, *Bicentennial History of Georgetown*, 284–290, and Foley, *Dream of an Outcaste*, 169–185.

28. PFH to Eliot, April 20, 1880, Eliot Papers, Box 69, Harvard University Archives, Cambridge, Massachusetts; Georgetown House Diary, November 27–29, 1878, AGU; PFH California Diary, November 30, 1878, PFH Papers 1:2, ACHC.

29. PFH California Diary, December 9 and 16, 1878, PFH Papers 1:2, ACHC. There are other similar passages in this diary.

30. PFH California Diary, December 27 and 30, 1878, PFH Papers 1:2, ACHC; Mullaly to PFH, January 10, 1879, PFH Papers 2:3, AGU. The meager success of this fund-raising tour is discussed in Curran, *Bicentennial History of Georgetown*, 286–288, and Foley, *Dream of an Outcaste*, 186–198.

31. Foley, in *Dream of an Outcaste*, 294–296, makes the unsupported assertion that Healy suffered from a form of epilepsy, and this is repeated in Curran, *Bicentennial History of Georgetown*, 319. The symptoms of which Healy complained throughout his life—headaches, a jumpy stomach, normal muscle pains, and "catarrh"—could have resulted from any number of causes, and there is no evidence to suggest epilepsy as their specific origin.

32. On his health and his extended stays in Maine, see, for example, Episcopal Diary, Febru-

ary 25–April 23, 1882, ADP; PFH to Richards, October 17, 1891, J. Havens Richards Papers 1:5, AGU; "Our Ex-President," *Georgetown College Journal* 10 (March 1882): 71–72. On his last years as president, see Curran, *Bicentennial History of Georgetown*, 319–320, and Foley, *Dream of an Outcaste*, 199–211. The "second founder" title is recognized in Dennis, "Rev. Patrick F. Healy, S.J.," 225–227.

33. See the diary Patrick kept during this trip, May 17–October 15, 1883, PFH Papers 1:4, ACHC. Throughout this diary, he consistently misnamed the ship the "*Corsica*."

34. PFH Alaska Diary, May 26, July 12, July 16, and July 31, 1883, PFH Papers 1:4, ACHC; Fred Healy Diary, July 31, 1883, Healy Collection (HM 47577), Huntington Library, San Marino, California.

35. PFH Alaska Diary, June 11, 12, and 23, July 8 and 12, 1883, PFH Papers 1:4, ACHC.

36. See the uneventful descriptions of his year in California in PFH Diary, October 1883–August 1884, PFH Papers 1:5, ACHC.

37. See his diaries for these years in PFH Papers 1:5–7, ACHC, and in PFH Papers 1:2–3, AGU. His remarks on the schoolchildren are in PFH Diary, February 3, 1898, PFH Papers 1:3, AGU. On his noticing of the slight against Georgetown, see PFH to Richards, November 27, 1891, J. Havens Richards Papers 1:5, AGU. Reports of his participation in the international Jesuit conference, all of them devoid of personal observation and comment, appeared in the Jesuit publication *Woodstock Letters* 21 (1892): 384–410, and 22 (1893): 27–38.

9. Sisters: Martha, Josephine, and Eliza

1. For a useful discussion of the portrayal of interracial women in fiction, see Elizabeth Fox Genovese, "Slavery, Race, and the Figure of the Tragic Mulatta, or, The Ghost of Southern History in the Writing of African-American Women," *Mississippi Quarterly* 49 (Fall 1996): 791- 817, and Judith R. Berzon, *Neither Black Nor White: The Mulatto Character in American Fiction* (New York: New York University Press, 1978). The most famous examples of such portrayals are the characters in Nella Larsen's *Passing* (New York: Knopf, 1929).

2. Marriage record, July 25, 1865, Saint Mary's parish, Waltham, AABO. There is also a copy of the civil marriage record in Marriage Records (1865), vol. 181, p. 171, ACM. Civil marriage records did not at this time specify the race of the parties. On Martha's contentment since leaving the convent, see JAH to "Reverende Soeur," February 1, 1864, ACND.

3. Unlike her two sisters, Martha seems never to have applied for a passport, so there are no reports of her complexion or other physical characteristics.

4. I have reconstructed the Cashman family from birth, baptismal, marriage, and death records in AABO, ACM, and the Massachusetts Registry of Vital Records and Statistics. I have also received valuable information about the family from Professor Thomas Riley of Fargo, North Dakota, and his siblings, the great-grandchildren of Jeremiah and Martha Healy Cashman.

5. I have traced Jeremiah Cashman's occupation and the family's residences, 1865–1920, through the annual *Boston City Directory* (precise title and imprints vary) in the Massachusetts State Library, Boston, and through the various Newton city directories and tax lists in the special collections room of the Newton City Library, Newton, Massachusetts. James Healy apparently sold his house in Newton about 1868, since his name drops off the town's tax rolls in that year. For the character of Jamaica Plain, see Alexander von Hoffman, *Local Attachments: The Making of an American Urban Neighborhood, 1850–1920* (Baltimore: Johns Hopkins University Press, 1994).

6. Student Diary, February 27, 1849, JAH Papers, ACHC; JAH to Martha Cashman, January 12, 1884, and February 4, 1884, JAH to McDonald, April 23 and 25, 1884, JAH to Pelletier, December 4, 1885, all in Letterbooks, ADP.

7. For a description of women's work in this period, see Glenna Matthews, *"Just a Housewife": The Rise and Fall of Domesticity in America* (New York: Oxford University Press, 1987), 98–106.

8. The story about subsequent generations of the family having to be told of their ancestry was related to me by Thomas Riley and his siblings in a personal interview with them on August 15, 1996. For the increasing identification of American mulattoes with the African American community at the end of the nineteenth and beginning of the twentieth centuries, see Williamson, *New People*, 2–3 and 62, and Fredrickson, *Black Image in the White Mind*, 234–235 and 277–278.

9. Careful, if not particularly informative, notations of the girls' school bills during this period are contained in the account books of the Pensionnat de Saint-Jean, ACND. See also JAH to "Reverende Soeur," February 1, 1864, and ASH to "Reverende Soeur," December 9, 1863, both in ACND.

10. Hilary Tucker Diary, May 1, 1863, and May 31–July 1, 1864, AABO. On the growing understanding of the home as a private refuge from the public world, see Mary P. Ryan, *Cradle of the Middle Class: The Family in Oneida County, New York, 1790–1865* (New York: Cambridge University Press, 1981), 232–234.

11. Smyrna Diary, January 6–May 17, 1868, JAH Papers 3.1, ACHC. It is unclear precisely which of the travelers kept this diary; most probably it was Mary Jane Healy. On the popularity of Smyrna as a tourist destination for Americans, see David H. Finnie, *Pioneers East: The Early American Experience in the Middle East* (Cambridge: Harvard University Press, 1967), esp. 20–44.

12. Smyrna Diary, March 11, March 19, March 25, and April 1, 1868, JAH Papers 3:1, ACHC.

13. *Sadlier's Catholic Directory, 1875* (New York, 1875), 127–133. On the work of sisters generally, see Coburn and Smith, *Spirited Lives*, and Mary J. Oates, "'The Good Sisters': The Work and Position of Catholic Churchwomen in Boston, 1870–1940," in *Catholic Boston*, ed. Sullivan and O'Toole, 171–200. The story of Josephine's decision to enter a convent is related in "Circulaire de la mort de Josephine Healy," July 23, 1879, Necrologies, 1861–1884, ARHSJ. This document contains much stylized language and formulaic narrative. Its usefulness in describing Josephine's particular experiences should not, however, be wholly discounted.

14. See Josephine's passport, #35578, December 28, 1867, State Department Passport Files, National Archives Microfilm #M1371, roll 3, frame 531. On the origin of orders of African American sisters, see Davis, *Black Catholics*, 98–115, and Morrow, "Outsiders Within," 35–54.

15. The work of the Good Shepherd sisters is described in Katherine E. Conway, *The Golden Year of the Good Shepherd in Boston* (Boston: Thomas Flynn, 1918). See also Katherine E. Conway, *In the Footsteps of the Good Shepherd, New York, 1857–1907* (New York: Convent of the Good Shepherd, 1907), 94–95 and 172–175; Lord et al., *History of the Archdiocese of Boston*, 3:372–375; and Holleran, *Boston's Wayward Children*, 127–136.

16. Foley, in *Beloved Outcaste*, 121–122, says racial prejudice excluded Josephine from the Good Shepherd order. The story is undocumented, and since Foley misidentifies the superior of the Boston convent, it may not be accurate.

17. The timing of her entry into the order has been calculated from several references in "Circulaire de la mort de Josephine Healy," July 23, 1879, Necrologies, 1861–1884, ARHSJ. On the origins of this community, see Soeur Mondoux, *L'Hotel-Dieu, Premier Hopital de Montreal, 1642–1763* (Mon-

treal: Therein Freres, 1941). An outline of the Hospitallers during this period is also provided in Edouard Desjardins et al., "L'Hotel-Dieu du Mont Sainte-Famille (1861–1973)," in *L'Hotel-Dieu de Montreal, 1642–1973*, ed. Michel Allard (Montreal: Hurtubise HMH, 1973), 57–72; see also Andre La Vallee, "Les Religieuses Hospitalieres de Saint-Joseph et l'Ecole de Medecine et de Chirurgie dans la Querrelle Universitaire (1843–1891)," in *L'Hotel-Dieu*, ed. Allard, 269–299.

18. The success of *Awful Disclosures* and its meaning for American nativism are described in Billington, *Protestant Crusade*, esp. 99–108, and in Franchot's more recent *Roads to Rome*, 154–161.

19. "Circulaire de la mort de Josephine Healy," July 23, 1879, Necrologies, 1861–1884, ARHSJ.

20. Josephine Healy to PFH, April 16, 1874, PFH Papers 2:2, AGU.

21. James noted her declining condition in his diary; see especially Episcopal Diary, September 6, 1878, and May 19 and 20, June 2, and July 20 and 26, 1878, ADP.

22. The notebook, labeled "Fleurs de Religion, . . . Villa Maria, 1860," is in JAH Papers, ADP; see also JAH to "Reverende Soeur," February 1, 1864, ACND.

23. "Profession de Elisa Mary Teresa Healey [*sic*], dite Soeur Ste. Marie Madeleine," July 18, 1876, ACND; Josephine Healy to PFH, April 16, 1874, PFH Papers 2:2, AGU. In those orders whose members took on new, religious names when they joined, names were assigned by superiors from a standard list of favorites. Eliza herself had no choice in the matter, and so we should not look for any particular significance in the selection of this name. On religious schools as "nurseries" for vocations, see Danylewycz, *Taking the Veil*, 116–119.

24. Expansion of the Notre Dame sisters is described in detail in Danylewycz, *Taking the Veil*, 74–75 and 123–125; see also tables 8 and 9. On the reputation of the sisters and the schools they ran, see also Doyle, *Marguerite Bourgeoys and Her Congregation*, 265–266.

25. For Eliza's official biography, see "Deces de Soeur Saint Marie Madeleine," Congregation de Notre Dame, *Annales de la Maison Mere*, 319–326, ACND. See Eliza's passport, #35579, December 28, 1867, in State Department Passport Files, National Archives Microfilm #M1371, roll 3, frame 531.

26. On the school at Brockville, see Sister Saint Alfred of Rome Baeszler, "The Congregation of Notre Dame in Ontario and the United States: The History of Holy Angels Province" (Ph.D. diss., Fordham University, 1944), 90–93, and *Histoire de la Congregation de Notre Dame*, vol. 10 (Montreal: Congregation de Notre Dame, 1969), 329–330. On the important role of music, art, and needlework classes in the economics of convent life, see Oates, "'The Good Sisters,'" 191–194.

27. On her successive assignments, see *Histoire de la Congregation de Notre Dame*, 249–252 (Sherbrooke), 274–275 (Montreal), 277–278 (Montreal), 325–328 (Ottawa).

28. Episcopal Diary, August 8, 1880; August 14, 1881; October 10, 1881, ADP. On the schools of the Notre Dame sisters in Maine, see also Baeszler, "Congregation of Notre Dame," 166–169, and *Histoire de la Congregation de Notre Dame*, 372–373.

29. On the administration of American sisterhoods, see Joan Lexau's somewhat dated but still useful *Convent Life: Roman Catholic Religious Orders of Women in North America* (New York: Dial, 1964).

30. The school at Huntingdon is described generally in *Histoire de la Congregation de Notre Dame*, 261–262; this account makes mention of the "kind generosity" of Bishop Healy.

31. Compare the apparent ease with which the Notre Dame sisters put Eliza Healy forward with the deliberate effort of another order, the Sisters, Servants of the Immaculate Heart of Mary, to conceal the mixed-race origins of their founder; see Marita-Constance Supan, "Dangerous Memory: Mother M. Theresa Maxis Duchemin and the Michigan Congregation of the Sisters, IHM," in

Sisters, *Building Sisterhood: A Feminist History of the Sisters, Servants of the Immaculate Heart of Mary* (Syracuse: Syracuse University Press, 1997), 31–67.

32. On the problems of Notre Dame, Chicago, see *Histoire de la Congregation de Notre Dame*, 384–388; Baeszler, "Congregation of Notre Dame," 151–156; and Harry C. Koenig, ed., *History of the Parishes of the Archdiocese of Chicago* (Chicago: Archdiocese of Chicago, 1980), 663–667.

33. On the conversion "epidemic" in Vermont and the origins of Villa Barlow, see Lord et al., *History of the Archdiocese of Boston*, 2:734–743. On the town's eventful history, see Robin W. Winks, "Raid at St. Albans," *Vermont Life* 15 (Spring 1961): 40–46, and Robert P. Ashley, "The St. Albans Raid," *Civil War Times Illustrated* 6 (November 1967): 18–27.

34. Almost nothing has been written about Villa Barlow during Eliza Healy's years there. See Helen Brophy, "Villa Barlow, 1869–1969," in the commemorative booklet *100 Years of Teaching in St. Albans, Vermont*, a copy of which is in the Saint Albans Historical Society. See also Henry G. Fairbanks, "Slavery and the Vermont Clergy," *Vermont History*, new series, 27 (October 1959): 309–312, and "Deces de Soeur Saint Marie Madeleine," *Annales de la Maison Mere*, 322, ACND.

35. The day-to-day routines of the convent and school are recorded in the Villa Barlow Annals, 1903–1919 (#328.300.3), ACND. See also "Deces de Soeur Saint Marie Madeleine," *Annales de la Maison Mere*, 322–323.

10. The Captain: Michael

1. MAH to Jackson, March 1893, Alaska File, USRCS, National Archives Microfilm #641, roll 3, frames 104–108 (hereafter cited as "Alaska File," with appropriate roll and frame numbers).

2. On occupational identity and the work of African American seamen, see Bolster, *Black Jacks*, and W. Jeffrey Bolster, "An Inner Diaspora: Black Sailors Making Selves," in *Through a Glass Darkly: Reflections on Personal Identity in Early America*, ed. Ronald Hoffman et al. (Chapel Hill: University of North Carolina Press, 1997), 419–448. On the nationalization of racial attitudes, see Leon F. Litwack, *Trouble in Mind: Black Southerners in the Age of Jim Crow* (New York: Knopf, 1998), esp. 476–496.

3. On Kimball and the reform of the Revenue Cutter Service, see Irving H. King, *The Coast Guard Expands, 1865–1915: New Roles, New Frontiers* (Annapolis: Naval Institute Press, 1996), 9–18.

4. For a description of one of these early assignments, see USRCS *Moccasin*, "Transcript of Journal," Logs of Revenue Cutters, Records of the U.S. Coast Guard (RG 26), Box 1565, NARA. Visits to Boston and Washington are noted in Bishop's Journal, November 12, 1865, AABO, and Jesuit House Diary, February 11, 1875, AGU. On Fred Healy's birth and baptism, see Birth Records, October 5, 1870, ACM (book 225, p. 154), and Baptismal Register, Cathedral of the Holy Cross, October 5, 1870, AABO. Albert Foley maintained (in *Dream of an Outcaste*, 223, and elsewhere) that Fred Healy was adopted after Mary Jane Healy had suffered an unbelievable nineteen miscarriages. This is completely false.

5. On the history of the territory and the government's neglect of it, see Ernest Gruening, *The State of Alaska*, rev. ed. (New York: Random House, 1968), 33–39, and Claus-M. Naske and Herman E. Slotnick, *Alaska: A History of the 49th State* (Grand Rapids, Mich.: Eerdmans, 1979), 57–65. Population estimates for this time period are very unreliable, but see the figures given in Gruening, 63 and 75.

6. Early Revenue Cutter Service interest in Alaska is described fully in Truman R. Strobridge and Dennis L. Noble, *Alaska and the U.S. Revenue Cutter Service, 1867–1915* (Annapolis: Naval Institute Press, 1999). See also Evans, *Coast Guard,* 106–109, and King, *Coast Guard Expands,* 22–53.

7. MAH to Clark, September 12, 1881, Alaska File, 1:351–361. On the other work of the *Corwin* and the *Rush* in this period, see Evans, *Coast Guard,* 124–129, and Gerald O. Williams, "Michael J.[*sic*] Healy and the Alaska Maritime Frontier, 1880–1902" (M.A. thesis, University of Oregon, 1987), 48–69. Williams's work is useful but marred by factual errors—not least in Healy's name—and by a frequently unsympathetic attitude.

8. MAH to Clark, September 12, 1881, Alaska File, 1:351–361.

9. See the two reports written by Healy: *Report of the Cruise of the Revenue Marine Steamer "Corwin" in the Arctic Ocean in the Year 1884* (Washington, D.C., 1889), and *Report of the Cruise of the Revenue Marine Steamer "Corwin" in the Arctic Ocean in the Year 1885* (Washington, D.C., 1887).

10. The painful story of Johnson C. Whittaker has been told in John F. Marszalek Jr., *Court-Martial: A Black Man in America* (New York: Scribner, 1972), reissued as *Assault at West Point: The Court-Martial of Johnson Whittaker* (New York: Collier, 1994). Another African American had managed to graduate from the military academy a few years earlier but was court-martialled and discharged shortly afterward; see Henry O. Flipper, *The Colored Cadet at West Point,* ed. Quintard Taylor Jr. (Lincoln: University of Nebraska Press, 1998; orig. pub. 1878).

11. Fred Healy Diary, July 25, 1883, Healy Collection (HM #47577), Huntington Library, San Marino, California. For Healy's equation of whites and "our" people, see his letter to the U.S. Commissioner of Education, December 17, 1894, Alaska File, 3:952–956. For generally disapproving comments about "half-breeds" in Alaska, see PFH Diary, July 12, 1883, PFH Papers 1:4, ACHC, and J. T. White Diary, June 27, 1889, transcript in U.S. Coast Guard Academy Museum, New London, Connecticut. For the popularity of this kind of language in this period, see Jacobson, *Whiteness of a Different Color,* esp. ch. 6.

12. MAH to Secretary of the Treasury, September 14, 1886, *Bear* Letterbook, Healy Collection (HM #47616), Huntington Library. On the ship's long, colorful history, see Evans, *Coast Guard,* 129–130, and King, *Coast Guard Expands,* 82–84. There is also a surprisingly large popular literature: Stella Rapaport, *The Bear, Ship of Many Lives* (New York: Dodd, Mead, 1962); William Bixby, *Track of the Bear* (New York: D. McKay, 1965); Polly Burroughs, *The Great Ice Ship "Bear": Eighty-Nine Years in Polar Seas* (New York: Van Nostrand Reinhold, 1970); and Robert H. Rankin, *Immortal Bear, the Stoutest Polar Ship* (New York: Putnam, 1970).

13. The logbooks for the *Bear* in this period, providing detailed accounts of each year's voyage, are all in the records of the Revenue Cutter Service, RG 26, NARA. There are also duplicate copies of some of the logs in the special collections room of the Oakland Public Library, Oakland, California. On the difficulties of Arctic navigation, see Healy, *Report of the "Corwin,"* 1885, 16.

14. Ludlow to all commanders, May 22, 1893, Alaska File, 3:156–166. The redoubled effect of killing seal mothers is described in White to MAH, December 10, 1894, Alaska File, 3:895–899. For a good description of seal hunting, see the contemporary reports in David Starr Jordan, *Reports on Conditions of Seal Life in the Pribilof Islands* (Washington, D.C.: Government Printing Office, 1898), 58–59; see also Gruening, *State of Alaska,* 87–90.

15. On the boarding of the *Ada,* see the logbook of the *Bear,* August 25–27, 1893, NARA. For an example of putting a man ashore to disrupt hunting, see the *Bear* logbook, June 17, 1888, NARA. The esti-

mates of the reduction of the seal population are in Charles S. Campbell Jr., "The Anglo-American Crisis in the Bering Sea, 1890–1891," in *Alaska and Its History,* ed. Morgan B. Sherwood (Seattle: University of Washington Press, 1967), 328–329.

16. The standard descriptions of the American whaling industry are Elmo Paul Hohman, *The American Whaleman: A Study of Life and Labor in the Whaling Industry* (New York: Longmans, Green 1928), and the more recent Margaret S. Creighton, *Rites and Passages: The Experience of American Whaling, 1830–1870* (New York: Cambridge University Press, 1995). On the role of blacks in the industry, see James Farr, "A Slow Boat to Nowhere: The Multi-Racial Crews of the American Whaling Industry," *Journal of Negro History* 68 (Spring 1983): 159–170.

17. For examples of the *Bear*'s work among the whaling fleet, see its logbooks, June 6–12, 1886, June 22 and July 31, 1888, and June 12–16, 1894, NARA.

18. Mary Jane Healy Diary, September 22, 1890, Huntington Library (HM #47579); *New York Times,* May 19, 1895; MAH to Jackson, March 1893, Alaska File, 3:104–108. See also the scrapbook (ca. 200 pages) of mostly-unidentified newspaper clippings maintained by Mary Jane Healy, Healy Collection (HM #47616), box 2, Huntington Library. Testimonials from the whaling fleet (dated November 12, 1888, December 2, 1889, and several undated), are also in the Huntington Library's Healy Collection.

19. MAH to Shepard, July 4, 1893, Alaska File, 3:280–283; PFH Diary, July 25, 1883, PFH Papers 1:4, ACHC; *Bear* logbooks, July 17, 1887, and June 24, 1890, NARA; MAH to Carlisle, July 4, 1893, Alaska File, 3:322–336; *New York Times,* August 11, 1892.

20. *Bear* logbooks, July 3, 1886, July 2, 1890, and May 1, 1891, NARA; Healy, *Report of the "Corwin," 1884,* 17; MAH to Clark, September 12, 1881, Alaska File, 1:351–361; MAH to Windom, September 14, 1881, Alaska File, 1:363–367.

21. Healy, *Report of the "Corwin," 1884,* 16–17; MAH to Commissioner of Education, December 17, 1894, Alaska File, 3:952–956; MAH to Clark, September 12, 1881, Alaska File, 1:351–361; *Bear* logbook, July 3, 1886, NARA.

22. Healy, *Report of the "Corwin," 1884,* 18; Healy, *Report of the "Corwin," 1885,* 16; Fred Healy Diary, July 11, 1883, Healy Collection (HM #47577), Huntington Library; Mary Jane Healy Diary, May 1883, Healy Collection (HM #47578), Huntington Library.

23. MAH to Jackson, December 10, 1893, Sheldon Jackson Correspondence, vol. 16, Presbyterian Historical Society, Philadelphia. For firsthand accounts of this entire project, see John C. Cantwell, "Captain Healy's Reindeer," *Marine Corps Gazette* (May 1935): 26–29, 58–60, and Sheldon Jackson, "The Arctic Cruise of the United States Revenue Cutter *Bear*," *National Geographic Magazine* 7 (January 1896): 27–31.

24. MJH to Jackson, October 20, 1890, Jackson Correspondence, vol. 15, Presbyterian Historical Society, Philadelphia. On the career of Jackson, see the rather pious biography by John T. Faris, *The Alaskan Pathfinder: The Story of Sheldon Jackson* (Chicago: Revell, 1926), and the more recent work by Norman J. Bender, *Winning the West for Christ: Sheldon Jackson and Presbyterianism on the Rocky Mountain Frontier, 1869–1880* (Albuquerque: University of New Mexico Press, 1996). Jackson and Healy are the principal characters in the fictionalized but generally accurate account of the reindeer project presented in part 7 of James Michener's *Alaska* (New York: Random House, 1989).

25. On the planning of the project, see MAH to Harris, December 6, 1890, Alaska File, 1:1532–1534, and

MAH to Jackson, December 28 and 31, 1890, Jackson Correspondence, vol. 15, Presbyterian Historical Society, Philadelphia. The logbook of the *Bear*, July 11–24, 1890, NARA, describes this period in general. See also Cantwell's memoir, "Captain Healy's Reindeer." Mary Jane Healy's account of buying and transporting this first group of reindeer is in MJH Diary (HM #47580), July 10–25, 1891, Huntington Library. The captain's frequently repeated commendation of Jarvis is in MAH to Shepard, February 23, 1893, Alaska File, 3:39–42.

26. JAH to Eugene Healy, October 4, 1884, Letterbooks, ADP. See also JAH to Pelletier, June 18, 1882, and JAH to Pelletier, October 29, 1891, both in Letterbooks, ADP, and JAH to McCarthy, November 20, 1877, JAH Papers, ADP. James's decision to leave his brother in jail is noted in Episcopal Diary, January 17, 1876, ADP.

27. MAH to Shepard, January 31 and February 21, 1893, Alaska File, 3:20–21 and 34–36; Eugene Healy application, February 2, 1893, ibid., 17. According to its historian, the short-lived facility at Barrow was "a model of governmental mismanagement and irresolution"; see John Bockstoce, "The Point Barrow Refuge Station," *American Neptune* 39 (1979): 5–21.

28. See Healy's report on the project, July 1893, Alaska File, 3:407–420; there is also a copy of this report among the Sheldon Jackson Papers in the Speer Library, Princeton Theological Seminary, Princeton, New Jersey. See also Lieutenant Jarvis's later report to the secretary of the treasury, July 30, 1899, Alaska File, 8:304–312. The whole project is also described in William R. Hunt, *Arctic Passage: The Turbulent History of the Land and People of the Bering Sea, 1697–1975* (New York: Scribner's, 1975), 176–182.

29. *New York Sun*, January 28, 1894; Humphrey to Carlisle, January 8, 1895, Alaska File, 4:10.

30. MAH to Shepard, April 29, 1893, Alaska File, 3:131–136; MAH to Jackson, December 19, 1890, Jackson Correspondence, vol. 15, Presbyterian Historical Society, Philadelphia; J. T. White Diary, June 23, 1889, transcript in Coast Guard Academy Museum. On the power of ship captains, see Herman Melville, *Benito Cereno* (New York: Library of America, 1984; orig. pub. 1855), 681; see also Greg Dening's useful *Mr. Bligh's Bad Language: Passion, Power, and Theatre on the Bounty* (Cambridge: Cambridge University Press, 1992).

31. *Bear* logbook, September 18, 1887, NARA; MJH to Jackson, October 20, 1887, Jackson Correspondence, vol. 15, Presbyterian Historical Society, Philadelphia; MJH Diary (HM #47578), May 19, 1884, Huntington Library; PFH Diary, June 18 and December 7–11, 1883, PFH Papers 1:4 and 1:5, ACHC.

32. MAH to Shepard, May 23, 1891, Alaska File, 2:84–89; Transcript of journal, USRCS *Moccasin*, December 10, 1871, Records of the Coast Guard (RG 26), Box 1565, NARA; John Early Diary, November 14–December 1, 1871, John Early Papers 1:9, AGU.

33. MAH to Shepard, April 28, 1890, Alaska File, 1:1309–1316; J. T. White Diary, June 27 and 30, 1889, transcript in Coast Guard Academy Museum; PFH Diary, December 17, 1883, PFH Papers 1:5, ACHC.

34. The full transcript of Healy's trial, March 3–22, 1890, and supporting documents are in "Charges against RCS Officers: Capt. M. A. Healy," Records of the Revenue Cutter Service (RG 26), box 11, NARA; hereafter referred to as "Trial, 1890." See also J. T. White Diary, July 8, 1889, transcript in Coast Guard Academy Museum.

35. On the involvement of temperance organizations, see Johnston to Windom, January 13, 1890; Eden to O'Connor, March 14, 1890; and Gray to Windom, March 24, 1890, all in Trial, 1890. The trial records also include a clipping from the San Francisco *Morning Call*, January 12, 1890, describing the mass denunciation meeting. The *New York Times*, January 20, 1890, reported the meeting under the headline "Disgrace to the Service! Atrocious Cruelty Practiced on Seamen."

36. Buhner's testimony and the ruling in the case are in Trial, 1890; see also MAH to Shepard, April 28, 1890, Alaska File, 1:1309–1316.

37. The *Bear's* logbook, April 27–November 14, 1895, NARA, gives no indication that there was anything out of the ordinary on this cruise. Captains ultimately controlled the keeping of the log, however, and this always affected its content.

38. The complete transcript and other supporting documentation of the trial is in "Charges against RCS Officers: Capt. M. A. Healy," Records of the Revenue Cutter Service (RG 26), boxes 10–11, NARA; hereafter referred to as "Trial, 1896." Reports on the trial appeared in the *New York Times*, November 3, 4, 20, and 30, 1895; December 2, 13, and 14, 1895; January 27, 1896; May 14, 1896; and June 10, 1896.

39. Quotations of the testimony are from the transcripts in Trial, 1896. Strobridge and Noble, in *Alaska and the U.S. Revenue Cutter Service*, 173–177, suggest that there were deep generational tensions among RCS officers in this period: junior officers felt their advancement blocked by senior men who would not (or could not) retire.

40. "Special Order, Revenue Cutter Service, No. 20," June 8, 1896, Trial, 1896. Efforts on Healy's behalf are evident in Jackson to MJH, February 20, 1896, Jackson Papers, Speer Library, Princeton Theological Seminary; PFH Diary, January–June 1896, PFH Papers 1:2, AGU; JAH to Hale, November 15, 1897, and JAH to Reed, November 1898, both in Letterbooks, ADP; and Hamlin Diary, February 9–11, 1896, Charles Sumner Hamlin Papers, Manuscript Division, Library of Congress; see also the "index-digest" of this diary, which contains additional recollections from Hamlin who, as assistant secretary of the treasury, was under pressure to reverse Healy's sentence.

41. See the logbook for the *McCulloch*, July 7–13, 1900, NARA; see also Coulson to Secretary of the Treasury, December 24, 1900, Alaska File, 9:61–73, and PFH Diary, July 15–18, 1900, PFH Papers 1:4, AGU. On the incident aboard the *McCulloch*, see Gary C. Stein, "A Desperate and Dangerous Man: Captain Michael A. Healy's Arctic Cruise of 1900," *Alaska Journal* 15 (Spring 1985): 39–45.

42. For the nonracial character of these insults, see the testimony of March 20, 1890, Trial, 1890; address of the official prosecutor, Trial, 1896; and MAH to Shepard, December 14, 1892, Alaska File, 2:932–935.

11. The Ends

1. Episcopal Diary, February 28, 1895, and June 28, 1896, ADP; JAH to Brownson, December 5, 1887, Henry F. Brownson Collection, AUND; Foley, *Beloved Outcaste*, 224–225; Meagher and Grattan, *Spires of Fenwick*, 115.

2. *Portland Eastern Argus*, June 5 and 6, 1900; *Portland Evening Express*, June 5, 1900.

3. The events of his death and funeral are described in PFH Diary, August 5–13, 1900, PFH Papers 1:4, AGU. See also the description in Foley, *Beloved Outcaste*, 233–240.

4. "Frederick Healy's Rash Marriage," *San Francisco Chronicle*, June 11, 1896; PFH Diary, June 16, 1896, PFH Papers 1:2, AGU; MJH to Jackson, October 28, 1898, Sheldon Jackson Correspondence, vol. 16, Presbyterian Historical Society, Philadelphia. There are some miscellaneous notes on Fred Healy's wife and children in the Albert Foley Papers, Box 7, Josephite Archives, Baltimore. I am grateful to Clay Young of San Francisco, a grandson of Fred Healy, who has shared with me his family's history.

5. MAH to Secretary of the Treasury, June 11, 1903, Alaska File, 9:846–847. For his last voyage, see his

reports to the secretary, dated July 7, August 19, and September 12, 1903, all in Alaska File, 9. There is a clipping of his obituary from an unidentified newspaper in the MAH Papers 1:2, ACHC. See also PFH Diary, August 31–September 3, 1904, PFH Papers 1:4, AGU.

6. PFH Diary, November 6, 1900, and September 15–16, 1903, PFH Papers 1:4, AGU. Several of Patrick's diaries contain random genealogical notes; see especially the diary for 1886–1887, PFH Papers 1:7, ACHC.

7. "Father Patrick F. Healy," *Woodstock Letters* 39 (1910): 387–389. See also the brief death notices (which contain some inaccuracies) in *New York Times*, January 11, 1910, and *Boston Pilot*, January 22, 1910.

8. See, for example, John J. O'Connor and Elio Gasparetti, "A Negro President at Georgetown Some Eighty Years Ago," *Negro History Bulletin* 18 (May 1955): 175–176, and Joseph Durkin, *Georgetown University: The Middle Years (1840–1900)* (Washington, D.C.: Georgetown University Press, 1963), esp. 296, note 1. Durkin made a deliberate effort to be open-minded about Healy's ancestry, proclaiming it not "of great and spectacular importance." Still, he eagerly asserted that Eliza Clark Healy had been "a household servant and not a common slave in the fields."

9. "Return of Death, Eugene A. Healey [*sic*]," March 30, 1914, Registry of Vital Records and Statistics, Boston. Foley, in *Dream of an Outcaste*, 275 and 293, summarizes what little is known of Eugene's later years. On the unsuccessful effort to find Eugene, see the notes appended to Patrick's will (originally dated January 5, 1904) in AMJP 79:4, AGU.

10. Her death is described in characteristically sentimental language in *Annales de la Maison Mere*, ACND. On the Staten Island school, see Baezsler, "Congregation of Notre Dame," 219–229, and *Histoire de la Congregation de Notre Dame*, 11:405–410.

11. "Standard Certificate of Death," May 18, 1920, Registry of Vital Records and Statistics, Boston. I am grateful to Thomas Riley, grandson of Bessie Cunningham, for further information about the family.

12. Litwack, *Trouble in Mind*, ch. 6.

BIBLIOGRAPHY

Archives and Manuscripts

Archives, Archdiocese of Boston; Boston, Massachusetts
Archives, College of the Holy Cross; Worcester, Massachusetts
Archives, Congregation de Notre Dame; Montreal, Quebec
Archives, Diocese of Portland; Portland, Maine
Archives, Georgetown University; Washington, D.C.
Archives, Harvard University; Cambridge, Massachusetts
Archives, Josephite Fathers; Baltimore, Maryland
Archives, Paulist Fathers; Washington, D.C.
Archives, Religious Hospitallers of Saint Joseph; Montreal, Quebec
Archives, Sacred Congregation de Propaganda Fide; Rome, Italy
Georgia Department of Archives and History; Atlanta, Georgia
National Archives and Records Administration; Washington, D.C.
Presbyterian Historical Society; Philadelphia, Pennsylvania
Princeton Theological Seminary, Speer Library; Princeton, New Jersey
U. S. Coast Guard Academy Library; New London, Connecticut
Yale University Library, Archives and Maunscripts; New Haven, Connecticut

Published Works

Abrahams, Roger D. *Singing the Master: The Emergence of African American Culture in the Plantation South.* New York: Pantheon Books, 1992.

Adams, James Truslow. "Disfranchisement of Negroes in New England." *American Historical Review* 30 (April 1925): 543–547.

Alexander, Adele Logan. *Ambiguous Lives: Free Women of Color in Rural Georgia, 1789–1879.* Fayetteville: University of Arkansas Press, 1991.

Allard, Michel, ed. *L'Hotel-Dieu de Montreal, 1642–1973.* Montreal: Hurtubise HMH, 1973.

Allen, Cuthbert. "The Slavery Question in Catholic Newspapers, 1850–1865." *Historical Records and Studies* 26 (1936): 99–169.

Applebaum, Harvey M. "Miscegenation Statutes: A Constitutional and Social Problem." *Georgetown Law Journal* 53 (1964): 49–91.

Appleby, R. Scott. *"Church and Age Unite!" The Modernist Impulse in American Catholicism.* Notre Dame, Ind.: University of Notre Dame Press, 1992.

Arfwedson, C. D. *The United States and Canada* (London, 1834); quoted in Lane, ed., *Rambler in Georgia,* 93–106.

Ashley, Robert P. "The St. Albans Raid." *Civil War Times Illustrated* 6 (November 1967): 18–27.

Aubert, Roger, et al. *The Church in the Age of Liberalism.* Translated by Peter Becker. New York: Crossroad, 1981.

Ayers, Edward L. *The Promise of the New South: Life after Reconstruction.* New York: Oxford University Press, 1992.

Baeszler, Sister St. Alfred of Rome. "The Congregation of Notre Dame in Ontario and the United States: The History of Holy Angels Province." Ph.D. diss., Fordham University, 1944.

Baker, Ray Stannard. *Following the Color Line: American Negro Citizenship in the Progressive Era.* New York: Harper Torchbooks, 1964; orig. pub. New York: Doubleday, 1908.

Bartley, Numan V., ed. *The Evolution of Southern Culture.* Athens: University of Georgia Press, 1988.

Bederman, Gail. *Manliness and Civilization: A Cultural History of Gender and Race in the United States, 1880–1917.* Chicago: University of Chicago Press, 1995.

Bellamy, Donnie D. "Macon, Georgia, 1823–1860: A Study in Urban Slavery." *Phylon* 45 (December 1984): 298–310.

Bender, Norman J. *Winning the West for Christ: Sheldon Jackson and Presbyterianism on the Rocky Mountain Frontier, 1869–1880.* Albuquerque: University of New Mexico Press, 1996.

Berlin, Ira. *Slaves without Masters: The Free Negro in the Antebellum South.* New York: Pantheon Books, 1974.

Bernstein, Iver. *The New York City Draft Riots: Their Significance for American Society and Politics in the Age of the Civil War.* New York: Oxford University Press, 1990.

Berzon, Judith P. *Neither White nor Black: The Mulatto Character in American Fiction.* New York: New York University Press, 1978.

Betts, John R. "The Negro and the New England Conscience in the Days of John Boyle O'Reilly." *Journal of Negro History* 51 (October 1966): 246–261.

Billington, Ray Allen. *The Protestant Crusade, 1800–1860: A Study of the Origins of American Nativism.* New York: Macmillan, 1938.

Bixby, William. *Track of the "Bear."* New York: D. McKay, 1965.

Blied, Benjamin. *Catholics and the Civil War: Essays.* Milwaukee: St. Francis Seminary, 1945.

Bloch, Julius M. *Miscegenation, Melaleukation, and Mr. Lincoln's Dog.* New York: Schaum, 1958.

Bockstoce, John. "The Point Barrow Refuge Station." *American Neptune* 39 (1979): 5–21.

Boles, John B. *Masters and Slaves in the House of the Lord: Race and Religion in the American South, 1740–1870.* Lexington: University Press of Kentucky, 1988.

Bolster, W. Jeffrey. *Black Jacks: African American Seamen in the Age of Sail.* Cambridge: Harvard University Press, 1997.

———. "An Inner Diaspora: Black Sailors Making Selves." In Hoffman, Ronald, et al., eds., *Through a Glass Darkly,* 419–448.

———. "'To Feel Like a Man': Black Seamen in the Northern States, 1800–1860." *Journal of American History* 76 (March 1990): 1173–1199.

Bonner, James C. *A History of Georgia Agriculture, 1732–1860.* Athens: University of Georgia Press, 1964.

Brown, John. *Slave Life in Georgia: A Narrative of the Life, Sufferings, and Escape of John Brown, a Fugitive Slave, Now in England.* 2nd ed. London: W. M. Watts, 1855.

Brown, Phil. "Passing: Differences in Our Public and Private Self." *Journal of Multicultural Social Work* 1, no. 2 (1991): 33–50.

Brown, Richard D. *Knowledge Is Power: The Diffusion of Information in Early America, 1700–1865.* New York: Oxford University Press, 1989.

Browne, Henry J. *The Catholic Church and the Knights of Labor.* Washington, D.C.: Catholic University of America Press, 1949.

Brownson, Orestes A. "Abolition and Negro Equality." *Brownson's Quarterly Review*, National Series, 1 (April 1864): 186–209.

Brundage, James A. *Law, Sex, and Christian Society in Medieval Europe.* Chicago: University of Chicago Press, 1987.

Buckingham, James Silk. *The Slave States of America* (London, 1842); quoted in Lane, *Rambler in Georgia*, 137–178.

Buckley, Thomas E. "Unfixing Race: Class, Power, and Identity in an Interracial Family." *Virginia Magazine of History and Biography* 102 (July 1994): 349–380.

Burma, John H. "The Measurement of Negro 'Passing.'" *American Journal of Sociology* 52 (July 1946): 18–22.

Burroughs, Polly. *The Great Ice Ship "Bear": Eighty-Nine Years in Polar Seas.* New York: Van Nostrand Reinhold, 1970.

Butler, John Campbell. *Historical Record of Macon and Central Georgia.* Macon: J. W. Burke, 1879.

Butsch, Joseph. "Catholics and the Negro." *Journal of Negro History* 2 (October 1917): 393–410.

———. "Negro Catholics in the United States." *Catholic Historical Review* 3 (April 1917): 33–51.

Campbell, Charles S., Jr. "The Anglo-American Crisis in the Bering Sea, 1890–1891." In Sherwood, ed., *Alaska and Its History*, 315–340.

Campbell, Stanley W. *The Slave Catchers: Enforcement of the Fugitive Slave Law, 1850–1860.* Chapel Hill: University of North Carolina Press, 1970.

Cantwell, John C. "Captain Healy's Reindeer." *Marine Corps Gazette* (May 1935): 26–29, 58–60.

Carroll, Mary T. A. *Leaves from the Annals of the Sisters of Mercy.* 4 vols. New York: Catholic Publications Society, 1881–1895.

Carter, Wilmoth A. "Epithets." In Thompson and Hughes, eds., *Race*, 375–379.

Cauce, Ana Mari. "Between a Rock and a Hard Place: Social Adjustment of Biracial Youth." In Root, ed., *Racially Mixed People in America*, 207–222.

Chalker, Fussell. "Irish Catholics in the Building of the Ocmulgee and Flint Railroad." *Georgia Historical Quarterly* 54 (Winter 1970): 507–516.

Chappell, Absalom Harris. *Miscellanies of Georgia, Historical, Biographical, Descriptive.* Atlanta: J. F. Meegan, 1874.

Clark, Dennis. "The South's Irish Catholics: A Case of Cultural Confinement." In Miller and Wakelyn, eds., *Catholics in the Old South*, 195–209.

Clinton, Catherine. *The Plantation Mistress: Woman's World in the Old South.* New York: Pantheon Books, 1982.

Coburn, Carol K., and Martha Smith. *Spirited Lives: How Nuns Shaped Catholic Culture and American Life, 1836–1920.* Chapel Hill: University of North Carolina Press, 1999.

Coleman, Kenneth, ed. *A History of Georgia*. Athens: University of Georgia Press, 1977.

Collison, Gary. *Shadrach Minkins: From Fugitive Slave to Citizen*. Cambridge: Harvard University Press, 1997.

Conway, Katherine E. *The Golden Year of the Good Shepherd in Boston*. Boston: Thomas Flynn, 1918.

————. *In the Footsteps of the Good Shepherd, New York, 1857–1907*. New York: Convent of the Good Shepherd, 1907.

Conyers, James E., and T. H. Kennedy. "Negro Passing: To Pass or Not to Pass." *Phylon* 24 (Fall 1963): 215–223.

Cook, Adrian. *The Armies of the Streets: The New York City Draft Riots of 1863*. Lexington: University Press of Kentucky, 1974.

Cornelius, Janet Duitsman. *"When I Can Read My Title Clear": Literacy, Slavery, and Religion in the Antebellum South*. Columbia: University of South Carolina Press, 1991.

Coulter, E. Merton. *Georgia: A Short History*. Rev. ed. Chapel Hill: University of North Carolina Press, 1960.

Creighton, Margaret S. "Fraternity in the American Forecastle, 1830–1870." *New England Quarterly* 63 (December 1990): 531–557.

————. *Rites and Passages: The Experience of American Whaling, 1830–1870*. New York: Cambridge University Press, 1995.

Curran, Robert Emmett. *American Jesuit Spirituality: The Maryland Tradition, 1634–1900*. New York: Paulist Press, 1988.

————. *The Bicentennial History of Georgetown University*. Vol. 1, *From Academy to University, 1789–1889*. Washington, D.C.: Georgetown University Press, 1993.

————. "'Splendid Poverty': Jesuit Slaveholding in Maryland, 1805–1838." In Miller and Wakelyn, eds., *Catholics in the Old South*, 125–146.

Daniels, John. *In Freedom's Birthplace: A Study of the Boston Negroes*. Boston: Houghton Mifflin, 1914.

Danylewycz, Marta. *Taking the Veil: An Alternative to Marriage, Motherhood, and Spinsterhood in Quebec, 1840–1920*. Toronto: McClelland and Stewart, 1987.

Davis, Cyprian. *The History of Black Catholics in the United States*. New York: Crossroad, 1990.

Davis, F. James. *Who Is Black? One Nation's Definition*. University Park: Pennsylvania State University Press, 1991.

Day, Caroline Bond. *A Study of Some Negro-White Families in the United States*. Cambridge, Mass.: Peabody Museum, 1932.

Degler, Carl N. *Neither Black nor White: Slavery and Race Relations in Brazil and the United States*. New York: Macmillan, 1971.

DeLaney, Theodore C. "Julia Gardiner Tyler: A Nineteenth-Century Southern Woman." Ph.D. diss., College of William and Mary, 1995.

D'Emilio, John, and Estelle B. Freedman. *Intimate Matters: A History of Sexuality in America*. New York: Harper and Row, 1988.

Dening, Greg. *Mr. Bligh's Bad Language: Passion, Power, and Theatre on the "Bounty."* Cambridge: Cambridge University Press, 1992.

Dennis, William. "Rev. Patrick F. Healy, S.J.: An Attempt at an Appreciation." *Georgetown College Journal* 41 (January 1913): 226.

Derks, Scott, ed. *The Value of a Dollar: Prices and Incomes in the United States, 1860–1989.* Detroit: Gale, 1994.

Dolan, Jay P. *The American Catholic Experience: A History from Colonial Times to the Present.* New York: Doubleday, 1985.

Dominguez, Virginia R. *White by Definition: Social Classification in Creole Louisiana.* New Brunswick, N.J.: Rutgers University Press, 1986.

Donald, David Herbert. *Lincoln.* New York: Simon and Schuster, 1995.

Douglass, Frederick. *My Bondage and My Freedom.* New York: Miller, Orton, and Mulligan, 1855.

Doyle, Sister Saint Ignatius. *Marguerite Bourgeoys and Her Congregation.* Gardenvale, Quebec: Garden City Press, 1940.

Du Bois, W. E. B. *The Autobiography of W. E. B. Du Bois: A Soliloquy on Viewing My Life from Its Last Decade.* New York: International Publishers, 1968.

Duffy, Eamon. *Saints and Sinners: A History of the Popes.* New Haven: Yale University Press, 1997.

Durkin, Joseph. *Georgetown University: The Middle Years (1840–1900).* Washington, D.C.: Georgetown University Press, 1963.

Early, Gerald, ed. *Lure and Loathing: Essays on Race, Identity, and the Ambivalence of Assimilation.* New York: Allen Lane, 1993.

Eaton, Clement. "Slave Hiring in the Upper South: A Step toward Freedom." *Mississippi Valley Historical Review* 46 (March 1960): 663–678.

Edelstein, Tilden G. "*Othello* in America: The Drama of Racial Intermarriage." In Kousser and McPherson, eds., *Region, Race, and Reconstruction,* 179–197.

Ellis, John Tracy. *The Life of James Cardinal Gibbons, Archbishop of Baltimore, 1834–1921.* 2 vols. Milwaukee: Bruce, 1952.

———, ed. *The Catholic Priest in the United States: Historical Investigations.* Collegeville, Minn.: Saint John's University Press, 1971.

Erikson, Eric H. "The Concept of Identity in Race Relations: Notes and Queries." In Parsons and Clark, eds., *The American Negro,* 227–253.

Evans, Stephen H. *The United States Coast Guard, 1790–1915, with a Postscript, 1915–1950.* Annapolis: United States Naval Institute, 1949.

Fairbanks, Henry G. "Slavery and the Vermont Clergy." *Vermont History,* new series, 27 (October 1959): 309–312.

Faris, John T. *The Alaskan Pathfinder: The Story of Sheldon Jackson.* Chicago: Revell, 1926.

Farr, James. "A Slow Boat to Nowhere: The Multi-Racial Crews of the American Whaling Industry." *Journal of Negro History* 68 (Spring 1983): 159–170.

Fields, Barbara J. "Ideology and Race in American History." In Kousser and McPherson, eds., *Region, Race, and Reconstruction,* 143–177.

Finnie, David H. *Pioneers East: The Early American Experience in the Middle East.* Cambridge: Harvard University Press, 1967.

Flanders, Ralph B. "The Free Negro in Ante-Bellum Georgia." *North Carolina Historical Review* 9 (July 1932): 250–272.

———. *Plantation Slavery in Georgia.* Chapel Hill: University of North Carolina Press, 1933.

———. "Two Plantations and a County of Antebellum Georgia." *Georgia Historical Quarterly* 12 (March 1928): 1–24.

Flipper, Henry O. *The Colored Cadet at West Point.* Edited by Quintard Taylor Jr. Lincoln: University of Nebraska Press, 1998; orig. pub. 1878.

Fogarty, Gerald P. *The Vatican and the American Hierarchy from 1870 to 1965.* Wilmington, Del.: Michael Glazier, 1985.

Foley, Albert S. *Beloved Outcaste: The Story of a Great Man Whose Life Has Become a Legend.* New York: Farrar, Straus, and Young, 1954.

———. "Bishop Healy and the Colored Catholic Congress." *Interracial Review* 28 (May 1954): 79–80.

———. *Dream of an Outcaste: Patrick F. Healy.* Tuscaloosa, Ala.: Portals Press, 1989.

———. *God's Men of Color: The Colored Catholic Priests of the United States, 1854–1954.* New York: Farrar, Straus, 1955.

Formwalt, Lee W. "A Case of Interracial Marriage during Reconstruction." *The Alabama Review* 45 (July 1992): 216–224.

Fowler, David H. *Northern Attitudes towards Interracial Marriage: Legislation and Public Opinion in the Middle Atlantic and the States of the Old Northwest, 1780–1930.* New York: Garland, 1987.

Fox Genovese, Elizabeth. "Slavery, Race, and the Figure of the Tragic Mulatta, or, The Ghost of Southern History in the Writing of African-American Women." *Mississippi Quarterly* 49 (Fall 1996): 791–817.

———. *Within the Plantation Household: Black and White Women of the Old South.* Chapel Hill: University of North Carolina Press, 1988.

Franchot, Jenny. *Roads to Rome: The Antebellum Protestant Encounter with Catholicism.* Berkeley: University of California Press, 1994.

Frankenburg, Ruth. *White Women, Race Matters: The Social Construction of Whiteness.* Minneapolis: University of Minnesota Press, 1993.

Franklin, John Hope, ed. *Color and Race.* Boston: Houghton Mifflin, 1968.

Fraser, James W., et al., eds. *From Common School to Magnet School: Selected Essays in the History of Boston Schools.* Boston: Boston Public Library, 1979.

Fredrickson, George M. *The Black Image in the White Mind: The Debate on Afro-American Character and Destiny, 1817–1914.* New York: Harper and Row, 1971.

Gabriels, Henry. *Historical Sketch of St. Joseph's Provincial Seminary, Troy, N.Y.* New York: U.S. Catholic Historical Society, 1905.

Gans, Herbert J. "Symbolic Ethnicity: The Future of Ethnic Groups and Cultures in America." *Ethnic and Racial Studies* 2 (January 1979): 1–20.

Gatewood, Willard B. *Aristocrats of Color: The Black Elite, 1880–1920.* Bloomington: Indiana University Press, 1990.

Geary, James W. *We Need Men: The Union Draft in the Civil War.* Dekalb: Northern Illinois University Press, 1991.

Genovese, Eugene L. *Roll, Jordan, Roll: The World the Slaves Made.* New York: Vintage, 1974.

George, Hardy. "Georgetown University's Healy Building." *Journal of the Society of Architectural Historians* 31 (October 1972): 208–216.

"Georgetown College." *Woodstock Letters* 1 (1872): 156–163.

Gergen, Kenneth J. "The Significance of Skin Color in Human Relations." In Franklin, ed., *Color and Race*, 112–128.

Gibbs, Jewelle Taylor, and Alice M. Hines. "Negotiating Ethnic Identity: Issues for Black-White Biracial Adolescents." In Root, ed., *Racially Mixed People in America*, 223–238.

Gienapp, William E. "Nativism and the Creation of a Republican Majority in the North before the Civil War." *Journal of American History* 72 (December 1985): 529–559.

———. *The Origins of the Republican Party, 1852–1856.* New York: Oxford University Press, 1987.

Gillard, John T. *The Catholic Church and the American Negro.* Baltimore: St. Joseph's Society Press, 1929.

———. *Colored Catholics in the United States.* Baltimore: Josephite Press, 1941.

Gilmore, Glenda Elizabeth. *Gender and Jim Crow: Women and the Politics of White Supremacy in North Carolina, 1896–1920.* Chapel Hill: University of North Carolina Press, 1996.

Gilroy, Paul. *The Black Atlantic: Modernity and Double Consciousness.* Cambridge: Harvard University Press, 1993.

Ginsberg, Elaine K. "The Politics of Passing." In Ginsberg, ed., *Passing and the Fictions of Identity,* 1–18.

———, ed. *Passing and the Fictions of Identity.* Durham, N.C.: Duke University Press, 1996.

Gist, Noel P., and Anthony Gary Dworkin, eds. *The Blending of Races: Marginality and Identity in World Perspective.* New York: Wiley-Interscience, 1972.

Glazer, Nathan, and Daniel P. Moynihan, eds. *Ethnicity: Theory and Experience.* Cambridge: Harvard University Press, 1975.

Goldberg, Milton M. "A Qualification of the Marginal Man Theory." *American Sociological Review* 6 (February 1941): 52–58.

Gossett, Thomas F. *Race: The History of an Idea in America.* New York: Schocken, 1965.

Green, Constance McLaughlin. *The Secret City: A History of Race Relations in the Nation's Capital.* Princeton: Princeton University Press, 1967.

———. *Washington: Capital City, 1879–1950.* Princeton: Princeton University Press, 1963.

Greenwood, Janette Thomas. *Bittersweet Legacy: The Black and White "Better Classes" in Charlotte, 1850–1910.* Chapel Hill: University of North Carolina Press, 1994.

Gross, William H. "The Missions for the Colored People." In *A History of the Third Plenary Council of Baltimore, November 9–December 7, 1884,* 71–74. Baltimore: Baltimore Publishing, 1885.

Grosvenor, Gilbert H. "Reindeer in Alaska." *National Geographic* 14 (April 1903): 127–149.

Gruening, Ernest. *The State of Alaska.* Rev. ed. New York: Random House, 1968.

Guibert, Joseph de. *The Jesuits: Their Spiritual Doctrine and Practice.* Translated by William J. Young. Chicago: Institute of Jesuit Sources, 1964.

Guignard, Michael J. *La Foi, La Langue, La Culture: The Franco-Americans of Biddeford, Maine.* Biddeford: Privately printed, 1982.

Gutman, Herbert G. *The Black Family in Slavery and Freedom, 1750–1925.* New York: Pantheon Books, 1976.

Hall, Basil. *Travels in North America* (Edinburgh, 1829); quoted in Lane, ed., *Rambler in Georgia,* 62–84.

Hall, Christine C. Iijima. "Please Choose One: Ethnic Identity Choices for Biracial Individuals." In Root, ed., *Racially Mixed People in America,* 250–264.

Halter, Marilyn. *Between Race and Ethnicity: Cape Verdean American Immigrants, 1860–1965.* Urbana: University of Illinois Press, 1993.

Handlin, Oscar. *Boston's Immigrants: A Study in Acculturation.* Revised and enlarged edition. New York: Atheneum, 1997; orig. pub. 1941.

Haney Lopez, Ian F. *White by Law: The Legal Construction of Race.* New York: New York University Press, 1996.

Hanna, William F. "The Boston Draft Riot." *Civil War History* 36 (September 1990): 262–273.

Harris, J. William. *Plain Folk and Gentry in a Slave Society: White Liberty and Black Slavery in Augusta's Hinterlands*. Middletown, Conn.: Wesleyan University Press, 1985.

Healy, Kathleen. *Frances Warde: American Founder of the Sisters of Mercy*. New York: Seabury, 1973.

Healy, Michael A. *Report of the Cruise of the Revenue Marine Steamer "Corwin" in the Arctic Ocean in the Year 1884*. Washington, D.C.: Government Printing Office, 1889.

———. *Report of the Cruise of the Revenue Marine Steamer "Corwin" in the Arctic Ocean in the Year 1885*. Washington, D.C.: Government Printing Office, 1887.

Heilbrun, Carolyn G. *Writing a Woman's Life*. New York: Norton, 1988.

Hennesey, James. *American Catholics: A History of the Roman Catholic Community in the United States*. New York: Oxford University Press, 1981.

———. "The Baltimore Council of 1866: An American Syllabus." *Records of the American Catholic Historical Society of Philadelphia* 76 (1965): 165–172.

———. *The First Council of the Vatican: The American Experience*. New York: Herder and Herder, 1963.

Herron, Sister Mary Eulalia. "The Work of the Sisters of Mercy in the New England States: Diocese of Portland, 1858–1921; Diocese of Manchester, 1884–1921." *Records of the American Catholic Historical Society* 35 (March 1924): 57–100.

Herskovits, Melville J. "The Color Line." *American Mercury* 6 (October 1925): 204–208.

Hill, Samuel S. *Varieties of Southern Religious Experience*. Baton Rouge: Louisiana State University Press, 1988.

———, ed. *Religion in the Southern States: A Historical View*. Macon, Ga.: Mercer University Press, 1983.

Hinckley, Ted C. "Sheldon Jackson and Benjamin Harrison." In Sherwood, ed., *Alaska and Its History*, 293–312.

Hine, Darlene Clark. "'In the Kingdom of Culture': Black Women and the Intersection of Race, Gender, and Class." In Early, ed., *Lure and Loathing*, 337–351.

Hinks, Peter P. "'Frequently Plunged into Slavery': Free Blacks and Kidnapping in Antebellum Boston." *Historical Journal of Massachusetts* 20 (Winter 1992): 16–31.

Histoire de la Congregation de Notre Dame. 10 vols. Montreal: Congregation de Notre Dame, 1941–1969.

A History of the Third Plenary Council of Baltimore, November 9–December 7, 1884. Baltimore: Baltimore Publishing, 1885.

Hitchcock, James. "Race, Religion, and Rebellion: Hilary Tucker and the Civil War." *Catholic Historical Review* 80 (July 1994): 497–517.

Hodes, Martha. *White Women, Black Men: Illicit Sex in the Nineteenth-Century South*. New Haven: Yale University Press, 1997.

Hoffman, Ronald, et al., eds. *Through a Glass Darkly: Reflections on Personal Identity in Early America*. Chapel Hill: University of North Carolina Press, 1997.

Hohman, Elmo Paul. *The American Whaleman: A Study of Life and Labor in the Whaling Industry*. New York: Longmans, Green, 1928.

Holleran, Peter C. *Boston's Wayward Children: Social Services for Homeless Children, 1830–1930*. Boston: Northeastern University Press, 1994.

Holmes, Derek. *The Triumph of the Holy See: A Short History of the Papacy in the Nineteenth Century*. London: Burns and Oates, 1978.

Horowitz, Donald L. "Color Differentiation in the American Systems of Slavery." *Journal of Interdisciplinary History* 3 (Winter 1973): 509–541.

———. "Ethnic Identity." In Glazer and Moynihan, eds., *Ethnicity: Theory and Experience*, 111–140.

Horton, James Oliver. "Freedom's Yoke: Gender Conventions among Antebellum Free Blacks." *Feminist Studies* 12 (Spring 1986): 51–76.

———. "Shades of Color: The Mulatto in Three Antebellum Northern Communities." In Horton, ed., *Free People of Color*, 122–144.

———, ed. *Free People of Color: Inside the African American Community*. Washington, D.C.: Smithsonian Institution Press, 1993.

Horton, James Oliver, and Lois E. Horton. *Black Bostonians: Family Life and Community Struggle in the Antebellum North*. New York: Holmes and Meier, 1979.

———. *In Hope of Liberty: Culture, Community, and Protest among Northern Free Blacks, 1700–1860*. New York: Oxford University Press, 1997.

———. "Race, Occupation, and Literacy in Reconstruction Washington, D.C." In Horton, ed., *Free People of Color*, 185–197.

Hunt, William R. *Arctic Passage: The Turbulent History of the Land and People of the Bering Sea, 1697–1975*. New York: Scribner's, 1975.

Hunter, Tera W. *To 'Joy My Freedom: Southern Black Women's Lives and Labors after the Civil War*. Cambridge: Harvard University Press, 1997.

Ignatiev, Noel. *How the Irish Became White*. New York: Routledge, 1995.

Inscoe, John C., ed. *Georgia in Black and White: Explorations in the Race Relations of a Southern State, 1865–1950*. Athens: University of Georgia Press, 1994.

Isaacs, Harold R. "Group Identity and Political Change: The Role of Color and Physical Characteristics." In Franklin, ed., *Color and Race*, 75–97.

Jackson, Sheldon. "The Arctic Cruise of the United States Revenue Cutter *Bear*." *National Geographic* 7 (January 1896): 27–31.

Jacobs, James H. "Identity Development in Biracial Children." In Root, ed., *Racially Mixed People in America*, 190–206.

Jacobson, Matthew Frye. *Barbarian Virtues: The United States Encounters Foreign Peoples at Home and Abroad, 1876–1917*. New York: Hill and Wang, 2000.

———. *Whiteness of a Different Color: European Immigrants and the Alchemy of Race*. Cambridge: Harvard University Press, 1998.

Jean, Marguerite. *Evolution des Communautes Religieuses de Femmes au Canada de 1639 a Nos Jours*. Montreal: Fides, 1977.

Jenkins, William T. "Ante Bellum Macon and Bibb County, Georgia." Ph.D. diss., University of Georgia, 1966.

Jenks, Albert E. "The Legal Status of Negro-White Amalgamation in the United States." *American Journal of Sociology* 21 (March 1916): 666–678.

Johnson, James Weldon. *The Autobiography of an Ex-Coloured Man*. New York: Vintage, 1989; orig. pub. 1927.

Johnson, Mark R. D. "'Race,' Religion, and Ethnicity: Religious Observance in the West Midlands." *Ethnic and Racial Studies* 8 (July 1985): 426–437.

Johnson, Michael P., and James L. Roark. *Black Masters: A Free Family of Color in the Old South*. New York: Norton, 1984.

Johnson, Walter. "The Slave Trader, the White Slave, and the Politics of Racial Determination in the 1850s." *Journal of American History* 87 (June 2000): 13–38.

Johnston, James Hugo. *Race Relations in Virginia and Miscegenation in the South, 1776–1860.* Amherst: University of Massachusetts Press, 1970.

Jordan, Brian. "Sources for African American Catholic Spirituality." *Journal of Religious Thought* 47 (Summer–Fall 1990): 29–41.

Jordan, David Starr. *Reports on Conditions of Seal Life on the Pribilof Islands.* Washington, D.C.: Government Printing Office, 1898.

Jordan, Winthrop D. "American Chiaroscuro: The Status and Definition of Mulattoes in the British Colonies." *William and Mary Quarterly,* 3d ser., 19 (April 1962): 183–200.

———. *White Over Black: American Attitudes toward the Negro, 1550–1812.* Chapel Hill: University of North Carolina Press, 1968.

Kauffman, Christopher. *Tradition and Transformation in Catholic Culture: The Priests of Saint Sulpice in the United States from 1791 to the Present.* New York: Macmillan, 1988.

Kennedy, Lawrence W. *Planning the City upon a Hill: Boston since 1630.* Amherst: University of Massachusetts Press, 1992.

Kennedy-Haflett, Cynthia. "'Moral Marriage': A Mixed-Race Relationship in Nineteenth-Century Charleston, South Carolina." *South Carolina Historical Magazine* 97 (July 1996): 206–226.

Kenny, Kevin. *Making Sense of the Molly Maguires.* New York: Oxford University Press, 1998.

Kich, George Kitahara. "The Developmental Process of Asserting a Biracial, Bicultural Identity." In Root, ed., *Racially Mixed People in America,* 304–317.

King, Irving H. *The Coast Guard Expands, 1865–1915: New Roles, New Frontiers.* Annapolis: Naval Institute Press, 1996.

Kinney, James. *Amalgamation!: Race, Sex, and Rhetoric in the Nineteenth-Century American Novel.* Westport, Conn.: Greenwood, 1985.

Klineberg, Otto. *Race Differences.* New York: Harper and Brothers, 1935.

———, ed. *Characteristics of the American Negro.* New York: Harper and Brothers, 1944.

Koenig, Harry C., ed. *History of the Parishes of the Archdiocese of Chicago.* Chicago: Archdiocese of Chicago, 1980.

Kousser, J. Morgan, and James M. McPherson, eds. *Region, Race, and Reconstruction: Essays in Honor of C. Vann Woodward.* New York: Oxford University Press, 1982.

Kuzniewski, Anthony J. *Thy Honored Name: A History of the College of the Holy Cross, 1843–1994.* Washington, D.C.: Georgetown University Press, 1999.

Lalli, Anthony B., and Thomas H. O'Connor. "Roman Views on the American Civil War." *Catholic Historical Review* 57 (April 1971): 21–41.

Lane, Mills, ed. *The Rambler in Georgia.* Savannah: Beehive Press, 1990.

Larkin, Emmet. "The Devotional Revolution in Ireland, 1850–1875." *American Historical Review* 77 (June 1972): 625–652.

Larsen, Nella. *Passing.* New York: Knopf, 1929.

Laslett, Peter, ed. *Bastardy and Its Comparative History.* Cambridge: Harvard University Press, 1980.

Lempel, Leonard R. "The Mulatto in United States Race Relations: Changing Status and Attitudes, 1800–1940." Ph.D. diss., Syracuse University, 1979.

Leonard, William C. "Vigor in Arduis: A History of Boston's African-American Catholic Community, 1788–1988." Ph.D. diss., Boston College, 1999.

Leslie, Kent Anderson. *Woman of Color, Daughter of Privilege: Amanda America Dickson, 1849–1893.* Athens: University of Georgia Press, 1995.

Levesque, George A. *Black Boston: African American Life and Culture in Urban America, 1750–1860.* New York: Garland, 1994.

Levy, Leonard W., and Harlan B. Phillips. "The *Roberts* Case: Source of the 'Separate but Equal' Doctrine." *American Historical Review* 56 (April 1951): 510–518.

Lexau, Joan. *Convent Life: Roman Catholic Religious Orders of Women in North America.* New York: Dial, 1964.

Lincoln, C. Eric. "Color and Group Identity in the United States." In Franklin, ed., *Color and Race,* 249–263.

Litwack, Leon F. *North of Slavery: The Negro in the Free States, 1790–1860.* Chicago: University of Chicago Press, 1961.

———. *Trouble in Mind: Black Southerners in the Age of Jim Crow.* New York: Knopf, 1998.

Logan, Rayford W., and Michael R. Winston, eds. *Dictionary of American Negro Biography.* New York: Norton, 1982.

Lord, Robert Howard, et al. *History of the Archdiocese of Boston in the Various Stages of Its Development, 1604–1943.* 3 vols. Boston: Pilot Publishing, 1944.

Lott, Eric. *Love and Theft: Blackface Minstrelsy and the American Working Class.* New York: Oxford University Press, 1993.

Lowell, Charles U. *The Quakers in Flushing, 1657–1937.* Flushing, N.Y.: Case, 1937.

Lucey, William L. *The Catholic Church in Maine.* Francestown, N.H.: Marshall Jones, 1957.

McBride, James T. *Incardination and Excardination of Seculars: An Historical Synopsis and Commentary.* Washington, D.C.: Catholic University of America, 1941.

McCusker, John J. "How Much Is That in Real Money? A Historical Price Index for Use as a Deflator of Money Values in the Economy of the United States." *Proceedings of the American Antiquarian Society* 101 (1994): 297–373.

McDevitt, Gilbert J. *Legitimacy and Legitimation: An Historical Synopsis and Commentary.* Washington, D.C.: Catholic University of America, 1941.

Macdonald, Fergus. *The Catholic Church and the Secret Societies in the United States.* New York: U.S. Catholic Historical Society, 1946.

McDonogh, Gary Wray. *Black and Catholic in Savannah, Georgia.* Knoxville: University of Tennessee Press, 1993.

McNamara, Robert F. *The American College in Rome.* Rochester, N.Y.: Christopher, 1956.

McPherson, James M. *Battle Cry of Freedom: The Civil War Era.* New York: Oxford University Press, 1988.

McWhiney, Grady. *Cracker Culture: Celtic Ways in the Old South.* Tuscaloosa: University of Alabama Press, 1988.

Mack, Kenneth W. "Law, Society, Identity, and the Making of the Jim Crow South: Travel and Segregation on Tennessee Railroads, 1875–1905." *Law and Social Inquiry* 24 (Spring 1999): 377–409.

Marsden, George. *The Soul of the American University: From Protestant Establishment to Established Nonbelief.* New York: Oxford University Press, 1994.

Marszalek, John F., Jr. *Court-Martial: A Black Man in America.* New York: Scribner's, 1972.

Matthews, Glenna. *"Just a Housewife": The Rise and Fall of Domesticity in America.* New York: Oxford University Press, 1987.

Meagher, Walter J., and William J. Grattan. *The Spires of Fenwick: A History of the College of the Holy Cross, 1843–1963.* New York: Vantage, 1966.

Mencke, John German. "Mulattoes and Race Mixture: American Attitudes and Images from Reconstruction to World War I." Ph.D. diss., University of North Carolina, 1976.

Merritt, Carole. "Slave Family History Records: An Abundance of Materials." *Georgia Archive* 6 (Spring 1978): 16–21.

Merwick, Donna. *Boston Priests, 1848–1910: A Study of Social and Intellectual Change.* Cambridge: Harvard University Press, 1973.

Miller, Randall M. "Black Catholics in the Slave South: Some Needs and Opportunities for Study." *Records of the American Catholic Historical Society* 86 (March 1975): 93–106.

———. "Catholics in a Protestant World: The Old South Example." In Hill, *Varieties of Southern Religious Experience,* 115–134.

———. "A Church in Cultural Captivity: Some Speculations on Catholic Identity in the Old South." In Miller and Wakelyn, eds., *Catholics in the Old South,* 11–52.

———. "The Failed Mission: The Catholic Church and Black Catholics in the Old South." In Miller and Wakelyn, eds., *Catholics in the Old South,* 149–170.

———. "Slaves and Southern Catholicism." In Boles, ed., *Masters and Slaves in the House of the Lord,* 127–152.

Miller, Randall M., and John L. Wakelyn, eds. *Catholics in the Old South: Essays on Church and Culture.* Macon, Ga.: Mercer University Press, 1983.

Mills, Gary B. "Miscegenation and the Free Negro in Antebellum 'Anglo' Alabama: A Reexamination of Southern Race Relations." *Journal of American History* 68 (June 1981): 16–34.

Misch, Edward J. *The American Bishops and the Negro from the Civil War to the Third Plenary Council of Balitmore (1865–1884).* Rome: Patrizio Graziani, 1968.

Mitchell, Margaret. *Gone With the Wind.* New York: Macmillan, 1936.

Mixon, Wayne. "Georgia." In Hill, ed., *Religion in the Southern States,* 77–100.

Mondoux, Soeur. *L'Hotel-Dieu, Premier Hopital de Montreal, 1642–1763.* Montreal: Therein Freres, 1941.

Morgan, Edmund S. *American Slavery, American Freedom: The Ordeal of Colonial Virginia.* New York: Norton, 1975.

Morris, Thomas D. *Southern Slavery and the Law, 1619–1860.* Chapel Hill: University of North Carolina Press, 1996.

Morrow, Diane Batts. "Outsiders Within: The Oblate Sisters of Providence in 1830s Church and Society." *U.S. Catholic Historian* 15, no. 2 (Spring 1997): 35–54.

Morton, Patricia. "From Invisible Man to 'New People': The Recent Discovery of American Mulattoes." *Phylon* 46 (June 1985): 106–122.

Mulkern, John R. *The Know-Nothing Party in Massachusetts: The Rise and Fall of a People's Movement.* Boston: Northeastern University Press, 1990.

Murdoch, Eugene C. *One Million Men: The Civil War Draft in the North.* Madison: State Historical Society of Wisconsin, 1971.

Murphy, Thomas R. "'Negroes of Ours': Jesuit Slaveholding in Maryland, 1717–1838." Ph.D. diss., University of Connecticut, 1998.

Myers, Henry J., and Leon Yockelson. "Color Denial in the Negro: A Preliminary Report." *Psychiatry* 11 (1948): 39–46.

Myrdal, Gunnar. *An American Dilemma: The Negro Problem and Modern Democracy*. 2 vols. New York: Harper, 1944.

Nash, Gary B. "The Hidden History of Mestizo America." *Journal of American History* 82 (December 1995): 941–962.

Naske, Claus-M., and Herman E. Slotnick. *Alaska: A History of the 49th State*. Grand Rapids, Mich.: Eerdmans, 1979.

Oates, Mary J. "'The Good Sisters': The Work and Position of Catholic Churchwomen in Boston, 1870–1940." In Sullivan and O'Toole, eds., *Catholic Boston*, 171–200.

O'Brien, David J. *Isaac Hecker: An American Catholic*. New York: Paulist Press, 1992.

Ochs, Stephen J. *Desegregating the Altar: The Josephites and the Struggle for Black Priests, 1871–1960*. Baton Rouge: Louisiana State University Press, 1990.

O'Connell, Jeremiah J. *Catholicity in the Carolinas and Georgia*. New York: Sadlier, 1879.

O'Connor, James I. *Dispensation from Irregularities to Holy Orders*. West Baden Springs, Ind.: West Baden College, 1952.

O'Connor, John J., and Elio Gasparetti. "A Negro President at Georgetown Some Eighty Years Ago." *Negro History Bulletin* 18 (May 1955): 175–176.

O'Connor, Thomas H. *Boston Catholics: A History of the Church and Its People*. Boston: Northeastern University Press, 1998.

———. *Civil War Boston: Home Front and Battlefield*. Boston: Northeastern University Press, 1997.

———. *Fitzpatrick's Boston, 1846–1866: John Bernard Fitzpatrick, Third Bishop of Boston*. Boston: Northeastern University Press, 1984.

———. "The Irish in New England." *New England Historical and Genealogical Register* 139 (July 1985): 187–195.

Olmsted, Frederick Law. *A Journey in the Seaboard Slave States, with Remarks on Their Economy*. New York: Dix and Edwards, 1856.

O'Malley, John W. *The First Jesuits*. Cambridge: Harvard University Press, 1993.

O'Malley, John W., et al. *Jesuit Spirituality: A Now and Future Resource*. Chicago: Loyola University Press, 1990.

Omi, Michael, and Howard Winant. *Racial Formation in the United States: From the 1960s to the 1980s*. New York: Routledge and Paul, 1986.

O'Toole, James M. *Militant and Triumphant: William Henry O'Connell and the Catholic Church in Boston, 1859–1944*. Notre Dame, Ind.: University of Notre Dame Press, 1992.

"Our Colored Catholics." *Historical Records and Studies* 28 (1937): 259–264.

Painter, Nell Irwin. "'Social Equality,' Miscegenation, Labor, and Power." In Bartley, ed., *The Evolution of Southern Culture*, 47–67.

Paradis, Wilfred. *Upon This Granite: Catholicism in New Hampshire, 1647–1997*. Portsmouth: Peter Randall, 1998.

Parrish, Charles H. "Color Names and Color Notions." *Journal of Negro Education* 15 (1946): 13–20.

Parsons, Talcott, and Kenneth B. Clark, eds. *The American Negro*. Boston: Houghton Mifflin, 1966.

Pascoe, Peggy. "Race, Gender, and Intercultural Relations: The Case of Interracial Marriage." *Frontiers* 12 (Summer 1991): 5–18.

Patterson, Orlando. "Context and Choice in Ethnic Allegiance: A Theoretical Framework and Caribbean Case Study." In Glazer and Moynihan, eds., *Ethnicity*, 305–349.

Pekkala, Salme, et al. "Some Words and Terms Designating, or Relating to, Racially Mixed Persons or Groups." In Thompson and Hughes, eds., *Race,* 52–57.

Perkins, George C. "The Civil Government of Alaska." *National Geographic* 9 (April 1898): 172–178.

Piper, Adrian. "Passing for White, Passing for Black." In Ginsberg, ed., *Passing and the Fictions of Identity,* 234–269.

Pleck, Elizabeth Hafkin. *Black Migration and Poverty: Boston, 1865–1900.* New York: Academic Press, 1979.

Potter, David M. *The Impending Crisis, 1848–1861.* Edited by Don E. Fehrenbacher. New York: Harper and Row, 1976.

Powderly, Terence. *The Path I Trod.* New York: Columbia University Press, 1940.

Putney, Martha S. *Black Sailors: Afro-American Merchant Seamen and Whalemen Prior to the Civil War.* New York: Greenwood Press, 1987.

Raboteau, Albert J. *Slave Religion: The "Invisible Institution" in the Antebellum South.* New York: Oxford University Press, 1978.

Rampersad, Arnold. "Psychology and Afro-American Biography." *Yale Review* 78 (Autumn 1988): 1–18.

Range, Willard. *A Century of Georgia Agriculture, 1850–1950.* Athens: University of Georgia Press, 1954.

Rankin, Robert H. *Immortal "Bear," the Stoutest Polar Ship.* New York: Putnam, 1970.

Rapaport, Stella. *The "Bear," Ship of Many Lives.* New York: Dodd, Mead, 1962.

Reidy, Joseph P. *From Slavery to Agrarian Capitalism in the Cotton Plantation South: Central Georgia, 1800–1880.* Chapel Hill: University of North Carolina Press, 1992.

Reports on Condition of Seal Life on the Pribilof Islands by Special Treasury Agents in Charge, and Others, from 1868 to 1895. Washington, D.C.: Government Printing Office, 1898.

Reuter, Edward Byron. *The Mulatto in the United States.* New York: Negro Universities Press, 1969; orig. pub. 1918.

Rice, Madeleine Hooke. *American Catholic Opinion in the Slavery Controversy.* New York: Columbia University Press, 1944.

Richards, J. Havens. "An Explanation in Reply to Some Recent Strictures." *Woodstock Letters* 26 (1897): 146–153.

Roediger, David R. *The Wages of Whiteness: Race and the Making of the American Working Class.* London: Verso, 1991.

Rogers, W. McDowell. "Free Negro Legislation in Georgia Before 1865." *Georgia Historical Quarterly* 16 (1932): 27–37.

Root, Maria P. P., ed. *Racially Mixed People in America.* Newbury Park, Calif.: Sage, 1992.

Ruchames, Louis. "Jim Crow Railroads in Massachusetts." *American Quarterly* 8 (Spring 1956): 61–75.

———. "Race, Marriage, and Abolition in Massachusetts." *Journal of Negro History* 40 (July 1955): 250–273.

Rudolph, Frederick. *Curriculum: A History of the American Undergraduate Course of Study since 1636.* San Francisco: Jossey-Bass, 1977.

Russell, Kathy, et al. *The Color Complex: The Politics of Skin Color among African Americans.* New York: Harcourt Brace Jovanovich, 1992.

Ryan, Mary P. *Cradle of the Middle Class: The Family in Oneida County, New York, 1790–1865.* New York: Cambridge University Press, 1981.

Sanders, Cheryl J. "Religious Conversion, Ethics, and the Afro-American Slave: Evaluating Alternative Approaches." *Journal of Religious Thought* 45 (Winter 1989): 7–20.

Sanders, James W. "Boston Catholics and the School Question, 1825–1907." In Fraser et al., eds., *From Common School to Magnet School*, 43–75.

Saxton, Alexander. *The Rise and Fall of the White Republic: Class Politics and Mass Culture in Nineteenth-Century America*. London: Verso, 1990.

Scanlan, Arthur J. *St. Joseph's Seminary, Dunwoodie, New York, 1896–1921*. New York: U.S. Catholic Historical Society, 1922.

Schneider, Mark R. *Boston Confronts Jim Crow, 1890–1920*. Boston: Northeastern University Press, 1997.

Schulz, Mark P. "Interracial Kinship Ties and the Emergence of a Rural Black Middle Class: Hancock County, Georgia, 1865–1920." In Inscoe, ed., *Georgia in Black and White*, 141–172.

Scontras, Charles A. *Two Decades of Organized Labor and Labor Politics in Maine, 1880–1900*. Orono: University of Maine, 1962.

Sharrow, Walter G. "John Hughes and a Catholic Response to Slavery in Antebellum America." *Journal of Negro History* 57 (July 1972): 254–269.

Shaw, Richard. *Dagger John: The Unquiet Life and Times of Archbishop John Hughes of New York*. New York: Paulist Press, 1977.

Shelley, Thomas J. "'Good Work in Its Day': St. Joseph's Provincial Seminary, Troy, New York." *Revue d'Histoire Ecclesiastique* 88 (April–June 1993): 416–438.

Sherwood, Adiel. *A Gazetteer of Georgia*. Macon, Ga.: S. Boykin, 1860.

Sherwood, Morgan B., ed. *Alaska and Its History*. Seattle: University of Washington Press, 1967.

Sisters, Servants of the Immaculate Heart of Mary. *Building Sisterhood: A Feminist History of the Sisters, Servants of the Immaculate Heart of Mary*. Syracuse: Syracuse University Press, 1997.

Smith, Julia Floyd. *Slavery and Rice Culture in Low Country Georgia, 1750–1860*. Knoxville: University of Tennessee Press, 1985.

Smythe, Mabel, ed. *The Black American Reference Book*. Englewood Cliffs, N.J.: Prentice-Hall, 1976.

Sollors, Werner. *Beyond Ethnicity: Consent and Descent in American Culture*. New York: Oxford University Press, 1986.

Spalding, David. "Martin John Spalding's 'Dissertation on the American Civil War.'" *Catholic Historical Review* 52 (April 1966): 66–85.

———. "The Negro Catholic Congresses, 1889–1894." *Catholic Historical Review* 55 (October 1969): 337–357.

Spickard, Paul R. *Mixed Blood: Intermarriage and Ethnic Identity in Twentieth-Century America*. Madison: University of Wisconsin Press, 1989.

Stapp, Carol Buchalter. *Afro-Americans in Antebellum Boston: An Analysis of Probate Records*. New York: Garland, 1993.

Stein, Gary C. "A Desperate and Dangerous Man: Captain Michael A. Healy's Arctic Cruise of 1900." *Alaska Journal* 15 (Spring 1985): 39–45.

Stern, Julia. "Spanish Masquerade and the Drama of Racial Identity in *Uncle Tom's Cabin*." In Ginsberg, ed., *Passing and the Fictions of Identity*, 103–130.

Stone, James H. "Economic Conditions in Macon, Georgia, in the 1830s." *Georgia Historical Quarterly* 54 (Summer 1970): 209–225.

Stonequist, Everett V. *The Marginal Man: A Study in Personality and Culture Conflict*. New York: Russell and Russell, 1937.

Strickland, Reba Carolyn. *Religion and the State in Georgia in the Eighteenth Century*. New York: Columbia University Press, 1939.

Strobridge, Truman R., and Dennis L. Noble. *Alaska and the U.S. Revenue Cutter Service, 1867–1915*. Annapolis: Naval Institute Press, 1999.

Stuart, James. *Three Years in North America* (Edinburgh, 1833); quoted in Lane, ed., *Rambler in Georgia*, 85–92.

Stuckert, Robert P. "Free Black Populations of the Southern Appalachian Mountains, 1860." *Journal of Black Studies* 23 (March 1993): 358–370.

Sullivan, Robert E. "Beneficial Relations: Toward a Social History of the Diocesan Priests of Boston, 1875–1944." In Sullivan and O'Toole, eds., *Catholic Boston*, 201–238.

Sullivan, Robert E., and James M. O'Toole, eds. *Catholic Boston: Studies in Religion and Community, 1870–1970*. Boston: Archdiocese of Boston, 1985.

Supan, Marita-Constance. "Dangerous Memory: Mother M. Theresa Maxis Duchemin and the Michigan Congregation of the Sisters, IHM." In Sisters, *Building Sisterhood*, 31–67.

Theobald, Stephen L. "Catholic Missionary Work among the Colored People of the United States." *Records of the American Catholic Historical Society* 35 (December 1924): 325–344.

Thompson, Edgar T., and Everett C. Hughes, eds. *Race: Individual and Collective Behavior*. Glencoe, Ill.: Free Press, 1958.

Three Catholic Afro-American Congresses. Cincinnati: American Catholic Tribune, 1893.

Toll, Robert C. *Blacking Up: The Minstrel Show in Nineteenth-Century America*. New York: Oxford University Press, 1974.

Toplin, Robert Brent. "Between Black and White: Attitudes toward Southern Mulattoes, 1830–1861." *Journal of Southern History* 45 (May 1979): 185–200.

Trisco, Robert. "Bishops and Their Priests in the United States." In Ellis, ed., *Catholic Priest in the United States*, 111–292.

Tushnet, Mark V. *The American Law of Slavery, 1810–1860: Considerations of Humanity and Interest*. Princeton: Princeton University Press, 1981.

U.S. Bureau of the Census. *Negro Population, 1790–1915*. Washington, D.C.: Government Printing Office, 1918.

Valuska, David L. *The African American in the Union Navy, 1861–1865*. New York: Garland, 1993.

van den Berghe, Pierre L., and Peter Frost. "Skin Color, Sexual Dimorphism, and Sexual Selection: A Case of Gene Culture Co-Evolution?" *Ethnic and Racial Studies* 9 (January 1986): 87–113.

von Hoffman, Alexander. *Local Attachments: The Making of an American Urban Neighborhood, 1850–1920*. Baltimore: Johns Hopkins University Press, 1994.

Warner, William W. *At Peace with All Their Neighbors: Catholics and Catholicism in the National Capital, 1787–1860*. Washington, D.C.: Georgetown University Press, 1994.

Waters, Mary C. *Ethnic Options: Choosing Identities in America*. Berkeley: University of California Press, 1990.

Wells, Robert V. "Illegitimacy and Bridal Pregnancy in Colonial America." In Laslett, ed., *Bastardy and Its Comparative History*, 349–361.

White, Deborah Gray. *Ar'n't I a Woman? Female Slaves in the Plantation South.* New York: Norton, 1985.

White, George. *Statistics of the State of Georgia.* Savannah, Ga.: W. T. Williams, 1849.

White, Joseph M. *The Diocesan Seminary in the United States: A History from the 1780s to the Present.* Notre Dame, Ind.: University of Notre Dame Press, 1989.

Wilkie, Richard W., and Jack Tager, eds. *Historical Atlas of Massachusetts.* Amherst: University of Massachusetts Press, 1991.

Williams, Carolyn White. *History of Jones County, Georgia, for One Hundred Years, Specifically 1807–1907.* Macon, Ga.: J. W. Burke, 1957.

Williams, Gerald O. "Michael J. [*sic*] Healy and the Alaska Maritime Frontier, 1880–1902." Master's thesis, University of Oregon, 1987.

Williamson, Joel. *New People: Miscegenation and Mulattoes in the United States.* New York: Free Press, 1980.

Winks, Robin. "Raid at St. Albans." *Vermont Life* 15 (Spring 1961): 40–46.

Wirth, Louis, and Herbert Goldhamer. "The Hybrid and the Problem of Miscegenation." In Klineberg, ed., *Characteristics of the American Negro*, 249–369.

Woods, Frances Jerome. *Marginality and Identity: A Colored Creole Family through Ten Generations.* Baton Rouge: Louisiana State University Press, 1972.

Woodson, Carter G. "The Beginnings of the Miscegenation of the Whites and Blacks." *Journal of Negro History* 3 (October 1918): 335–353.

———. *Free Negro Owners of Slaves in the United States in 1830* (New York: Negro Universities Press, 1968; orig. pub. 1924.

INDEX

James M. O'Toole was born in Worcester and raised in Leominster, Massachusetts. He has an A.B. and Ph.D. in history from Boston College, an A.M. in history from the College of William and Mary, and an M.S. in library science from Simmons College. He has served as the Acting State Archivist for the Commonwealth of Massachusetts and the Archivist for the Roman Catholic Archdiocese of Boston. He was a member of the history department and director of the archives concentration in the history M.A. program at the University of Massachusetts Boston and is currently associate professor of history at Boston College. He is a member of Phi Beta Kappa, a recipient of the M. Claude Lane Award from the Society of American Archivists, and a recipient of three Mellon Foundation Research Fellowships in Modern Archives at the University of Michigan. His numerous books and papers include *Understanding Archives and Manuscripts* and *Militant and Triumphant: William Henry O'Connell and the Catholic Church in Boston, 1859–1944*. His current research project is a social history of confession in the American Roman Catholic church. He lives in Milton, Massachusetts.